A System's Evaluation of
**Global History of
Indian Architecture**

Other titles of interest:

Habib Rahman: The architect of independent India
Prof. S. M. Akhtar

High-density housing for mixed-income groups
Ranjana Mital and Aneesh Nandi

Smart Urban and Rural Planning Techniques
Harmit Singh Bedi

Fixing Flawed Urban Planning: The Case of Delhi
B.G. Fernandes

Humane Approach to Urban Planning
Priya Choudhary

Geographic Information System for Smart Cities
Prof. TM Vinod Kumar and Associates

Local Area Planning in India
Rishi Dev

Metropolitan Governance: Cases of Ahmedabad and Hyderabad
Dr. Vinita Yadav

India's Urban Confusion: Challenges and Strategies
Edited by Dr. M. Ramachandran

Designing Better Architecture Education: Global Realities and Local Reforms
Dr Manjari Chakraborty

The Ekistics of Animal and Human Conflict
Rishi Dev

Water Conservation Techniques in Traditional Human Settlements
Pietro Laureano

The City Observed: Notes from an Unfolding India
Pallavi Shrivastava

Tirtha at Mukteswar: Understanding its Architecture
Dr. Ranjana Mital and Prabhjot Singh Sugga

A System's Evaluation of
Global History of Indian Architecture

Joy Sen
Akshata Mohanty

COPAL PUBLISHING GROUP
Inspiring for a better future through publishing

Published by Copal Publishing Group
E-143, Lajpat Nagar, Sahibabad,
Distt. Ghaziabad, UP – 201005, India

www.copalpublishing.com

First Published 2016
© Copal Publishing Group, 2016

This book contains information obtained from authentic and highly regarded sources. Reprinted material is quoted with permission. Reasonable efforts have been made to publish reliable data and information, but the authors and the publishers cannot assume responsibility for the validity of all materials. Neither the authors nor the publishers, nor anyone else associated with this publication, shall be liable for any loss, damage or liability directly or indirectly caused or alleged to be caused by this book.

Neither this book nor any part may be reproduced or transmitted in any form or by any means, electronic or mechanical, including photocopying, microfilming and recording, or by any information storage or retrieval system, without permission in writing from Copal Publishing Group. The consent of Copal Publishing Group does not extend to copying for general distribution, for promotion, for creating new works, or for resale. Specific permission must be obtained in writing from Copal Publishing Group for such copying.

Trademark notice: Product or corporate names may be trademarks or registered trademarks, and are used only for identification and explanation, without intent to infringe.

ISBN: 978-81-924733-2-1 (hard back)
ISBN: 978-81-924733-1-4 (e-book)

Typeset by Bhumi Graphics, New Delhi
Printed and bound by Bhavish Graphics, Chennai

Preface

The inspiration behind writing the book is contained in the two Forewords.

A system's understanding of architecture is the understanding of human evolution and its relationship with the growth and development of the science of the built and the unbuilt environment. Architecture, the science of human-made environment is based on the relationship. The pattern of the relationship is also the pattern of human civilization and that can be best retrieved from what is embedded in the pattern of its architecture over time. In Indian architecture, there has always been a propensity from within towards an outward expression carrying within the deeper imprints of the relationship.

From the ancient Vedic altars in times of extreme remote antiquity, the first geometry of construction was perhaps developed. And now, ages later, for instance, the pattern of any specific temple footprint today can be re-evaluated as a later derivative and a footprint of the origin.

At the core of human evolution is the user. The user of the built is first a limited soul, who can be better styled as an individual continuously expanding towards the becoming of an infinite individual. In the journey from the finite or the coded to the truth in the vast, and the rhythm of the infinite (Satyam ritam brihat), the encoded meta-structures of the universe itself, and its abstract geometry can be truly re-discovered. That is the goal of Indian architecture. It is in this journey, which is always an expanding one, the constructs of human evolution can be traced, as a step by step culmination, and as a process where there are open-ended exploratory attempts to harmonise all the preceding systems in history, across space and time. As a result, all later systems become a more perfect future system. It is applicable to religion, culture and science. There is no last word. If there is a last word, then it is a simple beginning of a higher and larger cycle of evolution.

The system's approach, as attempted by the book, is evident in the following words:

"If it be true that man is the evolution of a mollusc, the mollusc individual is the same as the man, only it has to become expanded a great deal. From mollusc to man it has been a continuous expansion towards infinity. Therefore the limited soul can be styled an individual which is continuously expanding towards the Infinite Individual. Perfect individuality will only be reached when it has reached the Infinite, but on this side of the Infinite it is a continuously changing, growing personality. One of the remarkable features of the Advaitist system of Vedanta is to harmonise the preceding systems. In many cases it helped the philosophy very much; in some cases it hurt it. Our ancient philosophers knew what you call the theory of evolution; that growth is gradual, step by step, and the recognition of this led them to harmonise all the preceding systems. Thus not one of these preceding ideas was rejected."

Swami Vivekananda
PRACTICAL VEDANTA
PART IV
(Delivered in London, 18th November 1896)

Indian architecture is a system's reflection of the cosmos as a built-environmental form. Its footprint forms the cradle of human evolution. The shapes of the footprints, its built-form and the functional semantics evolving out of the footprint are actually not static nodes but dynamic processes representing the step-by-step journey of the human evolution heading for infinity. It is the systems-driven step-by-step cumulative growth of evolutionary patterns across space and time heterogeneity, what we may call the pattern of global history. Thus Indian architecture, at the generic level, is a larger science of these patterns and their recognition. Hence, there is a need of an evaluation of what we may call a System's Evaluation of Global History of Indian Architecture. Thus through language and semantics of music; through development of the semiotics of a vast array of iconography and art expressing culture and the sciences, human evolution is an expression of the very step-by-step system's progress and Indian architecture, the living representative of the journey has always been a tangible representation of the very universal humane progress.

In this journey there are the two worlds – the world within and the world without. India as a civilization has originally garnered the systems of human psychology and inner evolutionary growth, what we may call the science of the microcosm. Some people call that Spirituality. In the West, the accepted term is Deep Ecology. Indian architecture is always an inward-to-outward process. The Greeks on the other hand, has been bearers of the external world that of the material sciences and technology. Their approach is from outside-to-inside, with the advent of the sciences.

The most interesting part is that the two have always formed a complete system. There are match points and there are also points of discordance. Evolution is a movement from the lower truths of discordance to the higher levels of systems building based on the recognition of the first match points. The idea is evident in the following words:

There are two worlds, the microcosm, and the macrocosm, the internal and the external. We get truth from both of these by means of experience. The truth gathered from internal experience is psychology, metaphysics, and religion; from external experience, the physical sciences. Now a perfect truth should be in harmony with experiences in both these worlds. The microcosm must bear testimony to the macrocosm, and the macrocosm to the microcosm; physical truth must have its counterpart in the internal world, and the internal world must have its verification outside. Yet, as a rule, we find that many of these truths are in conflict.

At one period of the world's history, the internals become supreme, and they begin to fight the externals. At the present time the externals, the physicists, have become supreme, and they have put down many claims of psychologists and metaphysicians. So far as my knowledge goes, I find that the real, essential parts of psychology are in perfect accord with the essential parts of modern physical knowledge. It is not given to one individual to be great in every respect; it is not given to one race or nation to be equally strong in the research of all fields of knowledge.

The modern European nations are very strong in their research of external physical knowledge, but they are not so strong in their study of the inner nature of man. On the other hand, the Orientals have not been very strong in their researches of the external physical world, but very strong in their researches of the internal. Therefore we find that Oriental physics and other sciences are not in accordance with Occidental Sciences; nor is Occidental psychology in harmony with Oriental psychology. The Oriental physicists have been routed by Occidental scientists. At the same time, each claims to rest on truth; and as we stated before, real truth in any field of knowledge will not contradict itself; the truths internal are in harmony with the truths external.

Swami Vivekananda
COSMOLOGY

In the Global History of Architecture, there is always a storyline of apparent clashes between the two parts – the Eastern and the Western, or say, the Indians and the Greeks. In this story of civilization there is nothing new. But the greater and the vaster untold story can be unfolded if a system's evaluation of the larger processes can be tapped that triggers an evolving holism where two apparently different lines of thoughts converge to form a system. Here are the words:

It is probably true quite generally that in the history of human thinking the most fruitful developments frequently take place at those points where two different lines of thought meet. Werner Heisenberg

In the step-by-step journey of system's building, every cusp or a meeting point can be seen as a point of assimilation, or an interface, both in space and time. A truly befitting word is Sandhi. And the way is what we may call the Tao, i.e. the way of the Saints, representing a multitude of great men and women of sustainable knowledge hunting and wisdom from across the world; hence, a global evaluation.

To begin with, the initial followers of the internal world may only understand the deep roots of the Tao but not its branches; and the scientists may understand only its outward branches but not its roots. But as the ancient wisdom says, "Science does not need mysticism and mysticism does not need science; but humanity needs both." It is equivalent to the integration of the left and right hand side thinking, concentrating on the external and internal worlds. Today, it is called the Neuro-plastic integration of analytics (ex-tuition) and intuition, held by the latest of contemporary bio and evolutionary sciences.

Through a spirit of assimilation or what we can hail as a cusp called a SANDHI between the two, the great aim of the present book is achieved. The aim is to put forth a new order, a greater order in thought and action. It is not an 'either or' paradigm. It is essentially an integration of science and tradition where the system's evaluation of the essence of Indian Architecture can be better attempted. Why? Here is the answer:

Mystics understand the roots of the Tao but not its branches; scientists understand its branches but not its roots.

Science does not need mysticism and mysticism does not need science; but man needs both.

Fritjof Capra
The Tao of physics

The book has attempted to assimilate the better of the two worlds. It has continuously drawn a pool of clues from every important phase in history – from the science of the built and the un-built, extracting the best from the analytical and deep intuitive sectors of human thinking and action. Assimilation or universal acceptance had always has been the life-line of India since eternity and that spirit was also partly evident in her counter-part, the ancient Milesian Greeks and at times, in the later chain of inheritance, the democratic and the liberal Euro-American approach recovered by France and later, by the new world. It is the pattern of assimilation, the system's building which the book has traced. The spirit of the system's building, which is also an evaluation, is SANDHI, through which a complete and a vaster meaning of the carrying capacity of human growth and evolution can be best retrieved from the science of the built and the unbuilt and the relationship between the two. To sum up the Intent:

'India of the ages is not dead nor has she spoken her last creative word; she lives and has still something to do for herself and the humane peoples'……but still the ancient immemorable SHAKTI recovering her deepest self, lifting her head higher towards the supreme source of light and strength and turning to discover the complete meaning and a vaster form of her Dharma (religion).

Shri Aurobindo
'Foundations of Indian culture

Have a pleasant reading.

Joy Sen, Ph.D.
Professor, Indian Institute of Technology Kharagpur
Principal Investigator, SandHI
Please see: www.iitkgpsandhi.org
January 2016

Contents

Preface v

Forewords xvii

1. **Introduction and organization of the book** 1
    1.1 Introduction 1
    1.2 A Cybernetic perspective 2
    1.3 A parable of a musical orchestra: Is architecture 'frozen music'? 5
    1.4 The Cybernetic perspective in architecture: Patterns of co-evolution 6
    1.5 Patterns of co-evolution: The system's outcome 8
    1.6 Organization of the book 11
    1.7 Acknowledgements 14

2. **A system's approach to evaluation** 18
    2.1 Introduction 18
    2.2 Part I: Evolution of system's approach 18
    2.3 Part 2: Complementary events and impacts 39
    2.4 Conclusions: Patterns of flow and measures 54

3. **System framework one: Phase I of global history of architecture** 60
    3.1 Introduction 60
    3.2 Basic system's dimensions 62
    3.3 Part one: System of unity of opposites 66
    3.4 Part two: Systems of historical–mythological recurrence – from India to Egypt 75

3.5	Part three: System of converging realization and belief systems	88
3.6	Part four: System of cooperative language systems	94
3.7	Part Five: System of inter-continental carriers and migrations	114
3.8	Part six: System of cooperative archaeology based on anthropology and iconography	121
3.9	Conclusions	160

4. System framework two: Phase II of global history of architecture — 173

4.1	Introduction	173
4.3	Part two: The missionaries of 'Dhamma' to the Mediterranean	196
4.4	Part Three: Architectural Parallels – Ancient Buddhism and early Christianity	204
4.5	Part Four: The legend of Therapeutes – Who were they?	211
	– 'Physicians, heal thyself' (Therapeutic purgation, Catharsis and Lutheran ideals)	211
4.6	Conclusions	233

5. System framework three: Phase III of global history of architecture — 259

5.1	Systems' framework three: Introduction	259
5.2	Section one: The legacy of the Korahites (Quraysh)	267
5.3	Section two: The contribution of the Kores	274
5.4	Section three: The making of European civilization	284
5.5	Section four: The birth of Iberian architecture	288

	5.6	Section five: Redepiction of the Garden of Eden: The Char-bagh	291
	5.7	Conclusions	304
6.	**System framework four: Phase IV of global history of architecture**		**316**
	6.1	Systems' framework four: Interpenetration and turning	316
	6.2	The cumulative causation of four phases	318
	6.3	Forwarding the transition	336
	6.4	Towards interpenetration: System's architecture	347
	6.5	One: Cosmic Architecture	350
	6.6	Two: Architecture of Evolution	355
	6.7	Three: Architecture of Deep Ecology	362
	6.8	Four: Architecture of the Cosmic Matrix	365
	6.9	Five: Architecture of Co-evolution	366
	6.10	Six: Architecture of the Mahat	375
	6.11	Seven: Architecture of Interpenetration	378
	6.12	Parallels in Iconography: Fractals and the Gandhaavyu–ha Sutra	392
	6.13	Conclusions: Cycles and lines – both and beyond	398

References	**403**
Index	**409**
About the authors	**423**

India of the ages...

Clusters of clouds move the celestial blue,
White and Black, not absolute, are their twin hue,
Differences in grey scales, only of dilution!
That Yellow Sun seeks departure,
As variety sets by clouds in commotion -

...The waves of individual signs temporarily espy,
Libra tries to balance Leo and Gemini...
To soar or to love and die -
(But finally) all disappear in the sky.

Deep below the Ocean sings an eternal hymn!
Not greatness on surface, but silence pervades her rim.
Bharat! — Your famous religion of the seas!
All waves: emotions and forms are your waters in time's breeze,
You calmly sing here - within and above, without any seize.

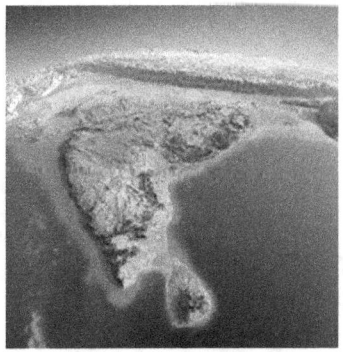

Swami Vivekananda

Forewords

Systems Approach (SA) is a recovery of **a holistic understanding** of humanity and its deep relationship with the environment and the cosmos around. The relationship between the two portrayed as a deep symbiosis of the microcosm and the macrocosm is as old as humanity itself.

The ancients, particularly in India and to an extent in Greece, have had traced the symbiosis between the dynamics of external nature or the macrocosm and that which is kinetic and evolving within the human body, the microcosm. An assessment of the symbiosis have often intensified in India and at times, diminished in the cycle of evolution and dissipation elsewhere. In other parts of the world, it has not only diminished but got diluted and degraded lower in grayscales of devolution.

In India, when it has intensified, the patterns have conformed essentially to a deep spiritual path seeking an inner liberty. As it de-intensified, the pattern has come down to the outward material level. In other parts of the world, it has exuded as the externalities and patterns of material priorities. It is like the Vedantic story of the two birds, who are always originally one, but are separated through a bifurcation in priorities – the spiritual and material liberties. But both are needed and to be integrated. There is a deep understanding of the two birds, when they are one and when they are not and also, where they defy each other. The FOREWORD is in two parts:

- The first one is entitled 'Vedas and Puranas', explains the three stages and the twin patterns of an increasing and

decreasing intensity and the third, which is deviation and denial.
- The second one is called 'Math-Pather-Tungata' meaning 'the Summits of impersonal realization and peripheries of personal ways to truth'.

The twin forewords are two translations of two separate works. Swami Ramananda is the author of both of them. If from the Swami, the author has received the spiritual initiation. The two forewords by the Swami are the two keys to unlock an understanding of the system's approach of civilizational patterns and recurrence, from a viewport of fixities/ order and another viewport of change/ freedom. It is the System's dynamics that the approach puts forward.

Part I

'Vedas and Puranas'

Evolution and returns to the cycle of recurring historic patterns

Introduction

'In the Vedic way, humanity becomes THAT: the absolute impersonal being, the Brahman by virtue of tapasya, which is an earnest and steadfast path of contemplation, meditation and rapture through yoga. And in the Puranic way, God, as the personified divine being comes to offer salvation to a devoted human mind. As a result, the human becomes an intimate divinized associate of the Supreme. **Vairagya or deep indiscrimination** is apathy for what is disjointed and transient and an affinity for what brings in unity or unification leading to the divine. **Viraha or intense longing** is an earnest true desire for the beloved evolving as a deep heartfelt longing for the Divine. Both are ways to reach the Supreme state of being. The two are considered as two distinct paths to Unity, Divinity itself. It is the deep realization of the two cornerstones of human evolution as held by Indians since times of remote antiquity.

Figure 1 In India it is the Double Bird of the Vedic Realization (see left); later becoming the double aspect of an impersonal Chaitya and the Purusha also symbolized as the Buddha, the Personal Saviour (see middle); in other lands, like Egypt, it became other doubles like the two status of Horus as the Son of Mother Goddess Isis in the Heavens and as a Falcon-like God (see right)

The Vedic way is hardly evident in other countries; the Puranic way is the predominant one in different forms in all other nations. But, the more puritan and original form of the Puranic way is seen alone in India. Whereas in other countries, the different forms of the Puranic way are mostly distant and diluted derivative of the original form, and they have been tailored to meet the easier and an opportunity-driven necessity of the multi-folded material existence, a reigning feature of the cultural patterns there. The focus of the derivation is often tailored by a 'personal-savior' prescription having a lesser or least emphasis on the necessity of a self-driven responsibility and diligence for an inner soul-searching and a deeper appetite for higher salvation. That is why there have had emerged a concept of 'Eternal Entombment' – a Sepulcher, where someone sleeps waiting through eternity for final mercy and permanent absorption in the 'Heaven'. It is often represented by the Garden of Eden and its impact on three religions constituting the Semitic tradition.

The two ways and a further trickling down

The Vedantic way is a sub-set of the Vedic way. In the Puranic way, human beings are unable to become that Absolute Being in the increasing absence of a self-driven diligence and perseverance. That is why there is a need of the Absolute as Personified Saviour, who will descend to the lower planes of human inability and incertitude to forward constant support, value-addition and recovery. Gradually and eventually, the 'path-finder' also becomes the 'end of the path'. The spirit and the duet of the 'path-finder' and the 'path-seeker' are expected to coalesce to a state of oneness, which is non-dualistic and absolute.

For the sake of clarity in the early stages of progression, the two paths are seen as the two distinct ways governed by non-dualism and dualism i.e. the Adwaita (a-duet) form of religious practice and the Dwaita (duet) form of religious followings, respectively. This Dwaita or the Dualistic form has been further diluted in other countries forming a third kind. Or, it can be said to have been fashioned down to accommodate the lower levels of the materially driven societies. That is why, even the Puranic way have often given away to the mundane, factional and selfish opportunities of individualism in the disguise of collective movement and proselytization.

But, the recovery of the higher moral, ethical and refined aesthetic sides of humanity has to be honestly emphasized. This is mostly missing in the religion of the other lands.

The two worlds, and is there a transition between them?

The absolute Brahman of the Vedic way has matured in the impersonal realization called 'Shiva' of the Tantras [the transition has taken place through the Krishna and Sukla Yajdgur Vedas]. The abstraction of 'Shiva' is of extreme greatness, as 'Shiva' is potent in all beings. In times today, the abstraction is all-assimilative. Either it is an impersonal abstraction of 'The Shiva' or it is 'The Buddha', and both cover all personifications, as evident in the contemporary and latest manifestation of Sri Ramakrishna.

'The birth of Sri Krishna is in the midst of a prison-cell is a parable of the state of bondage, helplessness, captivity. Why? The parable explains our own state in this world. His birth extends to embrace and co-exist with us here at this end of infinity, here amidst the current weak and helpless state of humanity. But from there the parable marches to the other imagery of Krishna as the 'Lord', seated in complete sovereignty and omnipotence – the Lordship of the blessed ever-upward spirals of divine cosmic interconnectedness and its play – the Golaka. To that great and the vast, which he represents, he is taking us all. In the pastures of Vrindabana, he is the player of the reed – the divine seven-perforated flute. Just not by his descent, but also by virtue of our ascent and upward struggles and urges for that vast – lies the implications of the real significance and applicability of a religion.

But in other countries, the part of self-diligence, the path of austere upward catharsis and therapeutics has eventually taken a back seat. Instead the Lord alone is portrayed as a single monolith of a sole personal savior defying the abstraction and transition of God both as and from the 'God of fear' to the 'God of love'. If 'God of Love' is also true, then how can a religion hail alone the bloody picture of the Crucifix as the highest ideal? Where is the role of Beatitude now as preached in Mount Olives? The words had been changed and manipulated accordingly to suit externalities.

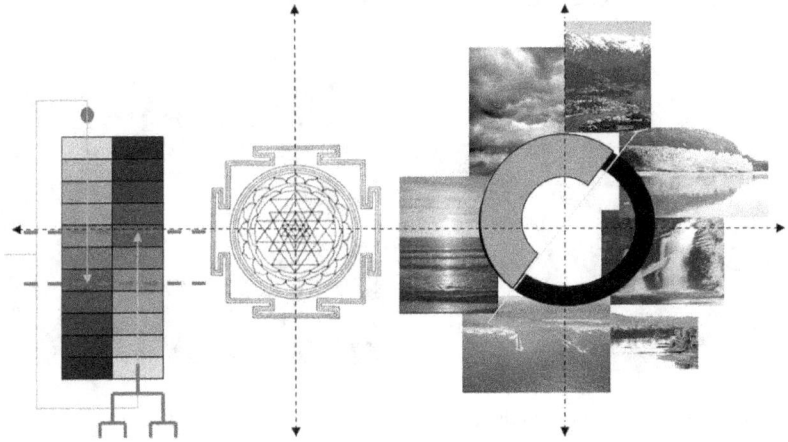

Figure 2 A return to scale in the ladder (intensities in grey scales: greater and lesser light); various interpenetrations of triangles (representing heat) forwarded by the ancient wisdom of the Vedas and a cyclic hierarchy of evaporation and anti-evaporation (condensation), as explained by science today

The Cyclic Return to the Highest Path

The Vedic way has said that any human being by virtue of the intrinsic divinity will be able to reach some day his or her highest state of self-esteem, that highest level of consciousness. It is 'Original Divinity'. It is the basis of Adwaita of the highest and complete kind.

Tat-tvam-asi ::: 'Thou Art That'

Tat-tvam-asi – *'Thou Art That'*: It is from this bedrock of Indian civilization, both a sovereign and an impersonal religion, to which the continuity of personal realization has been duly forwarded and returned to scale and hierarchy (see Figure 2). This is the way of the Rishis, who represent an impersonal lineage of realization called the Vedas, often seen as the Srutis.

And the other one is the Puranic way. In here, the impersonal realization is personified to begin with – seen as a Godhead, who reveals himself like a human being, stands beside the ordinary ones backing up their salvation, and recovering them from their dissipated and disjointed state. Here he becomes the Lord of salvation. Here the seed of 'Bhakti-bada' is planted. The path of devotion finally sprouts, blooms and emerges as the full tree of bliss, Ananda, whose roots are one and that Absolute. The two birds once separated become one (see Figure 3).

Figure 3 The two birds once separated by different intensities in priorities are originally conjoint

The beloved Lord has come down at the level of despair and helplessness. But it does not end here. From there, with his help from above and within (original divinity), humanity, bit by bit, being by being, step by step attempts to struggle and ascend and march forward. That is the highest message. Thus the combined effect of 'non-dualism'-driven and 'dualism'-driven spirituality have been the source of different approaches and cults in the Puranas and similar others. The continuum of Vedas, its sub-set – the Vedanta and its ramification, the various Puranas are stitched as one garland of various letters.

The bird below finally says to upper Bird: I am a part of you, the Lord; and Oh Lord, you are that and everything' (see Figure 3) It is mainly the case of India and her historical evolution.

Figure 4 Separation of the two birds
Affinity for Greater Light and expansion (upward arrow); and a departure for a lesser light, decay and degeneration (downward arrow)

The underlying differences and a return to scale

And that 'dualism'-driven spirituality, from the level of Puranas alone has led to different religious manifestations in other parts of the world and that too with dilution. What is still seen in India is its near-to-original or purer form of dualism-driven spirituality backed by the non-dualism strand.

But in other countries other forms are largely polluted by the materially driven conflicts and selfish opportunities prevailing and increasing. This is the pattern of the historical evolution of the rest of the world (see the lower arrow in Figure 4).

In effect it is the key to understand the underlying differences and understand the System's framework and the possibilities of a great return with scaling up the ladder' (see Figure 2).

Swami Ramananda
Santa Prasanga
(In the Divine Company of Saints)
Sadananda Ramakrishna Ashram
Dakshineswar, Kolkata

Part II

'Math-Pather-Tungata

The summit of impersonal realization and diverse peripheries of personal ways to truth' (excerpts)

'Practically, all religious systems are processes and attempts towards the rapture with that great impersonal realization. In the process of social organization, there is nothing that has a final say or the ultimate word. All religions, in effect, are trying to push forward continuously the great truth of evolution through variations in space-time towards that one great universal realization – the unity, the centrality, that core truth.'

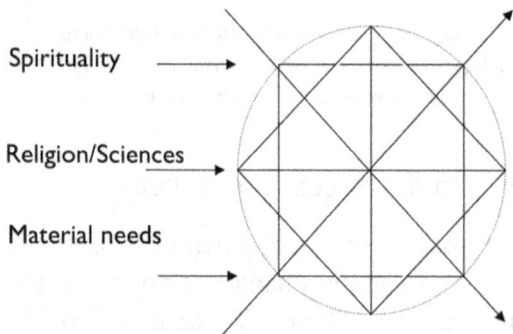

Figure 5 Diagonals (karna-sutras) and peripheries of change
(The System's Framework)

Note: The diagonal in the ascendant is driven by instinct, reason and inspiration that extend to material, moral/ rational and intuitive domains of materialism, religion/ science and spirituality respectively. In the descendant, there are higher involutionary dimensions.

'With respect to various national or regional viewpoints, every religious approach is an attempt, an experimental process of that truth immanent in existence. In that sense, the question that which approach or what viewpoint is closest to truth does not arise (whether they are from India or from the West). Also which is more perfect – is also an insignificant question. As an abstraction, spirituality, religion and various social systems (sciences, culture and material systems) can be seen as dynamic imageries of loci (fixed points) on a diagonal linking the peripheries of change and that summit of a great core – the realization itself' (see Figure 5).

'This viewpoint is neither in favor nor against any religious dogma or whim. This viewpoint is based on the points of the highest impersonal truth that any approach may have in its core and yet having other levels of functioning complementing the social variations over space and time.

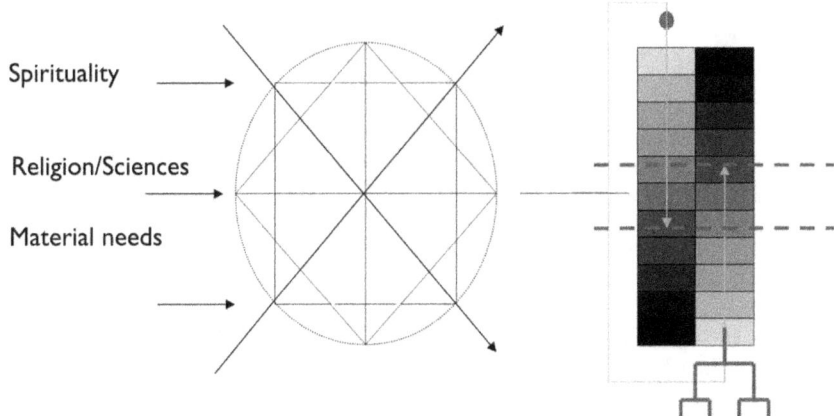

Figure 6 Diagonals (karna-sutras) and the grey scales/ shades (The System's Framework: Moving from lesser to greater truth)

Note: The diagonal in the ascendant, as the evolutionary dimension and the descendant represents involutionary mechanisms in a two-way ladder, which contains the infinite possibilities of progression, regulations and a change-order conjugate in the time-cycles of recurrences.

But at the same time, none of that too can be forwarded as a role model for imitation or replication as each of the others in their own way have been true in their own contexts and times. So it cannot be that way. It is the science of universal acceptance, which is larger than universal tolerance. Otherwise time-line progress and change in human evolution and the order and flexibility contained in the change In various shades and proportions (grey scales) cannot be regulated and accommodated within the system's framework, which is an eternal dynamic equilibrium (see Figure 6).'

Swami Ramananda
Santa Prasanga
(In the Divine Company of Saints)
Sadananda Ramakrishna Ashram
Dakshineswar, Kolkata

1
Introduction and organization of the book

1.1 Introduction

System's approach (SA) is a holistic approach of understanding. The approach streamlines how small parts or things or events influence one another within a sequence of events, which constitutes of to-and-fro causal relationships. The network of such relationships represents a whole, where more than the co-existence of parts, the pattern of relationship gains a higher significance. For instance, system's approach or SA looks at nature as a network of various natural systems. These networks include ecosystems in which various abiotic elements such as air, water, and the biotic configurations like plants and animals are seen as interdependent of each other and consequently, co-evolving. In another example, say, in human associations or organizations, systems may consist of people, organizational structures, and management processes and the systems can work and coalesce together to form a collective entity, which can also be termed as a sustainable whole. There are two important premises where:

1. SA is holistic but is not against reductionism, which takes an isolated standpoint or a partial view of a system. Like when someone is designing an air-conditioned hospital building, the design of laboratories bears no relationship with the microclimate of the local environment. On the contrary, SA is holistic but inclusive of the standpoint of various isolated systems, which finally become interconnected, interdependent and co-evolving, which is not the objective of a reductionist approach.
2. SA also bears the key to sustainability. The 'ability' to sustain to-and-fro relationships in various levels of interaction between sub-systems is the true basis of SA. Thus, the

design of an airport is synonymous with the planning of a city and vice versa; and as a result, an 'aerotropolis' can be better conceived, designed and monitored through a SA. As a result, the position of the airport with respect to the growth and development of a city and its surrounding region becomes mutual, co-evolving and a single system, and therefore, 'smart' and 'sustainable'.

Recently, the entire scientific world, ranging from social sciences to basic quantum and relativistic physics, and say, from ecology to trans-personal psychology, are being revolutionized by the system's approach. The system approach expands from a conventional reductionist paradigm of looking at linear causal relationships to a view port of looking at things or events in a wider and deeper perspective involving a non-linear or cyclic nature. The cyclic nature may stand for reversibility and variety of causes in the systems instead of a simplified one-way causal relationship. The approach therefore imparts a sense of holistic and interconnected truths as processes and networks rather than systems based on discrete variables or isolated events and components.

In applied and social sciences, a system's approach presents a system of interconnections between the evolution of human society and systems through a chain of to-and-fro relationship with environment itself. Architecture is a science of built environment, and the evolution of architectural systems likewise is an outcome of human–nature or behaviour–environment correlations, and often, these correlations are reciprocal, cyclic and complex. Under system's approach, therefore, it is extremely important to see the architecture as a co-evolutionary function of these correlations. This is the principal essence and concern of the present book.

1.2   A Cybernetic perspective

One word that bridges modern system's approach to ancient wisdom is 'Cybernetics'. The word 'Cybernetics' owes its roots from the ancient Greek word for steersman (kybernetes). Today, the word 'cyber' means 'informatics' or a system of streamlining complex sets of information codes representing a variety of relationships in one loop or 'matrix'.

Cybernetics in general system's approach is defined as the study of control within a system, typically using combinations of feedback loops or 'cyclical' relationships. Over the years, the advance of science and technology is based on an evolving order – First, Second and of late, the Third.

- First order Cybernetics relates to closed systems, and a common example may be that of the 'Carnot's cycle' or that of the relationship between a 'Flywheel' as a free-energy supplying system and an 'Engine' requiring that energy to run sustainably, and bear a continuous and reversible relationship with a flywheel. If one refers to the analyses from a built-environmental perspective, say the exploration of the City of Varanasi, the idea encompasses the physical-Cartesian level of the city – covering its geometry, the spatial measurable landscape and distribution of buildings; and physical network of built spaces and their functional relationship with a variety of users (Fig. 1.1).

- The Second order is an expansion of the First order where the observer perspective is involved imparting a role and reflection of human consciousness in the evolution of the so-called material world. Much of the current or cutting-edge thoughts in quantum physics are based on this strange but hidden relationship. Much of pioneering work of Erwin Schrodinger and Werner Heisenberg had set the earliest paces. Architecturally, it may be said the relationship becomes mental. The physical landscape becomes a ritual landscape. Habits and repetitions of user's journey to a certain *ghat* of Varanasi performing a specific oblation or 'ritual' every day constitutes the Second order (Fig. 1.1).

- Later, the Third order system's approach in Cybernetics is emerging, where the two, that the role of human consciousness and various systems in the material world bears a phenomenon of co-evolution. It is when a whole system acknowledges its surroundings in its growth and evolution. The hidden but reciprocal relationship between human behavior and external environmental changes begin to recur as a complementary and cyclic relationship.

Here, built-environmental design sciences appear to play a very important role. Architecture, the design of built environment, becomes a co-evolutionary representation of the two – behaviour and environment, or say, the internal and external worlds. What had been physical to begin with and ritual through repetitions and iterations now become an established impression or memory sequence. The sequence is mnemonic, and it arrays the cognitive and re-cognitive truth impressions that lead to the Third order, representing a deep ecology or grouping of relationships between 'habits' and 'habitations' established in a city like Varanasi (Fig. 1.1). Cognitive memory sequence becomes inspirational and deeper. It can be felt even by a person experiencing something for the first time but reacting in the words of a user of a thousand times. Such words are evident in the words of American Humorist-explorer Mark Twain:

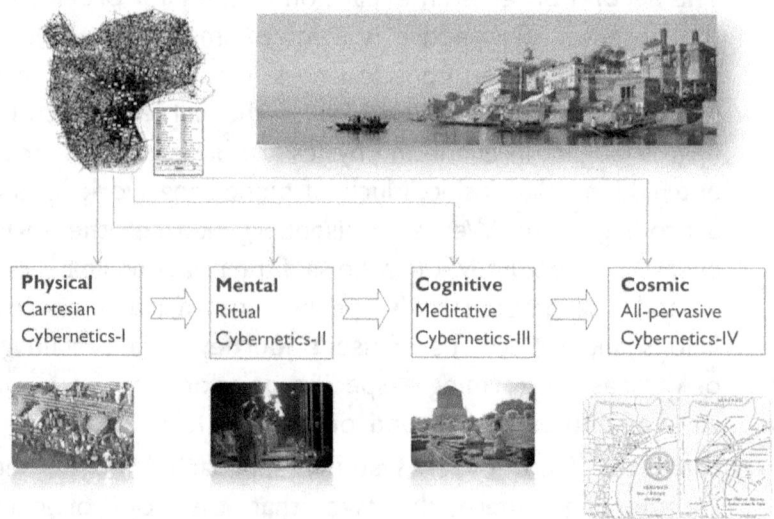

Figure 1.1 A four-phased Cybernetics flow – an exploration of Varanasi at the physical, mental, cognitive and all-pervasive (transcendental) levels
[*Source*: Developed by author]

"Benaras is older than history, older than tradition, older even than legend and looks twice as old as all of them put together".

In this sense a few underlying truths surface as the framework of the Third order:

- A whole system may redirect itself in order to adapt to its context.
- The designer or the user as the observer and the designed system co-evolve together; and this means that the observer can see his or herself as part of the system under deeper observation. Here the extent of observation becomes almost a nature of participation.
- Finally, there is the Fourth order thinking, which is penultimate. Here, the environment, which is external and the responding mechanism, which is internal, becomes one. The inter-relationship collapses to an ethereal unity, the bed of interconnectedness. If we refer to the case of Varanasi, it is the highest order in the rung of evolutionary experience. The involution of Varanasi and the evolution of an aspirant in Varanasi become complementary. They become reciprocal and completely co-evolving. They become one. They transcend individualities and become all-pervasive (Fig. 1.1).

1.3   A parable of a musical orchestra: Is architecture 'frozen music'?

In architecture, art and science of built-environmental design, all the orders of cybernetics are evident. The buildings and the environment are isolated experiences, representing the First order. In urban design, such experiences get connected, thereby representing the Second order. Slowly, experience for some becomes deeper, leading to creativity, innovation and adaptable changes in the environment, leading to the Third order. Often, one changes, rather than changing the environment, and the process thereby coming close to the Fourth order.

'Architecture', often said, is frozen music. The meters, microtones, and the rhythms of music are converted to visual proportions, something which Pythagoras had tried. The later Ionic, Tuscan and Corinthian orders of Greek columns originated from the various

Milesian orders (based on an urban centre of an ancient City called Miletus in Turkey in 1400 BCE), namely the Phrygian, the Lycia-n and the Dorian, which are basically musical notes and arrays of scales of octaves. The proportions (Fig. 1.2) that are generated as 'music' based on the sensory systems are also inevitable as 'proportions' of the human configuration – 'the anthropic' (Vitruvian Man) and centred on the human module – 'the anthropocentric' (Le Modular).

 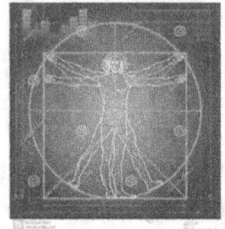 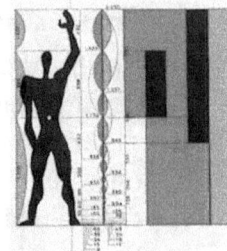

Figure 1.2 Systems of modulation in music and human proportions

Thus the system of architecture is actually a system of designed environment and designed behaviour, which is like an orchestra, an ensemble. Here, each player in a musical ensemble, for example, listens to each other player, and to his, or her, own instrument. In the whole ensemble, the inter-play is staged as a unified, emergent sound, as though all the instruments play as one. Thus eventually, architecture becomes a design process, which is a kind of *system transformation*.

1.4 The Cybernetic perspective in architecture: Patterns of co-evolution

The book proposes a system's evaluation of global history of Indian architecture. The evaluation is based on two important premises:

1. It both analyses and assimilates and finally forwards a chronological review of basic contributions and disseminations of Indian history of architecture in relationship with a larger setting of the world.
2. It interconnects the evolutionary phases of Indian architecture as a time-series or dynamic evaluation, thereby

exploring its closed system's relationship with that of global architecture, whose Western origin and cradle had been historically located in Greece. The Indian and the Greek variety represent both an opposite and, yet, mutually befitting a complementary dimensions of the co-evolution and dynamism of the two architectures.

Indian civilization and its architecture have had been essentially intrinsic. It is contemplative, and it fundamentally seeks a liberty or freedom of human spirit, of an inner order. The Greek mind and its evolutionary aftermath, i.e. the timeline and order of the entire course of Western civilization, is characteristically outwardly and extrinsic. The Greek mind and its descendants, i.e. the Europeans and the Americans, seek external social and political liberty. But both, the Indian or the Greek mind are one-sided and henceforth, in each of them, separately, the approach tends to reductionist, or portrays a 'one-way' linear approach to human progress.

- In the Indian approach, the external world is often 'underplayed', and the best of variety as available in the outer world is neglected or nullified. Consequently, the Indian approach seeks to transcend the phenomenal and reaches a state that is beyond. The 'sense' of heaven is transcendental, absolute and beyond the material world.
- The Greek mind had taken an opposite approach. To defy and deny the world above, and create a 'paradise' in the material environment is the sole social and political approach of the Greek mind driven by Western civilization.
- But the best is achieved, when the two comes together and they co-evolve to produce, in a system's loop, a far-reaching and long-term effect. And that is based on an ancient system's foundation, or an idea, which the book centrally upholds:

The idea is evident as follows:

Three mountains stand as typical of progress – the Himalayas of the Indo-Aryan, Sinai of Hebrew ('ibri), and the Olympus of Greek civilization. When the Aryans reached India, they found the climate so hot that they could not work incessantly, so they began to think: thus they became introspective and developed religion. They discovered that there was no limit to the power of mind; they therefore sought to master that; and through it they learnt that there was something infinite coiled in the frame we called man, which was seeking to become kinetic. To evolve this became their chief aim.

Another branch of Aryans went into smaller and more picturesque country of Greece, where the climate and natural conditions were more favourable; so their activity turned outwards, and they developed external arts and outward liberty.

- The Greeks sought political liberty. The Hindu has always sought spiritual liberty. Both are one-sided.
- The Indian cares not enough for national protection or patriotism, he only defends the religion; while the Greek and in Europe (where the Greek civilization finds its continuation), the country comes first.

To care only for spiritual liberty and not for social liberty is a defect, but the opposite is still a greater defect. Liberty of both body and soul is to be striven for. *Swami Vivekananda*

1.5 Patterns of co-evolution: The system's outcome

To care for spiritual liberty and material liberty at the same time is the complete ideal of human progress. It happens when and where ever the two opposite but mutually complementary forces meet to produce a holistic effect. In the following words, the confluence is best evident:

"These two gigantic rivers (Aryans and Yavanas), issuing from far-away and different mountains (India and Greece), occasionally come in contact with each other, and whenever such confluence takes place, a tremendous intellectual or spiritual tide, rising in human societies, greatly expands the range of civilization and confirms the bond of universal brotherhood among men."

The time-series is presented in four phases. Each phase represents a certain period of history, in its current cycle of global patterns and movements (Fig. 1.3). The book evaluates and summarizes these interconnections among them, which till date are an unexplored area of research and authorship:

1. Once in far remote antiquity, the Indian architecture and its cultural philosophy came in contact with that of the Greek and the intermixing led to the rise of the civilizations and consequent architecture of the Persians, the Romaic-Romany (Egyptian), and other great nations in West Asia. The role of an Indo-Persian (*Sura-Ashura*) conjugate played an important role. The role of Phoenicians, the ancient mariners, who moved westbound from eastern Persian Gulf represented a significant and last part of this period.
2. After the invasion of Alexander the Great, these two great forces had met again, as they deluged nearly half of the globe – from Western Asia to Eastern Europe. It produced the earliest architectures of Christianity prior to the Dark Ages in Europe. By this time, Phoenicians had established in the Levant – the 'Fertile Crescent' and Byzantium.
3. Again, a similar confluence took place resulting in the improvement and prosperity of Arabia – via the court of Baghdad. It laid the foundation of modern Western European civilization and shaped the impact of Renaissance through Gothic reformations, in Iberian architecture, i.e. in Spain and Portugal – from where the wave of reformation crossed the Atlantic. The Phoenicians had spread all over the Mediterranean and now they were the 'Moors'.
4. In our own days, such a time for the conjunction of these two gigantic forces has come again. The 'Moors' were now crossing the Iberian Peninsula (Spain and Portugal), and they were contributing to the evolution of modern American civilization and its architecture, which has crossed the Pacific and now is reaching the shores of the Asia-Pacific. This time, perhaps, the centre of the new architectural explosion is Asia. The centre is now moving along the Asia-Pacific and is heading from Japan to the heart of the Asiatic continental space.

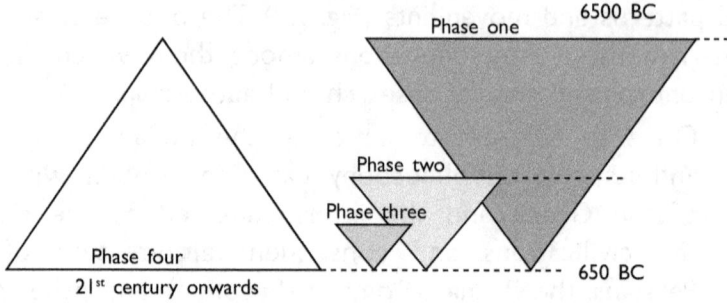

Figure 1.3 Time-line of the historical confluences – the four phases

The system's dynamism is the function of the four phases as the book envisages from the complete works of Swami Vivekananda. It comprises a global timeline and a global spatial framework. This is the first hand, the left hand of the book.

On the other hand, the system's framework forwards a right hand (Fig. 1.4), where the system's view has included the self-organization of Indian architecture complementing the global part, i.e. the part within the whole. On the whole, the left hand and the right hand constitute the spatial-temporal and the functional-built aspect of Indian architecture in relationship to global architecture. It is the key concern of the book.

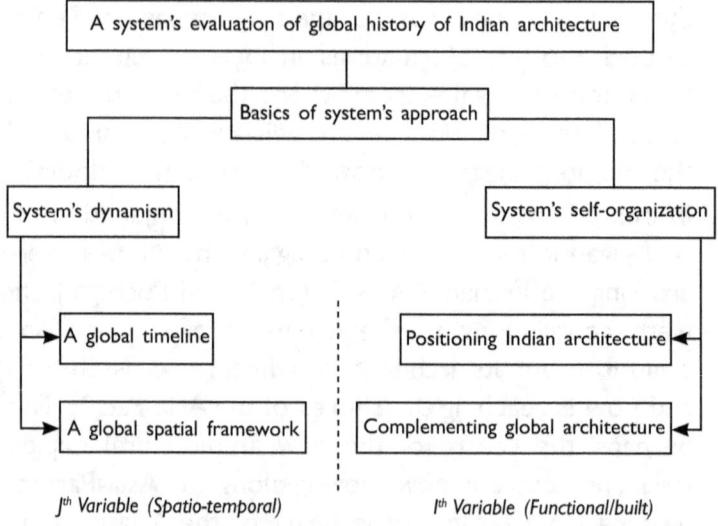

Figure 1.4 The system's framework

In the present book, the Greeks and their system of thought – democracy, economy, ecology, social structure, mathematics and sacred proportions covering natural sciences, cosmic geometry and architecture – represent the Western counterpart. On one hand, the Greeks represent the mother race or cradle that leads to the genesis of Western thought and actions; on the other hand, the Indians (people staying east of 'Sapta Sindhu' (pronounced 'Hindu' by the Persians and 'Indu' by the Greeks) represent the Eastern side of the global whole.

1.6 Organization of the book

The book is presented in six chapters.

The present chapter has been an overview of system's approach to architecture and in effect, it introduces the fundamentals and the reasons of why(s) and how(s) the book has taken this particular approach.

Chapter 2 presents the application of system's evaluation in Indian and global histories of architecture. Chapter 2 explains the unfolding that has taken place around this idea – a conjunction of the two most distinct and opposite priorities of human civilization. Yet they are binary and complementary representing the involution based (enfolding of a tree within a seed) and the evolutionary (unfolding of a tree from a seed outside) conjugate.

From Chapters 3 to 6, the system's evaluation is unfolded in the following four phases:

1. *Introduction and Evaluation of Phase I*
   Systems network: India and Greece – birth of West Asian architecture based on the ancient of interactions subsequent to the ramification of a remotely placed Vedic Age first in Aryabarta (India) and then in Airyan (Iran)
2. *Evaluation of Phase II*
   Expansion of architectural styles in Eastern Europe based on the developments in Anatolia
3. *Evaluation of Phase III*
   Expansion of architectural patterns and shapes from the Moorish beginnings of European Renaissance (after Dark Ages) in Western Europe and subsequent transition to the Americas

4. **On Phase IV**

A current expansion from the Western American centres towards the Asia Pacific and its expected aftermath: Birth of a new paradigm in architecture based on return or flow to 'Asia'

It is evident in the following order.

Chapter 3 draws evidences from the earliest phase of global patterns of architecture completing the contribution of India's earliest history. It can be termed as Phase I. It traces the earliest Indian and Greek interactions that led to the rise of Persian and Romanic civilizations. The outcome can be termed as the first Renaissance – a rebirth of human inquiry – a search for truth. It is evident in the following words:

'Once in far remote antiquity, the Indian philosophy, coming in contact with Greek energy, led to the rise of the Persian, the Roman, and other great nations'. – *Swami Vivekananda*
The Problem of Modern India and Its Solution

Chapter 4 draws the next set of evidences. The sources of these evidences belong to a much later period following the Alexandrian phase of interaction between the two ancient worlds. It can be identified as Phase II, the later Indo-Hellenic interactive phase that gave birth to the rise of Eastern Mediterranean Culture. This was the second Renaissance. It is evident in the following words:

'After the invasion of Alexander the Great, these two great waterfalls (Indian and Greek principles) colliding with each other, deluged nearly half of the globe with spiritual tides, such as Christianity'. – *Swami Vivekananda*
The Problem of Modern India and Its Solution

Chapter 5 traces the third phase which is the evolution of the Arabic-Moorish phase of global architecture. The chapter unfolds the medieval Indo-Hellenic phase revival in the Western Mediterranean, subsequently giving birth to the Euro-American civilizations, which are extensions in our present times. It is evident in the following words:

'Again, a similar commingling (of Indian and Greek principles), resulting in the improvement and prosperity of Arabia, laid the foundation of Arabia, laid the foundation of modern European civilization'. — *Swami Vivekananda*
The Problem of Modern India and Its Solution

Chapter 6 finally unfolds the return of civilization to Asia. Through globalization and completion of a full circuit, the modern phase or Phase IV had begun to consolidate from its early beginnings in the new world – 'The Americas'. It was the huge 'melting-pot' mushrooming at the turn of the 19th Century. The setting in the Americas culminated with a high pace of assimilation of the Eastern and Western dimensions, i.e. the Indo-Hellenic elements. The visible vehicle of this greatest of confluences is the ever advancing set-up of globalization and communication-information sciences.

In effect, much larger than the 'Renaissance' that had triggered the foundations of Modern European civilization (early Phase III) and a much deeper than the effect of a 'machine-industrial order' that has had shaped the Americas (later Phase three) is on its move. The pattern of the change has crossed the Western shores of the Americas and now they are consolidating along the entire coastline of the Asia-Pacific – from Japan to Korea, through China and Malaysia up to the tip of the ancient Lion's Gate 'Singapore'. And the force and the confluence of the two elements which is at the helm of the force are penetrating deep into the mainland of the most ancient continent, from where it had originated in its last cycle of change and renewal. It is best evident in the following words:

'And perhaps, in our own day, such a time for the conjunction of these two gigantic forces (Indian and Greek principles) have presented itself again. This time their centre is India'. — *Swami Vivekananda*
The Problem of Modern India and Its Solution

It is the fourth and an imminent Renaissance. The conclusion of the book explores the dimensions, opportunities and future embedded in the fourth and imminent Renaissance.

1.7 Acknowledgements

The writing of this book has become a reality as I came back to my cradle, where I was shaped and nurtured. It is my alma mater – The 'Indian institute of Technology Kharagpur'.

I like to put on record the valued interest and advice of our present Director, Professor Partha Pratim Chakrabarti and those I had received from a previous Director – particularly, Professor Amitabh Ghosh. I like to put on record the valuable contributions of the entire SANDHI team of IIT Kharagpur. Readers may refer: www.iitkgpsandhi.org.

Finally, I would like to acknowledge the source-inspiration of the true essence of this book, which is consolidated in the final chapter. The personality is Swami Ramananda, who have had been a very special man in many of our lives. It is from the Swami I have had received a unique concept of sustainability, a concept that is holistic, dynamic and India-centric. At the same time, it is also a concept that is just not a theory but a dynamism that can be planned and lived to celebrate the 'process of being and becoming'. In this sense, the concept is universal and all-embracing – accommodating areas of formalized planning and informal decision-making processes as an interlinked system or wholeness.

The undersigned sincerely acknowledges the experiences gathered from various deliberations (as conference and journal papers by the Author) in international planning conferences organized by the International Society of City and Regional Planners (ISoCaRP), Netherlands, in Athens, Greece (2002); in Bilbao, Spain (2004); in Istanbul, Turkey (2005). Also are the experiences drawn from interactions and deliberations in the Center of Sustainability Studies (IR3S), The University of Tokyo (2008) and international conferences on 'Eco-Balance' and 'Urban Engineering' (2008, 2010, 2012) in Tokyo, Japan, organized by the Society of Non-Traditional Technology, Tokyo, Japan, and others by the University of Tokyo and the Tokyo Metropolitan University; and interactions at Massachusetts Institute of Technology, Cambridge, USA (April 2015) and the National University of Singapore (October 2015).

The book presents a new age theme – a new wisdom that is more than centuries old. It retells the story of a paradigm shift happening in our own times. It forwards a shift from factor-driven reductionism to system's and life-driven approach to growth and development in civilization. It is a growing consciousness in the formation and life embedded in that formation which we call architecture – from 'architecture of the cosmos' to 'architecture of a building' and 'architecture of an electronic intelligent smart grid'. The spirit of architecture embraces it all.

System's approach is an ancient wisdom realized by the Indian sages. But that wisdom was lost. Today, with the advent of system's approach in science and technology, that wisdom is revived and now has reached a positional value that integrates the analytic and the synthetic method, encompassing both holism and reductionism. System's approach was first proposed under the name of 'General System Theory' by the biologist Ludwig von Bertalanffy. Bertalanffy noted that all systems studied by scientist in the classical viewports are closed, isolated and therefore reduced to partial truth as they do not interact with the outside world. Gradually, with the advent of system's approach in ecology and evolutionary biology, in non-linear chemistry and nano sciences, and in understanding the web of life in the cosmos, system's approach is coming close to an absolute value of a totality of things and its evolutionary possibilities. One subject that cross-cut all of it is the design of systems that we call 'architecture'.

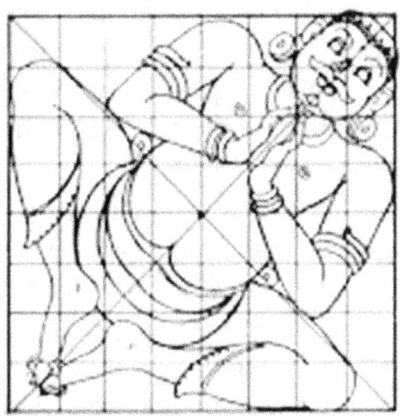 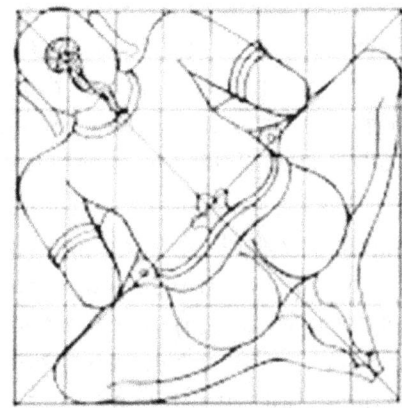

Figure 1.5 *Vastu Purusha Mandala* – An anthropocentric system of the universe

The conception and application of ancient Indian architecture is inseparable from her deep ecological realization coded in the involutionary and evolutionary perspectives of the Vedas. The *Vastu Purusha Mandala* of Indian architecture that governs the spirit of a specific and measurable building is also the pattern of a larger schema – the architecture of the cosmos (Fig. 1.5). The *Purusha,* the self-conscious sentient being (*Chaitya*, as evident in the cover design of the book), is both the spirit of the user and the building. On the other hand, it is also the same *Purusha*, the cosmic spirit behind everything. Thus, *Chaitya* is everything representing both a centre to everything and also the driving cause of the flux that constitutes everything. *Chaitya* is both being and becoming. This is the system's approach as coded in the mystery of poetry called the Vedas and un-coded in the Upanishads as a direct truth-realization called '*atma-vidya*'. The Buddhist architects employed this idea in their architecture and long before that it was stored in the *Bhagavata Puranic* version of the *Samkhya* and *Vedantic philosophy* coded by master-sage Kapila. But traces are decipherable even in Vedantic literature, mainly the *Shvetashvatara* Upanishad. Thousands of centuries later, the 'apsidal *Chaitya* cave' – the sacred innermost (*guha nihitam*) heart of hearts holding the inner 'Kingdom of the Divine' became the apsidal form of the Greco-Roman Basilica.

System's approach have had remained always as an ancient wisdom. For some it had become dormant and distant. From that remotely ancient origin, SA had made a journey West bound, from India to Persia and then to Anatolia, becoming sometimes bright and sometimes dull. From there it spread through the Dark Ages and was revived by the Renaissance master minds in 15th and 16th century till it reached the American soil.

The journey is portrayed as four phases, which the readers may enjoy. And while doing the reading, the reader may also feel a system approach that is operational – at the end and the beginning (alpha and omega) of each and every phase of the journey. Here, India and Greece are representatives of the two, the involutionary and evolutionary dimensions that constitute the dynamics of every phase.

The book makes a humble attempt to bring to light the greater truth. It hopes that the reading will unfold a vaster light that shall explain the journey of civilization and purpose of human cultural evolution in the making. The task attempted by the book has been carried out in light of an expanding ontology of becoming to a final being common to things and existence – pervading both the material and the spiritual and beyond.

Joy Sen, Ph.D.
Professor, Department of Architecture and Regional Planning (ARP)
Head, Ranbir and Chitra Gupta School of Infrastructure Design and Management (RCG SIDM)
Indian Institute of Technology Kharagpur 721302 INDIA

2

A system's approach to evaluation

2.1 Introduction

The present chapter forwards a system's evaluation of Indian architecture with that of the world. The evaluation is forwarded in two parts. Part I comprises of a detailed exploration of system's approach (SA) in light of the dimensions forwarded in Chapter 1. Part II complements the theoretical exploration on the approach through an array of examples and instances involving the greatest of contemporary minds.

2.2 Part I: Evolution of system's approach

A system's approach is a way of understanding how things or events or both, which are located across a large space, influence one another through a sequence of long stretches of interconnected events. In this sense, SA constitutes a holistic understanding of a super system of which individual things and events are parts or sub-systems. In SA, long stretches of events constitute timelines, and timelines are often further integrated with large space settings. SA therefore represents an integral dynamism of both, i.e. its spatial and temporal dimensions of the sub-systems.

Two examples can be cited to make the understanding clearer. First, through system's approach one looks at Nature as a network of various natural systems. The networks exist between the two ecosystems which are otherwise separated in a reductionist viewpoint. The two sub-systems are – one, in which various abiotic elements such as air, water prevail; and two, where the biotic configurations like plants and animals exist. In the system's viewpoint (SV), the two ecosystems are interdependent and are further considered to be co-evolving within an overall organization of things. The principle of organization can be seen as an array or a 'matrix' representing the territory or 'boundary conditions' of the system. In this example, the matrix represents Mother Nature, within which abiotic and biotic sub-systems are mutually interdependent and 'co-evolving', i.e. the evolution of the first one is interlinked with that of the other.

As a second instance, a system of human associations or organizations can be further cited. The system here is composed of organic sub-systems consisting of people, and functional systems like organizational structures, and management processes which work and coalesce together to form a collective work entity. The overall system finally becomes a sustainable whole, often representative of the human society. In this second example, the human society is the super system or the matrix.

In the two examples, it is evident that SA imparts a holistic system's viewpoint of the nature around us and also that of our present human society. It is also evident that the second example, i.e. a system of social organization is a sub-system of the first, i.e. Nature, by virtue of the boundary conditions of spatial and temporal dimensions. The spatial and temporal dimensions of large organizations or associations are smaller to that of Nature itself. So, in system's approach, there is also an idea of hierarchy of organization, where the larger system embraces the smaller. Also, the viewpoint underscores the relationship between various systems with regard to various set-ups, i.e. environmental, technical, economic, cultural and ecological. And there can be others, which are yet to be explored. Architecture, which is a system approach of integrating systems of art, sciences and technology of built environment, is one such unexplored area.

The present book proposes a system's evaluation of global history of Indian architecture, which is a relatively less addressed concern till date.

2.2.1   A contemporary concern

The book analyses and forwards a chronological review of the basic dimensions, contributions and disseminations of Indian history of architecture. The review takes into account a global context of space and time. The review happens in a way, perhaps not attempted before in any other book. The book presents an analytical framework in the form of a timeline covering historical shifts of these dimensions across space, ranging civilizations and continents and explaining an expansion of the system at the global level.

The timeline, that the book proposes, constitutes an evaluation of global history of Indian architecture by *interconnecting four important phases of Indian architecture*. While interlinking the four phases, namely – remotely ancient, ancient, medieval and modern, the analytical exploration of a global history of architecture is brought to view through a system's relationship of two major components or representations – one, the Indian architectural history along with the other one, that of Greece. India and Greece, for a system of many reasons, are considered to be the twin origins or, to an extent, the cradle of Eastern and Western counter halves of the world civilization and architecture. The following chapter brings to light the basis of the preceding statement or hypothesis proposed by the book. The book has been accordingly presented in six chapters:

1. An overview of system's approach and its significance in system's valuation of architecture
2. Specific application of system's evaluation of Indian history of architecture in the global context
3. Introduction and evaluation of Phase I systems network: India and Greece – birth of West Asian architectures
4. Evaluation of Phase II systems network: Expansion of architectural styles in Eastern Europe and the making of Greco-Roman architecture
5. Evaluation of Phase III systems network: From the early Moorish styles of architecture in Western Europe to its culmination in the Renaissance awaiting migration to the Americas
6. On Phase IV systems network: Transition through the American soil to what can be called a return to Asia; or a resurrection of the Asia-Pacific. The Phase IV forwards innovative green approaches to global architecture that were

once evident in the ancient codes: there is a birth of a new paradigm in architecture. It is towards a synthesis of futuristic solar utilitarian and green ecological dimensions drawn both from Indian and Western architectures. By 'ecology' we mean the term 'grouping' or 'coming together as a system' and therefore ready for the next leap, i.e. innovation and positive all-embracing change.

2.2.2 Basis of system's approach (SA)

System's approach (SA) is a holistic approach of understanding objects and events, which are otherwise reduced to isolated or disjointed framework of analyses. The approach streamlines how small parts or things or events influence one another within a sequence of events, which constitute various to-and-fro causal relationships among them.

In system's approach (SA), it is the network of such relationships that represents a whole, where more than a sum of the isolated co-existence of parts. Thus, the patterns of relationship between parts gain a higher significance in SA, and the framework of these patterns delineate a larger whole. Let us refer to the two examples cited in Preface. For instance, system's approach or SA looks at nature as a network of various natural systems. These networks include ecosystems in which various abiotic elements such as air, water and the biotic configurations like plants, and animals are seen as interdependent of each other and consequently, co-evolving. In another example, say, in human associations or organizations, systems may consist of people, organizational structures, and management processes; and the systems can work and coalesce together to form a collective entity, which can also be termed as a sustainable whole.

Recently, the scientific mind-set around the world, ranging from social sciences to basic quantum and relativistic physics and from ecology to trans-personal psychology, is being revolutionized by the holistic spirit of SA or system's approach. SA has helped the mind-set to expand from a conventional reductionist paradigm of looking at linear causal relationships only to a view port of looking at things or events in a wider and deeper perspective involving a non-linear or cyclic nature of relationships. The cyclic nature may stand for reversibility and variety of causes in the system instead of a simplified one-way or linear causal relationship. SA therefore imparts a range of interconnected truths viewed as systems of processes and networks rather than systems that are based on discrete variables or isolated events and components.

2.2.3   Important foundations

There are two important foundations of system's approach:

1. System's approach or SA is holistic but is not opposed to reductionism, which takes an isolated standpoint or a partial view of a system. Reductionism is like someone designing an air-conditioned hospital building, where the design of laboratories bears no reciprocal relationship with the microclimate of the local environment. As a result, the laboratories become capital-or-techno-intensive design ventures of advanced HVAC systems. On the contrary, in system's viewpoint, the machines within the laboratory will be sensitive to the built form of the laboratory; and the built form of the laboratory will be a part of the total hospital design, which will be further reciprocally sensitive to the site and surrounding, which are further parts of the larger local environment, having other buildings, natural systems and features embedded within. As a result, one layer of relationship at the level of smaller sub-systems will be interconnected, interdependent and co-evolving with others which are larger. Thus different levels of relationship which otherwise appear to be different in reductionist viewpoints, are finally accommodated and networked as ONE whole.
2. SA also bears the key to sustainability. Sustainability not so much as a goal, but more as a process. The 'ability' to sustain to-and-fro relationships in various levels of interaction among sub-systems is the true basis of SA and the key to sustainability. Thus, the design of an airport is synonymous with the planning of a city and vice versa; and as

a result, an 'aerotropolis' can be better conceived, designed and monitored through a SA. Concurrently, the position of the airport with respect to the growth and development of a city and its surrounding region becomes mutually co-evolving and 'sustainable'. A system's relationship between the city and the airport will make the city 'smarter' and the airport an 'aerotropolis'.

In applied and social sciences, SA or system's approach presents a system of interconnections between the evolution of human society and evolution of nature and that is explained through a chain of to-and-fro relationship through environment itself. In this regard, architecture is a science of built environment; and the evolution of architectural systems like art, sciences, technology and anthropometric sciences are outcomes of various human–nature or behaviour–environment correlations or interdependencies. Often, these correlations are reciprocal, cyclic and complex systems of network. The resultant understanding of the systems is the very basis of a system's evaluation of architecture.

A discussion of various recent developments in the social, evolutionary and technological sciences that paves the making of a system's approach and the necessity of a system's evaluation of other areas, relatively less explored or unaddressed, has been finally addressed in this book. A system's evaluation of a global history of architecture (a larger whole) in relationship with that of Indian architecture is a response to this concern. The present book has taken up this concern.

2.2.4 A systems' evaluation of architecture using spatial and historical dimensions

Under SA, architecture is a network of various scientific understanding explaining finally a complete science of built environment. At the root of the complete scientific understanding is a co-evolutionary and reciprocal functional process representing fundamental correlations between 'habits' as functions or responses of human mind and 'habitations' that are changes or stimulus coming from the environment. Often, the relationship is reversed.

Improvements in environment inspire the human mind. Human-mind-driven innovations emerge that improve the environment further. And the to-and-fro relationship between the two sides can proceed, co-evolve and grow. Thus, the relationship not only is reciprocal but also cyclic. Two aspects are evident:

1. *Improvements in environment represent the changes in the external world.* The changes are macrocosmic. The environment of a well-laden green park inspires the mind of a jogger, who can perhaps become a better writer or a musician; or say, the nature-based ambience of river-side developments can provide ample retreat spaces to inspire an engineering mind innovating new ideas of 'green design'. The inspiration, at times, comes from outside and the change happens within that leads to further changes outside.

2. *Improvements in the human mind represent changes in the inner world.* The changes within are microcosmic. The divine and elevated mind of the Buddha had once created the wonderful *viharas* – the green monasteries of ancient Buddhism; ages later, the inspired mind of poet Rabindranath Tagore creates a beautiful 'Santiniketan', a space for modern Indian university (Bharati) celebrating the spirit of world ethos (viswa), an ecological laboratory of experiments with human mind and nature and the interdependence between the two. And, there can be many other examples, that of Auroville and Arcosanti. But one can trace these traditions to times of remote antiquity, in the green forest traditions of education system, i.e. the 'Aranyakas' or the Vedic gurukuls, where ancient sages or rishis had laid the original seeds of mind-environment co-evolutionary approaches. In those traditions, a larger system's evaluation of green built environment over space and time had been processed. In all of them, the sources of inspiration have come from within, from the fathoms of the human mind; and the changes in the environment have obviously followed later, much later, in the outside, carving the built sciences of a tangible built environment. Thoughts precede and the built forms succeed. Improved

built environment can lay the foundations of further thoughts for improvement.

In SA or the system's approach, the two are therefore reciprocal and 'co-evolutionary'. SA sees them as ONE. The relationship between the inner urges of human mind or 'habits' and the built changes in the external world called 'habitation' are seen complementary to each other (Fig. 2.1). *In SA, 'habit–habitation' interdependence is the key of a system's evaluation of architecture.* It is a cycle, reversibility, if moderated and evolved, of a system of human habits and a system of human habitation and a larger system grown from the two based on their complementarities. *It is the principal essence and concern of the present book.*

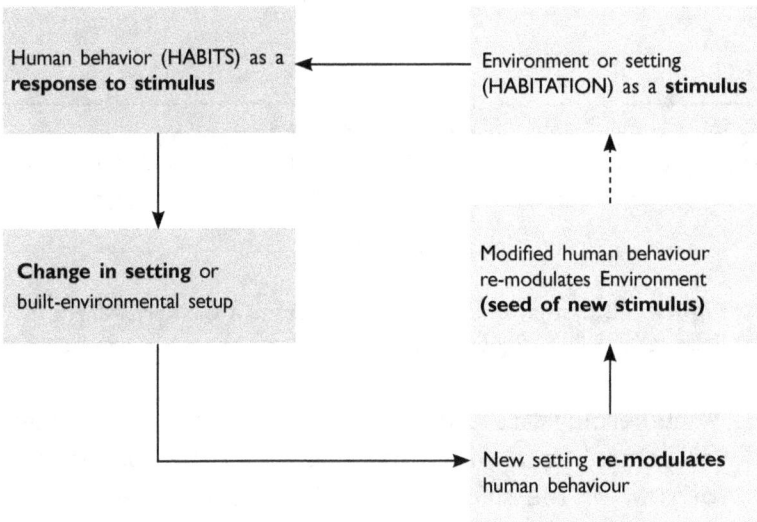

Figure 2.1 Habit–habitation complementarities

2.2.5 A cybernetic perspective

Let us forward a key word that bridges SA or system's approach to ancient wisdom. It is 'cybernetics'. The word 'cybernetics' owes its roots from the ancient Greek word for steersman (kybernetes). In ancient Indian texts, the synonymous word is 'Karna-dhara' (who is the oars-man or the Captain of the floating ship making a smooth course ahead). In Sanskrit, the word 'Karna' means 'the ear' or the sprout of the seed or the corn; and etymologically, the interrelated word is 'oar' or 'spike' or a 'ray'. The 'ray' represents the inner surge exuding to be the direction of relationship.

Today, the word 'cyber' means 'informatics' or a system of streamlining complex sets of information codes representing a variety of relationships in one loop or a whole of array, which is 'matrix'. In the ancient Indian example of *'Karna-dhara'* or the Greek steersman (kybernetes), the complementarities or the reciprocal balance is maintained between the two oars of the ship – one, on the left; and the other, on the right (Fig. 2.2). Thus 'cybernetics' employs a wonderful coordination between the array of iteration and logical sequence of strengths – either the left or the right oar, or both – which is represented by three principal factors:

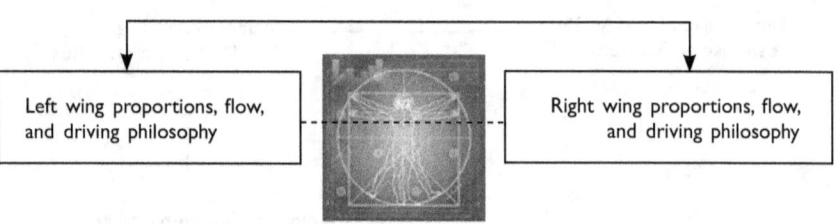

Figure 2.2 System of cybernetics (steersman or 'Karna-dhara') Balance or 'Libra' (Liberation from one-way biases or bondage)

1. A numerological sequence maintained by the logic of steering or control from within the ship (from the contained point of view or the ship). It is the idea of Kshetragya in Indian mathematical philosophy called *Samkhya*.
2. A procedural sequence of balance and progress maintained by the logic of float and buoyancy as 'feedback loops' (from the waves in the container or the larger receptacle, which is the imagery of the water channel – the river or the sea). It is analogous to the idea of Kshetra or the field in *Samkhya*; and finally,
3. A philosophical sequence depicting the objective or the overall aim of the journey based on an idea of origin (O) and destinations (D). Where is the ship from? Where is it heading for?

In other words, SA in the cybernetic perspective is represented by three dimensions of knowledge systems:
1. Mathematics – the component of the contained or the Kshetragya – the ith variable
2. Aerodynamics – the component of the field or the Kshetra – the jth variable
3. Philosophy – the overarching principle to the container (field) and the contained (seed) – the process which is a functional whole of the first two (ith and jth)

Now, the interaction among the three, i.e. Mathematics – the component of the contained or the Kshetragya; Aerodynamics – the component of the field or the Kshetra; and Philosophy – the overarching principle to the container (field) and the contained (seed), can have different depths or levels. These are often represented as 'orders'.

Cybernetics in general system's approach is defined as the study of control within a system, typically using combinations of feedback loops or 'cyclical' relationships. Over the years, the advance of science and technology is based on an evolving order – first, second and, of late, the third.

- First-order cybernetics relates to closed systems, and a common example may be that of the 'Carnot's cycle' or that of the relationship between a 'flywheel' as a free-energy supplying system and 'an engine' requiring that energy to run sustainably, and bear a continuous and reversible relationship with a flywheel. There is not much relationship with nature and the technology involved.
- The second order is an expansion of the first order, where the observer perspective is involved imparting a role and reflection of human consciousness in the evolution of the so-called material world. Much of the current or cutting-edge thoughts in quantum physics are based on this strange but hidden relationship. Much of pioneering work of Werner Heisenberg (Uncertainty Principle) and Erwin Schrodinger (Wave Equation) had set the earliest paces. Nature and technology, in other words, 'observer' as 'participator' and 'technology' as a 'medium' become an inter-twined medium.

- Of late, the third-order system's approach in cybernetics is emerging, where the two, that the role of human consciousness and various systems in the material world bears a phenomenon of co-evolution. It is when a whole system acknowledges its surroundings in its growth and evolution. The hidden but reciprocal relationship between human behaviour and external environmental changes begin to recur as a complementary and cyclic relationship. Here, the role of built-environmental design sciences appears to play a very important role. Architecture, the design of built environment, becomes a co-evolutionary representation of the two – behaviour and environment, or say the internal and external worlds. In this sense a few underlying truths surface as the framework of the third order:
  - A whole system may redirect itself in order to adapt to its context.
  - The designer or the user as the observer and the designed system co-evolve together; and this means that the observer can see him or herself as part of the system under deeper observation. Here the extent of observation becomes almost a nature of participation. Nature and technology become reciprocal and co-evolving with nature representing a ecology or 'grouping' of events and objects, which may be called holism, and technology forwarding a 'green ordering' that is best complementary to the holism (Fig. 2.3).
- It is better evident in the works of E. F. Schumacher, who terms this as a new level of wisdom and also points out that the problems of disorder in the socio-cultural and socio-economies extremes cannot be solved but can be transcended by this wisdom of balance. This growing wisdom, with time and experience, as he pointed out needs a combination of:
  - stability and change
  - order and freedom
  - tradition and innovation
  - planning and laissez faire

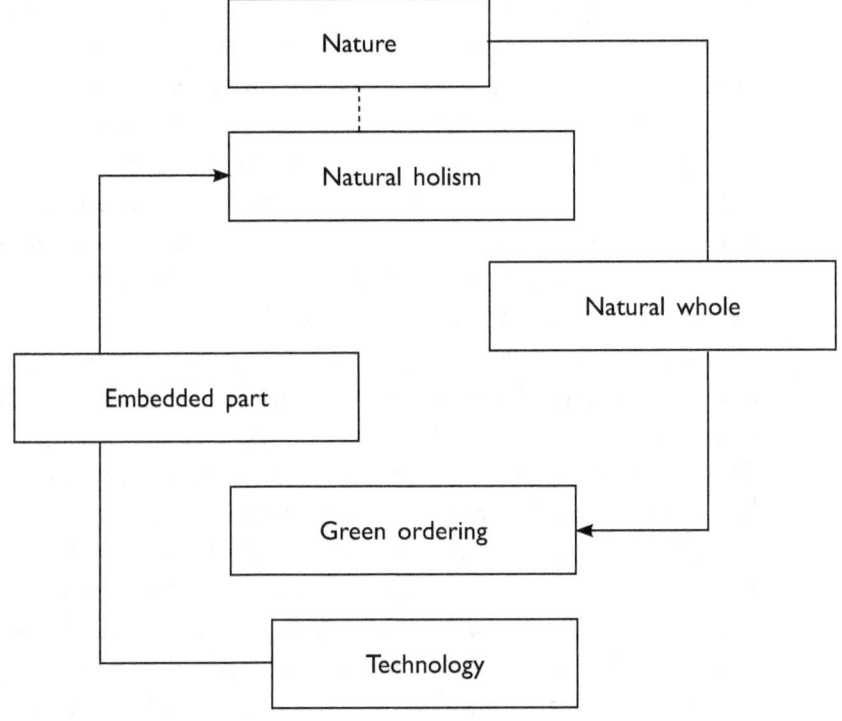

Figure 2.3 Third order of cybernetics: Co-evolution of nature and technology

2.2.6 Parable of an orchestra: Is architecture 'frozen music'?

Now, let us go back to the three components of cybernetics and re-present them from the point of view of elements of design:

1. *Mathematics* – It is the rhythm of progression maintained by the algorithm of design. In other words, it is the design input provided from Inside, by the creator–projector mind self-projecting on the design itself. It is like the captain who has designed the path, the course of the ship, the nature of the journey for all its passengers or users. *The key word is 'algorithm or inner code of design'.*
2. *Aerodynamics* – It is the interplay of the course of design in the external world maintained by a combination of formation – either through a frozen form or through continuous changes in form over time. If we take the example of the

ship, the complete dynamics is a resultant of the frozen form of the ship and its interaction with the course of the wind and the course of water (river or sea). It is the combination of how much of void and how much of consolidation are rightly put to an interplay over time. As a result, the boat makes its course. Here, the key word is the interplay of void and solids. In other words, it is the interplay of 'wind in space' and 'the fluidity of the form' as represented by 'water'. *In short, it is 'wind' and 'water'.*

3. *Philosophy* – It is the integrating principle that brings the inner 'algorithm of design' (mathematics) and the external expression of 'wind and water' (aerodynamics) together. The ultimate significance of the journey is a resultant of this integration. The inner and the outer worlds are put to perfect harmony. The will of the captain (steersman) is in harmony with the course of the ship and all (passengers) are perfectly happy with the ongoing journey. All players involved (the supply side) and evolved (the demand side) are in perfect harmony. The reciprocal relationship between the two worlds – the inner and the outer reach a stage of perfect harmony and a frame of integration emerges both at a surface containing 'all parts' and at a deeper level sustaining an interconnectedness as 'one whole'. The whole and the parts are frozen as one music (Fig. 2.4).

Figure 2.4 Third-order cybernetics: Frozen music
[*Source:* http://attainable-utopias.org/tiki/ThirdOrderCybernetics]

When a whole system acknowledges its surroundings, it reaches a stage called the third-order of cybernetics. It is best evident in the diagram of an orchestra, where:

1. Each player is in a musical networking or an ensemble. For example, every single player listens to each other player, and also to his, or her, own instrument; and his or her participant is a sum-total or interplay of the two.
2. The whole ensemble may then play as a unified, emergent sound, as though all the instruments play as one – the orchestra itself.
3. This is a kind of *system transformation*, where the captain (steersman) or the composer plays a unified transforming role in harmony with the audience.

The evolution emerges step by step. Initially, it is first-order cybernetics where everyone has a discrete position. The captain (steersman) is separate from the ship and yet to take over fully. The design of the ship is frozen but yet to sail forward in full course. The passengers are not yet full-fledged partners or players in the journey which is so enjoyable and absorbing. In first-order cybernetics, the subject and the object are separate, reduced to discrete blocks and all viewpoints impart a tendency to see systems as objects.

As evolution proceeds, second-order cybernetics takes over. The captain of the ship gets involved in steering the ship. The ship takes off to start the course based on inputs of the captain as a function of available wind and course of water. The order of the journey reaches a point of an internal dynamics of the system. A system becomes evident at this point.

Third-order cybernetics begins at this point. The internal dynamics of the system exceeds the boundaries as the ship satisfies the rhythm of the journey and the passengers become players and participants in the joy and satisfaction of the journey. The third-order transforms a system to a greater state of active-interactive element (a part) in a larger network of relationship between the captain, the ship, the sea, the environment and the passengers. A larger circuit or a network of relationship emerges.

Beyond this point, the larger circuit of relationship appears to be a greater and greater and more significant than parts or sub-systems in it. Individuality is slowly replaced by the totality of the system. In the Indian context, it is the idea of *Mahat* (collective or cosmic identity) that takes over *Aham* (individual or isolated identity), as per *Samkhya*. It tends to be fourth-order cybernetics when a system redefines itself. The focus shifts or expands. Expansion is the better word. It focuses on the integration of a system within its larger, co-defining context. Gradually, the network of relationship among systems becomes the system itself, becoming a circuit of things or systems. For instance, in Physics, in the area of Thermodynamics, the Carnot's cycle becomes more evident and significant than individual positions of temperature or pressure points of a system undergoing change. The overall flow of heat gain, heat losses, increase and decrease of disorder becomes more important than a single system in the cycle. There can be another example. In Tibetan Iconography, for example, individual gods or demi-gods play a lesser role, and they are absorbed into a larger circuit of changes and causation of the macrocosm or the universal scheme of patterns, which is often represented by various icons of the Mandala.

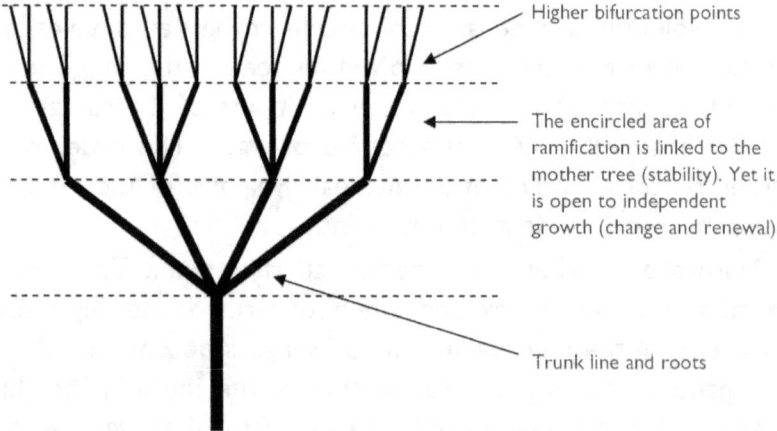

Figure 2.5 Fourth-order cybernetics: The network of cyclic relationships A system of flow: from (first fruits) seed to tree, tree to fruits, from new seed to returns

The two examples of the Carnot's Cycle in Physics and the Tibetan Mandala in metaphysical reality are significant modern and ancient examples of a non-linear network of relationships and patterns of relationships. In the two examples, the linear characteristics or location-based positions of individuals or parts or sub-systems are subdued; and instead, the dynamism of continuous changes and transformation in the overall pattern of universal changes takes over. In the system there are two processes: one, ramification (from unity to diversity), and two, interconnectedness (diversity to unity) becomes a complementary double intender (Fig. 2.5). Ramification of branches of a tree from roots and return to roots through the seed from its first fruits holding the possibility of the next-den tree is both a two-way intender of (a) dynamism over time (positional) and (b) an archetypal pattern (absolute) of the cycles of renewals and rebirths for fresh unending opportunities. This is the mystery of evolution of the next tree and the involution of a preceding seed from an 'original' tree that is a priori. Likewise, in tracing the pattern of the history of any civilization, the overall and the deeper truths are more revealed when one takes a system's approach or SA. The present concern is to conduct a system's evaluation of global history of Indian architecture. The basic questions are:

1. How Indian architecture as a system has evolved from within?
2. What has been the pattern of its interaction within a larger or global framework?
3. And, why it has been that way?

A cybernetic perspective of exploring the depths and spreads of Indian architecture and an arrival at the patterns of co-evolution of India with regards to the rest of the world holds a key to the right perspective. In doing so, the book takes a co-evolutionary standpoint of two principal components – one, the Indian dimension, which represents a major representation of the oriental architecture; and two, the Greeks, whose achievements in architecture has been a cradle to the West.

A precursory introduction to SA has been provided in the present chapter. However, a detailed discussion of the system's framework of evolution is provided in Chapter 3. The present chapter concludes by taking a cybernetic perspective, which is the very basis of the framework of the system's evaluation and this is also the very organization of the book.

2.2.7 A cybernetic perspective in system's evaluation: Patterns of co-evolution

The book proposes a system's evaluation of global history of Indian architecture and takes a cybernetic perspective. As said before, the perspective is based on three important aspects:

1. It analyses and forwards a chronological review of basic constituent dimensions, contributions and disseminations of Indian history of architecture in relationship with a larger setting of the world.
2. It interconnects the evolutionary phases of Indian architecture based on a time-series or dynamic evaluation. First, it explores its closed systems relationship with that of global architecture, whose Western half originates from its cradle located in the eastern Mediterranean, i.e. Greece.
3. The Indian and the Greek variety represent an opposite and yet mutually befitting and complementary dimensions of the co-evolution and dynamism of a global perspective of architecture.

The three aforesaid aspects correspond to the three basic questions:

1. How Indian architecture as a system has evolved from within? and
2. What has been the pattern of its interaction within a larger or global framework, whose Western counterpart has originated from Greece? Thus within the two larger systems, the East and the West, the two representative sub-systems of India and Greece are embedded, respectively. The dynamism of interaction at the global level is in effect the interaction between its Eastern and Western halves, which are further decomposed to the representative sub-systems

of Indian and Greek architectures (Fig. 2.6). Together, they form a pattern hierarchy.

3. And, what has been the dynamic outcome of these patterns of interaction? How the co-evolution of the two-halves has portrayed the growth and transformation of the whole, i.e. global architecture? The answers are hidden in Fig. 2.6.

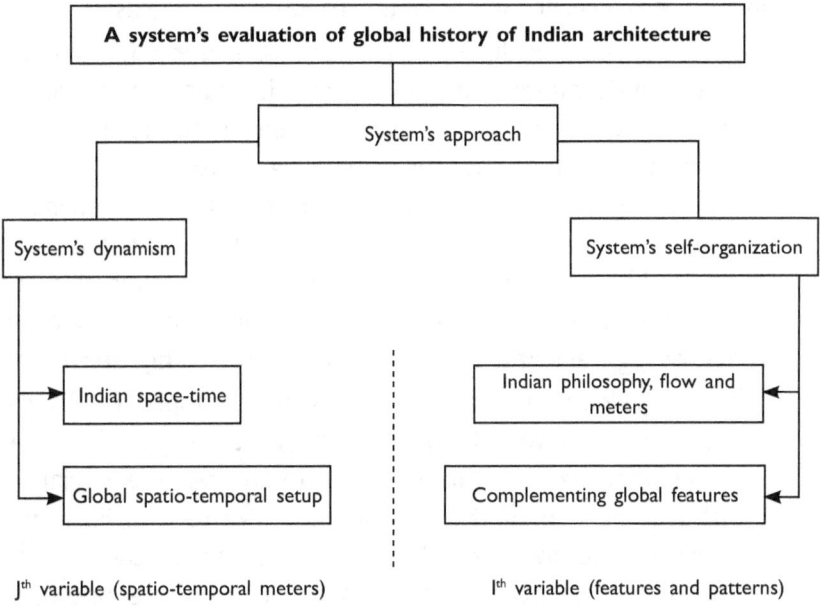

Figure 2.6 Dynamism of co-evolution of the East and the West and a making of a global pattern features at physical, mental, cognitive and all-pervasive levels

2.2.8 Complementarities and co-evolution: India and Greece – why and how?

Though an initial introduction to the system's framework of evolution has been explained here, but it is detailed in Chapter 3. The present chapter concludes explaining the very basis of the framework required for the system's evaluation. The evaluation has been conducted in four distinct phases, which constitute the dynamic framework of SA.

Indian civilization and its architecture have had been essentially intrinsic. It is contemplative, and it fundamentally seeks a liberty or freedom of human spirit, of an inner order. The Greek mind and its evolutionary aftermath, i.e. the timeline and order of the entire course of Western civilization, are characteristically outwardly and extrinsic. The Greek mind and its descendants, i.e. the Europeans and the Americans, seek external social and political liberty. But both the Indian and/or the Greek mind are one-sided and henceforth, in each of them, separately, the approach tends to reductionist, or portrays a 'one-way' linear approach to human progress.

- In the Indian traditional approach, the external world is often 'underplayed', and the focus is mainly intrinsic and introspective. The Indian approach seeks to transcend the phenomenal and the ever-changing external world and reaches a permanent state that is beyond. The 'sense' of heaven is transcendental, absolute and beyond the material world. The sciences that India has evolved over the ages are therefore the sciences of an inner world – of ethics, psychology, art and music, religions and mainly, spirituality.
- The Greek mind had taken an opposite approach. To defy and deny the world above, and create a 'paradise' here in the material environment had been the sole social and political passion of the Greek mind. Western civilization is a natural outcome of that. The sciences of the external world – social, political, economic and mainly, technological.

However, an aggregate evaluation of human mind has shown that the best is achieved only when the two come together and co-evolve to produce in a system's loop a far-reaching, a far more complete cause and effect of human growth and development.

In the global scale, the Indian mind represents the vertical or the 'depth' element, which is involutionary and descending. The Greek mind represents the complementary side – the spread or the 'horizontal' element that is moving continentally. Together they constitute the dynamism of human civilization based on:

1. changes and the leaps for further changes
2. turning of civilization in a cycle – horizontally
3. ascent of civilization – traversing level of changes vertically

Chapter 3 has expanded on the constitution of the dynamism, which is the basis of the present book. The ancient system's foundation of a complete system's approach (CSA), which is just not an idea, but a realization, maintained by a blessed few over different ages is what the book centrally upholds. However, the idea is best evident in the following description:

'Three mountains stand as typical of progress – the Himalayas of the Indo-Aryan, Sinai of Hebrew ('ibri), and the Olympus of Greek civilization. When the Aryans reached India, they found the climate so hot that they could not work incessantly, so they began to think: thus they became introspective and developed religion. They discovered that there was no limit to the power of mind; they therefore sought to master that; and through it they learnt that there was something infinite coiled in the frame we called man, which was seeking to become kinetic. To evolve this became their chief aim.

Another branch of Aryans went into smaller and more picturesque country of Greece, where the climate and natural conditions were more favourable; so their activity turned outwards, and they developed external arts and outward liberty.

- The Greeks sought political liberty. The Hindu has always sought spiritual liberty. Both are one-sided.
- The Indian cares not enough for national protection or patriotism, he only defends the religion; while the Greek and in Europe (where the Greek civilization finds its continuation) the country comes first.

To care only for spiritual liberty and not for social liberty is a defect, but the opposite is still a greater defect. Liberty of both body and soul is to be striven for'. (Fig. 2.7)

– *Swami Vivekananda*

Figure 2.7 Integral framework of the bases of two wings: Left wing (Material Liberty) and Right wing (Spiritual Liberty)

2.2.9 Patterns of co-evolution: System's outcome

To care for spiritual liberty and material liberty at the same time is the complete ideal of human progress. It happens when and where ever the two opposite but mutually complementary forces meet to produce a holistic effect. In the following words, the confluence is best evident:

"These two gigantic rivers (Aryans and Yavanas), issuing from far-away and different mountains (India and Greece), occasionally come in contact with each other, and whenever such confluence takes place, a tremendous intellectual or spiritual tide, rising in human societies, greatly expands the range of civilization and confirms the bond of universal brotherhood among men."

The time-series is presented in four phases. Each phase represents a certain period of history, in its current cycle of global patterns and movements (Fig. 2.8). The book evaluates and summarizes these interconnections between them, which, till date, are an unexplored area of research and authorship:

1. Once in far remote antiquity, the Indian architecture and its cultural philosophy came in contact with that of the Greek. The intermixing led to the rise of the civilizations and consequent architecture of the Persians, the Romaic-Romany (Egyptian), and other great nations in West Asia.
2. After the invasion of Alexander the Great, these two great forces had met again. It deluged nearly half of the globe – from Western Asia to Eastern Europe. It produced the earliest architectures of Christianity prior to the Dark Ages in Europe.
3. Again, a similar confluence took place resulting in the improvement and prosperity of Arabia – via the court of Baghdad. It laid the foundation of modern Western European civilization and shaped the impact of Renaissance through Gothic reformations, in Iberian architecture, i.e. in Spain and Portugal – from where the wave of reformation crossed the Atlantic.
4. In our own days, such a time for the conjunction of these two gigantic forces has come again. Traversing the modern

American civilization and its architecture, it has crossed the Pacific and now it is reaching the shores of the Asia-Pacific. This time, perhaps, the centre of the new architectural explosion is Asia. The centre is now moving along the Asia-Pacific and is heading from Japan to the heart of the Asiatic continental space.

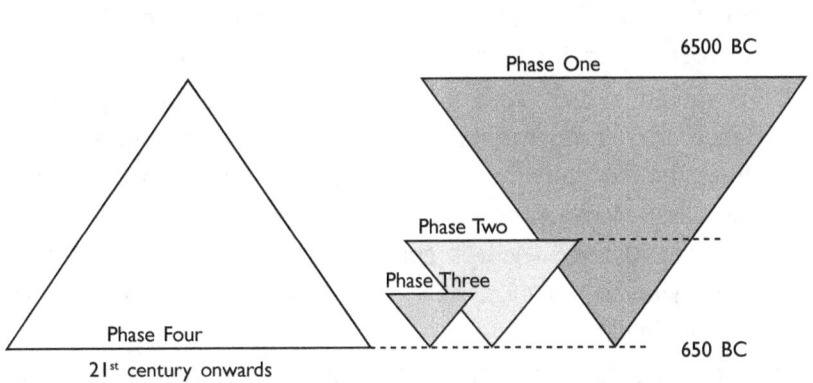

Figure 2.8 Time-line of the historical confluences – the four phases

2.3 Part 2: Complementary events and impacts

2.3.1 Introduction

In this part, a set of discussions have been forwarded from contemporary historic cases. The idea forwards a system of completeness that formulates architecture of the big and the small – the macrocosm and the microcosm.

The system's evaluation of Indian architecture with that of the world, as attempted by the book, is based on the aforesaid range – from small to big. The system's framework has been introduced in the two key Forewords to the book and a detailing coverage of an all-round features of the Indian architecture based on deep evolutionary sciences has surfaced in the last chapter. Four sets of discussion have been forwarded based on:

1. An initial historic dialogue between Indian yogi reformer Swami Vivekananda and electrical scientist Nikola Tesla in Chicago (1893)

2. Emerging paradigms in Evolutionary Sciences exceeding post-Freudian and non-reductionist psychological and ecological standpoints (works of C. S. Jung, Abraham Maslow, Ken Wilber and others: 1950 to till date)
3. A further dialogue between poet Rabindranath Tagore and scientist Albert Einstein (1930); and allied constructs by scientists David Bohm and John Wheeler in the 60s and 70s on 'the Anthropic' (human consciousness-centric) viewpoint of cosmos, architecture and human evolution
4. A system's approach based on a non-linear dynamism based on fundamentals of networks: interdependence, diversity, complexity; *boundaries*: scale and limits; cycles: recycling of resources and partnership; flow-*through*: energy and resources; *development*: succession and co-evolution; and *dynamic balance*: self-organization, flexibility, stability, sustainability.

The idea has been finally portrayed in the form of a cyclic stratification called the TREE. A TREE is a system's framework and a natural architectural archetype that is a living symbol of deep ecology and sustenance.

2.3.2 A system of completeness: Architecture of the cosmos

'Completeness' as a scientific abstract may be logically understood through theories and practice of the principles and elements of design called 'architecture'. Our concern here is to understand the fundamentals of the largest possible design – 'the architecture of the cosmos'. On the other hand, there can be smaller examples, say – the architecture of a building, or an even smaller one – the architecture of computer chips. The architecture of the cosmos can be best reviewed if the 'concept' is evaluated from different standpoints of natural and social sciences. The review has taken place in four sections.

The first section provides an analogy of Indian Cosmology and modern Electrical and Communication Sciences. This discussion is based on the historical dialogue of two most important personalities of the last century: (1) India's saint and reformer Swami Vivekananda and (2) renowned electrical scientist Nichola Tesla, who proposed and presented an alternative to direct current (DC) technology called the 'alternative current system' (AC). The discussion had happened during the Columbian Exposition celebrating the 'City Beautiful Movement' held at Chicago, USA, in 1893. The two of them discussed, converged and subsequently agreed upon three fundamentals that could bridge the ancient and modern viewpoints: (1) a pattern of life in this universe called the prana, which is analogous to modern concept of 'force'; (2) a framework of space accommodating the movement of life called the akasha, which is analogous to 'matter'; (3) the rhythm of life (prana) in space (akasha) seen over a long stretch of a creative cycle called kalpa, which is analogous to periodic cycles of 'time'. Our discussions shall reveal that these three ancient dimensions are acceptable in the modern scientific world.

Everything in this universe is a combination of 'force' and 'matter' (or of prana and akasha). We will begin to see a set of correlation imbedded in a simple logical see-saw:

- What is force? That which moves matter.
- What is matter? That what is moved by force.
- What is time then? That what records the stages of combinations of the two – in changing, i.e. increasing or decreasing intensities.

After the close of the Parliament of Religions on September 27, 1893, Swami Vivekananda was already a very accepted figure amongst the highest intellectuals of America, and subsequently, there was an invitation to the house of Elisha Gray, the noted inventor of electrical equipment. Later around September 28 and 29, 1893, Swami Vivekananda had gone to Highland Park. Some of the important guests at Highland Park were the British physicist Sir William Thomson (also known as Lord Kelvin); the German scientist Herman Von Helmholtz; and the French delegate to the International Electrical Congress, Professor Edourd Hospitalier. Swami Vivekananda met scientist Nichola Tesla in that gathering.

It was Swami Vivekananda, who was explaining Cosmology on the basis of three variables. First, prana, a life current constituting all dynamism from small to large; second, akasha, an all pervading space from small to large; and third and the last, kalpa, the single cycle of time representing a unitary cosmic creation and dissolution.

Recalling Tesla reaction to the invocation, the Swami writes:

".......Our friend (Tesla) was charmed to hear about the Vedantic Prana and Akasha and the Kalpas, which, according to him, are the only theories modern science can entertain. Now both Akasha and Prana again are produced from the Cosmic Mahat, the universal mind, the Brahma or Iswara. He (Tesla) thinks he can demonstrate mathematically that force and matter are reducible to potential energy. I am to go and see him next week, to get this new mathematical demonstration".

Two constructs emerged from what they had shared:
1. First, a conceptual framework of the parallels of Vedanta and Modern Science.
2. Two, the plans of Tesla outlining his advent in the later years in pursuit of the holistic truth as implied by the framework.

Meditation is a psychic depth where the soul of the person sojourns beyond the physical body (the pinda) and enters an inner (or the cosmic expanse – comparable to the Brahmanda). At times, the soul touches the transcendental unity beyond the cosmos and shines forever as the 'one and only one'. This journey is the very foundation of Vedantic Cosmology and also of Christian Eschatology. In the letter Swami Vivekananda further added:

"...In that case, the Vedantic Cosmology will be placed on the surest of Foundations. I am working a good deal now, upon the Cosmology and Eschatology of the Vedanta. I clearly see their perfect unison with modern Science, and that of the other will follow the elucidation of the one. I intend to write a work later on, in the form of questions and answers. The first chapter will be on Cosmology, showing the harmony between Vedantic Theories and modern science".

Swami Vivekananda had provided a conceptual system's framework (Fig. 2.9) in four ascending levels correlating the two:

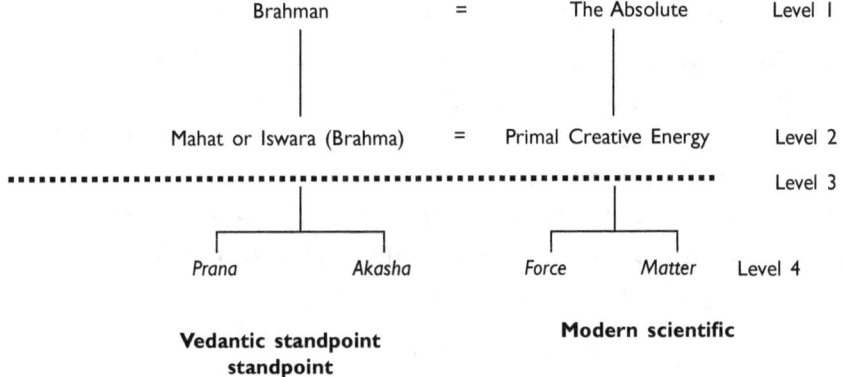

Figure 2.9 System's construct of the architecture of the cosmos (Indian and Western)

2.3.3 The system of trans-personating and spectrum

Recently great advances have been made in social, evolutionary and cognitive sciences. Key among them is the work on cognitive psychology in the post-Freudian years. They are of psychologists Carl Gustav Jung, Abraham Maslow and Ken Wilber. They present a recent recognition by modern psychology of the higher possibilities of human mind, i.e. possibilities which are beyond the superego, ego and the id (the material-carnal). This section brings forward these higher promises through new constructs called 'the psychic-transpersonal' and the 'spectrum-universal'. They make us understand the very basis of a larger scope of human life through proper usages of higher intelligence, values, ethics, conscience and consciousness itself.

Recognition by modern sciences

Since last century, few and commendable works have emerged. They are from fields of evolutionary biology, comparative ecology, cognitive psychology and built-environmental sciences. They come from the latest frontiers. And to our greatest delight, perhaps, they all are accepting this great proposition of the ancient. These current works propose a new viewpoint of human existence in relationship to *prakriti* or nature, either internal or external.

Inputs from cognitive psychology and evolutionary biology

Cognitive psychology and evolutionary biology are fundamental to inner and physical nature of beings. Of the two, in psychology important progresses have been made in the years that followed Sigmund Freud. The absolute authority of a 'natural selection processes and physical instinct like libido', as propagated by Freud, has undergone a 'paradigm shift'. The shift is characterized by the works of psychologists Carl Gustav Jung, Abraham Maslow and Ken Wilber.

Post-Freudian years: Carl Gustav Jung

Carl Gustav Jung, one of Freud's greatest disciples, had not conformed to classical Freudian notions only. Jung had opened up possibilities of the human libido beyond the 'carnal-sensual-physical'. Jung explained that wider and ethical domains of the human mind lied beyond the initial competitive processes.

Abraham Maslow and transpersonal objective

In later years, psychologist Abraham Maslow expanded on these wider domains as 'strands' of trans-personation where an initial self-centric individuality slowly opens to wider 'trans-personal' possibilities. These are the possibilities of collective community and ecological ethics, pan-altruism and philanthropy.

Holistic 'spectrum' of Ken Wilber

Abraham Maslow's work is called 'Towards a Psychology of Being' (1962). At a following point, one of the most comprehensive systems to integrate different psychological schools is the spectrum psychology proposed by Ken Wilber. It unifies (subsequent to the work of Abraham Maslow) numerous approaches, both Western and Eastern, into a spectrum of psychological models and theories that reflects the spectrum of human consciousness. Each of these levels, or bands, of this spectrum is characterized by a different sense of identity, ranging from the supreme identity of cosmic consciousness to the drastically narrowed identity of the ego. Ken Wilber distinguishes basically four levels: the ego level, the biosocial level, the existential level, and the transpersonal level 1.

Psychologist Ken Wilber has forwarded the possibilities of these multi-strands (that he called 'spectrums') of a fully blooming human personality. The layers of human psychology or the spectrums nearly match the ancient Indian wisdom of 'sapta-bhumi or sapta-chakras' (the concept of a septuplet matrix or the seven planes of consciousness) in Rajyoga. To draw an analogy, we may refer back to the Swami's works where once he says:

"...The true secret of evolution is the manifestation of the perfection which is already in every being; that this perfection is barred and the infinite tide behind is struggling to express itself. These struggles and competitions are but the results of our ignorance, because we do not know the proper way to unlock the gate and let the water in. This infinite tide behind must express itself; it is the cause of all manifestation. Competitions for life or sex-gratification are momentary, unnecessary, extraneous effects, caused by ignorance. Even when all competition has ceased (in the external frame), this perfect nature behind will make us go forward (in the internal frame) until everyone has become perfect. Therefore there is no reason to believe that competition is necessary to progress. In the animal the man was suppressed, but as soon as the door was opened, out rushed man. So in man there is the potential god, kept in by the locks and the bars of (refined) ignorance. When knowledge breaks these bars, the god (trans-personal man) becomes manifest".

Swami Vivekananda reinstated the ancient works of Indian evolutionist (Parinambadi) Patanjali, a yogi believed to have preached 1400 years prior to Christ, and his words is a key to the paradigm shift in cognitive psychology in the post-Freudian years. They also hold the key to the concept of a time-tested memory sequence called the 'Morphic resonance' (based on these earlier works of Carl Gustav Jung, Abraham Maslow, Ken Wilber and more lately that of Rupert Sheldrake) and a concept of wider evolutionary possibility called the co-evolutionary 'gene-culture' theory (works of EO Wilson, Herbert Simon, LL Cavalli-Sforza and MW Feldman). Let us review them one by one.

Cultural aspects of co-evolution
On the aspect of co-evolution, the 'cultural' dimension of human society has been considered as an equal or a more important dimension than the physical. Modern biologists and linguists contradicting classical

biologists have argued that the ability to learn and use language did not evolve from animal communication systems as a result of selective pressure for communication, but rather arose independently as a side effect of a uniquely human mode for organizing complex thought. Recent archaeological record documents the fact that ancient cultures have reliably inherited two kinds of information: one encoded by genes, the other by culture. The Indian viewpoint is founded on a similar co-evolutionary base that integrates the individual self-centric with the collective or the trans-personal.

Systems matrix in pan-ecological/environmental studies: Gaia hypothesis

The individual farmer in the field is a symbol and he stands for all. This collective (universal or planetary) standing have recently led chemist James Lovelock and the microbiologist Lynn Margulis to propose a holistic understanding. A unified whole is like any one of the many bees orchestrated for a single planetary purpose – the making of the honeycomb. This recognition takes us to a powerful myth, which the two scientists Lovelock and Margulis have termed 'The Gaia hypothesis', which stands for Gaia (Gaya) – the Mother Goddess of the ancient Greeks.

The Gaia hypothesis is founded on a unified energy vision of the mother's embryo that 'holds all in unity'. By her self-power, she sacrifices herself for our greater transformations. There are many ancient stories and myths of her descent into matter (the earth) so that everyone sprouts from the field like the 'ears of the corn'. These myths that grew round her stories bear a conjugate vision of the 'mother' and her 'sons' and the story of eternal love between the two.

2.3.4 Idea of 'Universal Anthropic Principle'

The universal man is the culmination of a development of a weaker level (can be relatively said to be in a state of bio-social entropy or mental disorder) of human existence to a stronger level (can be relatively said to be in a higher mental state having the capacity to work for self-improvement, quality and values). The discussion correlates 'the idea' and modern constructs drawn from latest evolutionary theories, psychology and ecology. This correlation takes the reader to 'the Anthropic principle', which is ratified by a discussion between the two great thinkers of our century: poet Rabindranath Tagore and scientist Albert Einstein.

The various combinations of prana and akasha give birth to different viewpoints of human mind. They vary in a scale of weak to strong, and from strong to stronger. One of the greatest combinations of prana and akasha is the ideal human being or the Complete Anthropic Principle (CAP) – also called the 'Supramental'. This has been discussed earlier in Chapter 3.

Through an ever-growing and ever-improving relationship between human life (prana) and surrounding space (akasha), this section essentially brings forward the intent of this book talking about a harmonizing symbiotic relationship between human consciousness and the nature around.

Scientist's Anthropic Principle

Stephen Hawking (1993) in his book Black Hole and Baby Universes have set the parameters of this principle. He says that some people have gone so far as to elevate these restrictions on the initial conditions and the parameters to the status of a principle, 'the Anthropic Principle', which can be paraphrased as 'things are as they are because we are'. Hawking says that as perennial version of the principle, there are a very large number of different, separate universes with different values of 'physical ' parameters and different 'initial' conditions.

Tagore–Einstein dialogue on the Anthropic Principle

In 1930, poet Rabindranath Tagore (T) and physicist Albert Einstein (E) had a discussion, which is closest to the Anthropic Principle. We present parts of that historic dialogue.

Einstein: There are two different conceptions about the nature of the universe: (a) the world as a *unity* dependent on humanity; and (b) the world as a reality independent of the human factor.
Tagore: When our universe is in harmony with man, the eternal we know it as truth and we feel it as beauty.
Einstein: This is purely a human conception of the universe.
Tagore: There can be no other conception. This world is a human world – the scientific view of it is also that of the scientific

man. There is some standard reason and enjoyment, which gives it truth, the standard of the eternal man whose experiences are through our experiences.

Einstein: Truth, then, or Beauty, is not independent of Man?

Tagore: No.

Einstein: If there would be no human beings any longer, the Apollo of Belvedere would no longer be beautiful?

Tagore: No................there is the reality of paper, infinitely different from the reality of literature. For the kind of mind possessed by the Moth, which eats that paper, literature is absolutely non-existent, yet for Man's mind literature has a greater value of truth than the paper itself. In a similar manner, if there be some truth which has no sensuous or rational relation to human mind, it will even remain as nothing so long as we remain human beings. Finally two great minds were in perfect agreement on a world view as a unity and dependent on the human perception.

Current thoughts on the Anthropic Principle

Timothy Ferris talks about a gradation of Anthropic Principle. Ferris says that 'nowadays the Anthropic Principle comes in three shades – weak, strong and 'participatory'.

- The weak Anthropic Principle (WAP) simply states a minimal or limited human development that allows the emergence of life.
- The strong version (SAP) goes further: it declares that the universe must be constrained so as to allow for life, or the universe must be such as to admit the creation of observers within it. In other words, if there are no observers, then there are no universes. So human perception becomes predominant.
- The participatory (PAP) is principally due to John Wheeler. It emphasizes the role of Quantum observer-ship in resolving potentiality into actuality and attempts to construct a new conception of the universe as observer-dependent. On this Hawking further adds that the Anthropic Principle can be given a precise formulation, and it seems to be essential when dealing with the origin of the Universe.

David Bohm's implicate order

Here comes a further interesting proposition by David Bohm. In the re-conciliation efforts of (micro) quantum laws and (macro) relativity principles, Bohm proposes an order of the Cosmos.

Bohm proposes a 'super-implicate order' beyond the two, i.e. beyond an existence of several vanishing universes in the black holes (the implicate order) and the emergences of baby universes from stellar nurseries (the explicate order). Bohm talks of an unfolding order inherent in the cosmic web of relations at a deeper, 'non-manifest' level, which is also that of the enfoldment. The two are perhaps happening at the same time.

2.3.5 Universe in a nutshell: The seed and the huge forest or Vrihad Aranyak

In the cosmic expanse, there are the riddles of the tree and the forest. In a picture of the forest itself, which one do we see? Is it the tree or the forest? If one is looking at the tree itself, then the 'attention' is not on the whole – the forest. If one is looking at the forest, then the 'attention' is not on the tree itself. But we know that N number of Trees (T) make up a forest F.

This means that $N \times T = F$, but this equation is not correlated to the dimension of ‹attention›, the very essence of the Anthropic Principle. From the Forest to the Trees is the ‹explicate order›. From the Trees to the Forest is the ‹implicate order›.

In a framework of ‹attention› as an underlying principle, it is very hard to concentrate simultaneously on the ‹Tree› and the ‹Forest›. This takes us to a more basic level of integrating the two opposites. Here comes the concept of a seed – *'vija'*.

In the seed form, we get the whole essence of universe in a nutshell. Here both the Tree and the Forest co-exist. The wisdom of sages had realized this seed. That is why they were called 'Siddhas' – the seed that is boiled – cannot be reaped, cannot be re-germinated – it stands outside the circuit of 'Trees' and 'Forests'.

System of seed and tree: network and reciprocity

The concept of a 'Tree' is etymologically Taru or bifurcation (troyi) in Sanskrit. The 'tree-form' is an abstract realized by the ancient sages and recognized later through logic and algorithm of modern computation sciences. The abstract has been concretized as a concept of completeness traversing entirety – root to branches; branches to root.

The Tree is complete as it encompasses everything – from roots to branches; from leaves to flowers; from flower to fruits; from fruits to seeds; from growth to death; and from death to re-germination of a new seed leading to another tree or more number of trees. That brings us to a 'forest of trees'. This is used in computational sciences. It also brings us to the ancient concept of *vrihad-aranyak* in the making. That is the realization of the Vedic sages. In the parable of the Tree, an ancient concept of sustainability has been unlocked and 'Concept of Completeness' has been logically unfolded and presented. The concept of the 'Tree' has been discussed in the following chapter to best understand the living history of India as a case of a unique evolution over time and space. In this concept, once we have in the forward linkage:

Tree ———— (Fruits): seed (s): ———— Tree (s) ———— Forest

Then we have the backward linkage:

Forest ———— Tree ———— (seed) ———— Forest itself

In other words, the seed holds the linkages between a previous set of forest and its trees and the following set of trees leading to another forest and so on…In the looping we see the reversibility or reciprocity (Fig. 2.10). In this reversibility the completeness of the cosmos (*the vrihad–aranyak*) in relationship to its origin and destination is looped and kept sustainable. This is the complete truth encompassing both the positional and absolute value of nodes in the framework. The pattern of cycles is an absolute archetype. Yet, the evolutionary possibilities are flexible, positional and free.

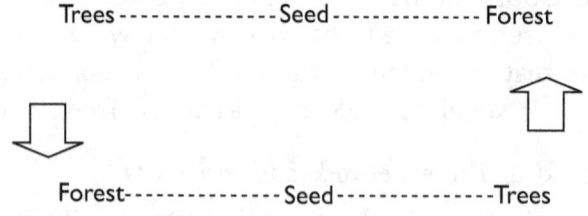

Figure 2.10 Stratification, ramification and unity

The EAF may also be seen as a sequence (Fig. 2.11) of junctions – or a sequence of nodes that links several functional levels or human activities namely:
1. The disjointed personal ego-intelligence level
2. From the personal level to the inter-personal level,
3. From the personal-interpersonal (bio-social) level to the existential and
4. From the existential level to the root level explaining both the trans-personal and the universal levels of interconnectedness

The idea of the three levels is based on advances made in the post-Freudian years. We have discussed this in our earlier section. The classical works of Sigmund Freud were limited to inferences drawn from experiments on a particular class of people conforming to retarded and animal-like instincts. From here, the three later works of Carl Gustav Jung, Abraham Maslow, and lately Ken Wilber have come a long way. All three of them have gone beyond the limited range of human functions and intelligence which was restricted to 'competitive animalism' and 'a survival instinct of the fittest'.

The concept of EAF – the TREE

The concept of EAF is presented through a construct called the TREE. The application of the TREE as a data structure is well known in the computational world. In this process the TREE is an epitome of sustainability – as it is a stratified data structure and a network of junction – both. TREE is sustainability itself – representing a continuous cyclic iteration represented by contraction (going back to root) and expansion (further extension from root; Fig. 2.12). The more widely accepted aspect of computational engineering application is the TREE where it is used as a tool of data structure based on the depths or levels of data, node of data centering at each level and allied concepts of topology or Graphing System (another system of data structure that is bigger than the TREE). In support of this concept, it has been said:

' ...Many aspects of the relationships between organisms and their environment can be described very coherently with the help of the systems concept of stratified order.... the relations between these systems levels can be represented by a 'systems tree'.

As in a real TREE (the lifeline of green consciousness), there are interconnections and interdependencies between all systems levels; each level interacts and communicates with its total environment. The trunk of the systems TREE indicates that the individual organism is connected to larger social and ecological systems, which in turn have the same TREE structure...from an evolutionary point of view, it is easy to understand why stratified, or multi-levelled, systems are so widespread in nature. ....They evolve much more rapidly and have much better chances of survival than non-stratified systems, because in cases of severe disturbances they can decompose into their various sub-systems without being completely destroyed (because higher nodes or the root is there). Non-stratified systems, on the other hand, would disintegrate and would have to start evolving from scratch'.

Figure 2.11 explains the Extended Anthropoligical Framework (EAF) achieved by the shift of conscious intelligence from the disjointed personal-ego level (or the weak Anthropic Principle) to the greater existential levels. Figure 2.8 explains the movements in the framework in a four-stage cycle. It starts from the full TREE with four depths or levels.

A priori and the recognition of TREE as a primal archetype

The principle of a priori forms the basis of cognition – the process of knowledge building is facilitated by re-cognition – the association of further intelligence of a future seed is with the older seed of intelligence – a priori itself. It is both absolute (sthithi) and positional (gati).

The importance of the principle of a priori runs through the history of Western European philosophy. The earliest ideas come from the days of the Platonic Socrates and the related works called Phaedo. The origin of Platonic Socrates in Phaedo is not traceable to the Olympian sources but to an even earlier archaic body of ancient knowledge system believing in the concept of transmigration and incarnation of knowledge and intelligence. These were called the Orphic school of thought that belonged to the proto-Greek settlements of mainland Asia.

- Half of classical Western sciences and technology are based on the concept of empiricism and Tabula Rasa emphasizing

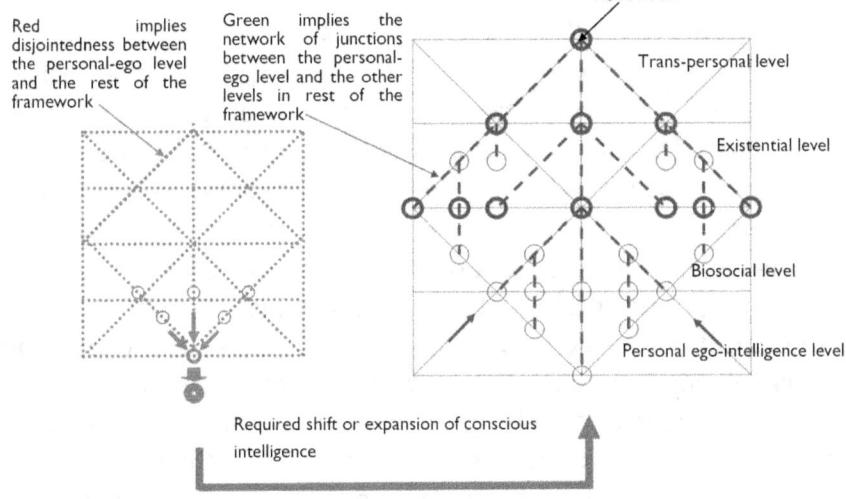

Figure 2.11 Extended Anthropoligical Framework (EAF) achieved through the required shift or expansion of conscious intelligence (Developed by the author)

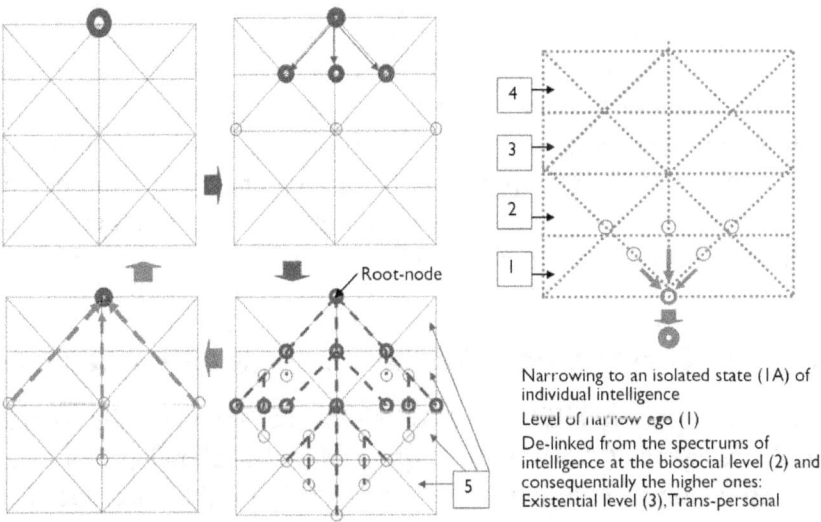

Figure 2.12 A four-stage cycle of sustainable dynamism evident in the stratified framework of the TREE

Starting from *bottom right* – full TREE (5) with four depths or levels; *Bottom left* – traversal through the four levels and tracing back to root node of TREE; *Top left* – Reaping of all levels (or contraction to the trans-personal level or the root-node); *Top right* – Sprouting or extension from the root node a 'clean slate' objective experience as the building blocks of knowledge and human intelligence.

- But the other increasing half still pertains to the ancient view. Particularly the psychological precepts of Socrates, Plato, Pauline Christianity, Kant and Spinoza belong to this group, which are strengthened by the works of Jung, Maslow and Wilber.

The idea of the TREE as a double intender forwards the absolute and positional significance of the twin interplay of involution and evolution. It is an ancient wisdom that surpasses the depth and gravity of anything else. The 'decimal' system (dasam) of India iterates the double intender as encoded in the flow – the parable of seed and the cyclic process. The significance of the development of both the absolute and positional number system is described by the French mathematician Pierre Simon Laplace (1749–1827) who wrote:

"It is India that gave us the ingenuous method of expressing all numbers by the means of ten symbols, each symbol receiving a value of position, as well as an absolute value; a profound and important idea which appears so simple to us now that we ignore its true merit, but its very simplicity, the great ease which it has lent to all computations, puts our arithmetic in the first rank of useful inventions, and we shall appreciate the grandeur of this achievement when we remember that it escaped the genius of Archimedes and Apollonius, two of the greatest minds produced by antiquity.»

2.4 Conclusions: Patterns of flow and measures

The discussion on TREE as a complete archetype of the widest social intelligence (WSI) can be presented in the following sequence. This concluding discussion is developed from the two lectures on 'microcosm' and 'macrocosm' delivered in New York, USA, on 19th and 26th of February in 1896 by Swami Vivekananda. The sequence begins with the seed and its germination; the cause (the previous seed) and effect (the future seed) of the growth of the tree; the cycles of its life, its turns, crests and troughs; the matching points; and the same plan, which is a pattern of the universe – the

external reality and the inner universe – the reality within us. It is presented in four parts:
1. The seed idea behind the design – the first order – driving philosophy, flow and meters
2. Cycles and regulations in design leading to second order
3. Design innovation and creativity reaching a system's framework
4. No design or no creation – it is fourth-order cybernetics: Self-manifestation

Measures of architecture: Seed idea and expression

- *Parable of the seed and the cyclic process:* What does man see around him? Take a little plant. He puts a seed in the ground, and later, he finds a plant peep out, lift itself slowly above the ground, and grows and grows, till it becomes a gigantic TREE. Then it dies, leaving only the seed. It completes a circle – it comes out of the seed, becomes the tree, and ends in the seed again.
- *Cycles of cause and effect:* The universe with its stars and planets has come out of a nebulous state and must go back to it. What do we learn from this? That the manifested or the grosser state is the effect, and the finer state, the cause.

Meters of cycles, turnings and regulating lines

- *The rise and fall of waves:* The TREE produces the seed, which again comes up as another TREE, and so on and on; there is no end to it. Water drops roll down the mountains into the ocean, and rise again as vapor, go back to the mountains and again come down to the ocean. So, rising and falling, the cycle goes on. So with all lives, so with all existence that we can see, feel, hear or imagine. Everything that is within the bounds of our knowledge is proceeding in the same way, like breathing in and breathing out in the human body. Everything in creation goes on in this form, one wave rising, another falling, rising again and falling gain. Each wave has its hollow; each hollow has its wave. The same law must apply to the universe taken as a whole, because of its uniformity.

- *The periodic nodes of turning or tropics:* There is one more fact about this rising and falling. The seed comes out of the TREE, but has a period of inactivity or rather a period of very fine un-manifest action. The seed has to work for some time beneath the soil. It breaks into pieces, degenerates (dies) as it were, and regeneration (resurrects) comes out of that degeneration.

Origin of design innovation and creativity
- *Out of what has the TREE been produced?* Out of the seed, the whole of the TREE was there in the seed. It comes out and becomes manifest. So, the whole of this universe has been created out of this very universe existing in a minute form. It has been made manifest now. It will go back to that minute form, and again will be made manifest. This coming out of the fine and becoming gross, simply changing the arrangements of its parts, as it were, is what in modern times called evolution.
- *Involution precedes evolution:* We have to go one step further, and what is that? That every evolution is preceded by an involution. The seed is the mother of the TREE, but another TREE was itself the mother of the seed. The seed is the fine form out of which the big TREE comes, and another big TREE was the form, which is involved in that seed. The whole of this universe was present in the cosmic fine universe.

The ancient designer and the new creator
- *A priori – Recognition of the involutionary principle in an evolutionary process:* This involution and evolution is going on throughout the whole of nature. The whole series of evolution beginning with the lowest manifestation of life and reaching up to the highest, the most perfect man (Anthropic Principle) must have been the involution of something else. The question is: The involution of what? What was involved?
- *Unfolding of involved a priori universal intelligence as evolving individual and social intelligence:* The TREE comes out of the seed, goes back to the seed; the beginning and the end are the same....applying the same reason to the whole of the universe, we see that intelligence must be the lord of creation, the cause. At the beginning that intelligence becomes involved,

and in the end that intelligence gets evolved. The sum total of the intelligence displayed in the universe must, therefore, be the involved universal intelligence unfolding itself.

Design as a self-extension of the designer: No design theory or creation but 'Manifestation'

- *Complete or perfect Anthropic Principle:* This cosmic intelligence gets involved, and it manifests, evolves itself, until it becomes the perfect man.
- *Macrocosm and microcosm are built on the same plan:* Applying the law we dwelt upon under macrocosm, that each involution presupposes an evolution, and each evolution an involution, we see that instinct – of the personal ego-animal level is involved or down turned reason. In this manner, each lower level is an evolution of a preceding involvement of a higher level. The latest scientific man admits that each man and each animal is born with a fund of experience, and all these actions in the mind are the result of past experience.

The entire system contains a reflection of the same plan ingrained in its parts and in the whole. The system becomes 'anthropic' or to be precise an 'anthropo-centric' consciousness and its evolutionary system-driven system (ES-D-S).

In recent years, there has been an increasing realization and application of networking of systems linked through a complex web of interdependence. It involves an exchange of matter and different forms of energy in continual cycles. Scientists and people concerned have begun to realize that linear cause-and-effect relationships exist rarely in ecosystems and the linear approach (as suggested by reductionism) is far from being useful to describe the functional interdependencies of the embedded social and economic systems and their technologies in the larger web of networking. The recognition of nonlinear nature of all system dynamics is the essence of any designed creativity, and the system is embedded as part of a deeper ecological awareness required for design.

The complexity of any design system is limited only if the system is rigid, inflexible, and isolated from its environment (Jantsch, 1980). As a realization of this limitation, there is the need for a holistic approach to design-creativity where systems, as parts, self-organize in continual interaction with their environment and show the capability of increasing their complexity by abandoning structural stability in favour of flexibility, open-ended evolution, and creativity. Hence, true or holistic efficiency of our technologies and social institutions will depend not only on their complexity but also on their flexibility and potential for change (Capra, 1990). Walter Weisskopf (1971) has pointed out in his book Alienation and Economics that the crucial element of scarcity in human life is not economic but existential. They are related to our needs for leisure and contemplation, peace of mind, love, community and self-realization, which are reached only through a greater and deeper range of ecological ethics. It is the deeper ethics that is the source of the holistic viewpoint. It demands a shift of our conventional values from the 'shallow' to the 'deeper':

1. Self-assertion and notion of competition to cooperation and social justice
2. Material expansion to conservation
3. Material acquisition to inner growth, which is the direct inter-dependent communion with the self within and the self of the universe

A holistic realization called 'deep ecology' has emerged in the West, which includes ideas of integral ecological economics and the need for an energy-sensitive sustainable world. The pointers of an 'over-view effect' have led to a new development paradigm of interconnectedness, where a web of integral planetary consciousness in terms of human activity and global climate in relationship to the Sun and the Cosmos is forwarded.

The 'ideas of dissipative structures', 'complexity' and 'chaos theory' have further augmented a deeper understanding of an integrated micro-bio-chemical and physical worlds. The concept of 'non-linear dynamism' and 'bifurcations' have augmented current studies in bio-informatics and genetic engineering. The new paradigm focuses more on deeper scientific advancements, which are to be more 'processes than goal' oriented. From factor-driven changes that are goal oriented, one shifts to holistic process-based systems-driven framework. Then, there is inspiration-driven innovation of the highest kind, where the designer self-manifests as the 'design' itself. In effect, it is an initial shift from the weak Anthropic Principle to a stronger type. Finally, it is 'participatory' and co-evolving. The entire system becomes 'anthropic' or to be precise an 'anthropocentric' consciousness and its evolutionary system-driven system (ES-D-S). Then the Anthropic Principle both in positional (gati) and absolute (sthithi) terms becomes complete.

Here, the networks stand for interdependence, diversity, complexity of parts in a whole, parts of a whole, and as parts representing the whole. It is the highest rung in cycles representing recycling of resources and partnership. It is the highest expression of flow-through ecology of energy and resources' exchanges and transfer. It is development of the highest kind that guarantees succession and co-evolution of the 'weak' becoming 'strong' and 'stronger' and not a 'survival of the fittest'. It is the dynamic balance between self-organization, flexibility, stability and sustainability.

3
System framework one: Phase I of global history of architecture

3.1 Introduction

The earliest Indo-Greco interactions had occurred in times of remote antiquity, and a system of the first civilizations, which stretched from Persia through Mesopotamia and the Anatolian highlands extending up to Abyssinia, evolved as a result. Figure 3.1 explains the evolution and ramification of them in three sub-systems. The sub-systems conform to the Biblical tradition of the Japhetic (in Central Asia), Semitic (in western Asia), and the Hamitic (in northeast Africa) branches emanating from an allegory of three geo-spatial lineages conforming to 'siblings' to sons of Noah, who is a primal ante-diluvium imagery of an anthropic survival from previous cycles of creation, as evident in the Old Testament. The Indian tradition of Seven (Sapta) antidiluvian Sages (Rishis) accompanying Manu (the primal man) bears a near similar tradition and has much in common with the epic of Gilgamesh, which was an early proto-Mesopotamian allegory of 'The Flood' myth, and perhaps, a link between the two.

The 19th line of Tablet I of the Epic of Gilgamesh makes an important observation. While erecting a sacred masonry (bricks) for building the first Mansion of divinity, the role of 'Seven Sages' are most evident as follows:

> "..And did not the Seven Sages themselves lay out its plans?"

In a recent book entitled 'A Global History of Architecture' (2007), the authors Francis D. K. Ching, M. M. Jarzombek and V. Prakash have quoted important lines from the Epic. From these lines a striking similarity between the three civilizations in terms of the 'sacred use of building units' (as found in the symbolic use of altar making with Istaka or bricks as mentioned in the Yadjur Veda) and common primordial role of the Seven Sages are undeniably evident:

'Go up on the wall of URUK and walk around, examine its foundation, examine its brickwork thoroughly.

Is not (even the core of) the brick structure made of Kiln-fired brick, and did not the Seven Sages themselves lay out its plans?'

The Epic of Gilgamesh (3000 BC)
Translated by Maureen Gallery Kovacs (Stanford)
Stanford University Press (1985)

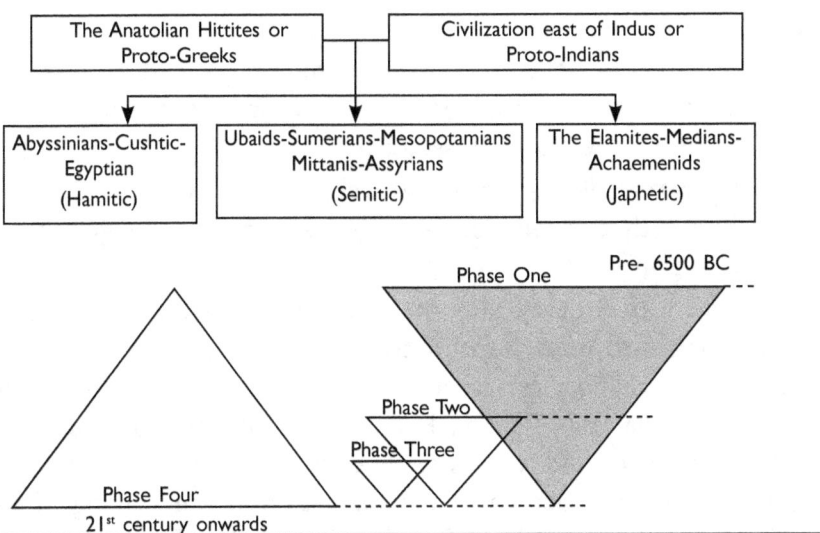

Figure 3.1 System of Phase I: Evolution of the first civilizations

Now, who are the Seven Sages mentioned in the Epic? The Epic of Gilgamesh is of course an epic poem, which dates from the UR, and it is often regarded as the first great work of literature beginning with five Sumerian poems about 'Bilga-mesh' (Sumerian for 'Gilgamesh'), king of Uruk. To search for the Seven Sages, we have to revert back either to India, in the earliest literature of the world, the Rig Veda or to Greece, in the tales of the Seven Wise Men. In both, there are evidences of creation of myths, floods, and recurring cycles of the four ages – from the Golden to the Iron Ages and so on.

'Sacred Bricks' in India is known as 'Avi-istaka' and Persian sacred text on Holy Fire is also known as 'Avistak' (later coded as Avesta). The Seven Sages are precisely guiding the sacred art of building, which is 'Architecture, meaning a combination of two words – one, the primal seed, i.e. Ark + *Takkhon* meaning the art of sculpturing or formulating out of abstract. In all, architecture here means 'primal building'.

An ancient system of anthropocentric realization is evident. The 'flood' stands at the cross-road of a 'pre-creation stage' and 'post-flood or creation stage'. The witnesses are raised human souls or sages. And the double intender is how the Seven Sages are:

1. tracing the seed, allegorically 'the first Word or creative impulse' that was handed over from a primordial state, i.e. prior to the flood (dissolution)
2. later re-building from that very seed in the period after flood, that is allegorically 'genesis' or 'the beginning of creation'

In Indian spirituality, the first one, which traces the whole system back, and goes beyond to the origin, is 'Yoga' or 'Death of Creation' (called First Death anthropocentrically). The second one is 'Kshema' or 'Tantra'. Kshema stands for continuity, life of creative flow and diversity. The two represent a system's dimension, of architecture of the cosmos and the making of the architecture of the temple after flood following the cosmic plan and its processes.

3.2   Basic system's dimensions

An ancient system of human or anthropocentric realization, which evolved from a two-fold aspect of reality – one, spiritual (represented by Yoga) and the other, material (represented by *kshema*) – had represented the key system's dimension. As the realization disseminated across civilizations, the material dimension had begun to predominate keeping the spirituality in background.

The inter-relationship between the two was sustained by a principle of transformation called *al-khemia* or Alchemy, which initially meant a spiritual transformation of the material world. In later times, it devolved further to become the material foundation of first logical science, which is 'chemistry'. The concept of Yoga and Kshema and its relationship with another observation drawn from recurring patterns or changes in the natural world of human evolution and devolution (known as involution) became the two cornerstones of the ancient world. Two quotations may be forwarded to best represent the two corner stones, respectively.

3.2.1 Corner stone 1: A conjugate system of the spiritual and the material – Yoga and kshema

'...when the Soul of Gold has been separated from its body or when the body, in other words, (the body or sema) has been dissolved, the body of the moon (soma) should be watered by its proper menstruum and reverberated, the operation being repeated as often as is necessary, i.e. until the body of the moon becomes supple, broken up, pure, dissolved and coagulated. This is done, not with common fire, but with that of the SAGES, and at last one must see clearly that nothing remains unresolved.

For unless the moon or earth (KA-BA) is properly prepared and entirely emptied of its soul, it will not be fit to receive the Solar Seed (EL); but the more thoroughly the earth (the body and the terrestrial) is cleansed of its impurity and earthiness, the more vigorous it will be in the 'Fixation of its Ferment'.

Sepharial
A Manual of Occultism: Chapter on Alchemy
Rider and Company, London

The entire ancient world stretching from India to Egypt was influenced by the principles of Alchemy. The life principle in the tangible and quantified material world, which is KA (incidentally, the first alphabet in Egypt and its Mansion and also the first consonant of Sanskrit that apex the tree of Indo-European Language system) had complemented EL (or Lah/ ilah), the principle in the abstract and intangible heavens. The principle that links the two i.e., KA and Lah (El) is BA. Hence, the text and treatise of Ka-Ba-Lah had evolved and impacted the entire ambit of deep ecology of the ancient world. Architecture, the science of built environment, developed from these principles. As a result, we begin to encounter a list of important words like Ka-Ba; Va-ka; Ka-La; Al-Alkh; Ba-el; Ky-be-le; Ka-la; Ba-B; Al-ilah and many others; and finally, Ka-ba-lah and Al-Ba-Kah that constitutes an important header text of all ancient civilization. The present chapter will begin to unfold the syntactical and cognitive linkages embedded in the deeper layer that forms these 'words'.

3.2.2   Corner stone 2: System of cycles and renewability

'In course of time the slow advance of knowledge, which has dispelled so many cherished illusions, convinced the more thoughtful portion of mankind that the alternation of summer and winter, of spring and autumn, were not merely the result of their own magical rites, but that some deeper cause, some mightier power, was at work behind the shifting scenes of nature......and as they now explained the fluctuations of growth and decay, of reproduction and dissolution, by the marriage, the death, and the rebirth or revival of the Gods, their religious or magical dramas turned in 'great measures of these themes. They set forth the fruitful union of the powers of fertility, the sad 'Death' of one at least of the divine partners, and his joyful 'Resurrection'...the resemblance of these ceremonies to the Indian and European ceremonies which I have described elsewhere is obvious......His affinity with vegetation comes out at once in the common story of his birth.

......the story that Adonis spent half, or according to others a third, of the year in the lower world and the rest of it in the upper world, is explained most simply and naturally by supposing that he represented vegetation (the corn) which lies buried in the earth (the tomb) one half (or one-third the year) and reappears above ground the other half (or two-third). Adonis has been taken for the Sun (or Mithras)......moreover, the explanation is countenanced by a considerable body of opinion amongst the ancients themselves, who again and again interpreted the dying and reviving God as the reaped (separated from body or earth) and sprouting (conjoined again to rain-fertilized body or earth) grain.'

Sir James G. Frazer
Fellow of Trinity College, Cambridge
Chapters 1–9, 'Adonis: A Study in the History of Oriental Religions',
Watts & Co. (London)

The search of some deeper cause, some mightier power, was at work behind the shifting scenes of nature led to the ancient realization of something that is non-linear and cyclic. Here, ancient realization comes close to the latest findings of modern science, something that pervades a system's approach to complexity, fractals in nature and the science of evolutionary biology and ecology. Ancient civilizations and the normative systems that they produced from religion to ecology were based on the recurring theme of a 'life-and-death-cyclic system approach', which we call LCA today. It remained and still remains as a more meaningful symbol in science today. The present chapter also unfolds the system's approach embedded in the deeper layer of the ancient wisdom, which is the other cornerstone.

3.2.3 A cooperative approach to systems inquiry (not comparative)

Given a premise of the deep systems embedded in the two conjugates of (a) yoga and kshema and (b) death and resurrection (or re-birth), a historic framework of Phase I (as evident in Fig. 3.1) has been proposed for an evaluation of global history with regard to Indian architecture. Till date, a methodology collaborating and integrating a system's approach based on the six following dimensions has been least suggested and explored:

1. Unity of opposites that pervaded the ancient world in the domain of art, iconography, language and literature, culture, technology and architecture
2. Ancient historic (positive) connections
3. Convergent realization and belief (normative) systems

4. Inter-linked and cooperative language systems
5. Inter-continental carriers and migrations
6. Inter-linked or cooperative archaeology based on iconography and anthropology

Instead of a comparative approach to historical ramifications and thinking of each civilization as divergent expression, the present book and this present chapter has reverted more to a study of convergences and common 'patterns'. It humanely assumes an underlying unity of human cognitive and semiotic evolution that perhaps had pervaded the entire ancient world. So instead of the term 'comparative', the system's approach prefers 'cooperative'.

The discussion and the system's evaluation begin with an exploration of a dynamic unity that embraced the 'deeper' in the ancient world and its ramifications (Fig. 3.1). It is the 'system of opposites', which can be better termed as 'a system of complementarities' like 'light and darkness' or 'spring and autumn', which are not opposites. They are complementary and dynamic parametric conditions of the design that is either activated as 'one full day' or 'one full year' considering iterations and sustainability of a perennial cycle of change and evolution. It forwards the ancient key to ensure sustainability – the key concern and discovery of the present chapter. It is something that historian Will Durant accepts as 'Our Oriental Heritage' before he explains the story of Western civilization.

3.3 Part one: System of unity of opposites

In effect, the present chapter depicts a system's dimension of the global pattern of civilization from the earliest phase of India's history. It can be identified as Phase one, as it traces the earliest Indo-Greco interactions that had led mainly to the rise of Persian, Romanic and other great civilizations. To repeat, what has been said earlier:

'These two gigantic forces (Aryans and Yavanas), issuing from far-away and different mountains (India and Greece), occasionally come in contact with each other, and whenever such confluence takes place, a tremendous intellectual and spiritual tide rising in human societies, greatly expands the range of civilization and confirms the universal brotherhood among men.

Once in far remote antiquity, the Indian philosophy, coming in contact with Greek energy, led to the rise of the Persian, the Roman, and other great nations'·

– Swami Vivekananda
Problem of India and Its Solution

It is generally an extremely difficult task to revert back to a period so distant, locked in far-remote antiquity. It is more so in the absence of proper inter-linked archaeological, literary and other evidences from such distant antiquities. But the task perhaps becomes simple and straight-forward, when certain icons are best selected that share a common body of opinion held by a greater majority of diverse cultures and regions of the very ancient world – spreading from Asia to Europe and Africa on the one hand and to the Americas on the other hand.

The body of opinion is with regard to basic natural and larger observations of life, death and that opinion, defeating the urges of changeability over time, perhaps remains the same as 'natural truths' and consequently valid in our modern times of technology and artificial systems.

Such a continuity, which can also be called 'sustainability', points to a deeper cause, a basic science of a higher and broader power, always at work from behind the shifting scenes of nature and human progress. This is the parable of natural life processes observed in vegetation and its growth, decay and re-growth. The parable quintessentially can be seen as 'the theme of the reaped and re-sprouting corn' that explains the array of seasons coming, going and resuming again in cycles establishing the very sustainability of life itself under the rays of the sun. Through this parable perhaps, a common source of different regional cultures of the ancient world can be best retraced. They are the system of iterations – in death and resurrection and in complementarities of evolutionary changes that is deeper and far-reaching.

3.3.1 System of cycles: Death and resurrection

There is a dynamic balance based on the cycle of seasons, harvest and the turning of the year (Fig. 3.2).

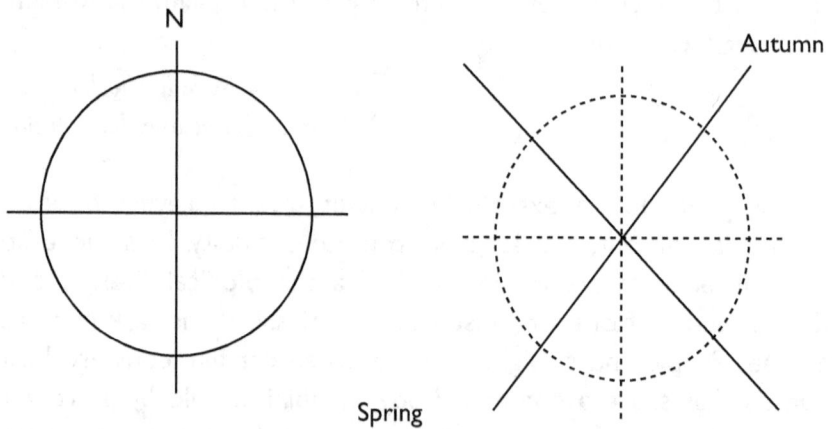

Figure 3.2 Spatial and temporal character of cycles

In the depiction the spatial and temporal features of the cycles are more significant. One, in space, like the figure in the left, cycle is an array of 'four quarters'. If seen as changes over time, like the right one, they are the four cyclic alternation of spring, summer, and autumn and winter (Fig. 3.2).

In the cycle of seasons the moving object is the sun, the source of all life, overall shinning equally on all but differentially in different times. The sun is making the projected movement on earth to sustain the full turn of the year. In the Vedic lore, it becomes the allegory of *samavatsara*, which not only represents the cyclic repetitive array of seasons, but also the rhythms and recurrence of 'death' and 'immortality'.

At summer, the sun reaches the highest point (solstice of day exceeding night) accumulating maximum heat in the northern hemisphere. Then the sun turns (tropics) downward and heads to forward winter in the northern hemisphere in the inverted solstice (night exceeding day). What does the turning of sun means in the wheel of change?

3.3.2 System of equal and opposite: Complementary conjugate

There can be a variety of interpretations and many are available from science. Perhaps one of the best comes from the last chapter and the concluding sutra of an ancient text called the *Yoga-sutra* by a sage named Patanjali. Along with the Yoga-sutra, we also refer to a recent work of ecological sciences called the Gaia's Hypothesis.

Gaia's Hypothesis is a collective (universal or planetary) standing recently led by chemist James Lovelock and the microbiologist Lynn Margulis to propose a holistic understanding[1] of our existence in relationship to a larger frame, say the universe. This is like a unified whole like the bees orchestrated for a single planetary purpose – the making of the honeycomb. This recognition takes us to a powerful myth[2], which the two scientists Lovelock and Margulis have termed 'the Gaia Hypotheses', where Gaia (Gaya) is the ancient Mother Goddess of the ancient Greeks.

3.3.3 System of Gaia's matrix

The hypothesis portrays a matrix – the womb of unification. Gaia Hypothesis is a unified energy vision of the mother's embryo that 'holds all in unity'. By her self-power, she sacrifices herself for our evolution or greater transformations. There are many ancient stories and myths of her descent into matter (the earth) so that everyone sprouts[3] from the field like the 'ears of the corn'. These myths that grew round her stories bear a conjugate vision of the 'Mother' and her 'sons' and the story of eternal love between the two. The Gaia myth provides an understanding of the exchange of energy between the mother and her son(s); and scientifically, this exchange can be seen as a science of heat-exchange

---

[1] This is taken from Lovelock, J.E. (1979) Gaia, Oxford University Press.
[2] From Chapter 9: The systems view of life in 'The Turning Point' (page 307, Flamingo, 1990).
[3] Such stories are heard all over the ancient world leading to the birth of the young male god (like Kumara or Adonis or Tammuz) which is achieved through the sacrifice of the Mother Goddess (like Kumari or Ishtar or Cybele). The ear of the corn symbolizes the resurrecting corn-spirit from the fertile waters. This has been discussed in Chapter 5.

called thermodynamics. Thermodynamics is based on reduction of disorder (entropy[4]) through a larger energy input from outside. The descent of sun rays is compared to the sacrifice of the Mother's energy for terrestrial growth and the ascent of sun is comparable to the recovery of life meaning the ascent of her son (or sons) from the lower world (Fig. 3.3).

Gaia's myth can be seen in the concluding sutra of Patanjali's Kaivalya-pada. In this sutra, the ascending son is the Purusha immanent in matter – waiting for release or resurrection. The descending Mother is Chiti-shakti, Gaia herself. The inversion and the turn is the fulcrum of natural law as evident in the sutra:

"......The resolution in the inverse order of the qualities, bereft of any motive of action for the Purusha (transcendent soul), is Kaivalya (or complete release from bondage of matter), or it is the establishment of the power of Knowledge (chiti-shakti) in its own nature".

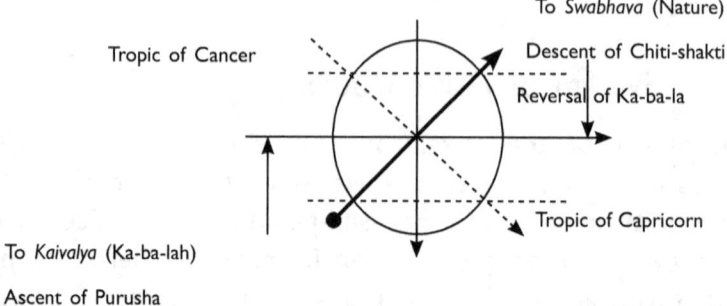

Figure 3.3 'Libra' or a balance of changes between spring and autumn
[Note: The counter arrow of summer (point on the Tropic of Cancer) and winter (point on the Tropic of Capricorn]. The two arrows are the two diagonals.

It is evident that liberated souls are the many *Purusha(s)*. Mother Nature is Gaia. The souls are reaped from the lower world and released into the higher plane. But the sacrifice and the descent of the Mother continue to fertilize the terrestrial world and continue the annual repetitive cycle of harvest in the coming years and the

---

[4] Readers may refer Chapters 2 and 11 in the book entitled 'Ecology: Principles and Applications' by J. L. Chapman and M. J. Reiss (1995), Cambridge University Press.

many subsequent reaping of future souls. So there is a continuous connection between the two – *the tie between her sacrifice and our resurrection!*

3.3.4   System of sacrifice and resurrection

"......Nature's task is done, this unselfish task which our sweet nurse, nature, had imposed upon herself. She gently took the self-forgetting soul by hand, as it were, and showed him all the experiences (iteration of good and bad and so on...) in the universe, all manifestations (the physical and the behavioral sides of all expressions), bringing him higher and higher through various bodies (the morphic sequence and the in-built resonance of wave-like experiential iterations), till his lost glory (the innate Purusha) came back, and he remembered his own nature. Then the kind mother (or Gaia) went back the same way she came, for others who also have lost their way in the trackless desert of life. And thus she is working, without beginning and without end. And thus, through pleasure and pain, through good and evil, the infinite river of souls (the time-tested sequence of experiences) is flowing into the ocean of perfection, of self-realization"

– Swami Vivekananda
Raj Yoga

Like a balance, the descent of the Mother force into the physical and the ascent of man from the physical are in constant balance, in constant harmony. It is like a fulcrum! A balance! A Libra! It is like a see-saw that we have referred earlier in this chapter. All ancient myths had explained it. In this chapter, we explain where and how they were done thereby unlocking the underlying common platform of that ancient world. It happened when a wave of thought from India had met another from Greece in such times of remote antiquity.

3.3.5   System of myth and history

There is a parable of the story of the birth of the son (Krishna) and the sacrifice of the daughter or the mother, on the different banks of river Yamuna is perhaps the historical truth or the mythical key – of times much prior to Buddha or Plato.

The explanation of the relationship between the ascent of the individual soul *(Purusha)* and the universal energy as Mother-power *(Chiti-shakti)* (Rig Veda: 7.68.8) can be seen in four stages. They are the spring, summer, autumn and winter. The Vedic wisdom goes further splitting the cycle into six seasons explaining the natural seasonal cycle seen in India (as visible in the six-spoke wheel, the sprouting corn and the symbol of reaped seed – the fertilizing bull in the Indus Valley Seal).

 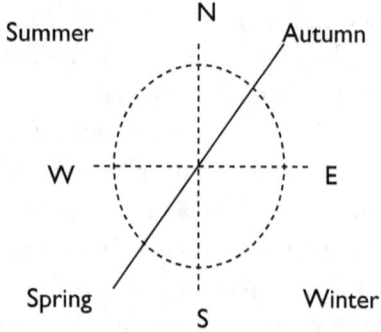

Figure 3.4 Sprouting corn and the six-season cycle depicted in Indus Valley seal
(Note: Conventional four-season four quarter cycle becomes six-seasonal iterations of Indian subcontinental six-season or Sara-ritu: Rig Veda: 1.164. Both the Vedic lore and seals of the Indus Valley civilization bear the same patterns.)

One can make the explanation simpler, and for this we may use the four-step iteration than a more detailed six sequence cycle:

1. *Spring (equinox):* Individual soul ascends (reaping from the terrestrial) as the universal energy descends from behind. These are the two in union. Heat builds up sufficiently to break off from winter (inertia or terrestrial bondage, say). Equity of day and night – descending power (night or moon) equalizes ascent (day or sun).

2. *Summer (solstice):* Summit of ascent or highest heat and the individual soul (Purusha) is one (in absolute rapture) with the universal energy (Chiti-shakti). Day exceeds leading to transcending limits of the increasing sun over

the moon. Moon is transcended. This is highest creation – spirit completely engulfing matter – chida-akasha. It is *sarva-bhutani-cha-atmani* (refer Isha Upanishad: 8 or Gita, Chapter 7).

3. *Autumn (equinox):* This is a reverse spring, when the wheel turns as the rapture in the highest heavens fashions *(Twastha)* out the thundering or all-pervading power. That power, from the highest seat, showers down the rains of another cycle, another fertilizing sequence – fosters *(Purusha)* the lower world again to equip another strand of aspiring souls – the future aspirants. Rain brings in moisture, coolness lowering the heat in the world. Day equals night. Autumn equals spring. This is the legacy of 'Spring and Autumn' – the wisdom of Chinese saint Confucius.

4. *Winter (solstice):* Night (or moon) exceeds day (or the sun). Life is set deep in the netherworld – in the inner rocks, below the soil – in the tomb of the terrestrial. The new seeds are again sown to create another world, another cycle of harvest. The creative inertness or the sepulcher is established. But one has to wait for another spring – the next wave of increasing heat. Sun is transcended. This is lower creation – establishment of matter encaging spirit – *Sarva-bhutastha-atmanam* (Isha Upanishad: 8).

5. *Spring again:* This is resurgence – Repetition or Resurrection. This is the lordship of four quarters (combination of 3/4 and 1/4 or 2/3 and 1/3). The lordship of the four nodes or the four quarters is discussed in the following section, in which are embedded the research clues of this chapter. But what is important to understand is that the wheel rolls on (Rig Veda: 1.164).

The combination of the quarters depends on the incidental rays of the sun on three sets of observed positions.

- They are either the poles – where it is half-summer and half-winter (see left in Fig. 3.5);
- in the temperate belt, i.e. from above the tropics of Cancer and Capricorn – where it is two-third and one-third (see middle part);

- Or in the tropical-equatorial belt – where it is three-fourth and one-fourth (see right part).

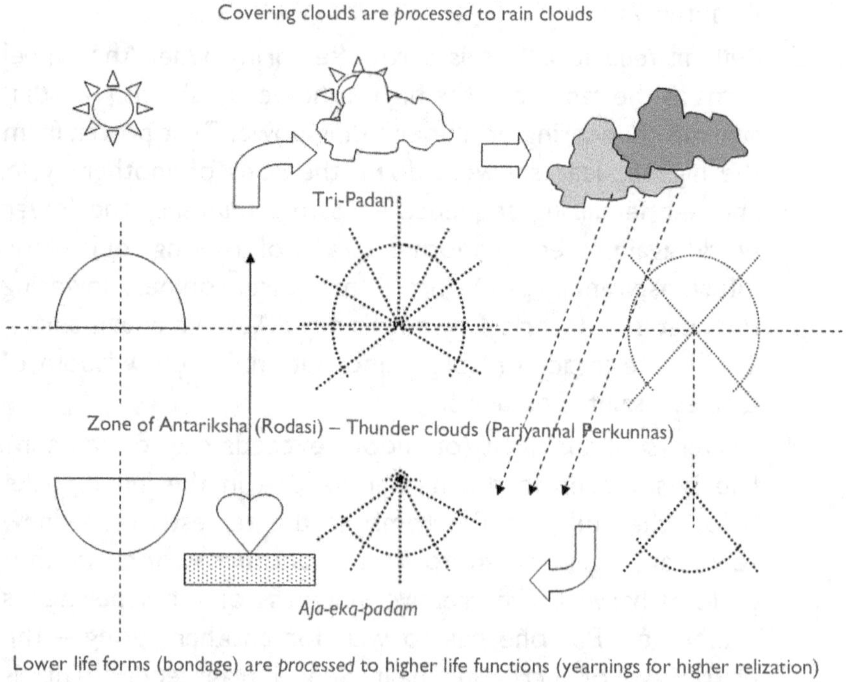

Covering clouds are *processed* to rain clouds

Tri-Padan

Zone of Antariksha (Rodasi) – Thunder clouds (Parjyanha/Perkunnas)

Aja-eka-padam

Lower life forms (bondage) are *processed* to higher life functions (yearnings for higher relization)

Figure 3.5 Relationship of upper and lower worlds (regions) through Antariksha (left – at Pole; Middle – Temperate; Right – Tropics)

(*Note:* The idea is based on Vedic Cosmology)

In the totality, the upper half symbolizes the upper world – the *Dyu* of the Vedas and the lower – *prithvi* of the Vedas. The link world is *Antariksha*, where the two tends to be one – which is merging and increasing equivalence of *Dyava-prithvi* or heaven-earth couplet. It is the operative zone of *Rudra* (zone of processing) and therefore known as *Rodasi* of the Vedas. This is an extremely important point in Vedic Cosmology, and particularly Cosmogony that underscores the ontology of creation – 'being and becoming'. It is the basis of all architectural renditions based on cyclicity (see Template 3.1).

It is evident in Fig. 3.5 that here in *Rodasi*, which are the thunder clouds. They are formed giving birth to thunderbolts (Vajra) and fertilizing rains (Madhu). In the Rodasi, in the layers of one darker cloud over the still darker is hidden the cyclic linkages of life itself. The water that is castrated from below leading to the descending dark clouds is showered back to earth in form of pollinating rains. The cycle of water is preceded by the cycle of heat – as the descending sunrays from above reciprocates the sprouting or ascending life-forms and rising water (vapor to form covering clouds) from below. The two-way linkage is the thunderbolt, *Vajra* linking both.

3.4 Part two: Systems of historical–mythological recurrence – from India to Egypt

It is important at this point to retrieve a commonality in the mythological overlap contained in the texts of the ancient world. A set of eleven features can be *initially forwarded* to unlock a common basis of the ancient world of Greece and India and everything that was formed from there. The common feature is the 'Concept of Four Quarters':

3.4.1 System of four quarters based on concept of three upper quarters or Tripadam – Aja-ekpadam (one lower quarter)

In the Vedas, the two halves are described as the upper triple strides of the solar world (*Aditya* highlighted by *Vishnu*). The lower strides are determined by *Rudra* (The plutonic upsurge from the nether and terrestrial world). The two are equinoctial to each other represented by the turning of the sun (the soul) based on Tropic of Cancer (higher world) and Capricorn (lower world) meaning the inter-reciprocal spiritual and material planes, respectively. Of the two, the upper half is governed by the ascending strides (day or heat-specific i.e. sun-based) of the three Vedas namely Rig-Krishna-*Yadjur-Sama* Veda. The lower half is governed by the descending strides (night or absence of heat-specific or moon based) represented by the *Atharva* and *Sukla-Yadjur* Vedas *(Vajsenaya)*. Of the two, the lower stride, which is represented by the Capricorn is the allegorical crocodile or *Makara* of India and is also the Chaldean or Semitic version of *Aja* or Horned Goat in Greece. In the Vedas, however, both are available.

The Persian-Semitic-Romaic tradition had concentrated on this symbol of Aja governing the lower corporeal (moon or soma part) only as against the upper spiritual half in the later Indian (Puranic) tradition. The goat is a symbol of the sun in India, where the day star is called *Aja Ekapad* ('the goat of the single foot'). Aja means not only 'goat', but mainly "unborn" (a-ja). As such, it is the symbol of primordial, unorganized matter, the same as *Prakriti*. The goat is also associated with the vajra, an image of the Fallen Sun. Interestingly enough, this association prevailed not only in India, but also in China, Tibet, and even in the Mediterranean world.

The symbol of the reconciliation of the lower half to the upper half is the resurrection from below determined by *Prajapati* (Lord of the terrestrial beings or *pra-ajas*) in the form of *Aja* (not born here) or the horned goat. This is the shield of the Lord known as the goat-skinned mask called the *Aegis* that Zeus-Jupiter of Greco-Roman world puts on his face. Similar symbolisms are available in the entire ancient Aegian sea world (Cyclades in Eastern Mediterranean) including *Agypptos* (which is the name of Egypt). The Indo-European term 'Gypsy' is a later derivative of that meaning people of the ancient Eastern Mediterranean. The original Indian Crocodile-Capricorn (the carrier of descending river Ganges) is the Gypsy *Mugger* or *Muzzer (Makara)* in the earliest of times. It also stood for *Mizara* or *Mishara* the ancient name of the entire Abyssinian world (Ethiopia, Somalia and Egypt) as known in the ancient times. This idea influenced the religions of ancient Egypt to a greater part of the eastern Semitic branch of religion, which is Islam, where mainly the symbolism of the goat-bearded Zeus or the Egyptian Pharaoh or the Persian Sage became 'an icon of the goat-beard' practiced by the followers of the much later religion of Arabia' (Fig. 3.6).

- Rig Veda: 7.35.13
- Book of Daniel (8.5f), Old Testament
- William and Mary Morris (1971). "Dictionary of Word and Phrase Origins", Harper & Row Publishers: New York

3.4.2 System of descent into lower quarter

The ascent of the *Prajapati* is counter-balanced by the descent of the *Adityas* – the undifferentiated Godheads of Light in the Vedas, of which *Vishnu* stands supreme. His descending strides are symbolized by the shades or steps (called *Chrome*) down *(anu-loma)* in the lower legs in the ladder of creation *(Ur)*. This is the descent of Gaya – *Vaishnavi Shakti*. In the Vedas, Vishnu descends or spreads from the highest pole *(Sumeru)* and the innermost seat *(Ur-u-gyuay)* in the highest sea of creation. Names of ancient civilizations and cities in the ancient Semitic world and the Americas like Ur, Uruguay have etymological roots in these ancient Vedic words.

- Rig Veda: 1.154.3 and 6

3.4.3 System of upper and lower Godheads (Sura and Ashura)

The ascendant and the descendent of the movements of the symbolic sun are termed as Sura and Ashura, in the original Vedic tradition. It is said:

'Great and unified is the basis and foundations of the forces of unity – 'Sura' or 'Devas', which is Mahat-deva Ashura (Ahura Mahadeo or Mazda of Persian tradition)'

Seer Prajapati Kausiki
Rig Veda: 3.55

From the days of the Vedas, till a time came, which is the age of Puranas, there was a split. It was a split of the unified meaning of the two, and it further led to the separation of Persia under a more ancient and distant *Atharvan* influence from India under a disjointed impact of the Tri-Vedic culture only. This led to inverted meanings of Suras (Devas) and Ashura (Titans) offered by the Semitic world with Persia with 'Pehlevis' in the apex of powers and the Indian world under the disjointed influence of another similar race called the 'Pallavas'. The ancient Assyrian world and its city of Ashur, the Indo-European (Scandinavian) lore of Aesir and the later derivation of the festival of Ashur-Day (also known as Muharam) in Arabia and Persia share the common roots.

- Rig Veda: 1.24.4; 1.54.3; 2.1.6; 3.3.4; 4.2.5; 5.12.1; 6.22.2; 7.2.3; 8.19.23; 9.73.1; 10.10.2
- John R. Hinnels (Ed.) (1984). Appendix C, Chapter on 'Islam', "A Handbook of Living Religions", Penguin.
- Edward Hale (1986). "Asura in Early Vedic Tradition", Motilal Banarsidass: New Delhi.

3.4.4 System of reconciliation in the lower half

The inner mysteries behind the symbolisms were always in the hands of a few only. They were maintained within the inner circles of *'mystae'*. Circles in Eleusinian Greece, Asia Minor, the Chaldees of Sumeria-Babylonia and various secret centers practicing Mithraism and Orphism are to name a few. They shared a common origin – the idea of a latent soul, originally divine, but entombed in the netherworld. This was the Orphic idea of Erebus, an ever-shining promise in the darkness of the netherworld from where one can rise again (terms like Erbium of the fire-lanthanide metal series are modern scientific examples). The term 'Orphism' has been derived from this original Vedic term, which is *'Ourba'* – meaning the hidden fire in the nether, terrestrial or dark world of matter and Neptune (sea). From here (the lower world) they rise as the 'Tritons' (The Titans of Greece), which is also from a Vedic source. They including the Roman Neptune or the Greek Poseidon share the symbol of rise and penetration, i.e. the Trident and finally the double trident or the Vajra.

- Triton in the Vedas: Rig Veda: 1.158.5
- Ourba in the Vedas: 8.102.4–6
- On 'Erebus' – Orphism, in Dionysus (Bacchus), the Dictionary of Symbols, Penguin.

3.4.5 System of lower quarter: tala (tail)

The lower worlds in Fig. 3.5, after the separation, are described as the *tala* – for example *patale, tala-tala, rasatala*. It is evident from the Orphic tablets of *Patale* (a region near the mouth of ancient Indus Delta); *Atalia* (the name of ancient Italy or ancient Etruscan-Sabian civilization); *Ana-atalia* (the region where the ancient Celto-Hellenic sources known as the Chaldees of Sumeria). At least a hundred of other names ending with *atala (atl')* or tala are available in the ancient Mediterranean. Ancient legends of *Atlantis* and *Atlantic*

Ocean, regions like Atlas Mountains of Morocco, Tunisia and Algeria, cities like *Tel-Amarna* of ancient Egypt and modern Tel-Aviv in the Middle East (West Asia) maintain the thread of continuity.

- 'Atlantis' in Dictionary of Symbols, Penguin
- Berlitz, C. (1981). Chapter 8, "Doomsday 1999", Granada

3.4.6 System of lordship of the third and fourth quarters: the Atharvans

It is evident from Fig. 3.5 that there is an original integrity of the two halves – *dyu* and *prithvi*, which is achieved by the lordship of the four quarters (discussed mainly in Chapter 2). The entire Semitic concept of this lordship is found in terms of two components: (1) the Circuitous journey and (2) the four quarters that are covered. This is the basis of the Garden of Paradise (*Para-desa* or a distant heavenly allegory based on the Pennsylvanian Indo-European Gypsy word – Yuletide at four quarters). The two components have shaped the concept of Circe (*Kirk* or Church) of later Indian Buddhist and Christian architecture on the one hand and the four-quartered Garden of Eden of Islamic architecture on the other hand, respectively. We shall review these two aspects in the following two chapters. An unified approach to empire building and settlement planning as found in ancient Sumeria and Assyria; in Egypt unifying the upper and the lower halves; and the making of similar ancient empires in Persia (by the Achaemenid emperors like Cyrus and Darius) and in India during the Mauryan and the Guptas share the same view.

An instance is the empire of Sargon of Agade, ancient Sumeria-Assyria, who unified the upper and lower empires of Assyria (Ashur) and Sumeria (Ur) and was known as the 'Lord of Four Quarters'. He also boasted of having subjugated the 'four quarters' – the lands surrounding Akkad to the north (Subartu), the south (Sumer), the east (Elam) and the west (Martu). Some of the earliest texts credit him with rebuilding the city of Babylon (Bab-ilu) in a new location. Thousands of years later, the Mauryan kingdom's famous pillar (patronized by Emperor Ashoka) or the cardinal plan of Moghul (Mongolian) architectural element like 'Diwan-i-Khas'. Important evidence is in Fateh-pur Sikri, India, where Emperor Akbar followed similar principles.

- Kramer, Samuel Noah (1963). "The Sumerians", Chicago University Press
- Burroughs, William J. (2006). "Climate Change in Prehistory: The End of the Reign of Chaos", Cambridge University Press
- Fagan, B. (2004). "The Long Summer: How Climate Changed Civilisation", Granta Books
- 'Yule at four quarters' – Church of Four Quarters: Artemis, Commonwealth of Pennsylvania, USA.

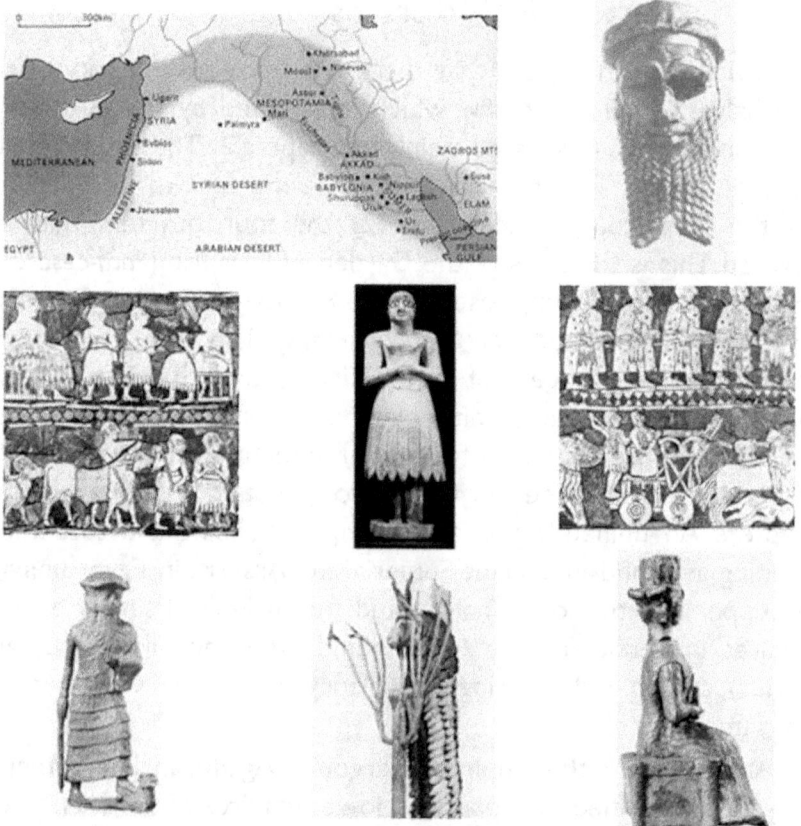

Figure 3.6 System development in early phase of Ubaid-Sumerian civilization
Top level – Empire of Emperor Sargon of Agade (goat-bearded lord of four quarters) unifying Sumeria, Assyria and Mittani (upper pictures) where Sargon the Great (Sharru-Kin) (2334–2279 BC). The actual spelling of his name was Sharru-Kin. According to legend his mother was of Kish, the name of a Sumerian city which traded with Indus Valley.
Mid-level – Cow (peace) and horse (war) processions of Tonsured figureheads of Sumeria
Lower level – Four-faced God; goat-head and cloak (Aegis) from Ur; and Goddesses of ancient Sumeria and Akkad. Similar goat-beards are found in Egypt right from earliest dynasties of Lower Kingdom (say Pharaoh Zoser)
[Source: The Oriental Institute, Chicago]

3.4.7 System of immortal lordship – from Garden of Odin: Adonis to the Garden of Eden with parallels in Orphic Eleusinian Mysteries

What is most important in the 'Four Quarters' or a 'Full Cycle' movement is the dynamism of a personified *Prajapati Brahman* transcending the universal limits and becoming the absolute impersonal *Brahman*, the impersonal is the whole basis of the lordship of four quarters and going beyond to the fifth and further. The way is that of purity and chastity – to realize the supreme like an ear of the corn. The evidences are available from both India and Greece – from Atharvan Mundaka Upanishad and the Hippolytic accounts of the Eleusinian Mysteries.

- 'Tapasa Chiyate Brahma..........samyag gyanena brahmacharya........Tat Parama Brahma veda brahmaiba bhabati......'
  (Atharvan Mundaka: 1.1.8; 3.1.5; 3.2.10)

The Absolute manifests like the 'Ear of the corn'.......the way is only facilitated by purity and abstinence from the sensual-carnal.... in the end the Brahman-seeker becomes Brahman itself.

- 'This ear of the corn...is the perfect light....he who has renounced all carnal generations, by night at El-Eusia, accomplishing by the light of the great flame the great and unutterable mysteries, says and cries in a loud voice – 'Holy Brimo has borne a sacred child, Brimos.'
- The Chthonian or Vegetation mystery of Greece is the rite of Brimo-Sabazius (older name of Dionysus) – refer to Indian and Greek counterparts of the same:

  Brahman = Brimos (Absolute)

  Shiva = Sabazius (Absolute personified)

  Vaka = Bacchus (The beatitude of the WORD)

  Dwi-ja = Dio-aegis or Dio-nysus (Double born or door)
- Hippolytus, Refutatio Omnium Haereium, V. 8; Chapter 5, "Comparative Religion – An Introductory and Historical study", E.O. James, Methuen & Co. Ltd.: London

The Vedic imagery has compared this to the overtaking of the self by the self itself – where the one who is eating (one who swallows) and the object that is to be eaten or swallowed is equivalent. This is equivalent to the seed or personified God-Head cutting the head *(Gardana)* of the other. This state of atonement (unity or rapture of the two) is allegorized in the form of a boiled grain or *Odana* – a term allegorized in the Vedas and mainly emphasized in the *Atharva Veda* and some earliest Upanishads. From this ancient allegory originated the symbol of four quarters. This is overtaking of the seed or the entire source of creation itself, which stands for the *Gardana* and hence equated as the highest level and represented as the supreme heaven. This in real tangible representation is the Garden of *Odona* or paradise itself. The lore and journey of Adonis in the two worlds and his Garden, the myth of Scandinavian Odin and his World-Tree (the term Wooden came from that) and finally the ideology and the architecture of the Garden of Eden share this common source.

- Atharva Veda
- Quran: Al-Zumar: 20, 73; Al-Rahman: 50; Al-Saad: 50
- Spenser's Garden of Adonis
  Josephine Waters Bennett, PMLA, Vol. 47, No. 1 (Mar., 1932), pp. 46–80
- Nassar, Hala. F. Islamic Garden of Four Quarters – Gardens underneath which Rivers Flow! Department of Landscape Architecture, West Virginia University

3.4.8 The turning of the wheel or the Mandala: Vedic Aswa-kranta (Ka-ba-lah or Kiblah) and Go-Kranta (reversal of Qiblah)

Evident in the Vedic lore, particularly in the Rig Veda, 7th Mandala, there is a clear distinction of this ascendant and descendent – in the galloping of the horse – signifying the core rays of the sun and the recovery of the cows – the periphery or the field of light or dawn. One is core power and the other, the stream of clarity or the light. Horse and cows are the twin allegory, respectively. One is Ka-Ba-Lah – the ascendant of creative consonants or cosmic vibrations that are perfected *(samskrita)* – which means towards the core or dissolution *(Laya-yoga* or *Yama-sutra)*. The other is its reversal Al-Ba-Ka, which is re-manifestation *(Kaya-yoga* or *Brahma-sutra)*. The link is Ba or Vayu-yoga, which is preserved by the diagonal connections or *Karna-sutras*. The Semitic wisdom of Judaism and

Islam accepts the two (Kabbalah and its reversal), respectively. Christianity is divided on it – for example the Monophysites and the Nestorians, one preaching a core that has an undivided Trinity (son of God alone) and the other a peripheral approach that divides the Trinity into three separate identities (son of Flesh). Both are true. *However, its separation had led to the twin paths of Abraham or Abiram-to-Isaac and Abraham or Abiram-to-Ishmael from where Christianity and Islam draw its original source.*

3.4.9 The Impersonal Indo-Iranian solar symbolism, and lately the cult of Mithra

Perhaps, the last of the research clue is the symbolism of solar seasonal cycles, as a whole within which the specific cult of Mithra and the cult of the DiosKouris (the twin riders of the horse or Vedic Aswinis) had become more important, over time. They had penetrated the entire European world and the coastlines of Africa, on the one hand and the eastern Mongoloid branch up to the Americas, on the other hand.

3.4.10 Iranian Zoroastrian 'Bahram' (Vedic – 'BRAHMN' and Orphic – 'BRIMO')

First and etymologically, it is noteworthy that the same letters are used in the words like Semitic patriarch 'Abraham' (mentioned as Abiram in Genesis, The Old Testament) or IBRAHIM (ABRHM), Bahram (BHRAM), and Brahma (BRHMA). Now let us look at the word 'BAHRAM' in some further details.

Secondly, the word Vahrām or Bahrām (modern Persian, var: Behrām; middle Persian: Varahram) is found significantly as the Zoroastrian concept of 'full or complete (up to the highest level or Brim) victory over resistance' and, as the hypostasis of victory, is one of the principal figures in the Zoroastrian pantheon of Yazatas. Armenian 'Vram' means victorious, fiery and stormy godhead connected with Vritta-hanta (verethragnan) Indra, the bearer of the thunderbolt of the Vedas. Based on the two evidences few observations can be drawn:

- *Traces of Bahram in ancient Airyan Vaeja (Iran):* Bahram's alter ego in the Avesta is Dāmōiš Upamana, and in the Bahram Yasht is addressed as *Verethragna* meaning 'smiting of resistance', related to Avestan verethra, 'obstacle' and *verethragnan*, 'victorious'. In the texts of the Avesta, in particular in the Bahram Yasht, which is one of the older sections of the Younger Avesta, Bahram has the attributes of a mighty force that overcomes all resistance. There, Bahram is addressed as *Verethragna*, "the most highly armed" (Yasht 14.1), the 'best equipped with might' (14.13), with 'effervescent glory' (14.3), has 'conquering superiority' (14.64), and is in constant battle with men and daemons (14.4, 14.62). In the Zoroastrian hierarchy of angels, Bahram is a helper of Asha Vahishta (Avestan, middle Persian: Ardvahisht), the Amesha Spenta responsible for the luminaries.
- *Astral implications of Bahram in head-crowns of Sassanids Kings:* In the astronomical and calendrical reforms of the Sassanids (205-651 CE), the planet Mars (representing masculine and patriarchal tradition) was named Bahram including some of their king's names (Bahram I to VI). Bahram also appears as wings, or as a bird of prey, in the crowns of the Sassanid kings. This iconography first appears in the crown of Bahram II which also bears the name of the divinity.
- *The Holiest of Fires:* The present-day expression Atash-Behram as the name of the most sacred class of fires – "Victorious Fire" appears in Middle Persian inscriptions such as the Kartir inscription at Kabah-i Zardusht, and now understood by the term Atash-Behram.
- *Traces in Southeast Asia:* The given official credence in Burma is that these names come from Sanskrit *Brahma*, which is the name of the Vedic God of creation *Brahma*. This interpretation of the name was spread to India by some Buddhist monks from Ceylon and, although the usage is no longer current, Burma was historically known in India as *'Brahma-desha'* ('Brahma-land') [Source: Background Note: Burma. Bureau of East Asian and Pacific Affairs (August 2005). Retrieved on 2006-06-11]. The empire of 'Pallava'

kings of India had extended in South Asia with king's name ending with *'Brahamana'* or later *'Varmana'* is a counter-part of the 'Pehlevis' (composers of Avesta) in ancient Persia. The word *'bahrama'* is a closer derivative of B(a)rahamana and V=B leading to heraldic 'Varmana' lion-kings in both Persian post-Pehlevi or Sassanid tradition and Southeast Asian Varman traditions. Varman or *Varma* is an honorific title and surname. Originally affixed to the names of Kshatriyas (royal Sage-Kings) in Southeast Asia, Varman was the official title of the Khmer kings of Cambodia. The king who built Angkor complexes was known as Jayavarman. The rajahs of Kerala/Tamil Nadu also used Varma or Varman and as a title and surname. Ample traces of long-standing tradition of *'Su-brahman-swami'* in South India associated with Kumara or Vishakha is major evidence in this regard.

- *Archaeological evidences of 'Bahram' from Rajasthan, India:* Evidence of Varman is a village in Sirohi District in Rajasthan state in India. It is 45 km from Abu Road. Its old name is Brahmana. It was a prosperous town in the past. The place was famous for Sun temple known as Brahmana Svamin. The temple is also called Surya Narayana and was built in the 7th century. It was a marvellous temple. During the reign of Paramara ruler Vikramasimha of Chandravati, the temple was rebuilt in 1299 AD by Lalitadevi, wife of Paratihara Raja Vinnada. There is a Jain temple and also the temple of Varmesvara (Shiva).

- *Amongst Mandeans (from ancient Sheba) of lower Iran and Yemen:* The ancient Mandeans and Sabians (Star worshippers) held Yurba is the power in darkness. *Yurba* appears to be Erebus of Orphism and the Ourba – the volcanic or Neptune-based subterranean fire of Vedas. It was Yurba who gave the Jews their power, and Abraham was of our people –we called him Bahram.

    Etymologically, one may research into the linkages of 'ibarahim = 'braham = Bahram. Bihram [Pr. Bih-ram] is named at baptism

    – *'I am baptized with the baptism of Bihram the Great'.*

This statement matches with *'Parama Brahman veda Brahmaiba bhabati'* of Vedas and *'Holy Brimo leads to sacred child Brimos'* of Eleusinian Mysteries in Greece. *Bihram* or Bahram (the Great) is often mentioned: his name suggests Indo-Iranian origin. The banner is sometimes called Bihram. Such traditions are still evident amongst the minstrels, fakirs, dervishes in Celto-Hellenic-Turkic region and perhaps the 'Sahajiya' or 'Bauls-Bards' of India.

- E.S. Drower (1937). "Mandeans of Iraq and Iran", Clarendon Press: Oxford (reprint Leiden: E.J. Brill 1962), pp. 266–269

3.4.11 Systems of Bauls (India), Dervishes (Turkey), Bards (Upper Eurasia) and Minstrels (Gaul or France)

There was and still a tradition of the 'non-conformist' or the non-institutional approach to spiritual tradition. It is the Baul or Faqir tradition in India, which embraced the original Gnostic elements of Vedas, and it remained in some avenues of later Hinduism, Tantric Buddhism and Sufi Islam; and it is still believed that authentic worship of God which takes place only deep within each person where 'God' the divine 'man of heart' is enshrined. They believe that church, temple, and mosque only stand in the way as minor tools. To the Baul, our bodies are the final temples – the shrine of the soul. This legacy is attached to the Islamic Sufi tradition of Baharampur – a place where great spiritual and cultural personalities like Lalon Shah Fakir, Shri Chaitanya-Nityananda and poet Rabindranath Tagore are connected. In the seminal Hebart Lecture in London (1933), Tagore first applauded Lalan Shah as a mystic poet who discovered 'soul' and the meaning of 'man'. Tagore said that I discovered that 'man' from the songs of Lalan who said that *'ai manushe ase se mon....'* that which means the 'man is within yourself where are you searching Him' (Folkore II, Calcutta, 1961).

- *The tradition of Lalon Shah and roots of 'Bahram' in undivided Bengal:* Lalon Shah, one of the greatest mystic poets of this sub-continent, was born in the year 1774 in the village Harishpur, under the present District of Jhenaidah in Bangladesh; and he imbibed all Gnostic elements of Vedas

(Tantra) and that of Sufi mystics like Shah Sultan Rumi, Hajrat Shah Jalal, Shah Sultan Makka, Shah Sultan Mahishwar, Khan Jehen Ali, Shah Ismail Gazi, Shah Makdum, Hajrat Jalal Uddin Tabreji and absorbed the essence of 'Nadia-Murshidabad' lineage of Vaishnavism in charge of Sri Nityananda, the associate and complementary part of Shri Krishna Chaitanya. This lineage took specific character under the leadership of Shri Nityananda, followed by his son Birbhadra and a Muslim woman known as Madhab bibi. The idea of spiritual egotism – the allegory of *Hamsah* – the spiritual spark in us – the bird of flight or *'achin-pakhi'* is the key essence or *'marma'* and the key to oneness leading to *maramiya* internally and *Sahajiya* externally with the supreme in the complete sense of mind, soul and body, where the body stood as the microcosm reflecting the universe or the macrocosm. This was and still preached by the Sufi mystics finding complementary resonance in the Vedic concept of Atman and Brahman leading to a 'complete victory' over one self:

> 'The spirit within me is smaller than a mustard seed,
> The spirit within me is greater than this earth
> And the sky and the heaven and all these are united.
> It is Brahman (Bah-ram).'

Traces of this tradition perhaps remain imbedded in the areas and regions around Bahrampur, in the renewed context of an undivided Bengal. Such assimilations have perhaps come out the best in the traditions of many – like Kabirji, Sai Baba of Shirdi and Sri Ramakrishna Paramhamsah in recent Indian spiritual traditions and the poetry of Rabindranath Tagore. This is again referred in Chapter 5 discussing Phase III – rise of Arabia and revival of Persian wisdom.

The eleven features constitute a first system's foundation to the beginning of an inter-mixing of the two civilizations, India and Greece:

'These two gigantic forces (Aryans and Yavanas), issuing from far-away and different mountains (India and Greece), occasionally come in contact with each other, and whenever such confluence takes place, a tremendous intellectual and spiritual tide rising in human societies, greatly expands the range of civilization and confirms the universal brotherhood among men.

Once in far remote antiquity, the Indian philosophy, coming in contact with Greek energy, led to the rise of the Persian, the Roman, and other great nations'·

– Swami Vivekananda
Problem of India and its solution

3.5 Part three: System of converging realization and belief systems

Important features of a Westward migration of the Vedic lore to the making of an earliest stock of the religion of Zarathusthra and the Old Testament tradition can be made evident. The migration, of course, is not a harmonious progression but a schism or a separation from the mother stock – where new waves of religion and material principles begun to deviate more and more from its roots. As a starting point, three important features may be forwarded to best establish a set of converging realization and belief systems:

The origin and a separation from the integral Vedic lore

An ancient split between the pillars of 'Sura' (Indians) and 'Ashura' (Persians) was carried out by an idea of the corporeal emphasis by the Persians and finally expanded by anti-transmigratory belief system of the soul by the Semitic branches. Later-Indian (Puranic) 'a-baidi' = Semitic 'Ubaid' = 'ibadi' tradition of Arabia = Chthonian words like abada (Khorsa-abada, Persia). They are the true origins of one symbolic fixed and high citadel (acropolis) and many low Arcadian pastures and produce of plenty in all ancient Greek settlements.

Origin of Impersonal truth (Vaidic) = Personified version (A-badi)

(A-purushyea or the Impersonal) = Abada (personified culture)

Celestial fixed point (Akshara or Acro) = Terrestrial Agro-culture

This is the basis of Vedas and Puranas as discussed in the Foreword. The Later Persian and Semitic religions are based on the second approach only. In India, Puranas or Smritis have the impersonal and universal Gnostic backdrop and never dependent on the imagery of a single Messiah or prophet, whose existences are subject to historical verification. In the religions outside India that dependence is there leading to higher degree of institutionalized, proselytized and politicized approach to mass religious dissemination.

3.5.1 The creation of the Semitic stock from Persia

The *'ibri'* or *'afriti'* may be the origin of the Hebrew race as a whole. The key is the lost or apparently dormant wisdom of the *'afri'* or *'apri'*-sukta' of the Rig Veda (Mandala seven, sukta 2) is an explanation of the nine levels of the Sumerian *Ziggu-rathu* (Ziggurat) and the basis of the Sepharial *(Kabala)* as a branch of the later Judeo-Christian tradition of mysteries. The sukta recurs once in every *Mandala* of the Rig Veda and spells out a 'nine + one + one = eleven-stepped' ascending journey of the individual soul. The term means – 'affinity for or favorably connected to the other side' – the separation of material and the spiritual. The later Semitic word *'ibri'* is a derivative.

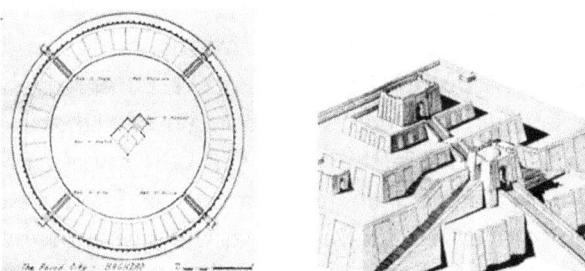

Figure 3.7 Four quarters of ancient Baghdad city: the four gates led to Khorasan (NE), Basra (SE), Kufa (SW) and Syria (NW); Quadrangular traditions of Ziggurat at UR – birthplace of Semitic Patriarchy (3000 BC)

Vedic *Apri* = Zoroastrian *Afrigi* = Semitic *'ibri'* = (H)-*ebrew* = Celtic (H)-*ebrides* = Iberian peninsula – Celto-Hellenic or Gaulish) = Moorish *Afriti* (Africa) = *'eufriti'* (Euphrates).

- Works of M. Haug (1884), "Essays on the Sacred Language, Writings and Religion of the Parsees", London, Trubner – Philo Press (1971), Amsterdam.
- Rig Veda: 3.4

3.5.2   Lordship of four quarters

Gardens are symbols, icons of the cosmic archetype – the macrocosmic whole engrafted on the microcosm, the earth. To the heavenly paradise, it is a pre-figuration and a preparatory set-up for upward resurrection of the 'First dead' (Aspirant souls) to those spiritual levels in the heaven. The great Sufi thinker Abu Yakub Sejeshani observes: the word Jannit in ancient Persia stood for Paradise, which means a state beyond filled with fruition; of fecundity in expression and fullness; of immortal juvenile expression represented by scented plants with flowers drawing 'elixir' from the streams of running water representing ambrosia or Amrita. In that sense, the mystic Islamic tradition calls the supreme, Al-ilahas, a perfect gardener. Another part of the Semitic tradition, Christianity labels God himself as the divine Garden. Particularly, St. John of the Cross had earmarked the City of God based on the cardinals of the cross, the garden or God himself.

In the origins of the Semitic tradition, mainly in Judaism, there is a deeper esoteric line of thought-realization called the Kabalistic tradition. The tradition calls the garden – Parades. Parades, as per the Indo-European language tradition, means garden and often a state, a domain or a distant land that is revered as a higher realm of knowledge and bliss. Pardes is the domain of higher knowledge and the four consonants in the word (P,R,D,S) correspond to the four rivers, which flowed from the Garden of Eden described in the first chapter of the Old Testament, the Book of Genesis (2: 10ff) or creation itself.

In addition to the birth of the tradition of garden in the Semitic tradition, one has to look to lands further east, namely Persia or Iran, i.e. ancient Airyan – the celebrated land of the Aryans. It was in Persia, the garden embraced metaphysical and socio-physical attributes also. Love for gardens became the pleasure of great Achaemenind emperors like Cyrus (Kurus) and Darius (Darayush) in times as early as 700 BCE. Of the two, Cyrus had built his famous garden of Pasargadae, which is till date, the seat of his sepulcher, the tomb awaiting divine resurrection from earth, for the heavens. Till today, Persian carpets are embroidered on the 'checkers' (square patterns) of these ancient gardens called the 'space of four divine quarters' or simply, the 'Chahar-bagh'. The word 'Chahar' means 'four' in the eastern or 'Satem' stream of Indo-European language system that covers both ancient Indian and Persian sub-language systems. And 'bagh' means garden, which metaphysically represents 'Bak' or 'vak', the word of God in India. Thus Par-deus meant a distant land often signifying a 'celebrated divine' realm of the east, an idea that the Gypsies had cherished as they travelled westbound. In ancient Egypt, the famous 'Book of the Dead' contains the word several times. The term Egypt, incidentally, is derived from '(A)-gypsia' meaning the land where the Gypsies had finally settled.

History tells that Cyrus and his son, Darius, had built an intercontinental road from Susa in Western Persia (close to the Tigris and Euphrates valley) to Sardis in Anatolia (Turkey). Travellers from the ancient Near East (Western Asia: the Fertile Crescent) and Asiatic Greece (Caria, Lydia, Lycia, and Phrygia) used to come to these gardens of Persia in the ancient times thus making the road as world's first international highway and attributing the ancient Persian empire as world's first gigantic urban empire that stretched from the western banks of the Indus to the eastern shores of Danube. Emperor Alexander had treaded this route to reach India a few centuries later.

Now, what is contained in these gardens as a cultural landscape, as a mosaic of mystic treasure? The squares or 'checkered' patterns are themselves filled up with heavenly flowers and green shrubs – that more than a millennium later became the basis of the sacred 'Ishmaeli diagram' portraying the infinite lace of creation by the Supreme, i.e. Al-ilah in Islamic tradition. More than two thousand years later, these patterns inspired the great works of AIA Gold-medal winner American Architect Sir Christopher Alexander (1979), who worked out his famous 'pattern language systems' for the built environment. In between, these patterns continued to evolve through the advent of Moorish Islamic architecture in Iberia (Spain and Portugal), mainly by the Nasrid sultanate. From Iberia, it continued to inspire the rest of Europe, and mainly Gothic architecture in France throughout the entire course of early dark ages (7th to 13th century AD).

Centuries later in Persia, the typical Sassanid park was arranged in the form of a cross (200 BCE). The features were the four arms meeting at right angles, with the palace in the center. The quadrangular pattern corresponded to the cosmological notion of the universe divided into four quarters and watered by four rivers flowing from the representative earthly paradise. Finally, the pattern became the heart of Islamic tradition, mainly in the form of 'char-bagh' representing many of the Moghul gardens in India, of which the Humayun's tomb and its later representative in marble, the famous 'Taj Complex' are just the two of many. The Koran (18:55) particularly forwards the divine implications of death and resurrection in a garden, which is the prototype of paradise holding the entombment, a link between the two.

However, in traditions that are perhaps pre-historic, gardens were famous in the entire ancient Near East including Anatolia or oldest Asiatic Greek settlements. They are evident amongst the gardens of the 'Ancient Gods', who were somehow pagan to the more formalized and institutionalized order of Semitic traditions. One of these ancient gods was 'Adonis', who lamented, died and was resurrected in a garden. Thus the garden of 'Adonis', who was a mysterious pagan corn-god, still stands as a possible source to the origins of the Garden of 'Eden'.

From 'Adonis' to 'Eden', there are enough evidence and a trace of a long journey of religious and iconic evolution; and this is however not the scope of the present chapter. But what this chapter seeks is to highlight is the celebration of life and death contained in the deeper cycle of renewal and sustainability, implied in the deep ecological patterns of these ancient gardens of Adonis. Adonis symbolized as the ‹corn god› (vija) re-sprouted (spring forth) after it was reaped following a Passover festival (after winter). The journey from ‹reaping to re-sprouting› represented the cycles of agriculture and the changing seasons in a year, and the return of the next year, the next spring. These cycles actually portrayed the deeper mysteries of death and resurrection, and they were often portrayed by a lot of ancient religions in Egypt, Greece and

Anatolia. From one spring, through summer, to autumn, and from there through winter to the next spring is an eternal journey of the four seasons, the four quarters, the four cardinals in a cross-like form delineated as a landscape, an icon of perfection. This landscape of perfection is ‹the Garden of Eden›.

Thus to trace origins of an icon as important as the Garden of Eden, one has to take an inter-continental, trans-cultural and cross-religious perspective. Such a viewpoint will certify how different cultures and religions, either related or not related to each other, arrive at a commonality of cosmic truth and truth-realization. This is what we mean by the ‹impersonal universal› often termed as the ‹Sanatana› – a lore that finds a special place in the ancient Vedic lore and then up to Buddhism; and also from pagan West Asian or East European religions to the later big three of the Semitic group, Judaism, Christianity and Islam. Even in the ancient Meso-American religions, it has a place, for instance, in the quadrangular Mayan calendar. In all of them, the iconography of the Garden and the Lordship of the four quarters persists, and has secured a central place or hope called the idea of Pardes or Paradise.

A proper interpretation of the immortal tradition of Paradise as a garden can be best attempted if we do not place the more ancient traditions on an isolated realm of the past having no continuity, but try and establish a holistic vision of tracing its evolution at every steps and niche of history – to which a later religious belief is perhaps another additional step added to the larger ladder of time and human history heading for the future.

3.5.3 The connection between Kali and Al-Kali

Lastly, it is the tradition of Ancient near West – the wisdom of the *Kalidi* or Chaldees (origin of early Babylonian astral lore), from where the Caledonian or Culdee (Celtoi) elements of Europe can be safely derived. The key word is 'Kali', which in Arabia is Al-kali, i.e. the burning fire (Volcanic) – source of later word like 'Caldera' (subterranean inferno).

Kali (Vedic) = Chi-Lin (Chinese) = Al-Kali (Arabic) = Calliope (Greece) = Kelly/Killi (Iberian/Caledonian)

This Westward dissemination can be further made evident by the following discussions in the subsequent system's approach.

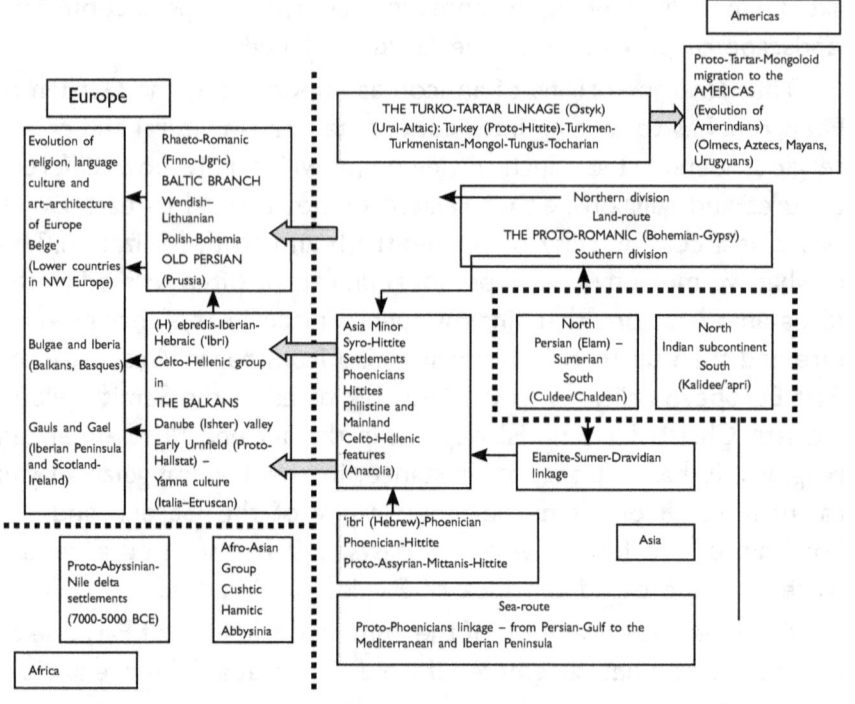

Figure 3.8 Inter-connected language systems

3.6 Part four: System of cooperative language systems

3.6.1 Indo-European language systems

The first proposal of the possibility of common origin for the various languages had (Fig. 3.8) come from the Dutch linguist and scholar Marcus Zuerius van Boxhorn in 1647. Boxhorn discovered the similarity among Indo-European languages, and supposed the existence of a primitive common language which he called "Scythian". He included in his hypothesis Dutch, Greek, Latin, Persian, and German, later adding Slavic, Celtic and Baltic languages. However, the suggestions of van Boxhorn did not become widely known and did not stimulate further research.

The hypothesis re-appeared in 1786 when Sir William Jones first lectured on similarities between four of the oldest languages known in his time: Latin, Greek, Sanskrit, and Persian. Systematic comparison of these and other old languages conducted by Franz Bopp supported this theory, and Bopp's Comparative Grammar, appearing between 1833 and 1852, counts as the starting-point of Indo-European studies as an academic discipline. Since then many scholarships have come in. Three components of the Indo-European carrier are evident:

1. Indo-European Gypsy (Tatar-Hittite) connection;
2. Indo-European Phoenicians (Dravidic-Elam) originating from the Persian Gulf and celebrated 'Land of Phewenet or PUNT'; and
3. Northern Mongoloid connection (Tatar-Mongol) – continental shift to Americas (Red Indians)

3.6.2 System of land migration: Indo-European Gypsy

The origins of the 'Gypsies' (The Romas) – as a principal westward carrier (Asia to Europe and more specifically, from Indo-Persia to Anatolia and further beyond into Austria) – has been first observed by a set of scholars and well documented by Prof. A. L. Basham in his seminal work 'The Wonder that was India'. Recently National Geographic Scholar Peter Godwin, National Geographic April 2002 (page 72ff.), says:

'The origins of the Gypsies, with little written history, were shrouded with mystery. What is known now from the clues in the various dialects of their language, Romany, is that they came from Northern India to the Middle East a thousand years ago, working as minstrels (spirituality) and merceneries (war), metal smiths and servants. Europeans misnamed them Egyptians, soon shortened to Gypsies. A clan system, based mostly on their traditional crafts and deeply fragmented and fractious people, only really unifying in the face of enmity (like one of the most horrifying ones, anti-semiticism) from non-Gypsies, whom they called Gadje (Gazi). Today Gypsey activists preferred to be called ROMA, which comes from the Romany word for 'man'.'

'One theory suggests that the ROMA left India to help repel Islamic attack (acting as early Christian merceneries – probably assisting the 'Templars' in Bulgaria and greater Danube Valley bordering the Eastern Byzantium). Passing through Persia and spending centuries in the Byzantium Empire (the entire region around the interface of South-eastern Europe and Western Asia – that changed from early Persian Empire to that of the Greeks (under Alexander and after him) till the extension of Eastern Roman Empire), the moved north in the 1300s (as Europe came out of Dark Ages – probably the Gypsies shaped the guild, foundries, presses and smiths activity – the seed to the Industrial Revolution and making of European Culture through the Indo-Persian components).'

National Geographic Scholar Erla Zwingle (September 2002, page 80ff) identifies the traces of the race of 'RUM' (ROM) of the Greek-Byzantim origin in the Upper Black sea – in the mysterious land of the COLCHIS (which is the source of Greek mythology, the tales of Argonauts, the Golden Ram (Aries or Lamb of God) and the twin Dioskouris (Aswins) accompanying them). Erla Zwingle says:

'When Constantinople fell to the Ottoman Turks in 1453, most of the Greek Christians who remained in the Black sea gradually converted to Islam. The RUM are their descendents, and although they are Muslim Turks, their private, unwritten language, RUMCA, is a form of Greek.....These Black sea people share foggyungly mountains.....the mountains press against the coastline, in some places plunging into the sea ....villagers have always traveled back and forth between the shore and the peak, and for centuries several important caravan routes through the mountain passes linked Trabzon to the luxurious cities of Persia and even INDIA....the coast has always meant trade, travel and prosperity.'

Thus continuity to routes of Alexander to India and Persian imperial highway from Sardis (Anatolia) to Susa is evident linking the Indo-European Hittite (Khatti) kingdom in Anatolia around 1700 BC (Fig. 3.9).

The absence of a written history has meant that the origin and early history of the Romani people was long an enigma.

Cultural anthropologists have historically hypothesized an Indian origin of the Roma based on linguistic evidence. Genetic data confirms this. The Roma are believed to have originated in the Punjab and Rajasthan regions of the Indian subcontinent. They began their migration to Europe and North Africa via the Iranian plateau long back, under different periods of history, facilitated by various reasons, as highlighted in the end of this chapter (Fig. 3.10).

- Angus F. Gypsies (Peoples of Europe) 2nd edition.
- Donald K. (1998). Historical Dictionary of the Gypsies (Romanies), Scarecrow Press.

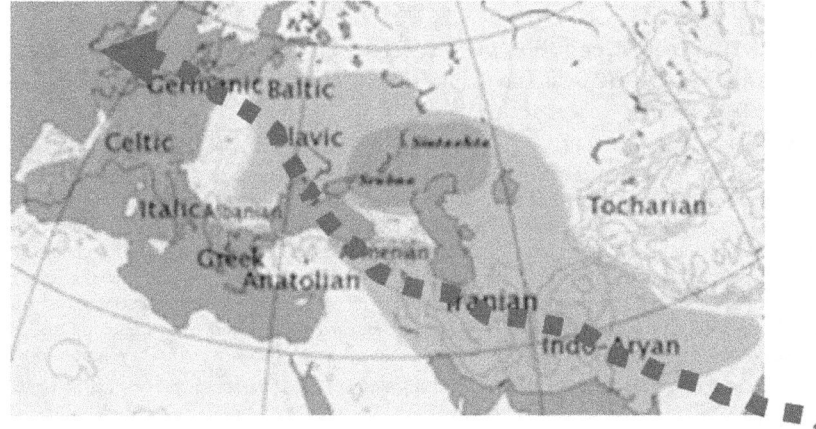

Figure 3.9 Movements of Gypsies (Roma – Romany – Rum) from Central Asia

- Grierson, G. A. 1887. Arabic and Persian references to Gypsies. Indian Antiquary 16: 257–258.
- Woolner, Alfred C. 1913–1914. The Indian origin of the Gypsies in Europe. Journal of the Panjab Historical Society 2: 136–141.
- Sampson, John. 1923. On the origin and early migrations of the Gypsies. Journal of the Gypsy Lore Society, Third Series, 2: 156–169.
- Woolner, Alfred C. 1928. Aśoka and the Gypsies. Journal of the Gypsy Lore Society, Third Series, 7: 108–111.
- Hancock, I. F. 1998. The Indian origin and westward migration of the Romani people. Manchaca: International Romani Union.
- Kenrick, Donald. 1993. Gypsies from India to the Mediterranean. Toulouse: CRDP Midi Pyrénées.
- Kenrick, Donald. 1994. Gypsies: from India to the Mediterranean. Paris.
- Origins and Divergence of the Roma (Gypsies) – David Gresham et al. (2001) by The American Society of Human Genetics; Centre for Human Genetics, Edith Cowan University; Western Australian Institute for Medical Research, Perth, Department of Genetics, Stanford University School of Medicine, Stanford, CA; and many European Centers including Human Genetics Centre, Medical Faculty, University of Vilnius, Vilnius, Lithuania.

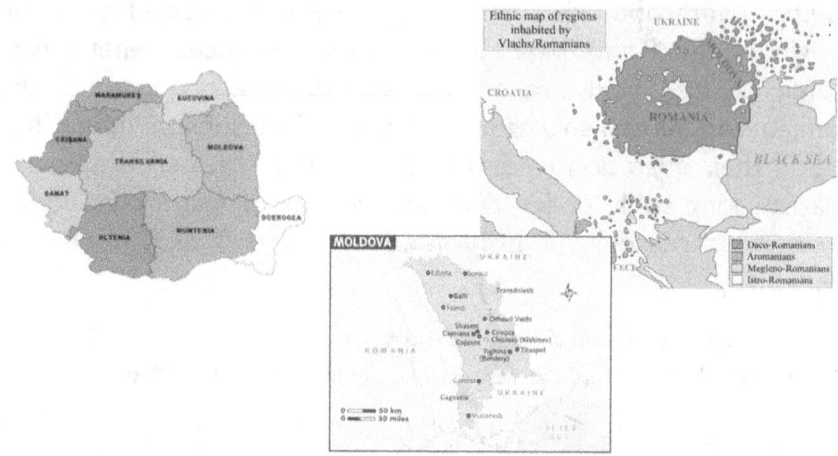

Figure 3.10 Key concentration of westward migration of Indo-Iranian Romany to Romania, CRISANA belt and CHISNEU, Moldova to Celtic VINDOBANA (Vienna), Transylvania

(*Note:* This dissipation occurred over a long period 3500–500 AD – having a common origin but leading to various diversified cultures and transformed language systems – from here the Indo-European contribution of the original Gypsy elements can be traced towards the making of Celto-Hellenic elements, that was the cradle of Anatolian (Hittite), Etruscan (Romanic-Italian), Slavic-Baltic (Lithuanian-Germanic) and Celtic (French Iberian language systems). All cooperative research linkages of art-architectural and cultural-folk-linguistic systems that lead to the evolution of the cult of Mithra-Adonis-Tammuz-Kumarbi and ultimately the idea of the death and resurrection of the 'sun' or the 'inner soul' had stretched from West Asia to Eastern Europe and they are to be posited and intra-reviewed within this movement of the ROMA and the gradual historical evolution of the Celto-Hellenic (Peruse-Pharisee-Parisian or Gaulish) element to understand the original linkages.)

3.6.3 System of marine linkages: Phoenicians and the land of Punt

The origin of Phoenicians from West Asia, mainly the coastline from Indus to Euphrates (Persian Gulf) is evident from Herodetus's book of histories:

'The Phoenicians, who had formerly dwelt on the shores of the Persian Gulf, having migrated to the Mediterranean and settled in the parts which they now inhabit, began at once, they say, to adventure on long voyages, freighting their vessels with the wares of Egypt and Assyria. They landed at many places on the coast, and among the rest at Argos, which was then pre-eminent above all the states included now under the common name of Hellas. Here they exposed their merchandise, and traded with the natives for five or six days.......'

The Phoenicians (a Greek name for them, known to the Hebrews as Phut) were originally – 'Puntians' (from which their name derives) a mercantile, Sea People. They were the ancient Mediterranean Sea's (and beyond) best navigators (their talents hired by Egyptians and Persians alike). They are classified as one of the nations in the four directions from Israel Gomer being the north, Persia or India to the east, Cush to the south, and Put to the west. The Land of Punt, also called 'Pwenet' by the ancient Egyptians, at times synonymous with Ta netjer, the 'land of the god', was a fabled site in eastern Africa and "was the source of many exotic products, such as gold, aromatic resins, African blackwood, ebony, ivory, slaves and wild animals" including monkeys and baboons. Information about Punt has been found in ancient Egyptian records of trade missions to this region.

The ancient Egyptians were also called Punt Ta netjer, meaning 'God's Land'. This designation did not mean that Punt was considered a 'Holy Land' by the Egyptians; rather it was used to refer to regions of the Sun God, i.e. regions located in the direction of the sunrise. These eastern regions were blessed with precious products, like incense, used in temples. The term was used not only in reference to Punt, located southeast of Egypt, but also in reference to regions of Asia east and northeast of Egypt, such as Lebanon, which was the source of wood for temples.

In an essay entitled 'Aryans and Tamilians', Swami Vivekananda has given us a clue. Referring to the earliest ethnic connections between the original Indians (Tamilians or Dravidians) and Akkado-Sumerian and Egyptian races[5], he asserts:

'.... We are glad that he (referring to the works of Pandit Savariroyan in his times) boldly pushes forward the Akkado-Sumerian racial identity of the ancient Tamilians...we would suggest, also, that the Land of Punt of the Egyptians was not only Malabar, but that the Egyptians as a race bodily migrated from Malabar across the ocean and entered the delta along the course of Nile from north (or say Alexandria) to south, to which Punt they have been always fondly looking back as the home of the blessed'.

---

[5] Pages 301–302, Complete Works, (Vol IV, 1995).

On several studies and research done on Egypt separately, direct trade and cultural linkages from Egypt and the revered 'Land of Punt' (The Land of God) has involved antique waves of migration. In this connection, readers may refer to a website[6] for the following quotation:

'...The question about the geographical location of the mythical "God's country" of Punt (above the name in hieroglyphics) has been a subject to scientific discussions for a long time, not only from an Egypt-logical point of view, but also from the view of the African archaeology, because the region around the Red Sea formed probably the base for the principal trade ways between the Mediterranean area and India in later, Greek and roman, times.'[7]

Another work the following quotation may be referred regarding the Land of Punt, a probable origin or destination-source of Phoenician trade, is:

'.........Their fine metal and ivory work indicates wide commercial activity: copper came from Cyprus, silver and gold from Ethiopia and maybe from Anatolia, although there were copper and iron mines in Wadi Araba, which Solomon exploited amply, ivory from India or Punt. All this shows the importance of the Red Sea route, which gave access both to the African coast and India.'

[http://www.cedarland.org/trade.html]

Readers may also refer National Geographic Magazine August 1974, p. 172, where scholars have established King Solomon's 'Ships of Tarshish (Tarsus)' (1 Book of Kings. Old Testament, 10:23) carrying spices, gold, cedar woods, apes, peacock coming from distant Ophir or Punt, and through these observations the scholars have concluded that the celebrated Land of God and fertility to be India as there are those peacocks and apes and spices.

The land of 'Punt' has been identified as India[8] and Persia. Here is a special note comes from Margaret A. Murray from her detailed research book entitled 'The Splendor that was Egypt' (page 222 in Appendix I, Sidgwick and Jackson):

---

[6] http://www.maat-ka-ra.de/english/punt/puntlage.htm
[7] Duke, R.; MDAIK 6, 1968; Fattovich, R., SAK supplement 4, 1991; El-Abbadi, M., bulletin de l'Institut d'Egypte, 1994
[8] This discussion may be referred to 'The Ancient History of the Near East', H. R. Hall: Methuen & Co: London.

'.... I have pointed out that there was probably trade with India, Persia and other eastern countries; these being grouped together by the Egyptians under the name of the Land of Punt.....a sketch of the Bandoor Cock shows that so much communion with India that an indigenous bird could be so well known in Egypt as to be sketched.....the Cheetah or the leopard, which appears to be peculiar to India, is among the products of Punt brought to Egypt by queen Hatshetput.'

Other than the trade-linkage is the linkage of spirituality and religion. At the root of these linkages is the inception of Egyptian culture from the Deltaic Nile had its earliest beginnings and this led to the foundations of the ancient city of Alexandria (known as Al-*ikkhan-dariya*). '*Ikkhan*' and '*Dahariya*' are symbolic words of Vedic origin. Both means a visual meeting point of the infinite and the finite – tangibly symbolized through the meeting point of a river (*rashmi* or thread-line or *tantu*) and the ocean – known as the 'estuary' [or 'Ishtar']. It is to be noted that the Greek name of Alexander is derived from this ancient Indo-Iranian source. To understand this linkage, we have to look deeply into the ancient landmass where the two continents had met – Asia and Africa.

- G. Rawlinson, Phoenicia (1889, repr. 1972); R. Weil, Phoenicia and Western Asia (1980); S. Moscati, ed., The Phoenicians (1989).
- Ian Shaw and Paul Nicholson (1995). "The Dictionary of Ancient Egypt", British Museum Press: London, p.231
- Breasted, John Henry (1906–1907). Ancient Records of Egypt: Historical Documents from the Earliest Times to the Persian Conquest, collected, edited, and translated, with Commentary, vol. 1–5, University of Chicago Press.
- Ancient History. Sourcebook: Herodotus: Hellenes & Phoenicians, c. 430 BCE.

3.6.4 System of ancient ties: Phoenicians-Moors in Asia and Africa

There were the civilizations of the inner ancient lands of inner Africa located in Abyssinia or Ethiopia and Egypt and they were named uniquely 'CUSH'. They also represent the tribes of CUSH occupying lands (Egypt and Ethiopia) in this part of inner Africa known as 'Cushitic' (Book of Genesis 10: 6–8, The Old Testament).

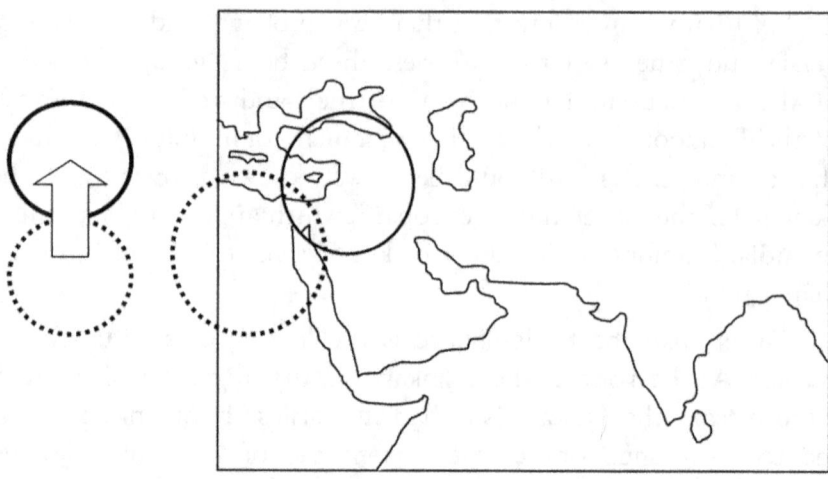

Figure 3.11 (1) The land of LAB (Libya and SEMITIC LEVITICUS – the parable of Sarah – the Promised or Free Land) – Fixed line circle
(2) The land of CUSH (EGYPTIAN ABYSSINIA – the parable of Hagar: Slave or Bonded Land) – Dotted line circle
(Note: the arrow shows the parable of Exodus (from Entombment or Bondage in Corporeal matter) to Resurrection (free or promised state of consciousness)).

On the other hand are the outer or northern rings of lands stretching from the northern Libyan coastlines to the Fertile Crescent of Asia (Lebanon), which were mythically grouped and seen as the 'Land of the High' – the 'promised land' or the Levant (after LAB). The spiritual tradition of the Old Testament can be traced to a principal movement (exodus) from bondage to freedom (from matter to spirit). In support of this allegorical journey, the geographical movement was from the 'initial lands given by God after deluge (CUSH)' to the more stable or 'promised lands (LEVANT)' for spiritual freedom, divine sovereignty and purity in Atonement (LEVITICUS and the Book of Numbers: 1: 1–3, The Old Testament).

This journey of the Semitic race, we all know, was achieved under the initial leadership of Musa (Moses) and fulfilled finally by *Yeshua* (an early Semitic name called Joshua and an origin to a later word called Jesus).

In any spiritual scripture or epic of the world, be it Iliad or the Ramayana or the Koran, there is always a story of a geographical journey, which is only fulfilled through an inner journey of the individual person. The story of the crossing of the 'sea of Reeds' (Red Sea) under the leadership of Moses conveys a similar message. In Ramayana there is the journey from North *(Ayodhya)* to South *(Sri Lanka)*. In Mahabharata, it is to the north *(Mahaprasthana)*.

Between the two ancient lands of LAB (the outer ring containing Alexandria and Lower Egypt) and CUSH (the inner lands of Higher Egypt going up to the source of Nile in Central Africa), the new waves of religion were born. And these waves were paradigm shifts. The shifts had both geographical (the collective socio-political side of religion) and internal (the psychological evolutionary side of the individual). There were two in them. In both the shifts there were the two sides (Fig. 3.11):

- System of earliest migration by the Egyptians
- A further shift from the Egyptian standpoint developed by the Semitic race

3.6.5 System of early migrations to Egypt

In all probabilities, an entire race had migrated from the revered Land of Punt (Indo-Persia). The earliest of this race was about to found a parallel legacy of Sage-Kings known by the popular names – RAMASES (RAM + ISIS, where Ram is the Egyptian Sun-God Amun-Re and Isis is the Great Mother and therefore RAMASES is the divine incarnate of Sun-God on earth).

The juxtaposition of the three words, CUSH, LAB and RAM is definitely intriguing. If there is any single piece of mythical literature that contains all the three names, it is the well-known tale of 'Sage-King RAMA' and his allegorical wanderings compared to the wandering of the Aditya or the inner sun *(ayana)* – hence the name *Ramayana*. The names of LAB and CUSH, the two sons of RAMA come distinctively in the last chapter of the Indian Epic. There the story ends with a note of pessimism that highlights a descent or a departure of the daughter of earth (SITA) into the bosoms of her mother (Mother *Vasundhara*), i.e. the netherworld *(patala* or matter).

Scholars round the ages have argued that this last chapter

is definitely a later addition and a spiritual anti-thesis to original Indian traditions. Why is it so? It is due to a real symbolism of Epic *Ramayana* that has to end with the defeat and death of the tyrant RAVENA and 'the subsequent union of RAMA and his divine consort SITA'. In Indian ethos, it has to been always that way. It has to end in *Sringara* – the highest note of the union of *Purusha* and *Prakriti* – the divine conjugate. In simple words, the note of conclusion has to end with optimism, glorified in light and bliss.

The Indian *Ramayana* contained in this last part the story of the descent of SITA into dark matter and the associated story of LAB and CUSH. This in India is considered a spiritual departure and definitely a later deviation. Many believe that it is probably a product of troubled times in India characterizing the very decline of the Vedic Age. The addition of this story to the original epic was the result of a schism between an emerging group, who were trying to defy the essence of the Epic and the original message contained in the mother faith (Vedic lore) and the original Epic; and ultimately forward a greater importance of 'matter over spirit' (beginning of original sin and its derivative *Mayavada*) as against 'spirit over matter' (original divinity). This process of the religious and cultural Diaspora shifted as a race from India and reverted to the inverted theme of matter and spirit. We can now understand the observations made by Swami Vivekananda:

'.... We are glad that he (referring to the works of Pandit Savariroyan in his times) boldly pushes forward the Akkado-Sumerian racial identity of the ancient Tamilians...we would suggest, also, that the Land of Punt of the Egyptians was not only Malabar, but that the Egyptians as a race bodily migrated from Malabar across the ocean and entered the delta along the course of Nile from north to south, to which Punt they have been always fondly looking back as the home of the blessed'.

Swami Vivekananda also mentions both the nature of the paradigm shift (from the Indian original) to the earliest Egyptian forms (in his article entitled 'The Necessity of Religion'). The Egyptian form evolved as a changed version of the root idea of a spiritual double – the concept of the self (atman) in the body and the self (Visatman) of the universe.

3.6.6 System of India's spiritual double: Another version in Egypt
(Elements of transmigration – KA and BA)

In the original Indian form, the relationship between the two is seen and emphasized as the ascendant. It is the freedom of the self from the individual body to the body of the universe and finally beyond. In the Indian case the upward journey is always emphasized as the path of an ascendant of Sun *(uttarayana)* – the human journey. In simple terms it follows the inner levitation principle of fire or *Agni* (the igneous vital spirit or *prana*). The descendent signifies the journey of Godheads, archangels or avatars – which is not a common man's concern. Hence it is always hidden.

In the Egyptian case, there was a major deviation. In the Egyptian form, the reverse view/emphasis emerged – the descendent becomes more important. Here a principle of the elixir of immortality (anti-thesis to fire or *pyra*) is characterized through a descent of spirit into matter and leading to consequential resurrection of the entombed body (matter itself). This is explained by the *'Soma-Sema'* doctrine emphasizing the 'somatic' or the corporeal principle.

It took slightly different versions with the passage of time with different groups. With ancient Egypt, it is like the story of Sita in the last part of Indian Ramayana. The theme became even more predominant in a later tradition of two figures of the Old Testament, the first lady of patriarch ABIRAM (Abraham) of Chaldees named Hagar and her later mortal son Ishmael – Galatians: 4.21–33). From Egypt it then shaped later religious development in Arabia.

On the other hand, it shaped a slightly different story in the Mediterranean version of the Eleusinian mysteries of 'Kore' where the descent of the mother-goddess Demeter was facilitated to free her daughter Persephone from the subterranean bondage of Hades. So a principle of freedom (or a purpose of ascent) was re-attached or further emphasized compared to the descent. In other words, descent is only a prelude to ascent. This became the later foundation of the Christ principle (New Testament) (2 Timothy: 2.8; Romans 10.5–7) formed out of the further developments in the Mediterranean. It emphasized the other lineage promoting the full resurrection of spirit from matter. This theme matured through the lineage of the other lady of Patriarch ABIRAM named Sarah and her blessed divine son Isaac – Galatians: 4.21–33). That contributed to historic Christianity.

3.6.7 System of Al-Baka: Lost wisdom of Mother Goddess

It is from this inversion, the whole body of Egyptian and subsequent Semitic spiritual beliefs are founded – the concept of eternal sepulcher and final resurrection are all strongly rooted. From this inversion also comes the further concept of anointment [(waxing or christening achieved through mummifying) and the resurrection of the body for final transfiguration (which is resurrection itself)]: On this Egyptian version of the Double, Swami Vivekananda says[9]:

'...With the ancient Egyptians[10], the first idea of the soul is that of a double. Every human body contained in it another being very similar to it; and when a man died, this double went out of the body and yet lived on. But the life of the double lasted only so long as the dead body remained intact, and that is why we find among the Egyptians so much solicitude to keep the body (waxed mummies) uninjured'.

The Egyptian concept of a double[11] (with large variations from the Indian and slightly from the Sumerian) had very important

---

[9] It may be a breaking away from the main body of thoughts. For instance, contrary to Vedic Sky-God and Mother Goddess, Egypt had Father Sky and Mother Heaven. Egypt also had contrasting red color for Death and Black for life unlike Indian and other oriental beliefs. Also Egypt had a reverse attribute of Lower (Northern Egypt) and Upper (Southern Egypt) unlike Uttara-khanda (above Vindhyas) and Dakshina-khanda (below the Vindhyas mountains) in India or Sumero-Akkadians (Assyrian). For India, the inner process of spirituality is ascending and from corporeal to the non-corporeal. For Egypt, it was a descent into Earth, into Hades or Erebus. This has been discussed in Chapter 5.

[10] Page 58, Complete Works (Vol II, 1995).

[11] The Indian concept of Double is just opposite to the Egyptians where the coupling of the Ka and the Ba is independent of the body and partially dependent so long it is not internally purified. This double in another word is the Jivatman (microcosmic self) of Samkhya and Param-atman (Macrocosmic self) of Vedanta. The Sumerian concept of double was possibly partly Indian and partly Egyptian and through many agrarian reforms (Eleusinian mysteries of Orphism) it led to the concept of twice-born Bacchus-Sabazius or Dionysus. These concepts of twice born or Dwija in the Vedas (following Second or Lower mortal and First or Upper immortal death as mentioned in Revelations of St. John, New Testament) later became the concept of 'Word in Heaven' and 'word made flesh'. The Upper and Lower symbolisms of ancient Egypt and Sumero-Akkadians were spatial-political responses to such concept of a 'divine' empire on earth.

contributions towards later development of all later Semitic faiths. The concept of 'EDEN' (the Garden of Adonis), an eternal garden of Paradise and a primordial source of eternal afterlife and resurrection are permanently attained was carved out this concept of double.

It is to be noted that in this double laid the ancient spiritual idea of mortal entombment (sepulcher connected to spiritual or First Death, which is not ordinary or mortal (second) death) and a complete freedom achieved through transformation of the corporeal body, i.e. resurrection[12] (from or within the Tomb). Also in this double lay the duality of Egyptian Isis (Ultimate heavenly spirit or the Virgin Mother) on the one hand and the twin role of father Osiris (the Father of the Underworld or Hades) and son Horus on the other hand. It is in and through the three earliest Egyptian divinities, the double led to a concept of 'Trinity' that significantly influenced the further spiritual developments[13] in the Mediterranean world.

The concept of an Egyptian God-King was seen as a heavenly 'Word'. The word was made flesh and born as the 'Son of Man'. Horus or the divine Son of God was also the son of human beings. Horus was therefore represented by the corporeal God-like existences called the *'Puras'* or 'Pharaohs'. Through an integration of 'Word' and 'Flesh', the concept of 'Eucharist' (sacraments of bread (body), wine (spirit)) and an anointment (christening or waxing[14] by the Moon or divine mind) was formulated to render a principle of 'Christ' (akin to the Divine principle like Egyptian Horus or Sumerian Adonis). This led to the theme of a resurrected King and his Kingdom of God on earth, where he raises everything – the universal to that Kingdom through his personal resurrection. Thus

---

[12] This is analogous to the concept of Jivanmukti as opposed to Videhamukti in Vedanta.

[13] The later schisms of the Christian Monophysites and Nestorians regarding the unification of the Trinity or not was geographically centered at Alexandrian Egypt and Syria in Asia. It is to be noted that in these fundamental differences laid the essential differences of the concept of double of the Egyptians and the Sumero-Akkadians. The conflict was between the concept of 'Word of God as Pure Divine Light' and that of the 'Word of God in Flesh'. The later was victorious leading to a personal savior Myth of Christianity.
(Readers may refer to 'Monophysites heresy' in later Alexandria and Papal Rome during Constantine's rule in Byzantium)

[14] This is equivalent to 'Soma' of the Vedas and has equivalence to 'Sim' (or Sin) Moon God of Akkado/Assyria to whom the principal Ziggurat (like stepped Pyramid of Saqqara, Egypt) was dedicated.

the universal and the personal are integrated – the theme of 'one body and many parts'. This is the concept of a 'personal saviour'.

With the development of historic Christianity probably the concept of a Semitic 'Isaiah' or *Yeshua*[15] of the Old Testament was further integrated with the ancient concept of Egyptian double. His Mother, Isis, determined the highest significance of the son. In the later Mediterranean case, 'Virgin Mary', who is the matrix of the 'Word of God' and 'everything' – the universe itself became the blessed lady to conceive the 'Word'.

3.6.8   System of Matrix: God as the mother

The central concept of the Matrix is that she conceives the cosmic word. In that matrix, through the deliverance and the glory of the 'Word', the glory of 'All' is recovered. The 'fall of man' (paradise that was lost) is restored. Eternal paradise is restored either through resurrection of Christ in the eastern Mediterranean or in the Arabian version through the Garden of Adonis or 'Eden'.

But what was gradually lost during these developments is the vision of the Great Lady – the highest sacrifice that has restored the Garden or helps resurrect Christ. She is the epitome of that universal sacrifice. She is the Matrix of one body and many parts. The Matrix holds the macrocosm, which is a consummation of all microcosms. She is the Mother – The Virgin – The Mare or 'Mary'[16] – or The Madonna – who had conceived by the Holy Spirit (like the Egyptian Isis or Sumerian Ishtar) the 'Word of God. Yet the Mother and son is one. Ishtar and Adonis, Isis and Horus or Mary and Christ are the conjugate – the pair. Essentially the two are one, as the Madonna is embracing Christ in her womb eternally. Therefore the Bible says:

"...In the Beginning, there is the word. The Word is with God. And the Word is God" (John).

---

[15] One may see a lineage of Prophet Isaiah (from Old to New Testament) and his (their) saying (s) ultimately behind the figure of the Christ. They have a mention in the apocalyptic Gospels of the Dead Sea Scrolls.

[16] It means the Sea and the Horse (the Sea Horse or Black Mare) or the Arabic Barb horse (Black Kelpie). See Chambers Dictionary.

A similar observation document in recent history is forwarded herewith:

'...Here under this tree, in the valley, I just had the greatest realizations of my life.......................... In the beginning is the word... the microcosm and the macrocosms are built on the same plan. Just as the individual soul is encased in the living body, so is the universal soul in the living Prakriti (Nature) - the objective universe. Shiva (i.e. Kali) is embracing Shiva. This covering of the one (soul) by the other (nature) is analogous to the relation between an idea and the word expressing it: they are one and the same...thought is impossible without words. Therefore, in the beginning was the Word...'

'...This dual (double) aspect of the Universal soul is eternal. So what we perceive and feel is this combination of the eternally formed and the eternally formless'.

Swami Vivekananda - 3 visits to Almora by G. Sen (RK Kutir, 1985) and Notes of Swami Akhandananda -

'On the realization of Swami Vivekananda at Kakrighat, Almora'

3.6.9 System of immaculate conception: Virgin Mary

In the long article entitled 'The EAST and the WEST', Swami Vivekananda provides a vital clue:

'...Here is the selfsame Old Shiva seated as before, the bloody Mother Kali worshipped with the selfsame paraphernalia, the pastoral Shepherd of Love, Shri Krishna, playing on his flute. Once this Old Shiva, riding on his bull.... traveled from India, on the one side to Sumatra, Borneo, Celebes, Australia, as far as the shores of America, and on the other side, ...in Tibet, China, Japan, and as far as Siberia...The Mother Kali is still exacting her worship even in China, and Japan; it is whom the Christians metamorphosed into Virgin Mary, and worship as the Mother of Jesus the Christ'.

So what is this image of Kali that the Swami thinks the Christians metamorphosed into Virgin Mary? What is that very image of the Mother Matrix that is still worshipped in China and Japan? And what is this bloody sacrificial embodiment within which the 'Word' is made flesh for universal resurrection of 'all'? So, who is she being both Kali and Mary? Recent scholarship provided by Penguin Dictionary of Religions[17] supplies the answer. While detailing a special Icon, which originated in the East and later influenced the west, the Dictionary says the following:

'...In Christian Iconography, it stands for the Virgin who has conceived by the Holy Spirit.... In the Middle Ages, it became the symbol of the word of God made flesh within the womb of Virgin Mary.........

...It was a symbol of power, basically expressed by its horn, as well as of magnificence and purity...it's dance is one of rejoicing, highly popular in the Far East at the Mid-Autumnal Festival...as a variant of Dragons in its role of the Lord of the Rains. With its single horn set in the middle of its forehead, it symbolizes a spiritual arrow, a sun ray (original), the SWORD of God, divine revelation or the Godhead penetrating its creation. This fabulous beast originating in the East and associated with the 'Third Eye' (Triambaka), with attainment of Nirvana and with a return to the centre and to the Monad, was ideally fated for the Western Hermetic the path to Philosopher's Gold – the inner transmutation (resurrection) effected when the primordial hermaphrodite is recreated. In China, it was called CHI-LIN, meaning the unity of opposites: Yin and Yang'.

Now, who is this fabulous Icon that the Swami is talking about? And what is this fabulous creature that the current scholars are pointing out? In National Geographic (p.122) Scholars of June 2000 we find a revealing answer:

'...........Among the (many) animals carved on seals....one is most often depicted is imaginary: A UNICORN[18] – pieces with one-horned (horse-like or fabulous) animals have been found throughout the Indus realm, leading Richard Meadow of Harvard University and M. Kenoyer of the University of Wisconsin to believe the UNICORN

---

[17] This is from page 1054–1056, "The Dictionary of Symbols", edited by Jean Chevalier and Alain Gheerbrant; translated by John Buchanan Brown (Penguin, 1994).
[18] She is possible the black sea horse etymologically represented as the spirit of the deep waters: marsh/marine with German 'mare', Old Slavonic 'Mora', Russian and polish 'Mora', Old Irish 'Marah', Lithuanian 'Maras'...or later Poseidon's horse or the fountain of Hippocrene and Pegasus associated with waters in Greek Mythology and finally the Aswinis (Baraba or Ourba) of the Vedas. There is an etymological connection between Aqua (water) and Eqqus (horse) (Penguin Dictionary on Religions on 'Horse'; Penguin Books, Paris (1982)).

was the symbol of a powerful community (of Ancient Indus Valley Civilization 3600-1700 BCE)'.

Possibly in times of remote antiquity, India had carved her out – this symbol of universal sacrifice amidst hundreds of Indus Valley seals[19] (Fig. 3.12). Later she is seen again in Babylonia with her horns on the Ishtar gate. The gates are dedicated to the one-horned spirit of the Mother Goddess – Ishtar. In the ancient Near East, she was known in different names. Isis, Rhea, Demeter, Astarte, Diana, Athena and the 'Kore' are to name a few. Finally, she became our beloved 'Madonna' – the Virgin Mary – the mother of the Christ principle.

3.6.10 System of universal sacrifice

Her universal sacrifice makes her the CHI-LI (N)[20] of China and the Ka-Li of India to possibly the great Muse of epic battle, war and victory called the Calliope of Ancient Greece. She carries the sword of death. The sword stands for her universal sharpness of warfare, death and destruction on the one hand and that of wisdom, love, immortality and ambrosia on the other hand. She is the great Mother – the Madonna of Civilization. She is the unity of the ascendant – the fire (agni or Angira) or death principle (Yang) and the descendent – the life or immortalizing principle of soma or anna (Yin). Therefore she is the totality – 'spring' and 'autumn' – of seasonal cycles and sustainability of life in this universe. That is why she is known as CHI-LI (N)[21] of China and the KA-LI of India. The iteration and the cyclic unity of the rise (spring) and fall (autumn) come through the following:

---

[19] The author had prepared a pre-cursory exhibition work on this Indus Valley theme called the 'Madhu Vidya 2000' (displayed at Academy of Fine Arts, Gaganendra Pradarshanalaya (Kolkata Information center)) and then Madhu Vidya 2002 (displayed at India Habitat Center, New Delhi) and finally at Institute of Culture, Ramakrishna Mission, Golpark with media references in major newspapers like:
- The Statesman, August 6, 2000: Exhibition column: 'Making of a culture'.
- Downtown: The Statesman: August 18, 2000: 'Back to the Future'
- Metro: The Telegraph: July 24, 2000: 'The Secrets of the Unicorn
- The Indian Express (New Delhi): News 3, page 3, January 2, 2001, and 'An IIT exhibits interest in the Indus Valley'.

[20] CHI= Ka or Universal Spirit or Life Current and Li=Universal Law of correspondence.
[21] CHI = Ka or Universal Spirit or Life Current and Li = Universal Law of Correspondence.

- The principle of *Chi* is the underlying transcendental reality but involved in everything. It is the principle that self-condenses from that Great Void, the formation of gross matter, and disperses to de-form all of that to subtlety and final dissolution into that Great Void, which is full of Chi[22] otherwise [(Chang Tsai (1958)].
- The principle of Lin[23] is the overlying immanent principle of organization that takes back everything to that reality. It is the essential 'law' of natural patterns of combinations and re-combinations to perpetually run the cyclic purpose – the way – the Tao. This is the universal law to which parts of a larger whole have to conform by virtue of their existence as parts (these many) of the whole (That one).

The Unicorn is a representation of this double intender of the twin principle of 'CHI' and 'LIN'. Do we have a proof of this somewhere else other than Chinese philosophy? For that we have to re-look at the geo-spatial terrain of the ancient Indus Valley. It has been made evident in Fig. 3.13, which is a further development of Fig. 3.5.

Figure 3.12 Sprouts or corn-head dress in various forms:
(a) Zoo-morphic versions – Indus Valley seals and Ishtar Gate (pictures above)
(b) Anthropo-morphic versions – Indus Valley seal and Egyptian Pharaoh

---

[22] Chang Tsai quoted in Fung Yu-Lan (1958), 'A Short History of Chinese Philosophy', McMillan, New York, p.279.
[23] Quoted from citations in J. Needham (1956), 'Science and Civilization in China', Cambridge University Press, London, pp. 558, 567.

The Penguin Dictionary on Symbols gives a final word on the Unicorn:

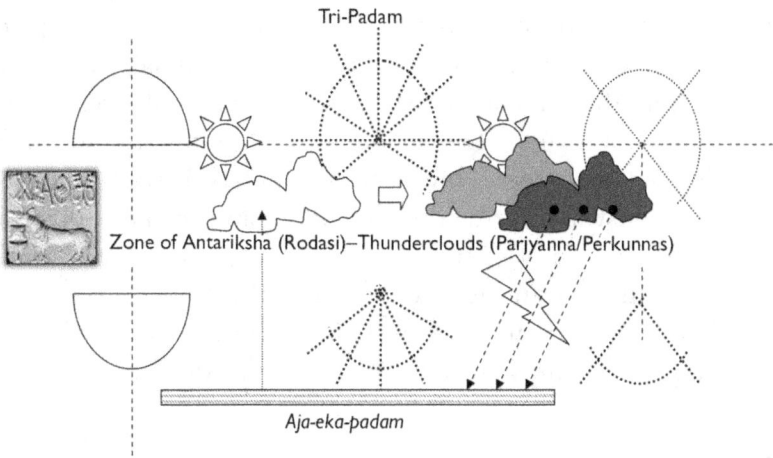

Figure 3.13 UNICORN or Rodasi: The integrity of the upper and the lower – super and sub-structures – Cosmic architecture and its sustainable cycles
(Note: The Unity of the Heavens and Earth are best achieved and allegorized by the formation of thunderclouds – the Thundering Flash of Lurid Light, the Angara is the residual – the thunderbolt and the downstream fecundating rains – the life-giving waters; this is assured by Sun, whose heat vaporizes the water from below to form covering clouds. With time, the thunderclouds (NIMBUS) give birth to Fire (Vajra) and Water (Immortality) and rains come down again to re-charge earth and fertilize. Thus the two worlds are continuously united this way. This is the parable of unity of Yin and Yang – CHI-LIN – The UNICORN or 'Rodasi' (Rudra-shakti) of the Vedas (Refer Rig Veda: 1.164.all and 'Rodasi sukta' in Third Mandala (Kausiki) 3.55.11–22)).

'The Unicorn also did battle with the Sun and with eclipses swallowing them......The Unicorn dance is one of rejoicing, highly popular in the Far East at the Mid-Autumn Festival. However, in it the Unicorn only seems to a variant of the Dragon in its role of 'LORD OF THE RAINS' (Refer the Vedic connectivity at Antariksha – Rodasi – where the Heaven and earth constantly exchange to produce THUNDER CLOUDS). The battle with the sun, responsible for disastrous droughts, might explain this approximation. Like the Dragon, the unicorn might be born at the 'constantly changing pattern of the clouds', the faithful harbinger of fecundating rains.

'......With its single horn set in the middle of its forehead, a Unicorn also symbolizes a Spiritual Arrow (Like RUDRA of the Vedas – in the RUDRA-PRAJAPATI-ROHINI Myth, as discussed in the Foreword), a sun-ray, the 'SWORD of GOD', divine revelation or Godhead penetrating its creation (activating the counter LOOP)......the single horn may also symbolize a stage upon the way of differentiation, from biological procreation (sexuality) to psychic evolution (a sexual oneness) and to sexual sublimation......Yet, at the same time the Unicorn is the symbol of physical virginity (seen from the physical plane). This fabulous beast originating in the East and associated with the 'Third Eye' (Triambaka), with attainment of Nirvana and with a return to the centre and to the Monad, was ideally fated for the Western Hermetic the path to Philosopher's Gold - the inner transmutation (resurrection) effected when the primordial hermaphrodite is recreated. In China, it was called CHI-LIN, meaning the unity of opposites: Yin and yang'.

3.7 Part Five: System of inter-continental carriers and migrations

3.7.1 Migration of Mongoloid tribes to the Americas

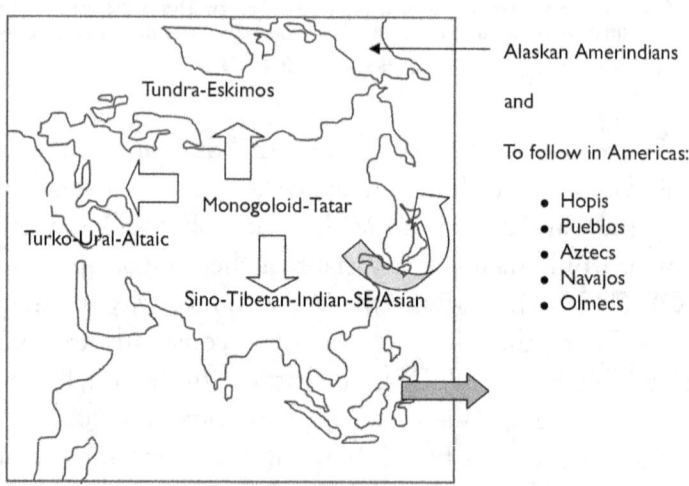

Figure 3.14 Predominantly East-bound and other exoduses of Asiatic Mongoloid-Tatar tribes – creation of Red Indians – (1) the upper arrow indicating the northern land-route via Bering Strait and (2) the lower arrow indicating the equatorial route via the East Asian-Polynesian islands

It is evident now by virtue of advanced genetic researches that not only the entire stock of Red-Indians (Indians of Americas) bore strong resemblances with that of the 'Mongoloid' features of Asiatic counterpart but show undeniable evidences of a 'mother stock' from where they had migrated in successive waves (Fig. 3.14). A recent article named 'First Americans' in the issue of the National Geographic (January 2015, Vol. 2, Issue 6) has researched the eastbound migration from Asia to America around 32000 years ago. Two quotations may be cited here to best establish the point:

1. In the introductory chapter, Harold Osborne authoring 'South American Mythology' (Hamlyn, 1988) says: 'Only slightly later 'nativist' views were put forward which took the form of locating the Biblical creation and the Garden of Eden in the New World. These claims have not stood up to criticism and it is now generally accepted to be pretty well beyond dispute that people first entered America by migration across the Bering strait during last phases of final glacial period, probably about 20,000 BC......the native people of America, who were of predominantly Mongoloid stock, immigrated from the region of Siberia and slowly spread from Alaska southwards, reaching Tierra del Fuego not later than about 5,000 B.C.'
2. Irene Nicholson in her introductory chapter authoring 'Mexican and Central American Mythology' (Hamlyn, 1988) provides a wider migratory possibility involving the sea-route via the Polynesian islands in the Pacific. Ms. Nicholson comments: 'The main mythology of the high Mexican tableland was not created by the Aztecs but by their Nahua-speaking predecessors......the pre-Hispanic Mexican population was composed of a variety of stock. There were Nahuas on the high central plateau, Olmecs and Totanacs along the Gulf coast, Mixtecs, Zapotecs and Huastecs farther south......where these various peoples originally came from is uncertain......but there has been all manner of theories, including the idea that they came from Asia across the Bering straits and migrated southwards – the opposite theory being that which the Kon-tiki expedition

tried to prove: that migrations would have been feasible eastwards from Polynesia (from mainland Asia and then) to South America. There is no reason why migrations should not have taken place in both directions at various times in history.'

A study of skulls excavated from the tip of Baja California in Mexico suggests that the first Americans may not have been the ancestors of today's Amerindians, but another people who came from Southeast Asia and the southern Pacific area.

- 'Cerumen in American Indians: Genetic Implications of Sticky and Dry Types' Nicholas L. Petrakis, Kathryn T. Molohon, and David J. Tepper, Department of Epidemiology and International Health, and the George Williams Hooper Foundation, University of California School of Medicine, San Francisco.
- The Origins of Native Americans: Evidence from Anthropological Genetics by Michael H. Crawford
- WHO ARE THE FIRST AMERICANS? Stefan Lovgren for National Geographic News, September 3, 2003

If this is true, then there will be enough grounds to trace some similarities in folk-anthropology and socio-normative belief systems of times antiquity. Here are some clues that lead to such constructive anticipations and also prove the extents of such antiquities, as such migrations took place thousands of years before the known Indus or Egyptian civilizations. Though a sufficient amount of future researches need to go into the heart of this matter. Still a great deal of first-hand evidences can be drawn definitely drawn. We can broadly construct three major groups of such evidences:

1. *Folk-anthropology:* The icon of a seasonal dying and resurrecting god as the corn-god and goddess and the seasonal festivals associated with the Godhead can be drawn from all Amerindian folk-literature. This gives birth to the season cycles and the icon of a four-quarter calendar, mainly that of the Mayans. Here is a small list of references:

2. *Etymological:* A set of etymological over-laps can be broadly drawn and they have been very sketchily provided as following:

   - *Ama* (Moon) = The resemblance with the first of the twin rivers of *Amu-Darya* and *Sur-Darya* (the river of Moon and Sun in plateau of Uzbekistan draining from north of Karakoram and Pamirs mountains to Aral sea in North of greater

Persia) = Mythical matriarchal tradition of Lady Moon is called 'Ama': hence the Ama-jana race of matriarchal lineage = representing the ancient Amazons of Anatolian Greece = the races in the valley of river Amazon in South America. The various Asian and Mediterranean Mother Goddess (like Ishtar, Lilith, Lolita and Tara) are associated with the Moon.

- Resemblance of the word Maya (celebrated Vedic and later Indian race) = Maya (one of the principal Amerindian races). Both are primal race realizing the number zero (cipher). Principal Maya city like *Yukatan* (Yuktan peninsula in Central America) is etymologically Indo-European based on a key word 'Yoke' (Yoga) and its derivative 'Yucta' – a geographical part that unites or Yokes the two Americas in the two hemispheres. The nearest European word is 'Juxta' (Juxtaposition).

- Resemblance between the Sanskrit word Ahi = Ohio (the name based on legendary snake mound leading to the name of the State of Ohio, USA). Even Old Testament has an ancient tradition of the Serpent – coded in Genesis (Lilith or primordial serpent – agent of creation equivalent to Indian and Eurasian-Russian Lolita, whose symbol is the Sripura or Sipur or double Tripura or the Triangle having direct resemblance with the Star of David; the tradition of Aaron and Moses's serpent countering the Egyptian serpent). Scholars have traced the Vedic word – *Ahi* in the wisdom of *Ahikar*.

- Resemblance between two important peaks of Mount Annapurna – one in Asia – *Maccha-puccha* (Tibet) = the other in South America, *Maccha-pucha* (Inca) – both meaning the Fishtail. Ancient Amazonian Greece had a similar Goddess by this name *Anna-pariena*.

- Resemblance between two words and places – that of *Uruguay*, an ancient symbolic name of Vishnu or the transcendental Godhead (Vedic) = that of the country *Uruguay* in South America. Sufficient research need to go in at this point in the vicinity of archaeological artefacts of Polynesian Island.

- Iconic similarities have been observed between the ancient Indus Valley script = the Script discovered in the statues of Polynesian Easter Island.
- The word *Tantu* is a word of Vedic solar symbolism meaning a solar ray – a ray of creation – a cosmic loom or weft – a rayon (like Sun God Re of Ancient Egypt). It represents the cosmic weft and Loom = the similar word *Tonatiu* meaning the Amerindian Solar God and 'Tonantzin' – the Mother Goddess. The city and its symbolism of Tonatiuhican are based on the etymological roots (Mayan and Nahua lore).
- The ancient name of Kali-Purina = source of the Older Amerindian name of modern California in USA. In this connection, the word Kala-hrada (mythical river in India) = matches the river Colorado (Amerindian name in Grand Canyon). Ancient words like Culdee (Celtic) and Chaldean (Sumerian) are nearby derivates.
- The ancient connections with 'Araucanian' plateau of Chile (Kalli) in South America and the Eastern Asian sea-board people of *'Arakan'* peninsula of South Asia (Malay-Myanmar). A deeper research need to go in to link this connection and one has to rope in the spread of Indian spirituality and associated architectural legacy (based on the Vedic lore of Vajra and the associated wisdom of Mandalas regarding Vajrayana and the cult of Brahma – leading to the heraldic lion-kings of 'Varmana' in Kamboja and Siam (Cambodia and Siam) of Southeast Asia). This has to be comprehensively executed in the light of architecture of the ancient Dravidian Pallavas and the school of Amravati that flourished in Krishna-Cauvery belt of Southern India at a time of remote antiquity. This was in collaboration with Gandhara-Kamboja School of Art-Architecture in Western Kashmir, where the Pehlevis of ancient Iran of the Atharvan Zoroastrian school and followers of the cult of the 'Lord of Four Quarters' i.e. Brahma had played a pivotal role. Five basic clues may be drawn:

i. The reasons behind the common etymology of Kamboja (Cambodia, Southeast Asia) = Kamboja (Kandahara or Gandhara, the region that linked Indus Valley with Elam and Khorasan, ancient Persia)
ii. Similar etymological connections of Pehlevis (Persia) = Pallavas (India)
iii. Connections between words like fire-traditions of 'Bah-ram' (Persia) = that of 'Brahman' (India) = and 'Varman' (South Asia). The esoteric corporeal or lunar (soma-sema) traditions of *Al-Khemia* of *Akka-manishiya* of Parasiya (Achaemenid of Persia) and Khmer(s) of South Asia) are to be assimilated. The ancient science of 'Al-chemy' and its offshoot, the later medieval alchemistry of Europe, is the other dimension. Also it is the study of lower *('atl)* base and earth metals and their transmutation possibilities. This is the symbol of the *Double-Axe* (*Khanitra* or earth-penetrating heavenly *Vajra*) – a symbol (Fig. 3.15) that was the key of many chthonian religious traditions in ancient Mediterranean islands (Crete), Egypt, Anatolian Hittites, Sumeria and ancient India and perhaps, amongst the Ural-Altaic people extending up to the Amerindians – the basis of which is 'Orphism'. The Volcanic (Falcon) or Plutonic tradition of Fire-Smithies (found in the allegorical Hephaestus of Grecian myths and traditions of Idean Dactyls of 'Kaberoi' practiced in the islands of Lemnos, Imbros and Samo-trika (Samo-thrace) is to be linked. The workings of the fire-smithies are on the base-metals (known as *Dhatu-garbha*) of the underworld, where underworld stands for lower human consciousness and this understanding holds the key – the key to the wisdom of transformation of ordinary body-senses to divinized sense-aesthetic possibilities *(Divya Nandan Tatya)* and the ultimate resurrection of the 'soma' *(Vajra-Mandala)*. In the Vedas, it stands for the power of *Kala-agni-Rudra* of the Vedas. In Tibetan wisdom it is also called *Kalachakrayana*.

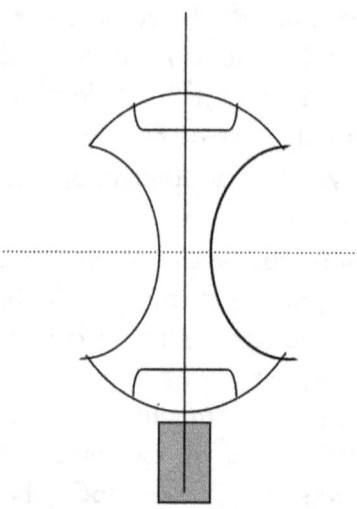

Figure 3.15 Making of the symbol of the Double Axe (Khanitra)

  iv. 'Lion-King' heraldic traditions of West Asia and Egypt and that of South India and Southeast Asia. Much of these traditions are still evident as architectural.
  v. To arrive at the final linkages of migration of elements to first generation Amerindians, the four preceding points have be reviewed in light of the traditions of 'Druids' of Celto-Hellenic world – 'Shamans' of Ural-Altaic traditions and 'Dravidian alchemic traditions' of Vedic India.
3. Iconographical: Ichnographically, the three most important evidences that can be matched are (Fig. 3.16):
  i. the ideas of a Thunder-bird (the *Vaj* (Swena) or Buzzard-Falcon symbolizing the lightening-like life-force in action)
  ii. The relationship of the Falcon with the slaying of the coils of Cosmic Chaos (as the icon of the Serpent separating heaven and earth) – matching the dual of *Vajradhari Indra* and *Vrtra* symbolism of the Vedas.
  iii. The cult of Jaguar-skin/mask cloaked God-head – the connections with cult of Shiva and Sabazius.

- The Penguin Dict.ionary of Symbols, edited by Jean Chevalier and Alain Gheerbrant (in French); Translated by John Buchanan-Brown (1996) in sections on 'Thunder', 'Soma', 'Falcon'.

Figure 3.16 Evidences of Eastward migration to the Americas
1. Thunder God (Greece) – Thunder-bolt (Tibet) – Thunderbird on totem-pole (Red-Indians of British Columbia) – (see upper strand)
2. Circuits of the Year – West Asian – Tibetan – Mayan – (see middle strand)
3. Corn Godhead – Eleusinian – Asiatic – Aztec – (see lower strand)

3.8 Part six: System of cooperative archaeology based on anthropology and iconography

'The origin of the mystery ceremonies does seem to be India: or, at least, the place and time when the Brahman priesthood started its initiation. The ceremonies were based upon the Hindu myths but the procedure followed in training the aspirant is strikingly similar in Egypt. And Egypt profoundly influenced Greece.'

– Arkon Daraul
Secret Societies

3.8.1 Atharvans – Origin of Indo-Iranians (Airyan-Vaja)

First, one has to revert back to the genesis of Persian civilization – the times of Prophet Zarathusthra and the origins of the 'Pahlavi' race as a whole. At the end of that period, we have historic evidences of Emperors *Kuru* (Cyrus) and *Darayuush* (Darius) – from 700 BC[24] and later. By that time, the Persian Empire, as recorded by the Greeks, was world's first gigantic empire, which had spread from the western borders of Indus valley to the upper Mediterranean Danube (River Ishter). Many religious, social and cultural waves had moved across from the east to the west taking advantage of the length and breadth of world's first empire. Here are a few. An important evidence is the earliest religion of Persia (Parasiya) called the Religion of the Atharvans or Divine Fire Priests (or Magi). Much of this religion is still recorded as an extension of the Atharva Veda[25], the forth cardinal Veda of the Indian spiritual tradition. As evidences in the most sacred book of the Pahlavis, called the 'Yasht' (sacred fire ritual or the Vedic Yagna), we get this reference:

'Usta-no zato Atharva, yo Spitamo Zarathusthra' (xiii. 94).

(Fortunate are we that the great teacher the Atharvan was born, Spitama Zarathusthra)

In the Vedas, the Atharvans (Atar-bahram) and the Bhrigus (Kavya Ushana) are the patron fire priests and their legacy along with the cult of 'Vivashwan' (Vivasgwa) (Aditya or resurrection – refer Gita 4:1) and Yama (Jamshid) (death and sacrifice) is the very basis of the sacred literature of Persian 'Avesta'. That is the original Indo-Iranian root (page 195, The Penguin Dictionary of Religions, 1984).

3.8.2 A system of Iranian counterpart of the Atharvans

We certainly know that Av. 'Athravan' is equivalent to Skt. 'atharvan'. Thus the term had a common Indo-Iranian origin and must have existed even in pre-Gathic times. There is, thus, no reason to

---

[24] Refer sections on Indo-Iranian roots in Persian Mythology by John R. Hinnells (Hamlyn).
[25] Evidences of the Atharvan foundations are traced through works namely 'The Religion of Zarathusthra' by Irach Jehengir Sorabji', Theosophical Publishing House, Chennai (1920), where in Chapter II in the ancient Pahlavi text of Yasht 13.94, the Prophet is hailed as the supreme First-Born Atharvan and it matches with the opening verse of the Mundaka Upanishad. Another great work is entitled 'The Hymns of Atharvan Zarathusthra' by Jatindra Mohan Chatterji and published by the Parsi Zoroastrian Association, Calcutta in 1967.

deny that 'aathravan-s' existed in Zarathustra's time. And further, not much weight should be given to its absence from the texts.

- S. K. Hodiwala (1924). Indo-Iranian Religion, Journal of the K. R. Cama Oriental Institute, Vol. 10
- K. F. Geldner (1925). ZAOTA, in Indo-Iranian Studies in Honour of Dastur Darab Peshotan Sanjana, London
- J. S. Taraporewala (1991). The Divine Songs of Zarathustra, Bombay

Âthravans or atharvans, descendents of Atharvan, a legendary Indo-Iranian *rishi* (sage) who introduced the fire ritual and is the supposed author of Atharva Veda, are the fire-priests who performed the soma/haoma ritual in the Rig Vedic lore, and *atharva-angiras* formed the sacerdotal class or race of men. This shows their pre-Zarathushtrian presence. However, the term has since declined in Hinduism. In Zoroastrianism, however, it has held the highest position. The term occurs almost 40 times in the later Avesta. It was the first of the four professions (Y: 19.18). The Hom Yasht (Y 9-11) says that Keresâni (a legendary ruler), who stopped *atharvans* from operating in his land, was dethroned by Haoma (here personified for the purpose) (Y 9.24). Paradoxically, Krshânu (Indic pronunciation of Keresani) of the Vedas is a guardian of soma in heaven. The two versions are a sign of Indo-Iranian schism in which the Iranian haoma priests seemed to have deposed the ruler of the original cult and to have established their supremacy.

During the latter part of the Gathic period, we see the Ratu hold a new title – *Aethrapaiti*. It means the master of an aethra, and therefore teacher. The term still remains in the Avesta, as an *Aethrapaiti* is the teacher who teaches the Gathas and its philosophy only. The disciple is called *Aethrya*. The Avesta shows that Zarathushtra's father raised horses (Yt 23.4; 24.2). The eulogy stating that Zarathushtra is the "foremost" âthravan, warrior, and prospering settler only shows his complete reformation of the three professions. The famous stanza of *'Ushtâ nô zâthô âthrava yô Spitâmô Zarathushtrô—Hail* to us, for an *âthravan*, Spitama Zarathushtra, has been born,' (Yt 13.94) only indicates that the composer of the eulogy was an *Atharvan* who obviously preferred to hail Zarathushtra as the foremost 'reformer' of his particular profession.

- Bulsara, Sohrab J., Aerpatastan and Nirangastan, Bombay, 1915

- Ali A. Jafarey, THE ZOROASTRIAN PRIEST IN THE AVESTA, 1992. The texts within quotes is an extract from "Glimpses of the Atharvaveda in the Avesta," a paper read by the author at "The Atharvaveda Conference, held by the International Foundation for Vedic Studies, U.S.A., Dag Hamarskold Auditorium, United Nations, New York; July 14–16, 1993

3.8.3 Atharvans – An etymological extension in Azerbaijan

Azerbaijan is the name used by the Republic of Azerbaijan and the Iranian region of Azerbaijan. This name is originated from pre-Islamic history of Persia, derived from Atropates, an Iranian Median satrap (governor).

- Historical Dictionary of Azerbaijan by Tadeusz Swietochowski and Brian C. Collins, ISBN 0-8108-3550-9 (retrieved 7 June 2006)

Historically, the Turkic-speaking people of Iranian Azerbaijan and the Caucasus often called themselves or were referred to by some neighbouring peoples (e.g. Persians) as Turks, and religious identification prevailed over ethnic identification. When Transacaucasia became part of the Russian empire, Russian authorities, who traditionally called all Turkic people Tatars, called Azeris Aderbeijani/Azerbaijani or Caucasian Tatars to distinguish them from other Turkic people, also called Tatars by Russians [8]. Russian Brockhaus and Efron Encyclopedic Dictionary also refer to Azerbaijanis as Aderbeijans in some articles.

Etymological clue: Aderbeijani = Ateropatene = Atherobaidani

According to various works on Turko-Tatars, it is suggested that Aderbaijani Tatars (Iranians by type) are mainly Aderbaijans. The modern ethnonym Azerbaijani/Azeri in its present form was accepted in 1930s.

- Brockhaus and Efron Encyclopedic Dictionary. "Turks". St. Petersburg, Russia, 1890–1907
- Russian Brockhaus and Efron Encyclopedic Dictionary, published in 1890, states the following in the article called "Azerbeijan": Azerbeijan or Aderbeijan – fire land

'Atrupatkan' in Pahlavi and 'Aderbadekan' in Armenian are the north-western province and the richest trade and industrial region of Persia. It borders Persian Kurdistan and Iraq of Adjam (Media) to the south, Turkish Kurdistan and Armenia to the west, Russian Armenia (Southern Trans-Caucasian), from which it is separated by the Aras River, to the north, Russian province of Tashil to the east and Persian province of Gilan near the Caspian Sea.

It is to be noted that this important historical land centered 'Baku' and lands north of Zagros, the mountains of Persia. These places bear the ancient historicity and the origin of the chthonian cult of Dionysus or Adonis that swept the ancient world from India to Transylvania. The name of that cult is 'Bacchus-Zagreos'.

3.8.4 System of chthonian death and rejuvenation (Odin-Adonis-Eden)

The key word is *Odona*, which means pure boiled seed or corn. In the Vedas and particularly the Veda of the *Atharvans* (Eleventh Section), the complete knowledge of the Absolute or Brahman is compared to a seed corn, which is boiled and therefore free of any earthly bondage. This is called *Odana*. Since the Vedic times, many names can be found in later Indian traditions. They include the name of the father of Buddha, *Suddhodana* (which means Pure Corn) and also his son *'Siddhartha'* (which means the essence of the boiled corn – *'Siddha'*).

3.8.5 System of festivals of Adonis in West Asia

In Persian and near eastern traditions come the most powerful cult of Adonis[26] (found in all ancient pre-Christian myths of Anatolia and the near eastern religions) and Odin (a principal cult of all Indo-European Scandinavian and Lithuanian tales). Both Adonis and Odin are vegetation deities, connected to the soil, or of 'deep waters' or a cosmic 'Tree' (Garden of Eden or Yggrasil) of which they are the seed. Both are rooted in the word – the *Odana*, which means a pure boiled corn (*Siddha vija* in Sanskrit) or the seed. It is from the cult of Adonis and his Gardens sprang the tales of the primordial Garden dedicated to Adonis (or Eden).

---

[26] The book entitled 'Adonis' – A Study in the History of Oriental Religions by Sir James G. Frazer (1932), Watts and Co. (London), discusses the common underlying symbolism of all ancient agrarian festivals from India to Egypt.

3.8.6 System of Chthonian Celtic-Caledonian festivals

The mythical Garden of Eden is the Garden of paradise or eternal heavens where eternal resurrection is forwarded. This is the heart and origin of all Semitic traditions and the entire book of Genesis (Old Testament) springs from this tale. The myth of a dying and a resurrecting Godhead is symbolized by the 'seed-corn'[27]. The myth had crosscut all religions – from Asia to the Celtic lands in Iberia (Spain/France) and Ireland/Scotland, probably a thousand years or more preceding Christianity. The festival of seed-corn vegetable god 'Sabazius-Dionysus' is a similar derivative.

3.8.7 System of Chthonian Egyptian Sed festival

Eventually they had formed the foundations of the 'Sed' festival, the most ancient agricultural harvest festival of Egypt shaping the after-life mystery symbolisms[28]. It also shaped an entire cult of death and resurrection celebrated or observed by the ancient Celtic world around a mound also called the 'Sid'.

3.8.8 System of Chthonian basis of Orphic lore

If we look deep into similar seasonal agrarian festivals of India, we shall also see continuity. Megasthenes and Arrian had made an ancient account of this continuity. They had come to India after the invasion of Alexander the Great and to their surprise they could trace the roots of the most prominent cult of the Greek Pantheon. It is that of 'Dionysus-Bacchus' to 'Sabazius' found in Shiva of India[29], which was also the central theme of Orphism. Orphism influenced the philosophy of ancient Milesians and early

---

[27] For symbolic agrarian festivals of 'Ear of the Corn', one may refer National Geographic June 1960.

[28] They are the symbolisms of Uraeus (Head serpent dress), Trinity of Horus-Isis-Osiris and the Triple logic of the Ka (immanent life force) – Ba (Bios or Soul force) – El (The upper macrocosmic heaven). Interested readers may refer National Geographic Cover Article in October 2002. It is from this backdrop later Greco-Roman mysticism and Hebrew Gnosticism (Kabalah) were derived.

[29] There are some mentions of these phases in Arrian's Indica and Megasthenese's account on India. It is about a peculiar invasion of father Bacchus (comparable to Old Shiva) in and between Greece and India around five thousand years prior to their entry as writers.

Ionians. The greatest of names include Pythagoras, Heraclitus and Plato.

From the Orphic lore, three important etymological linkages can be traced:
1. Mediterranean or Orphic Brimo and Brahma from India
2. Orphic-Grecian Sabazius (older version of Dionysus) and Shiva from India
3. Father Bacchus (Zeus or Jupiter) and Vachaspati (or Brihaspati)

The basis of these linkages can be finally traced in Mithraism.

3.8.9   System of Chthonian Indo-Iranian Mithraism

A later religion of the most commonly known solar cult of the Vedas, called the Mithra[30] (Mithras), was associated with the doctrine of death and resurrection of Mediterranean. He was known by many names:
1. Victorious Sun God of the sky (Sol Invictus).
2. The chthonian or vegetation God called the earlier 'Sebazius' or 'Zagreus' or 'Brihmo' (or Bromios, which are the many early names of Dionysus), who was an earlier form of Greek God Bacchus or Dionysus (p.392, The Penguin Dictionary of Classical Mythology);
3. Tammuz and Adonis, who were also intimately connected with the Eleusinian mysteries of a maiden/virgin 'Kore' (Demeter and/or Persephone)); and lastly Orphism (a doctrine of Erebus, Hades, mass worship, transmigration of souls, the wheel of life and salvation beyond the wheel through ascetic and contemplative life[31]).

---

[30] This is from the 'The Mysteries of Mithra' by Franz Cumont, Dover Publications, N.Y.

[31] One may refer F. Cumont's Oriental Religions in Roman Paganism. In Chapter XV, Bertrand Russell confirms this by saying: '...Then came, as a result of Alexander's conquest, a great influx of oriental beliefs. These, taking advantage of Orphism (The doctrine of Infernal EREBUS, Metempsychosis, transmigration of soul and final Eleusinian Chthonian mysteries) and the mysteries, transformed the outlook of the Greek-speaking world, and ultimately of the Latin-speaking (Roman) world also. The dying and resurrected (agrarian corn spirit) god, the sacramental eating, ...came to be part of the theology of the pagan Roman world' (page 466, Chapter X, A History of Western Philosophy, Unwin paperbacks (1987).

By the earliest period of the Christian era (or probably before that by virtue of the Persian Empire extending right through Eastern Europe), Mithraism as a cult was spread all over Europe from Danube to Seine and Thames (see Template 3.2).

It has been said that Mithraism, the popular oriental cult, was so strong that if the West had not become Christian, it would have become Mithraic[32]. The complementarities of Mithraism and ancient Mediterranean Sabazius (Bacchus) are evident from a popular invocation found on various bas-reliefs of the Western European world having Mithraic temples (Figs. 3.17 and 3.18).

Figure 3.17 Archaeological remains of Indo-European archaeology
- Mithraism in Persia (left and middle); in Italy, Europe (right) – upper strand
- Storm God (Empire of Hittite-Mittani – mentioned in the early Chapters of the Old Testament) holding the Vajra (Trident) – see middle strand
- Double Trident – Twin Winged Gods and Vajra – signs found among Assyrians (West Asia), Hittites (Eastern Mediterranean) and Egypt (Africa)

---

[32] This is observed by John R. Hinnells in 'Persian Mythology', p.78, Hamlyn (1985).

Figure 3.18 Mithraism sites in
- Top – Dura Europos (Euphretes); Karlsruhe in Nuenheim Museum, Germany; Hadrian's Wall Mithraeum at Housesteads, Carrawburgh and Rudchester;
- Middle – Double-faced Mithraic relief. Rome, 2nd to 3rd century CE. Louvre Museum, Paris – front: Mithras killing the bull, being looked over by the Sun god and the Moon god; and back: Mithras banqueting (Supper) with the Sun god and Mithras and the Bull: This fresco from the mithraeum at Marino, Italy (3rd century) shows the tauroctony and the celestial lining of Mithras' cape
- Site of cross-shaped Mithraeum in London, UK; Brocolita, Fort of Carrawburgh, Germany

The invocation reads:

'Nama, nama Sebe-zio'

(Sabazius or Sheba-ji – the other name of Bacchus or Mithras)

- F. Cumont, "The Mysteries of Mithra", Dover Publications: N.Y., p.151

[(Any expert on Indian language would know that this is an act of pranama (nama meaning a gesture of obeisance and courtesy in India) local Indian hymn or invocation commonly attributed to Seba or Shiva, who out of veneration is called *Shivaji* or *Sebazeo* (hence the *suffix zeo* or *ji*). Even today, the cult of Sabazius is based on the double-U or 'W' – a Tridentate like symbol – an ancient symbol of Trinity used by the worshippers of Shiva and even *Vishnu*. The similarities have been observed by Megasthenes in his book on India (Book IV. Fragment XLVI, part 7–8: account of Dionysus, Herakles and Sibae)].

The relationship between ancient Indo-Iranian Bull-Mithras (Sabazius-Dionysius) cult from West Asia and the subsequent evolution of earliest Christian rites like seven Churches or Stages (see below) of Initiation, symbolism of Unleavened Bread, sacrificial Blood and Wine (Eucharist), Cross cardinals and Crucifix, the anointment by Holy Spirit (Mary) and Last Supper, Yuletide, Resurrection of Winter Sun-God (Spring and Easter) has been noted by a series of scholars:

- A Rehn (1921). "The Relation Between Mithraism and Christianity", University of Chicago, Divinity School
- H Salahi (1979). "Mithraism and Its Similarities to Christianity", California State University
- RN Wells (1946). "A Study of Mithraism and of Its Effects on Christianity", Duke University
- KP Robinson-Campos (2006). "Mithraism and Christianity: Myths and Origins", University of New Mexico
- DR Morse (1999). Mithraism and Christianity: How are they related, Journal of Religion and Psychical Research
- E Winter (2000). "Mithraism and Christianity in Late Antiquity – Ethnicity and Culture in Late Antiquity", Swansea: London
- JJ Hoffmann (1923). "Mithraism and Early Christianity", Northwestern University
- MS Whitman (1933). "Similarities in the Content and Practices of Early Christianity and the Mithra Cult", University of Idaho
- R Beck (1998). "The Mysteries of Mithras: A New Account of Their Genesis", The Journal of Roman Studies
- Luther H. Martin (1989). Roman Mithraism and Christianity, Numen

The symbolism of the Bull-killings is found in all Mithraic and Gallo-Roman pictures. There is a beautiful bronze-plate kept in Wiesbaden (Germany), but found in Heddernheim (left) which has a marvelous symbol. You can see a sun, there under a victorious man standing upright on a bull. The man is supposed to be Zeus-Jupiter-Bacchus (Jupiter from Syria) – in the form of a statue of *'Taranis-Jupiter'* standing on the bull, waving a double axe or Vajra, which is evident in Fig. 3.15.

3.8.10 System of evolutionary symbolism of seven stages

The mysteries of Mithras have an original basis in the Vedic lore, in the seven planes or gates of initiation, but mostly taking the ascendent – or the male patriarchy. In Fig. 3.19, traces of these seven planes of initiation (the origin of later seven sacraments of Christianity like matrimony, holy rapture and so on) have been presented both to decipher the note of iconography and the purpose of folk-anthropology-based evolutionary purpose of human evolution. It begins with the 'Raven' – the sacred crow or cuckoo – whose beak symbolizes the base of the spinal cord – the coccygeal point *(Kaki-mukha)*. The inner energy is initiated – the disciple (the symbolic bride) is the nymph in which the Guardian spirit (*Guru* as bridegroom) begins to play – the guiding archangel. The following stages are advanced stages of this interaction of which is the seventh or the last one is the rapture or unity of the two – where holy 'Brimos' leads to 'Brimos' solving the task of being and becoming. This is true spirituality or gnosis.

1. The Coccygeal – the Raven – Corax – the initiation (powered by Caduceus or Double Loop – support from above or within)

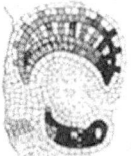

2. The Nymphs or the Bride – state of longing or Love

3. Miles – The Fury soldier (the process of Catharsis – evolving diligence and Tapasya)

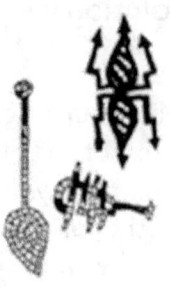

4. Reaching the sole ascendant – Leo – from where it is two-way – Vajra or Thunderbolt

5. The state of soul-realization is attained. This is Purusha (Person) or Persee (origin of Persia / Pharisee / Farsi) – reaching the crown or by transcendence of the Moon (right hand)

6. The Courier (Movement) of Sun – (H) Elio-Dromu (Drum) – The Tauroc (the carrier of Torch – messenger again, who descends) – the immanence of the Sun (left hand)

7. Ascent and descent are equivalent = The Lordship or Father (words like Peter or Patri): Rapture or extreme Atonement – Bromius (The Final Transcendental) – The Supreme impersonal Lordship

Figure 3.19 Seven stages of Mithraism

[*Source*: Mithras, the Secret God, M.J. Vermaseren, London, 1963]

The seven stages are common to the Vedic lore *(Sapta-bhumi)*; the seven gates of ancient Sumerian myth – Ishtar's descent and ascent of Tammuz and later Eleusinian Mystery (Demeter or Kore); the seven planes and circuits of the Ka'aba at Mecca (Qiblah and its inversion); the seven Churches in the Book of Revelation of the New Testament and the seven wells/Rams or Ears of Corn of Beersheba in the Old Testament. This is also the wisdom of seventh heaven that is at the root of Indian architectural shape grammar.

Mithraism on the western front, as a predominant solar cult, shaped Christianity. On the other hand, in Asia, it shaped another religion, Islam. Here, of the above, the extremely important one is the role of the moon – Soma, as known in the Vedas, the ambrosia of Gods – the elixir *(al-iksir)* of immortality – the Madeira of the Heavens.

3.8.11 System of Chthonian immortality (Corporeal counterpart of Elixir of life: Soma)

The presence of different Indo-European Gods (including Mithras) has been found in a much larger region in Sumeria or later Mesopotamia to the eastern Mediterranean Anatolia. This was particularly among the Mittanis, the Hittites and Philistines around 1700–1100 BC.

Scholars of 'The Encyclopedia of Religion' (1987), Volume 9, Macmillan, N.Y, page 380 (edited by M. Elide) have traced 'the background and source of European Mithraism in Asia Minor, where Persian communities and their priests (Magi in the western version and Atharvan of the original eastern version) had established by 700 BC (or even earlier) the western frontiers of an inter-continental Achaemenid empire. They had later provided the Zarathusthra doctrine of a 'future savior' *(Saoshyant)*. This formed the basis of the story of three Magi coming to Bethlehem and blessing the 'new born' (Gospel of Matthews (2:1–12). In this idea of the future savior, a newborn was built in the idea of the divine godhead taking the sole responsibility to resurrect the world. The responsibility on part of the world was lesser or none.

In the idea of the newborn, that of its resurrection built with the resurrection of the world (or its believers) and an idea of eternal heaven or immortality itself were at the root of the later religions – called 'Puranas' in India and similar in other worlds. The single word that played a key role in these ideas was a divine grace, a holy spirit, an oil of redemption and salvation, which in the Vedas was known as 'soma' – the drink of the immortals – *'amrita'* of the Vedas or 'ambrosia' in Greek mythology. In the Vedas, however, it was a universal drink of many Gods, open to all, including men who became *Rishis* by drinking it. But in the later Puranic religions, the idea shifted from a process of 'being and becoming' to 'a personal savior-dependent myth-based religious structure', where the 'Avatar' or the 'Messiah' began to play a predominant role.

What exactly was this soma in the universal sense of the Vedas no one remembers now. Almost everyone in the post-Vedic period began to confuse it with an external agency, perhaps a medicinal plant. But right in the original lore of the Vedas both the true nature of 'soma' and the probabilities of many giving confused with its true meaning and mixing up with the juice of an earthly plant has been provided. In the 10th Mandala of the Rig Veda in sukta 84, the first three sutras give the pointer. 'Soma', as the sutra points out, is only accessible through an open-ended effort or 'tapasya' – meaning spiritual diligence aiming for universal salvation – the process of being and becoming, where humanity, by virtue of his own ability, becomes 'God' by knowing 'God' thereby establishing his or her original divine connections. The Sutra says:

'Somena adityam balina......'

[Soma is the nectar of heavens, its spiritual light, the Adityas – the undifferentiated Ashuras of Vedas. It is also the power of the Constellations, the stars, at the lower world where 'Soma' (as moon) is coupled with stars (or Venus). People confuse and think soma to be an herbal plant, but is truly the life-line of the cosmos].
In an essay entitled 'Vedic Religious Ideals', Swami Vivekananda says:

'...these hymns are sung in praise of different Gods......one is called Indra, another Varuna, another Mithra, another Paryana and so on......various mythological and allegorical figures come before us one after another – for instance, Indra, the thunderer, striking the serpent (vritta), who has withheld rains from mankind......and they had a popular plant called soma. What plant it was nobody knows now; it has entirely disappeared.....'

In this section, we have attempted to forward a few important clues to explain the lost nature of this 'soma' in other lands than India. These are probably the lands to which the knowledge was transferred, got dispersed....and finally disappeared. Deep in this doctrine of 'soma' – meaning the 'elixir' of immortality, signified by the mystic inner moon lies hidden the knowledge of the other one – that of *Tapasya*. This is the equivalent and complementary principle of 'soma', which is *'agni'*, through which the cycles of 'karma', that of life and death and life again are determined explaining distant concepts like metempsychosis and transmigration of souls. Such concepts are still a major part of Indian religions but almost fully in other lands. 'Agni' is the fire of life that burns everything but remains immortal and continuous – born again and again. It is called the *'Jatavedas'* – having the continuous knowledge of cosmic sustenance and all life-form in it. Through 'Agni', we may arrive at the other meaning and implication of fire, not just as something that burns and kills but as some that sustains and makes everyone live beyond a limited meaning of one body, one life, one form and one small-time period. In the unlimited or composite meaning of many lives, many bodies, many forms and a large time period – perhaps very large like an ayana (aeon), the true meaning of immortality or 'soma' is founded.

3.8.12 System of Soma – the doctrine of immortality in the Vedas (Evidences of transmigration and collective immortality)

The doctrine of Metempsychosis and transmigration is found in the earliest of India's scripture – the Rig Veda (3rd Mandala)

'Janame janame nihito Jataveda Viswamitra........'
(Rig Veda: 3.1.21)

The Sages *Kaushiki Viswamitras* have realized Agni as the all-knowledgeable wisdom capacitated fire as the continuum of soul from one birth to the next through which the continuity of space-time evolution of consciousness is maintained.

Evidences on metempsychosis and transmigration of souls, and the idea of collective souls are available from the Study of the Doctrine of Metempsychosis in Greece. It ranges from Pythagoras to Plato by Herbert Strainge Long, Author(s) of Review: Edwin L. Minar, Jr in *The American Journal of Philology,* Vol. 71, No. 4 (1950), pp. 447–449 that traces long decides for a parallel, independent (or inter-dependent) development in Greece and India. Herodetus in Book V on Histories, 3f refers to ORPHISM having possible sources from Asia (Indica) Mysteries. These are available from the two papers from the Eranos Yearbook, edited by Joseph Campbell, bollingen series XXX. 2/Princeton:

- The Mysteries of the Kabeiroi – C. Kereyni
- The Orphic Mysteries and the Greek Spirit – Walter Wili

A short outline of this extremely important evidence is forwarded by Fig. 3.19 where a list of evidences from various works in Penguin Dictionary of Religions (PDR) has been collated. This figure leads to the discussion of the two important doctrines of collective unity of souls and planes of existence. One, the idea of 'soma-tawy' – an idea that was at the beginning of Egyptian civilization; and two, the idea of 'soma-sema' doctrine of Orphism that influenced and shaped the Milesian philosophers and structured the constructs of Platonic and Pythagorean ideas of Cosmogony (Figs. 3.20 and 3.21).

3.8.13 System of Soma-Tawy doctrine of Egypt (Origin of the principle of Soma-sema of Milesian philosophers, Greece)

The Semitic tradition has its ancient roots in the Moon Goddess, 'Sim' (Sin) or 'Shem' – closest to the 'Soma' of the Veda, one of the three allegorical words:

1. *Soma* (highest stage of meditation) – Rig Veda: 9th Mandala
2. *Haoma* (intermediate stage of meditation) – Rig Veda: 8th Mandala
3. *Japha* (early stage of mantic *(mantra)* tradition – prelude to meditation)

```
┌─────────────────────────────────────────────────────────────────┐
│                   The concept of 'Aswatara'                     │
│      (Black and White Yadjur Veda – Swet-aswatara Upanishad)    │
│      (The double seed of death and resurrection – parashakti)   │
│      'Eka Hamsah Salile madye...nanya pantha' (Fire-swan in waters) │
│      (Born of deep waters but independent of it – knowing it is the only │
│                        way = Adonis)                            │
└─────────────────────────────────────────────────────────────────┘
                                │
┌─────────────────────────────────────────────────────────────────┐
│          ISHTAR (ASHTORETH) –'OISTERRE (LADY OF EASTER)         │
│   (The twin-fold Goddess of War (Death) and Love (Immortality or resurrection) │
│       Consort (Virgin) of Baal/Tammuz/Osiris/Adonis/Shiva/Christ │
│          The concept of resurrection of the Corn-Goddess: Ishtar │
└─────────────────────────────────────────────────────────────────┘
```

The inner Mediterranean Group of mainland East, Central and NW Europe	The Mediterranean Group of ancient mariners (Eurasia and North Africa)	The Persian Gulf-Red sea group of ancient mariners (Ancient West Asia)
Balts, Letts, Lithunia and all of Prussia (Peresia: Pharasia; Farasia) • Evidences of cremation till medieval ages, beliefs of transmigration (Association with Holy Oak) – right up to crematory (Ship funeral) custom of Scandinavia • Language predominantly Indo-European (IE) • Connections with mainland Greece (Mycenaean) and earliest Hall stat civilization (Central Europe) – forming the Galatian (Hittites) – Gaulish (France) – Gaelic (Ireland/Scotland) chain of Celto-Hellenic chain of IE group	Philistines (people identified with 'Peleset' (pelesta or Palesta) by the Egyptians (Sea People or Pelasgics): • Evidences of cremation, beliefs of transmigration [at 'Azor (Ashur)] • Connections with Egypt, Anatolia (Hittites), mainland Greece (Mycenaean) and Crete (Minoan)	Phoenicians (People of coastal Syria-Palestine mainly in Ras Shamra (Ugarit). Their deities had characteristics variously attributable to Egypt, Anatolia (on the Mediterranean side) and Mesopotamia (ancient Sumeria): • Deities of Baal (corn God of Death and Resurrection) and his consort (Ishtar); Resheph (Rishav); Anath (Lady of Heaven); (H)oron (Aron or Aaron – light of underworld) • Evidences of cremation, beliefs of transmigration

```
┌─────────────────────────────────────────────────────────────────┐
│     The trans-migratory foundations of soul in Orphism          │
│   (Precursor to Milesian Philosophers, Pythagoras, Plato        │
│        and later Catharsis (Neo-Platonism)                      │
└─────────────────────────────────────────────────────────────────┘
```

Figure 3.20 Idea of cremation and transmigration

Figure 3.21 Soma-tawy symbolism of ancient Egypt symbolizing the unification of Earth and Heavens and externally represented by that of Upper (Southern) and Lower (Northern) Egypt (see left)

The royal symbolism was the seat of the falcon thunder-bird 'Horus' or the divinized 'Son of Man' – the Pharaoh (see middle) and is a close derivative of Vajra (see right)

These are the steps to spirituality in Indian tradition. In all probability, the allegorical interpretations of the man who survived with his ark the first flood is *'Naiaha'* or Noah, whose three sons are Shem, Ham and Japheth. It is from Shem or Soma, the entire Semitic tradition owes its roots. The soma-tawy tradition was the basis of Egyptian wisdom, and it shared the same basis as that of Orphism, which as a basic 'soma-sema' doctrine influenced everyone in Greece – from Plato to Pythagoras and Plotinus – shaping the corporeal (soma) – resurrection (sema) principle of Christianity derived from greater ancient Egypt – or the Land of descending sun, i.e. Ethiopia (Abyssinia).

The basis of Trinity, Earth, Heavens and the unity of the two or Mother Heavens – Isis, Father – Earth – Osiris and son – Horus (The falcon thunder bird) led to the foundations of 'Trinity' in early Christianity.

- Pijoan, Joseph, An outline History of Art, University of Chicago.
- Artifacts from University of Pennsylvania Museum, Philadelphia, USA

3.8.14 System of triple foundations of Sabazius (Thriambic meters) (Trinity or the idea of Triambaka of Vedas)

Much of these traditions have strong roots in the iambic verses (syllable-based) of ancient Mediterranean tradition. Closest were the hymns of Bacchus (Dionysus-Sabazius or the Greek god of Wine or Holy Spirit). The hymn was called 'Thriambus' from which the meaning of ecstasy and victory coined the later Christian word 'Triumph' (sound of trumpets) or the notes of the Archangels. The Book of Revelation in the New Testament is a later derivative of this. The origins are considered pagan today. But secular scholarship knows that they were ancient Orphic beliefs that influenced a generation of important men from Pythagoras to Plotinus and his neo-Platonism that shaped later Christian philosophy.

The original word is Dithyrambic: A frequent epithet of Dionysus, possibly meaning "he of the double door", i.e. twice born, alluding to his premature birth. These are the two births – one at the corporeal end and one later at the upper divine end. This is allegorically the Vajra (that the Hand of Sabazius) is holding (Fig. 3.22).

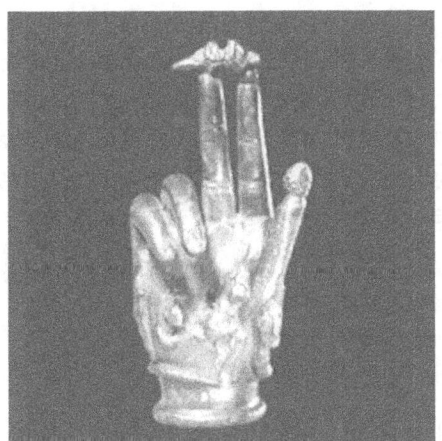

'Hand of Sabazius'
Votive hand decorated with religious symbols

Roman, 2nd or 3rd century AD; Found at Tournai, Belgium

Figure 3.22 In Sanskrit, Kara (Indo-European Chiero) – Idean Dactylic fingers – Hand of Kyrios-Sabazius (later Kyrios Shabuoth or Sabbath – the Host of Heavens – hailed among ancient Yemeni) – that emanates power (Dikksha or dictum)

The term also refers to the solemn odes and hymns sung to Dionysus at his festivals. An ancient Greek mystery religion arising in the sixth century BC from a synthesis of pre-Hellenic beliefs with the Thracian cult of Zagreus and soon becoming mingled with the Eleusinian mysteries and the doctrines of Pythagoras.

- Refer weblink: http://www.pantheon.org/articles/d/dithyrambos.html
- Cumont, Franz. "Oriental Religions in Roman Paganism" (1956) and "Afterlife in Roman Paganism" (1922), Dover Publications: New York

The cult was venerated in ancient Mount Ida (Idam or ID) of ancient Romaic-Greece (Mycenae and parts of Italy like in Cortona, Etruria and Sabine). The importance of the word 'Kora' or 'kara' is evident in Indian and other religions:

- The Eastern Ghats of India (Dravidian) still bear the ancient name Korah-mandalam. Modern states in that region like Kerala or Karakul (Modern Pondicherry) are derived from this. The root meaning is Korah – the rays of the sun – rays or looms (Coir).
- Polynesian matriarchal terms like 'Corraborri' or Dravidian Indian terms like 'Korravai' (Mother Goddess) come from the same source.

Note: The cult had spread from Persia to Samothrace, Lemnos and Imbros – the basis of Orphism. He forms the basis of the 'sacred palm' – Kore (Eleusinian Mysteries) or Kara (Asiatic words like Kara-Koram, Kara-kum, Kara mountains of West India stretching through north of Persia and Azerbaijan up to Anatolia). This is a verb root that is linked to Sabeans of Ancient Yemen and Arabia much at the beginnings of the Semitic wisdom – a root from where the key word Al-Kara (Koran) has been derived.

- Barbara G. Walker on the 'Star of David', the Kabalah & Tantrism
- The Wordsworth Encyclopedia of World Religions (1999), Wordsworth Editions
- A Handbook of Living Religions (1988) edited by John R. Hinnels, Penguin Books.

Sir Bertrand Russell (1988) points out the fact that he and other scholars like John Burnet had gone ahead to state the striking similarity between these beliefs and those prevalent in India at about the same time. The ancient Orphism (the Doctrine of Erebus or Hell and transmigration of soul was close to Indian religions) founded community worship that was precursory to Churches, i.e. religious communities to which anybody, without distinction of race or sex, could be admitted by initiation (refer page 43, chapter one in 'A History of Western Philosophy', Unwin Paperbacks). This secular worship then had become the very heart of different later religions including ancient Buddhism.

3.8.15 System of immortality in Orphism – its oriental roots

It is by and large accepted by scholars[33] that Pythagoreanism was a movement of reform in Orphism. From Pythagoreans, sprang the genius of Plato, Origen and later neo-Platonism of Plotinus. Much of later Christian philosophy is imbedded in Plotinus and also the later schools of Baruch Spinoza and German philosopher Schopenhauer. The root is Orphism, which was a movement of reform in the worship of Dionysus. And the cult of Dionysus (Sabazius) was that of an original Asiatic mystery cult imbedded in the pre-history of Anatolia and in the ancient Near East. The principal linkage was the 'cult of Mithras' that had spread from Persia to different parts of Europe as early as 600 BC. In Anatolia he was 'Kyros Sabazius'; in Greece he was 'Bacchus Sabazius'; and in Rome he was 'Jupiter (Zeus) Sabazius'. F. Cumont (1956) says:

'This ancient divinity of Thraco-Phrygian tribes (Turk-Riga) was by an audacious etymology, which goes back to the Hellenistic epoch (300 BC and earlier), identified with 'Yah-we-eh Sabaoth' (Sibboth), the Lord of Host of the Bible (Old Testament). The Kyrios Sabaoth (Sabbath) of the Septuagint was regarded as equivalent of the Kyrios Sabazius (Sebazius)'[34]

- Albinus, Lars (2000). The House of Hades. Aarhus.
- Burkert, Walter (2004). Babylon, Memphis, Persepolis: Eastern Contexts of Greek Culture. Cambridge, MA.
- Guthrie, W.K.C. (1952). Orpheus and Greek religion. London.
- West, Martin L. (1983). Orphic Poems. Oxford.

---

[33] By F. Cumont, John Burnet, Stewart Perowne and others
[34] Refer the books 'Oriental Religions in Roman Paganism' (1956) and 'Afterlife in Roman Paganism', Dover Publications, New York.

- Robert Parker (1995). "Early Orphism". In The Greek World, Anton Powell (ed.).

3.8.16 System of immortality or the symbolic Sabbath (roots in Sheva or Seba)

Sabazios is the nomadic horseman sky and father god of the Phrygians. In Indo-European languages, such as Phrygian, the '-zios' element in his name has a common root with 'deus' (god) or Zeus. Though the Greeks associated Phrygian Sabazios with Zeus, representations of him, even into Roman times, show him always on horseback, as a nomadic horseman god, wielding his characteristic staff of power.

- Saboi is the term for those who are dedicated to Sabazios, i.e. to Dionysos, just as those [dedicated] to Bakkhos [are] Bakkhoi. They say that Sabazios and Dionysos are the same. Thus some also say that the Greeks call the "Bakkhoi Saboi".
- As the worship of Dionysus spread the wine cult throughout the world, the Bacchae of the Goat-like Bacchus (from Buccus – buck – male goat) joined the Sibyls of Thrace who were known as Sabazius.
- The castrated Galli-priests (cult of Great Mother Kabala – Matar Cybele in Eastern Mediterranean and Crete) of Attis performed much the same ritual of sending the castrated Adonis-Attis-Dumuzi (Anatolia and West Asia) to the underworld and the renewals again (pollination). This is the 'Double door' – Dorje or Vajra.
- The twin Indo-European legacy of CASTOR and POLLUX (Aswinis or Nasatyas of Vedas, Orphism, Mithraism and all Indo-European derivates) are based on this concept of double door – of castration (Death) and pollination (Resurrection).

We therefore see that the highest concept of Biblical 'Sabbath' is an Indo-European derivative of a state of highest spiritual transcendence called 'Sibbatwa' (the highest and perfected impersonal state of meditation later personified through the cult of Shiva or Siba). This may be linked through the ancient settlers of 'Saba' (Hebrew: Sheba), the Arabian Sabeans – associated with worship of 'stars' and its lord – 'Saba' (Sheba), the host of heavens. Hence are the words 'Shavuoth', an Old Testament festival after Pentecost and the idea of a 'savior' – from verb 'save' (the sieve or refinement of quality and value).

In light of 'Kyros Sabazius' of Anatolia, 'Bacchus Sabazius' of Greece and Jupiter (Zeus) Sabazius' in Rome, one will venture to hope for a probable connections with the ancient 'Sabines' of Italy. It is from this source King Solomon and his probable consort, Queen of 'Sheba' had obtained their seal – the famous ancient star of Old Testament – 'the Star of David' (or the Seal of Solomon). It is also called the 'Magen Star' claiming even eastern or Persian Magi-based origins. And the roots of the Magi wisdom are that of the Persian Atharvan fire-priests and their cult of 'Atar-Ba-haram'. In this connection one may review the linkages through Arabia – SHEBA, the ancient region of Yemen and the connections that pave the roots of both the Old Testament and the Koran. The evidences come from three principle words:

1. Saba or Sheba – Land of Sabeans worshipping Kyrios Sabaoth – the host of heavens – based on the story of Abraham connected with the 'Well of Seven' called the Well of Beersheba. It is found in the Book of Genesis in the Old Testament.
2. The idea of *Shibboleth* – the ear of the corn symbolism and the associated legacy of Queen of Sheba and her connections with the worship of stars – Stars of David and Solomon. This is also found in the Book of Genesis.
3. The derived idea of *Sivan* (Judean Calendar) and S'aban (Arabic Calendar). This is found in chapters like Kings, Judges, Esther and others in the Old Testament and in Sura 34 and 15 of the Koran.

3.8.17 System of immortal life principle (Sheba or 'seven' in genesis 21.29, the Old Testament (The well of seven – Beer-sheba))

'And Abimelech said unto Abiram (later Abraham) – 'what mean these seven ewe lambs which thou hast set by them? And he said, for these seven ewe lambs shall thou take of my hand, that they may be a witness unto me, that I have dug this well. Wherefore he called that place Beersheba; because there they swore both of them.'

(Genesis 21.29)

The Hebrew word for Seven (Sheva) and Shava look identical – they differ only in pronunciation (vowel points also known as 'Shibboleth' in the Old Testament). These words are metaphors. The Well is called Beersheba because it is the Well (Beer) of Sheba (Seven or Oath). The Hebrew word for seven is שבע (Sheva) and roots that are closely related to it. This word is often transliterated as Sheba, with a hard Bet (b). The importance of the word 'seven' comes through seven angels with seven final plagues is also explained in terms of fullness in Revelation 15.1, the New Testament:

'And I saw another sign in heaven, great and marvelous, seven angels having the seven last plagues; for in them is filled up the wrath of God.'

In the Old Testament, the roots of 'Sheva' come as follows:
- Abimelech said to Abraham, 'God is with you in all that you do.' Genesis 21:22
- 'He called the place Beersheba (the Oath or Well of Seven).' Genesis 21:31

3.8.18 System of Seven ears of the corn and the stream of life (shibboleth)

In Genesis further in Chapter 41, the word 'Shivan' or 'seven' is explained through a dream of the seven reaped or empty corn and the fullness of the ripe ear of the corn. The conversation takes place between Josephus and the Pharaoh, and Josephus explains its symbolism:

'And it came to pass at the end of two full years that Pharaoh dreamed: and, behold, he stood by the river..... And he slept and dreamed the second time: and, behold, seven ears of corn came up upon one stalk, rank and good..... And the seven thin ears devoured the seven rank and full ears. And Pharaoh awoke, and behold, it was a dream....... The seven good kin are seven years; and the seven good ears are seven years: the dream is one. And the seven thin and ill-favored kin that came up after them are seven years; and the seven empty ears blasted with the east wind shall be seven years of famine.'

In this connection, one has to bring in the other Hebrew word Shibboleth meaning a 'flood or a stream of life' like the 'ear of corn' in Judges 12.4–6. It was the password used by the Gileadites to distinguish their own men from fleeing Ephraimites, because Ephraimites could not pronounce the -sh- sound. A similar wisdom was also the heart of Eleusinian mysteries and 'Sibylline' gospels of ancient Greece that was predominantly a matriarchal (KORE as Demeter /Persephone and sacred Priestess) tradition. The connections can be extended as a Celto-Hellenic linkage to Etruscan Italia, i.e. the Sabine. Detailed research needs to go with regard to establish this linkage. Two additional important linkages are:

- Shiva (India) = Sheba or Saba (Yemen, Arabia) = Sib or Zeb (Father of Osiris, Egypt) = Sabazius (Greece) = Cib (Amerindian Tree of life-stream)
- The Indo European word for the sustainable stream of life and continuity: 'SIB-LINGA' or 'Sibling' (the symbol of divine phallic like structures or columns of Light – Vedic *Skambhas* – where the upper crown is known as 'ritasya budhna'. This is the rue uncoiled rhythm of fully established light) and the lower crown as 'Ahir-budhna', the coiled or serpentine base of latent light in all of us, respectively.

3.8.19 System of seven from the land of sheba (saba or shivah)

Sheba (in Hebrew) or Saba (in Arabic) or Shivah (in Old Testament): In Hebrew, words can be broken down into their roots called a ‚shoresh.' That root consists of primarily consonants, as vowels are often added in Hebrew through the use of dots and dashes below or above the letters themselves. Long story short, my point is that the same word can often be pronounced several different ways. So the root letters of S, V, and H can be pronounced Sevah, Sebah, Shevah, Shebah, Shivah, Shibah, and so on.

Saba', Hebrew Sheba, ancient kingdom of southwestern Arabia (now the Republic of Yemen) was mentioned in the Bible, most notably in the story about the meeting between King Solomon and the queen of Sheba (refer to traditions of David and Solomon in 1 Kings 10:1–13, The Old Testament). The inhabitants of Saba', the Sabaeans, spoke a language in the Arabic group of the southern branch of the Semitic languages. We know that the Phoneicians maintained the trade linkage between the extreme eastern end of the Persian Gulf (Indus and Malabar Coast of India) via Arabia to the eastern Meditearranean and North African Abyssinia from times of remote antiquity. The connections have been discussed in the context of Phoenecians and *the celebrated land of 'Punt'*, at the beginning of this chapter.

According to Jewish and Islamic traditions, ruler of the 'Kingdom of Saba' (or Sheba) was in southwestern Arabia. In the Old Testament account of the reign of King Solomon, she visited his court at the head of a camel caravan bearing gold, jewels and spices. The story provides evidence for the existence of important commercial relations between ancient Israel and Arabia. In the Koran, it is mentioned as Saba' (Sheba) – Lord or Host of Heavens. The Surah takes its name from verse 15 in which the word Saba' has occurred, which implies that it is the Surah in which mention has been made of Saba' (i.e. the Sabeans) and SURA 34 as a whole – Sheba – Lord as Supreme host of heavens [leading to the Tridentate or w-like (ʊ) sign of *Al-illah* (shortened to Allah)].

The Wordsworth Encyclopaedia of World Religions (1999) recollects the 'Land of SEBA' as the people at the North-east of Africa – today what is Greater Ethiopia (ancient Cush) and Libya (ancient LAB). At Isaiah 43.3, the Dictionary says that it is linked with Egypt (falling between the ancient lands of Cush and Lab broadly known as Abyssinia). In a similar listing Isaiah 45.14 (The Old Testament) it has 'SABEANS' in place of SEBA, indicating that the people of SEBA were called SABEANS (p. 931). While explaining 'SHEVA', the dictionary extends the connections in pre-Islamic Arabia (p. 946). Both the connections from North-east Africa ('afriti) to Yemen ('abridi), there stand the mercantile connection within which the deeper cultural and religious connections are further deeply rooted. At this point it will be relevant to revert the first chapter of Megasthenes's INDICA we get a continuous connection of the 'Land of SHEBA' to Indica, i.e. India. He says:

'The ancient Greeks, till even a comparatively late period in their history, possessed little, if any, real knowledge of India......they must, however, have known of its existence as early as the heroic times, for we find from Homer that they used even then articles of Indian merchandise, which went among them by names of Indian origin, such as kassiteros (kassa), tin, and 'ibri (ivory). But their conception of it......they imagined INDICA to be an eastern Ethiopia, which stretched away to uttermost verge of the world, and which, like the Ethiopia of the west, was inhabited by a race of men whose visages were scorched black by the fierce rays of the sun.'

Scholar John W. McCrindle in his book 'Ancient India as described by Megasthenes and Arrian' (2000) explains as a footnote to above where Homer in his Odyssey I, 23–24, explains the Ethiopians as two branches – as Western Ethiopians are described as one part of the land of the 'setting sun' and the other, INDICA, as the 'land of rising sun' – and this had to be interpreted both in the material and the allegorical sense. We can now understand the discussion that we had on the Phoenicians based on observations made by Swami Vivekananda:

'.... We are glad that he (referring to the works of Pandit Savariroyan in his times) boldly pushes forward the Akkado-Sumerian racial identity of the ancient Tamilians...we would suggest, also, that the Land of Punt of the Egyptians was not only Malabar, but that the Egyptians as a race bodily migrated from Malabar across the ocean and entered the delta along the course of Nile from north to south, to which Punt they have been always fondly looking back as the home of the blessed'.

The cult of Kyrios Sabazius – the Lord or the Host of Heavens provides the following clues:
- *The Calendar in Judaism:* Month of Shivan (seven) in the Lunar Calendar of the Old Testament. During this month

of Pentecost and the few weeks after that in the following month of 'Tammuz', a period begins known as the daytime fast and that is known as 'Shivah Asar Be-Tammuz'.

- *The Calender in Islam:* Month of S'aban (seven) in the Lunar Calender of the Arabian Yemen people (Sabians) – the Mandeans, Korahites and Christians of St. John in Arabia.
- *The Calendar in Christianity:* It followed the Solar Calender based on the *Seven steps of Mithraism* from Indo-Iranian lore. In that sense, the solar spiritual element of Judeo-Christian tradition (Line of Abiran-Isaac) is separate but equal-opposite and therefore complementary to the lunar (soma-sema) corporeal element of Judeo-Islamic tradition (Line of Abiram-Ishmael).
- The *Samvatsara* – allegorical calender in the Vedas: Here there are both the Solar and the Lunar [the two *Aswinis* and the weft-loom out of the Circe (Kirk) of Day and Night] and hence a complete relationship between the corporeal and the non-corporeal is found through the doctrine of *Karma* (causation of transmigration of souls, reincarnation and metempsychosis).
- The symbolism of the Seventh day of rest or absolute rapture – Sabbath (Shavouth or shavot or Shibbath) – explaining the full rapture of the initiate with Lord Sabazius or Siba-zius. This is the origin and basis of the Semitic wisdom.
- The linkage with words: Seive (a strainer or a separator): Save: Safe – Sift: separating out wisdom (Sophia) from ignorance. Possibly, the word **'Sufi'** has roots in this etymological foundations = the symbolic Lamb's wool that separates warmth of knowledge (Spring) from the coldness of lack of knowledge (Winter). The word *Sheep or Sufi (Lamb's wool)* is perhaps from *S'aba or Sheba*. This we shall explore at the begining of the next chapter – the ancient cult of *Agnus Dei*.

George Stanley Faber in his book entitled 'The Origin of Pagan Idolatry Ascertained from Historical Testimony and Circumstantial Evidence' (1816) has directly correlated the following as a cause (Indian) and effect (Hebraic-Greco-Roman world) relationship:

1. Vedic Tradition of 'Shiva' = Semitic development of 'Sabaoth'
2. Sibaji (Vedic / Puranic) = Sebazius / Sabazius (Lord or Host of Heavens)
3. Vak (Vedic Word of God = Bacchus (Semitic Word of God)
4. Brahman (Vedic) = Bromius (Eleusian / orphic)
5. Triambaka (Triple eyes or perception) = Bacchus Thriambic (Dactylian meters)

3.8.20 A triple system of Sabazius-Bromius-Tammuz

The cult of Mithras (Mithraism) was therefore an extension of the Indo-Persian 'solar *(Sol Invictus)* cult' imbedded in the original Vedas and Avesta literature. This was almost synonymous[35] with that of Dionysus (Thracian or Turco-Bacchus or Anatolian Sabazious-Bromius), which was a cult of divine intoxication and ecstasy, and it had strong roots in the folk-anthropology of settlements in Anatolia[36] and the ancient Near East[37].

It is within this esoteric mystery of Anatolian highlands that we might discover the roots that we are looking for. The most important of all these mystery cults was that of 'Tammuz' or 'Tamisu', who is intimately connected with the cult of Kumarbi of ancient Anatolia. This on 'Kumarbi' we have had our discussions earlier. We will finally concentrate on 'Tammuz'.

3.8.21 System of double intender: Cult of Tammuz

The cult of Tammuz comes from an agrarian rite of a dying and rising theme related to the symbolisms in seasonal cycles and life on earth itself. The cult had chthonian (related to arable/underworld) fertility and growth implications, which were observed and practiced by all agrarian communities throughout the ancient Near East. Such

---

[35] Refer chapter on 'Moses and Mithras' (1988) in 'Roman Mythology' by Stewart Perowne, Hamlyn.
[36] John Pinsent's 'Greek Mythology', page 12, where the parallels between the 'first born' (The son) has been established between Greek version of Dionysus and that of the texts survived in the Hittite capital in Asia Minor (1200 BC).
[37] Refer http://www.leaderu.com/everystudent/easter/articles/yama/htm and allied books by E. O. James (The Ancient Gods) and James Frazer (The Golden Bough).

communities had spread from Persia, Assyria, Sumeria/Mesopotamia, Abyssinia, Egypt and Anatolia. We have previously discussed the Indian version of this great Godhead of fertility and growth, which is the cult of *'Kumar'* or *'Scanda'*. Let us discuss the Anatolian version.

The Anatolian legend of 'Adonis' or 'Kumarbi' has two parts. One is the 'divine' aspect and the other 'the mortal or the subterranean' aspect. One, it is the absolute image in the heavens and the other that image that is born here and is moving here and then seeking a release from the earthly terrestrial. The dual nature of 'Adonis' had provided the concept of a 'son of Light' and 'a son born of matter or mortal man'. They are also found in a slightly different version in the Old Testament through the duals of 'Sarah and Isaac' and 'Hagar and Ishmael', which we have time and gain discussed earlier.

In the Kumarbi legend, the second or the mortal aspect was called 'Tamisu' or Tammuz. The name probably at a later point became the name of a Jewish calendar month around June–July following the month of 'Sivan' or the Pentecost festivals of seasonal harvest symbolisms.

It is said that just over five weeks after Pentecost there is a three-week period of intense mourning, and this period begins with a daytime fast called 'Shivah Asar Be-Tammuz'[38] from where it goes up to month of Elul (August–September), the last calendar month.

Judaic New Year is again celebrated at Tishri (September–October), the month of post-Autumn. Traditions of ancient Judaism are just the mirror opposite of that we generally have in India (a New Year celebration beginning with post-Spring). In fact, in India, there is a deeper implication of the festival of the Mother Goddess celebrated twice – one by a mortal man called *'Ravena'* – during month of *Chaitra-Vaisakhi* or *'Vasanti'* in spring equinox; and the other – by a divine intervention – by Lord 'Rama' – during *'Aswin'* or *'Haimanti'* in Autumnal equinox. Why is it that way?

One shall to find out these deeper implications later ....
This is just a theoretical pointer.

---

[38] Refer 'A Handbook of Living Religions' edited by John R. Hinnells, Chapter on 'Judaism', page 36, Penguin Books (1984).

3.8.22 System of cycles of Tammuz

In the Arabic calendar instead of Judaic Shivan (Pentecost) and Tammuz (fasting), we get Sha'ban (Shivan in Arabic) and Ramadan (or Ramazan in India known for month of fasting). Ramadan is the probable equivalent of Tammuz.

The cult of Adonis (the Lord) is equivalent to the ancient cult of Tammuz whose roots are far more eastern than Anatolia, i.e. they are found in Ancient Sumerian mythology in the Ubaid traditions of archaic Mesopotamia. His name means 'the true son' or 'the earthly son, who is born of deep waters'[39] (Chapter 1, page 5, in 'the Myth of Adonis' by James G. Frazer (1932)).

In the religious literature of Babylonia, Tammuz appears as the youthful lover of Mother Goddess Ishtar (the Sumerian equivalent to Venus and Judaic Esther) and stands for the embodiment of the complete reproductive and creative power of nature.

In the story of this divine conjugate i.e. 'Tammuz-Ishtar', a cyclic recurrence was found. Every year Tammuz was believed to die, passing away from the cheerful earth that was previously sprouting up (the ear of the corn) to the gloomy subterranean world, and every year his mistress Ishtar continued the search of him. Thus life on earth succumbed to drought and fasting and loss of fecundity and mortal inertia of earthly doom. Hence the name of month called Tammuz.

After desperate search and torment in the infernal regions, Ishtar restores Tammuz to glory as fertilizing rains come in and the company of the two is restored. The two attains the original seat in the upper world, where their true and original divinity is restored.

3.8.23 System of original divinity: Tammuz in Orphism

This was also the key theme of Orphism, the theme of original divinity (1) and a descent of that original divine spark to mortality (2) and continuity through the next possible resurrection (ascent) to heaven (3). The cycle (1-2-3-1 and so on………) is continuous

---

[39] This is from the book "The Myth of Adonis", Chapter 1, page 5, by James G. Frazer (1932), Watts & Co. London.

because we are 'originally divine', as the original roots of the race in the supreme heavens keep the joy of creation forever:

In one of the discovered Orphic fragments of 'patale' (petelia, an Indo-European word meaning the subterranean), we find these lines. This may be compared to Fig. 3.23 below:

'I am a child of earth (Soma or Moon) and of starry (Star) heaven;

But y race is of heaven alone. This ye know yourselves,

And lo, I am parched with thirst and I perish. Give me quickly...

The cold water flowing from the lake of memory,

And of themselves they will give thee to drink from the holy well-spring.

And thereafter among the other heroes thou shalt have lordship.....

(Tablet of 'Petelia', Orphic Text, translated by Professor Gilbert Murray)[40]

 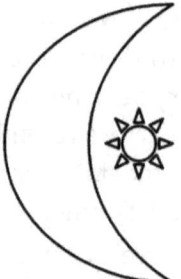

Figure 3.23 The Fifth Stage of Initiation – Moon (Crescent) and the Star (Venus)

Associated are other important words connected with the Indo-European root from where the geo-spatial connotations of ancient places in the Mediterranean and Anatolia were derived. They are:

- 'atalia' – older name of Italia;
- Ana-atalia or older name of Turkey;

---

[40] This is quoted from 'A History of Western Philosophy' (1979), pp. 38–39, Chapter I, Sir Bertrand Russell, Unwin Paperbacks.

- All ancient wells as source of water and life called Tella – like Tel-aviv, Tel-Amarna and many more.
- Other marine or subterranean words are 'atalaia-anta' i.e. Atlantic (in the depths of the subterranean sea) and the legacy of 'Atlantis' are also based on such ancient connections.

In ancient time, the lower Indus valley and lower Ganges valley were known as 'Petelia' to which the Orphic myth is probably connected. The highest points of the origins of river in the mountains were analogous to the heavens and the lowest points were the estuary and further beyond considered to be a lowest 'tail' point of the river entering the subterranean realms (refer Fig. 3.23).

Hence, in Indian myths we get the allegory of tala, atala, patala, rasatala and many other mythological descriptions of the subterranean and similar terms are also found in the Orphic Greek textual description of the fire in that subterranean called 'Ourba' (in Sanskrit) and 'Erebus' (Hades) in Greek.

This is mentioned in Megasthenes 'Indica' (Account of India).

Charles Berlitz (1982) in his book named 'Doomsday 1999' (pp. 136–137, Granada Books) has traced the word 'atalia' to many traditions in North Africa, particularly the ancient Phoenicians (their colony in Tunisia, Morocco) and later Moors (Berbers) of the ancient world.

3.8.24 System of upper and lower world: Parable of Kora (Kore)

The story is the annual disappearance of the spirit of life (activated by the symbolic reaping of the corn-goddess Demeter) to the netherworld (patalia) and its further reappearance in the upper heavens (the re-sprouting of the corn or 'shibboleth') of Persephone is a parallel Greek version[41]. The story is either of a specific Persephone (KORE) or the general case of any virgin young girl called 'the Kore' and her mother. The coupling of two in the upper

---

[41] Refer pp. 12–13, Greek Mythology (1988), John Pinsent, Hamlyn series.

world (Zeus) and the lower world (Hades) provides the two-way cycle and the story of death and resurrection in the Greek version, which was then matriarchal.

Thus Kore, who is the daughter of mortal man, is also the daughter of divine nature (the bridegroom of Zeus). She is also the eternal ancient Virgin – the mother of the Universe and the mother of all 'sons' of God.

3.8.25 System of death and resurrection: the parable of Corn spirit
(Blowing in (reaping or death) and blowing out (sprouting or resurrection))

The blowing out of the universe as the moving image of unity and the return of the universe or the 'world' itself (representing the entire universe and all life in it) to its roots is found in the symbols of the sprouting and the reaping of the corn. The Vedic roots of this parable have been discussed in Chapter 2.

Corn represented the seed, which is the epitome or 'Vija' of the universe; and it is a concept found in India from the earliest days of the Upanishads (Mundaka Upanishad: 1.1.8), where the absolute truth or 'Brahman' is compared to a corn. In the Vedas, it is a boiled corn served as a complete food of the supreme. It is called ODANA. This Vedic parable has also been discussed earlier.

The twin agricultural seasons of 'autumn' and 'spring' represents the twin half-circles (like the Chinese *Yang and the Yin*) of the full cycle of Cosmic Time. Like ancient India and China, it had also formed the common basis to almost all ancient civilizations of the ancient Mediterranean and African worlds.

In the Vedas they are explained through two important principles:
1. The principle of an original (out flowing or inflowing) cosmic breadth (called Matarishwan in the Vedas) and
2. The formation of the 'cosmic word' or the 'Logos' (Prajapati or Isha).

The first principle is symbolized in the form of the 'Mother' and the second, as the son, who is transcendentally the husband or the father in the heaven, and in immanence it stands as the aspiring lover and symbolized as the son in the highest or divine sense only (refer Table 3.1).

The two principles form the basis of many myths of ancient world.

Here is a short list:

Table 3.1 Mother–son (consort) conjugates in ancient civilization

Cult name: Son–Mother	Origin
CHI–LIN (unity of Yin and yang)	Chinese
Kumar–Kumarika	Indian
Adonis–Aphrodite	Greek
Attis–Cybele	Asia Minor
Dionysus–Demeter/Persephone	Eleusinian (earlier Greek)
Horus–Isis	Egyptian
Tammuz (or Dammuzi)–Astarte (Ishtar or Ashtoreth)[42]	Ancient Near East (Phoenician origin)
Christ–Mary	Christian symbolism

The origin of Easter is believed to have come from Goddess of spring 'Oisterre' or 'Ishtar'. The descent of Ishtar into the netherworld from the heavens and the resurrection of an entombed godhead called 'Tammuz' (equivalent to Adonis or Dionysus) simply symbolize the blowing out and the blowing in of the cosmic word or 'Logos'. This is the concept of 'Easter' carved out of early Asiatic wisdom and accepted by the Mediterranean world. Tammuz represents the embodied soul imbedded in the bondage of matter but ready for a fresh release activating another half-cycle of a sustainable creation going back to its roots. The cycle goes on like a self-activated 'fly-wheel' keeping life and hopes of resurrection eternal and perpetual (the story of Phoenix). Imbedded in the word 'Tammuz' is the Indian concept of cosmic time (or Kalpa). The final research clue on time comes from the works of Swami Vivekananda on Cosmology and Samkhya philosophy.

---

[42] It is to be noted that the concept of 'Easter' (Spring) comes from this ancient goddess Eoster/Ishtar.

Figure 3.24 Glimpses of various images of Mother Goddess – Demeter (Kore) – top left; Serpent Goddess – Crete; Ishtar in Sumerian Royalty; Indus Young Virgin (Kumarika)

3.8.26 System of descent of Ishtar and the ascent of Tammuz

'To the Land of No Return, the realm of Ereshkigal,

Ishtar (Astarte), the daughter of the Moon, set her mind.

Descent to the dark house, the abode of Irkalla.....

As for Tammuz, the lover (and son) of her youth,

Wash him with pure water; anoint him with sweet oil to make him rise....'

From ancient Near Eastern Texts Translated by E.A. Speiser and George A. Barton, Archaeology and the Bible,

7th ed, pg 530f.

Note the left Seal from Sumeria (2000 BC) and a later right one – a Garnet cylinder seal showing Ishtar Neo-Assyrian, 720–700 BC – from Mesopotamia). The anointing relationship between Ishtar and Tammuz can be traced to similar later relationship between Mary of Magdala and Christ. The basis is the two parts of human existence – earthly and divine – the essence of Orphism (Fig. 3.24).

3.8.27 The Vedic origin of Kore-Tammuz

Rooted in the concept of Tammuz is a double intender. It is the Orphic realization/notion that every soul was partly divine (rooted originally in the infinite) and partly earthly (rooted here in the bondage of matter). This was corroborated by similar observations in natural cycles of spring and autumn. Accordingly the 'twice-born' concept was born. From Dionysus of Greece to Adonis or Tammuz in Anatolia or Mesopotamia, the concept is rooted in the Vedas as the foundation of a 'Dwija' – the Sages who are born twice – later as an Olympian (heavenly) and first as a Titanic (earthly)[43].

3.8.28 Blowing in and the blowing out (Concept of space-time)

The blowing in and the blowing out of the life principle (signifying the descent into matter and the ascent or release of spirit from matter) are described on the basis of Prana and Akasha. On this Swami Vivekananda comments:

'...When the kalpa begins, after an immense interval, the 'anidavatam' (unvibrating stage) commences to vibrate and blow after blow is given by Prana to akasha. ...The akasha, acted upon by repeated blows of prana, produces Vayu or vibrations. This Vayu vibrates, and the vibrations growing more and more rapid result in friction giving rise to heat or Tejas. Then the heat ends in liquefaction, Apah or Jalah. Then that liquid becomes solid (gross inertia or the stage of TAMMAS) and it goes back in exactly the same way"[44].

---

[43] This has been explained vividly in Shri Aurobindo's work 'On the Vedas'.
[44] From Cosmology, pp. 435–436 (Vol 2, Complete Works)

Instead of the 'Mother' (Shakti) and the 'child' (Kumara), we may ideally impersonate them as 'nature' and 'the individual'.

It is out of nature, the soul rises as it evolves from an animal state of Dionysus (Zagreus or one bonded or dormant in its abysmal depths and symbolic of the chthonian netherworld mystery cults[45]) to an upper or divine state (Sabazius). Swami Vivekananda further observes:

'According to Kapila's philosophy (the principle of Numbers or Samkhya), all souls can regain their freedom and their natural rights like omnipotence and omniscience. But the question arises: Where is this bondage? Kapila says it is without a beginning...everything in Nature is constantly changing, but the soul never changes; so, as nature is always changing, it is possible for the soul to come out (rise or resurrection) of its bondage... (Nature is without any beginning or end, but not the same as soul, because nature has no individuality (in other words, soul has individuality or unity as it is non-changing)"[46]

Swami Vivekananda further adds:

'...this nature consists of three elements, called Sattva, Rajas and Tamas. These are not qualities but elements, the materials out of which the whole universe is evolved.'[47]

'...The combinations which you call nature, these constant changes are going on for the enjoyment of the soul, for its liberation, that it may gain all its experience from the lowest to the highest. When it has gained it, the soul finds it was never in nature, that it was entirely separate...that going to heaven (rise) and being born again (descent back to Hades) were in Nature, and not in the soul. Thus the soul becomes free[48].'

---

[45] On this, Sir James G. Frazer in 'The Myth of Adonis' (Watts and Co, London, 1932) says that "...Nowhere, apparently, have these rites been more widely and solemnly celebrated than the lands which border the eastern Mediterranean. Under the names of Osiris, Tammuz, Adonis and Attis, the people of Egypt and western Asia represented the yearly decay and revival of life, especially of vegetable life, which they personified as a god who annually died and rose from the dead" (p.4). (In page 166ff., Sir Frazer traces the linkages of this symbolic seed corn with festivals among many tribal villages of Eastern India and compares Gouri/Vassanti to Isis or Ishtar with an equivalent Kumara (son).

[46] From Cosmology, p.440, Complete Works of Swami Vivekananda

[47] From Sankhya and Vedanta, p.454, Complete Works of Swami Vivekananda

[48] Ibid, p.457

But this is not all. Swami Vivekananda finally adds:

'...the souls are many according to Kapila's philosophy. (But) The Vedanta says that the soul is in its nature Existence-Knowledge (consciousness)-Bliss absolute[49] .....the omnipresent, the infinite, cannot be two[50]......Hence, there can be but one infinite, that is, one Purusha"[51].

Thus we clearly see Samkhya as a resolution of force (soul) and matter (nature) in the planes of multiplicity and microcosm. Here, there is going and coming from a dualistic standpoint. In here, there is a twin concept of duality of death and resurrection[52]. Ishtar or Mother Nature has to sacrifice itself for the liberation of the soul or her son Tammuz. Ishtar has to descend into Hades to resurrect Tammuz. To a divine lover, she becomes both the mother and the beloved. This is in the divine sense. Similar standpoints can be framed to review the two Mary(s) and Christ the Jesus:

(1) Virgin Mary and
(2) Mary of Magdala

In the story of Ishtar and Tammuz, Ishtar as the Mother is also the Ishtar the beloved. Is it also true for Mary, the mother and the lover of Jesus? Who knows? Further research shall say.........

3.8.29 System of Gnosis: the basis of deep ecology or spirituality called 'GNOSIS'

At the level of true spirituality, gnosis emerges and in India we call that an Advaitic standpoint, as there is no coming and going. There is no death or resurrection and the unity is expressed as one word or 'logos'. The 'word', which was with God in duality, is now God itself in absolute rapture and as essential unity. This is the highest sacrament – matrimony or unity of the conjugate. Here the nature of soul reflects the true nature. From a monotheistic standpoint, Ishtar is one with Tammuz. Mary is one with Christ.

---

[49] Ibid, p.457
[50] Ibid, p.460
[51] Ibid, p.461
[52] As explained in Isha Upanishad

Mary is the Christ. This was the belief of the Cathars. Swami Vivekananda relating macrocosm and microcosm (the two-fold aspects of 'Tammas') says:

'...That self when it appears behind the universe (or Brahmanda) is called God. The same self when it appears behind this little universe, the body (or pinda) is the soul"[53].

The higher level is the Akhanda Tamas (undifferentiated unity of the material universe) and the lower aspect is Khanda Tamas (differentiated state of our mortal standpoint). The higher one, which is imbedded in transcendence, is the 'moving image of infinity'. The other and the lower one is a stage of our phenomenal world. Thus in this higher of two levels, we get the idea of 'Tamas' or 'Tammuz' or Platonic 'Timeus'. Today we call TIME in its complete sense and that power which brings us close to that sense of TIME is KALI.

The sequence of explanation is forwarded from Templates 3.3 to 3.9. Template 3.3 points out the fundamentals of the Unicorn symbolism as evident in the Ishtar gate of Mesopotamia and its deep systems evident in the manifestation of the ancient Mother Goddess 'Ishtar' (The Star Goddess of Arabia: Sabeans), which is explicit in Template 3.4. The idea of the 'Sacred Feminine', once characteristic of the ancient world, from India to Egypt, died everywhere except in India and remained subtly as the 'Madonna', the Unicorn of esoteric Christianity.

Finally Templates 3.7, 3.8 and 3.9 trace the igneous (Agni) or the Pyrrhic/Furious side of the Leviticus principle. The principle is an extension of a certain branch of the Atharva Vedic tradition of India which moved westwards and subsequently matured as the ancient tradition of the Persian Pehlevi priests called 'the Athaurvans' based on the original preaching of its historical called Prophet Zarathustra.

3.9   Conclusions

The present chapter has forwarded a system's approach to trace and delineate a Phase I historic continuum of the interactions of

---

[53] Ibid, p.461

two civilizations – the Indians and the Greeks. The approach is based on a historic framework of Phase I (as evident in Fig. 3.1) having a binary set of double intenders or conjugates namely, (a) yoga and kshema and (b) death and resurrection (or re-birth). The framework leads to a system's approach required for an evaluation of global history with regard to Indian architecture can be dealt through a system's approach to study of:

1. Unity of opposites which are actually 'complementary to each other' that pervaded the ancient world: in art, iconography, language, culture, technology and finally architecture; these are the first root principles: the chthonian principles – the very foundations of the research inquiry have been presented with an analytical insight. The principles to begin with are natural, agrarian, terrestrial, herbal or chthonian. But at a deeper level, they form the very science of a thermodynamic balance observed everywhere in life on this planet in relationship to sun and the cosmos. The principles are *the patterns of the seasonal cycles and natural growth* in the external universe and a corresponding human function facilitating the very purpose of civilizational growth and individual evolution. This section concludes with an extremely important allegory – the de-mystification of the equinoctial cycle of sun in relationship to earth leading to an inner understanding of a similar cycle of growth and evolution imbedded in an individual. In effect, the pattern is the dynamic whole of a sum total of several linkages between matter and spirit, which is represented by earth and heavens in the bigger sense. It is in this knowledge of the unification of the two (a downward movement of all-pervading spirit towards making of local matter and the resurrection of that space or matter to all-pervading spirit again) was borne of the confluence of the two tidal forces – that of very ancient Greece and India, in times of remote antiquity.

2. *Ancient historic (positive) connections:* An example is the wisdom of this unification through a material symbolism of the 'Lordship of Four Quarters'. This symbol shaped almost

all major physical expressions of overall settlement patterns and building systems, political and economic functioning and the imbedding of social systems in civilizations of ancient Persia, ancient Rome and others then. The discussion under this section culminates as it points out the key linkages of India with the world via Persia on the western front and Southeast Asia and Indo-China on the eastern front. Here it unlocks the meaning of a key vital word "Bahram' and links the lost connections between the two fronts – much of which can be traced through their settlement patterns and built-architectural systems even today, however scanty and damaged they may be. The architecture of ancient Sumeria, Assyria, Anatolia and Egypt in the west and that of Southeast Asia in the east is perhaps deeply rooted on this vital connection of 'Bahram' – associated with the cult of 'Brahma' and his allegorical lordship or power over the four quarters of the cycles of sun *(Brahma-jamala)*.

3. Convergent realization and belief (normative) systems which are further expressed in terms of:
   - inter-linked and cooperative language systems
   - inter-continental carriers and migrations
   - inter-linked or cooperative archaeology based on iconography and anthropology
   - inter-relationships of material and spiritual semantics in terms of the two sets of complementarities: (a) death and resurrection and (b) yoga and kshema (tantra)

First, among the details are the land-routed dissemination of the major Indo-European carriers – the 'Romas' or 'Gypsies', who remains at the helm of Celto-Hellenic dissemination. Also a similar role played by the Phoenicians as the ancient Indo-Iranian mariners from the entire Persian Gulf linking the celebrated 'Land of 'Sheba' or 'Land of Punt' or 'Ophir' or often called 'Molock' with the 'Celebrated Land of God or Spirituality' – located in South Asia. At this point, the discussion is reinforced by forwarding a third dissemination taking place beyond the eastern front. This was both through the upper land route through China, Korea, Bering Strait to the Americas and a similar sea-route through Indonesia and

Pacific Polynesia to the shores of Americas. Traces of original Vedic elements and the cult of 'Shiva' have been made evident in the context of the Amerindian religions of the Mayans, Incas, Aztecs, Pueblos and many others.

Under the second platform of archaeological iconography and folk-anthropology, the key evidence has been provided to establish the origins of Orphism in the Vedas and its cult of 'Kyrios Sabazius' shaping the later religions of the Semitic world through an intermediate patriarchal cult of 'Tammuz-Adonis-Mithra'. But at its root remained the lost matriarchal tradition – *'Aditi-Saraswati-Illa-Bharati-mahi-Matariswan'* of the Vedas and others in the Mediterranean world. The key however is 'Kali' and the evidence of the 'Unicorn' built around the ancient Indian Mother Goddess. With these initial pointers and first generation of evidences, the chapter perhaps has recovered that period imbedded in times of great remote antiquity – against which the eastward exploration of Alexander the Great was a later and a consequential response. These are evident in the descriptions of Indica by Megasthenes and Arrian, where a connection between the two lands have been frequently referred to, a few thousand years prior to the Macedonian invasion of the East. It is therefore evident that 'These two gigantic forces (Aryans and Yavanas), *issuing from far-away and different mountains (India and Greece), occasionally come in contact with each other, and whenever such confluence takes place, a tremendous intellectual and spiritual tide rising in human societies, greatly expands the range of civilization and confirms the universal brotherhood among men. (And) Once in far remote antiquity, the Indian philosophy, coming in contact with Greek energy, led to the rise of the Persian, the Roman, and other great nations'.*

The aforesaid contact between the Indians and the Greeks in times of far remote antiquity has been marked out as Phase I of the system's approach, which the present chapter has traced.

Template 3.1 Application of cyclic wisdom in architecture (Composed by author)

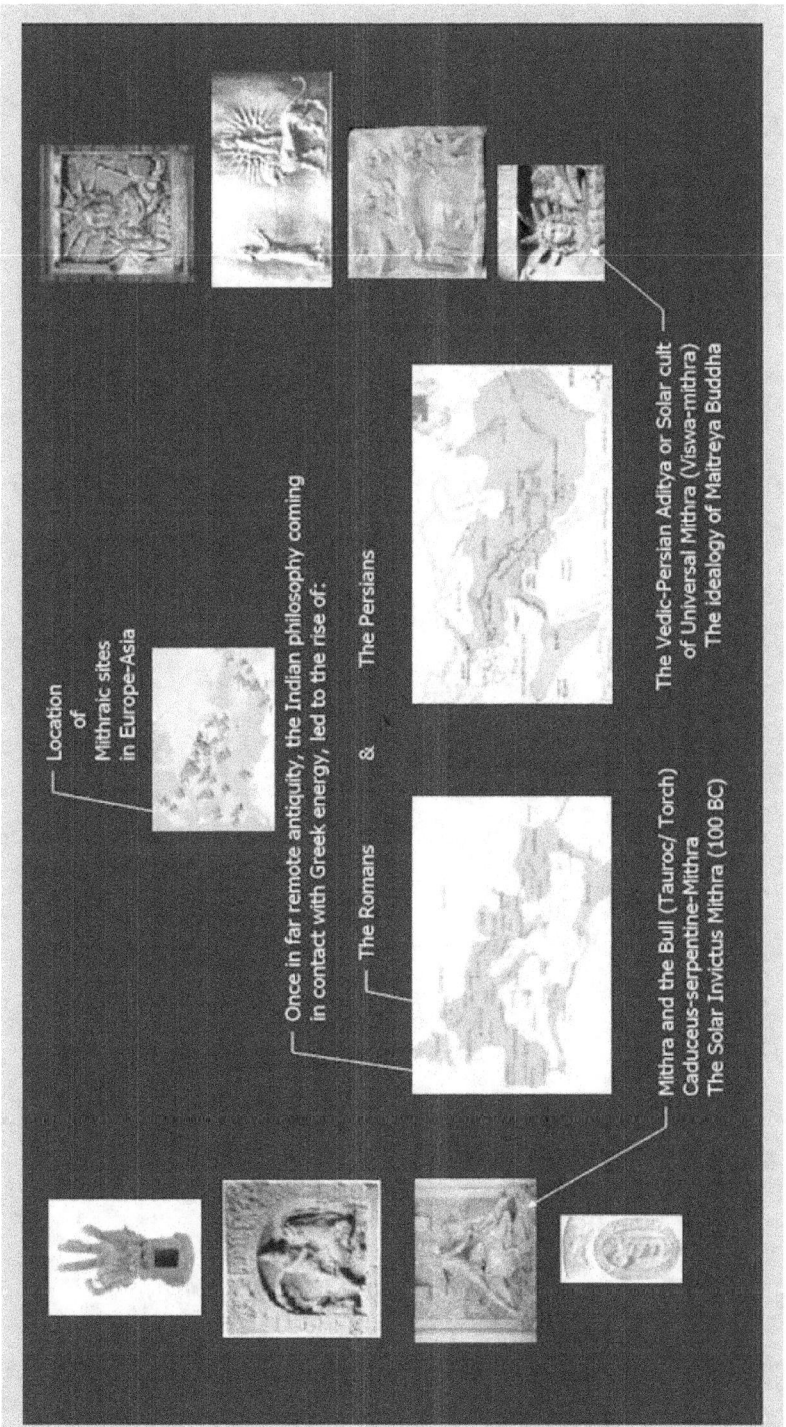

Template 3.2 Location and features of Mithraic sites in Eurasia (Composed by author)

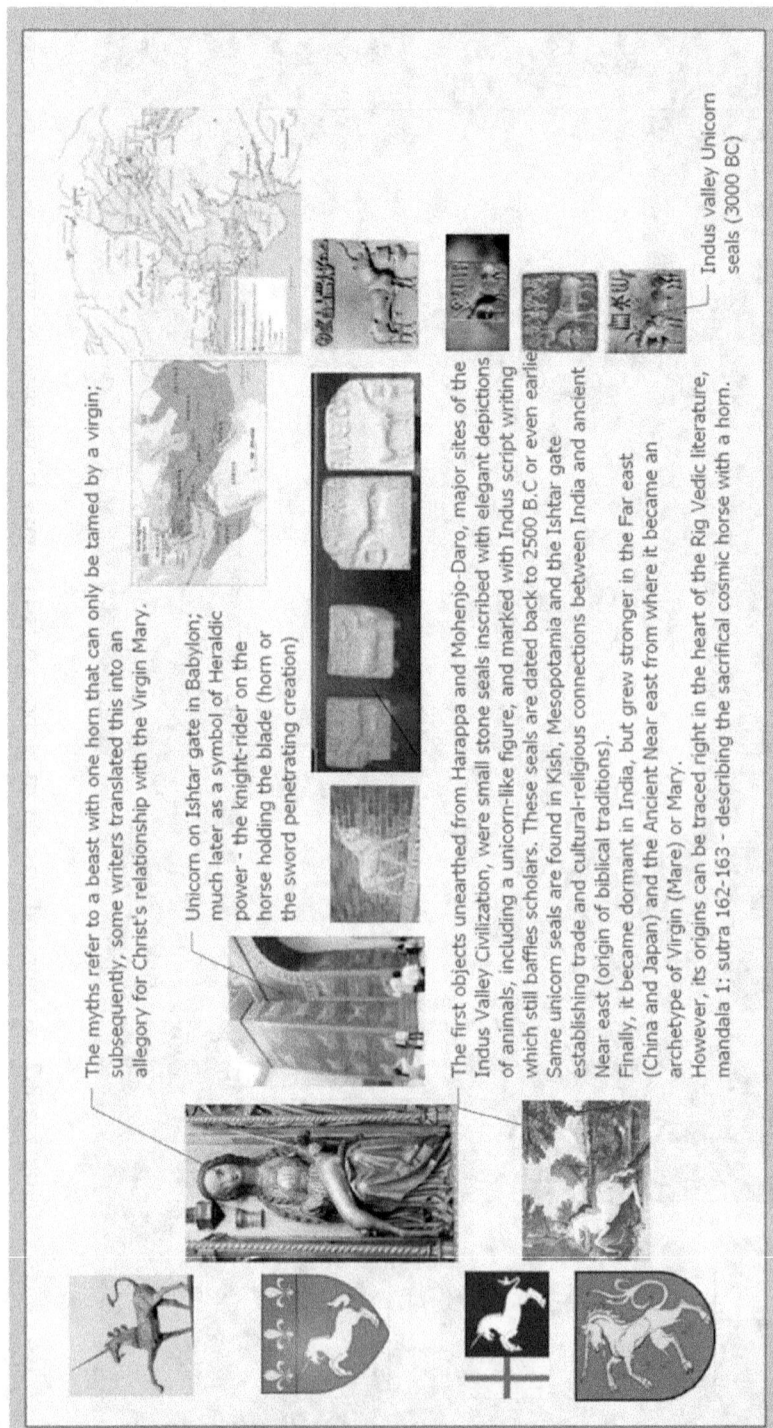

Template 3.3 Fundamentals of the Unicorn symbolism (note Ishtar gate) (Composed by author)

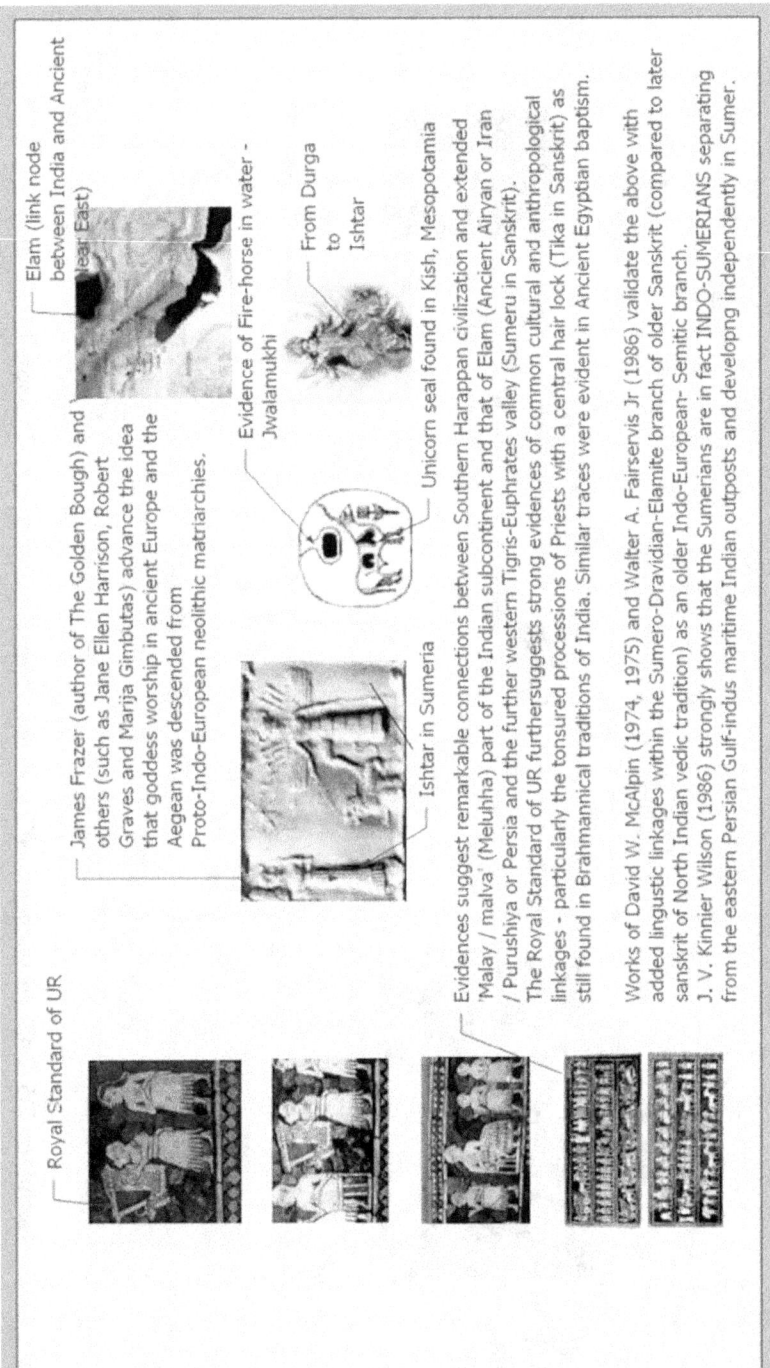

Template 3.4 Unicorn symbolism – Ishtar in Sumer and Durga in India (Composed by author)

System framework one: Phase I of global history of architecture

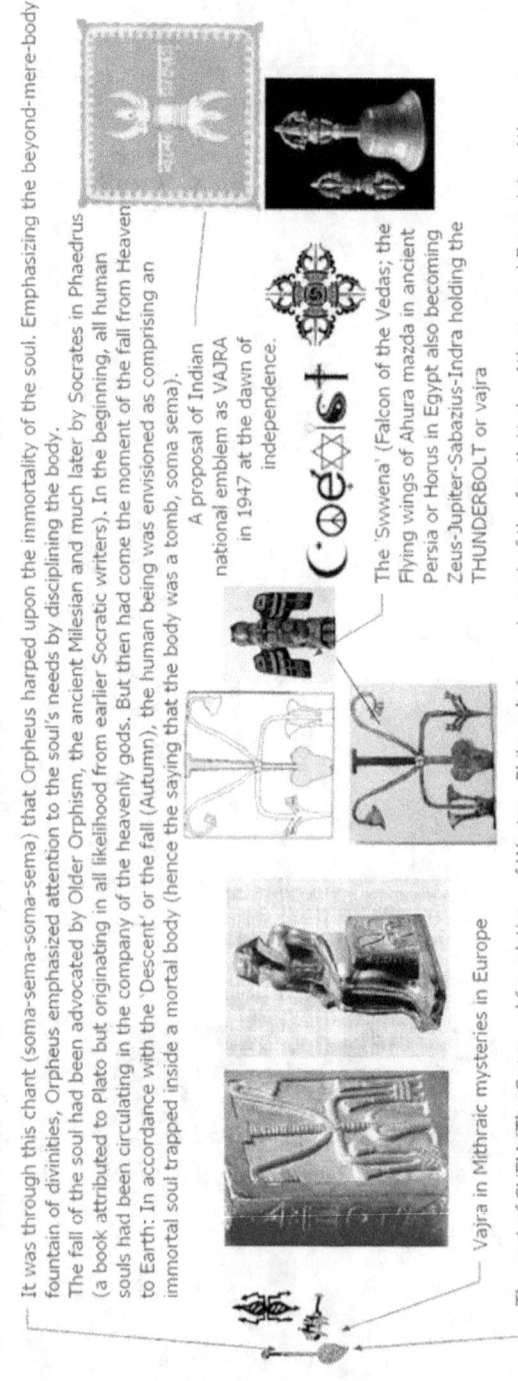

It was through this chant (soma-sema-soma-sema) that Orpheus harped upon the immortality of the soul. Emphasizing the beyond-mere-body fountain of divinities, Orpheus emphasized attention to the soul's needs by disciplining the body.
The fall of the soul had been advocated by Older Orphism, the ancient Milesian and much later by Socrates in Phaedrus (a book attributed to Plato but originating in all likelihood from earlier Socratic writers). In the beginning, all human souls had been circulating in the company of the heavenly gods. But then had come the moment of the fall from Heaven to Earth: In accordance with the 'Descent' or the fall (Autumn), the human being was envisioned as comprising an immortal soul trapped inside a mortal body (hence the saying that the body was a tomb, soma sema).

A proposal of Indian national emblem as VAJRA in 1947 at the dawn of independence.

The 'Svwena' (Falcon of the Vedas; the Flying wings of Ahura mazda in ancient Persia or Horus in Egypt also becoming Zeus-Jupiter-Sabazius-Indra holding the THUNDERBOLT or vajra

Vajra in Mithraic mysteries in Europe

The root of SHEM (The Corporeal foundations of Western Philosophy) – an impact of the fourth Veda –Atharva and Zoroastrian Atharvan systems (U-Baid or I-badi) systems of Semitic philosophy of the Vedic Asura as opposed to Spiritual or non-corporeal Sura)
- The idea of Somatic (Corporeal or liquefying or solidifying principle of Soma) as opposed/ complementary to Agni (the non-corporeal of Fire/ Igneous levitating or evaporating principle)

The sema-tawy is an ancient symbol of the union of the Two Lands, Upper and Lower Egypt. It is composed of the heraldic plants of the Two Lands. Lilies, for the south (Upper), and papyrus, for the north (Lower), are knotted around the hieroglyphic sign for 'union'. (reflects the ancient Cosmogony of Seers around the world - the integral 'Dyva-Prithvi' (Upper and Lower worlds integrated)

Template 3.5 Unicorn symbolism (Cross) and 'soma-sema' doctrine (Composed by author)

- The Sed festival also known as Heb Sed or Feast of the Tail) was an ancient Egyptian ceremony that celebrated the continued rule of a pharaoh; primarily rejuvenate the pharaoh's strength and stamina while still sitting on the throne, celebrating the continued success of the pharaoh – based on the symbolism of the death and resurrection (rejuvenation) of the corn-spirit (chthonian). Pharaoh is seen as the material projection of supreme Corn-spirit (Osiris or Demeter's son or Sabazius-Adonis).
  In the New Testament: 'And he said, 'Where unto shall we liken the kingdom of God? or with what comparison shall we compare it? It is like a grain of mustard SEED (SIDH of India or SID of the Celtic tradition), which, when it is sown in the earth, is less than all the seeds that be in the earth: But when it is sown, it groweth up, and becometh greater than all herbs, and shooteth out great branches; so that the fowls of the air may lodge under the shadow of it.' Mark 4:26-32
  Suddha-ODANA (Boiled seed) or Siddha-Artha (Worth of Spiritual growth)

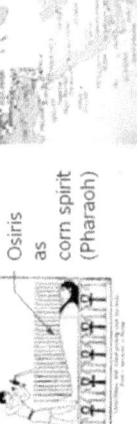

- Meso-American Corn goddess
- Greek corn goddess

Osiris as corn spirit (Pharaoh)

- The Land of Punt, also called Pwenet, or Pwene by the ancient Egyptians, was a trading partner known for producing and exporting gold, aromatic resins, African blackwood, ebony, ivory, slaves and wild animals and birds like peacock, bandoor cock. Information about Punt has been found in ancient Egyptian records of trade missions to this region. The earliest recorded Egyptian expedition to Punt was organized by Pharaoh Sahure of the Fifth Dynasty (25th century BC) although gold from Punt is recorded as having been in Egypt in the time of king Khufu of the Fourth Dynasty of Egypt.
  John Henry Breasted (1906) establishes from ancient records that the ancient Egyptians called Punt Ta netjer, meaning "God's Land". This referred to the fact that it was among the regions of the Sun God, that is, the regions located in the direction of the sunrise, to the East of Egypt. These eastern regions' resources included products used in temples, notably incense gold, aromatic resins such as myrrh, ebony and elephant tusks. Egyptians were very careful to describe Indian as the land of the Gods; so that there lies no controversy about it. Hence let us safely agree that the Land of Punt which Egyptians referred to was indeed India or a sovereign province of India. The Greeks called present day Punjab as "Paenta Potemia" meaning the land of five rivers. This was the scene of the famous highly developed culture of Mohenjo Daro and Harappa which had trade relations with Egypt. Punt is often mentioned along with another region called Ta-Netjer (tA-nTr) "The Land of the God". It is believed that Punt may have been a part of Ta-Netjer.
  Ta-Netjer (tA-nTr) = Tantra (land of divine weaving – in which the serpent, the sun, the swan and the Lotus/ lily are very important.

Template 3.6 Unicorn symbolism – parable of seed-corn: reaping and sprouting (Composed by author)

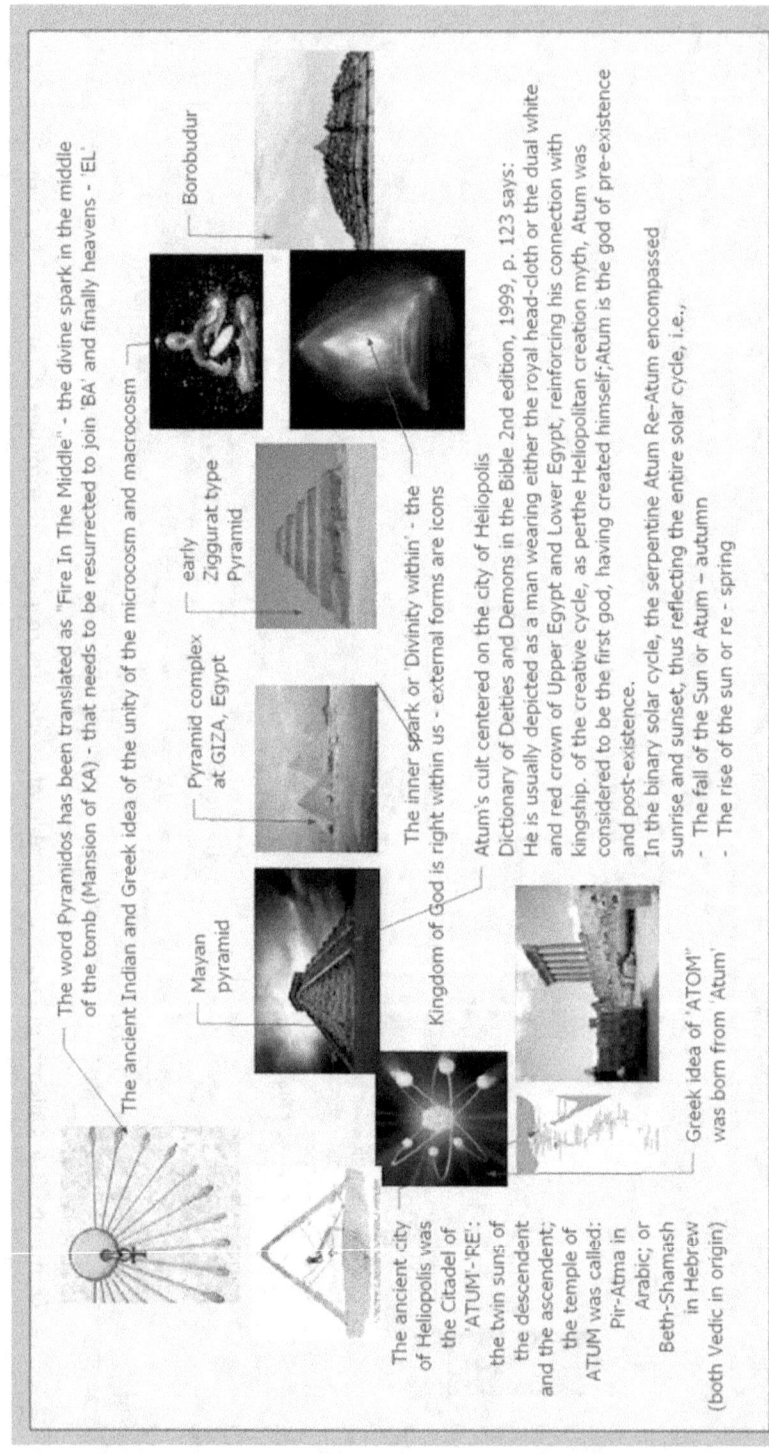

Template 3.7 The concept of Agni (anti-thesis to 'Soma') – Pyrrhic/Fire principle (Composed by author)

System framework one: Phase I of global history of architecture

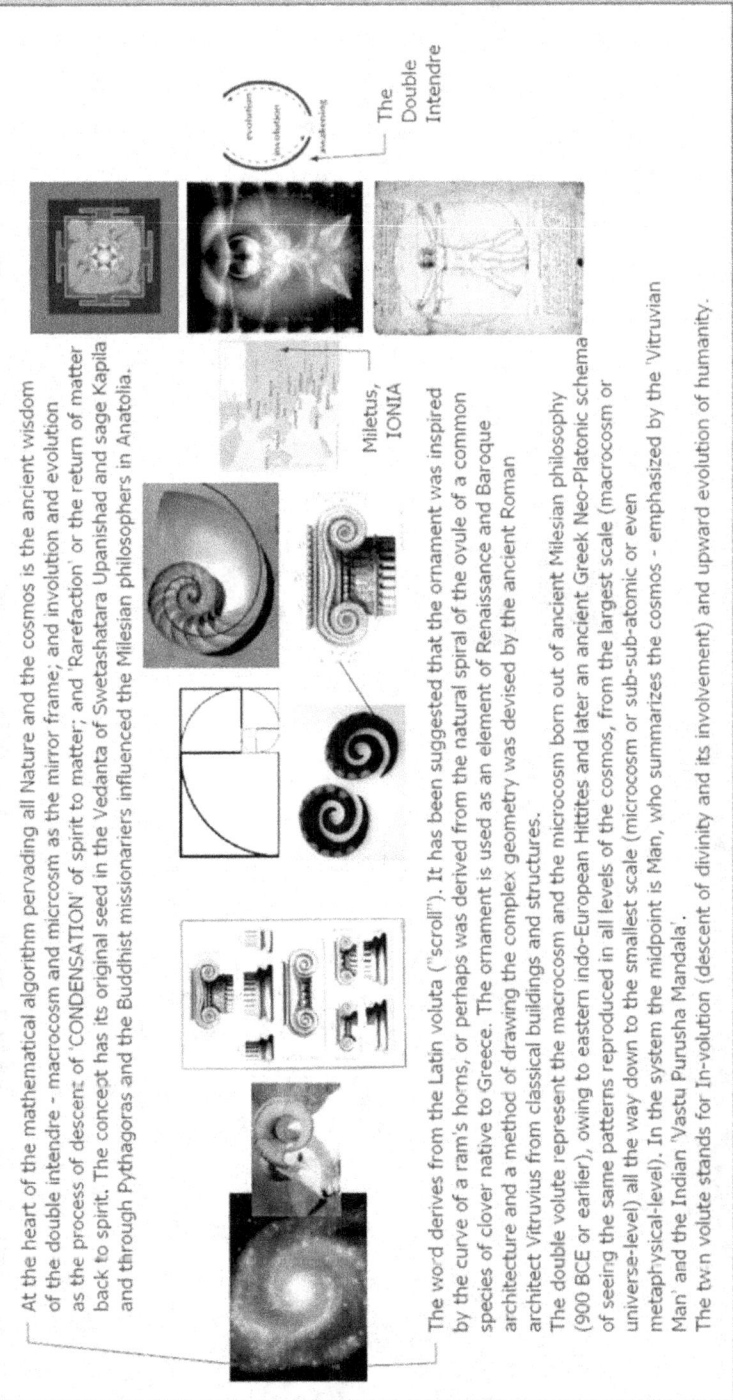

At the heart of the mathematical algorithm pervading all Nature and the cosmos is the ancient wisdom of the double intendre - macrocosm and microcosm as the mirror frame; and involution and evolution as the process of descent: 'CONDENSATION' of spirit to matter; and 'Rarefaction' or the return of matter back to spirit. The concept has its original seed in the Vedanta of Swetashatara Upanishad and sage Kapila and through Pythagoras and the Buddhist missionaries influenced the Milesian philosophers in Anatolia.

The word derives from the Latin voluta ("scroll"). It has been suggested that the ornament was inspired by the curve of a ram's horns, or perhaps was derived from the natural spiral of the ovule of a common species of clover native to Greece. The ornament is used as an element of Renaissance and Baroque architecture and a method of drawing the complex geometry was devised by the ancient Roman architect Vitruvius from classical buildings and structures.

The double volute represent the macrocosm and the microcosm born out of ancient Milesian philosophy (900 BCE or earlier), owing to eastern Indo-European Hittites and later an ancient Greek Neo-Platonic schema of seeing the same patterns reproduced in all levels of the cosmos, from the largest scale (macrocosm or universe-level) all the way down to the smallest scale (microcosm or sub-sub-atomic or even metaphysical-level). In the system the midpoint is Man, who summarizes the cosmos - emphasized by the 'Vitruvian Man' and the Indian 'Vastu Purusha Mandala'.

The twin volute stands for In-volution (descent of divinity and its involvement) and upward evolution of humanity.

Template 3.8 Ear of the Corn: Involutes (involution) and evolutes (evolution) (Composed by author)

The ancient land of the ATHAURVANS (Ajerbaijan)

The most important evidence is the earliest religion of Persia (Parasiya) called the Religion of the Atharvans or Divine Fire Priests (or Magi). Much of this religion is still recorded as an extension of the Atharva Veda, the forth cardinal Veda of the Indian spiritual tradition. As evidences, in the most sacred book of the Pahlavis, called the 'Yasht' (sacred fire ritual or the Vedic Yagna) we get this line: 'Usta-no zato Atharva, yo Spitamo Zarathusthra' (xiii, 94). (Fortunate are we that the great teacher the Atharvan was born, Spitama Zarathusthra).

In the Vedas, the Atharvans (Atar-bahram) and the Bhrigus (Kavya Ushana) are the patron fire priests and their legacy along with the cult of 'Vivashwan' (Vivasgwa) (Aditya or resurrection -- refer Gita 4:1) and Yama (Jamshid) (death and sacrifice) is the very basis of the sacred literature of Persian 'Avesta'. That is the original Indo-Iranian root (page 195, The Penguin Dictionary of Religions, 1984).

THE LEGEND OF JWALAMUKHI
(FIRE HORSE) & ITS ASSOCIATION WITH
THE ANCIENT INDUS VALLEY UNICORN

The descriptions of 'Jwalamukhi' as a 'fire-horse' are evident in an ancient text called the 'Kalikapurana' (42nd section, slokas 136-196).
The first evidences are in the Rig Veda 1: 162-163. The fire stands for the inner flame of any cosmic personality – a Mahayogin, personified as Shiva – the full blaze of pure psychic power standing over any individual or disjointed desires.
When any Mahayogin i.e., a person who has attained Shivattwa (Sabbath) is disturbed by the external material passions (kama), there bursts off the flames of his fiery inner power - sending forth a 'sword like jet of an all-engulfing' divine fire from his or her 'Third eye' (Triambaka = comparable to Thriambic of Sabazeus-bacchus].
It leads to calcinations (burning off to ashes) of the passions of flight (phoenix allegory).
Finally, the cosmic fire is condensed in the form of a Horse and stored in the depths of the Ocean by the great Sages (Saptarishis and Hiranyagrabha/ Brahma-purusha).
It is the parable of the Unicorn, evident in Jwalamukhi, standing as the epicenter of the Indus Valley Civilization.

Inscriptions of Jwalamukhi (Holy Fire) in Temple of the province of Bhagavan ("Fields of the Gods"), i.e., "Fire Gods"), Baku, Ajerbaijan

Template 3.9 The first westward movement from India: Legacy of Athaurvans (Composed by author)

4

System framework two: Phase II of global history of architecture

4.1   Introduction

The second phase of Indo-Greco interactions took place in the interfaces of Western Asia and the Eastern Mediterranean, what we call the Asia Minor. The interactions consolidated further westbound, along the shoreline of ancient Turkey and further in islands of Eastern Mediterranean. The consolidation was triggered only after Alexander the Great had treaded eastbound, to reach the very borders of Indus Valley and India. But it had a past, which is presented in the previous chapter, as system's framework one. It is on the first one, the present chapter traces and earmarks a further movement towards the Eastern Mediterranean.

Two books describing the ancient territories and communities in India in relationship with those in Asia Minor were coined as "Indica", authored by Megasthenes and Arrian. The ancient chronicles are perhaps an earliest and authentic description of India by the two Greek historians. They forward deeper implications of these consolidations and also giving precedence of continuity from the earlier ones.

In Megasthenes' Indica, there are powerful evidences of an important godhead. His name is Father figure Bacchus, who has surfaced almost in all ancient Near Eastern mysteries under various names – Bacchus, Bromius and most popularly, Dionysus-Adonis. It will be worthwhile to begin the probe with excerpts from the two chronicles on India and finally attempt a validation by another seminal work by a noted philosopher-historian of our own times, Sir Bertrand Russell.

To begin with, a step-by-step retrieval from these ancient records can be conducted to continue the system's recovery forwarded in the last chapter, particularly in Part 6: System of Cooperative Archaeology based on Anthropology and Iconography, and the contents of Table 3.1. The recovery as attempted in the last chapter in light of the later historical excerpts is a precursor to the journey of Alexander the Great to India, and it will lead to the system's recovery two, as attempted by the present chapter:

4.1.1 Excerpts from Indica: Recasting the dates of a two-phase recovery

To begin with the Indica of Megasthenes, we may arrive at a set of strong evidences of the two phases of systems recovery as attempted by this book – one more than 6000 years back and another taking place following the entry of Alexander to India. Interestingly, the dates of the earlier recovery match with the ancient dates of Prophet Zarathustra, the Atharvaun Sage of Persia, whom every Greek philosopher from Diogenes to Plato places around 6500 year prior to the beginning of Christian era. It is an important point to be noted, and it requires a re-casting and a re-formulation of Indian history in relationship to that of the Greeks and the Persians. Let us begin with the first two quotes:

> For the Indians stand almost alone among the nations in never having migrated from their own country. From the days of Father Bacchus to Alexander the Great, their kings are reckoned at 154, whose reigns extend over 6451 years and 3 months.
>
> FRAGM. L. C. Plin. Hist. Nat.VI. xxi. 4–5.
>
> *Of the Ancient History of the Indians*

> Father Bacchus was the first who invaded India, and was the first of all who triumphed over the vanquished Indians. From him to Alexander the Great 6451 years are reckoned with 3 months additional, the calculation being made by counting the, kings who reigned in the intermediate period, to the number of 153.
>
> *Solin. 52. 5.*

Megasthenes goes further to retrieve the ancient Pandyans (Pandu races of India, as described in the Puranas and particularly, the Mahabharata and geographically in the Pandulena-Nasik-Trambakerswar zone of the Western Ghats today, which is still famous for its caves and vineyards):

Many writers further include in India even the city Nysa and Mount Merus, sacred to Father Bacchus, whence the origin of the fable that he sprang from the thigh of Jupiter (22).

FRAGM. LVI. Plin. Hist. Nat. VI. 21. 8-23. 11.

List of the Indian Races

The Pandaean nation is governed by females, and their first queen is said to have been the daughter of Hercules. The city Nysa is assigned to this region, as is also the mountain sacred to Jupiter, Meros by name, in a cave on which the ancient Indians affirm Father Bacchus was nourished; while the name has given rise to the well-known fantastic story that Bacchus was born from the thigh of his father.

FRAGM. LVI. B. Solin. 52. 6-17.

Catalogue of Indian Races.

In Arrian's Indica, we get a more detailed description of the twin foundations of Dionysus, synonymous with Bacchus, in India and in Greece. Arrian also forwards the symbolic succession of line in India – the Spatembas (akin to Swetambaras) and the Boudyas (akin to generations emanating from Buddha himself):

When Dionysus had arranged these affairs and was about to leave India, he appointed as king of the land Spatembas, one of his companions, the man most versed in the mysteries of Bacchus. When this man died his son Boudyas succeeded to his kingdom. The father reigned fifty-two years, and the son twenty years. Cradeuas, the son of Boudyas, succeeded to the throne. From this time for the most part the kingdom passed in regular succession from father to son.

Arrian, "The Indica" in Anabasis of Alexander, The Indica, E. J. Chinnock, tr. (London: Bohn, 1893), Ch. 1–16

4.1.2 The Bacchic-Dionysiac element: Origin, evolution and impact

Bacchus as he is broadly known is the Roman god of agriculture, and wine is analogous to Greek Dionysus. History has confirmed that he was an addition to the twelve Olympians; having an origin in the Asia Minor mysteries and more so, having a specific feature in the ascetic Orphic and Pythagorean lore. It is mentioned in many ancient oracles that Bacchus before his position in the Olympus, wandered the world for many years, going as far as India to teach people how to grow vines – the mystery of wine or divine ecstasy! Amongst the Orphists of the ancient Greek religion, Dionysus is considered a saviour! Bertrand Russell, in his work ' History of western Philosophy', makes a step-by-step recovery, at least to an extent, the origin, pattern and ways of 'Bacchus-Dionysus' as a saviour:

> There was, however, in ancient Greece, much that we can feel to have been religion as we understand the term. This was connected, not with the Olympians, but with Dionysus, or Bacchus, whom we think of most naturally as the somewhat disreputable god of wine and drunkenness. The way in which, out of his worship, there arose a profound mysticism, which greatly influenced many of the philosophers, and even had a part in shaping Christian theology, is very remarkable, and must be understood by anyone who wishes to study the development of Greek thought. Dionysus, or Bacchus, was originally a Thracian god. The Thracians were very much less civilized than the Greeks, who regarded them as barbarians. Like all primitive agriculturists, they had fertility cults, and a god who promoted fertility. His name was Bacchus. It was never quite clear whether Bacchus had the shape of a man or of a bull. When they discovered how to make beer, they thought intoxication divine, and gave honor to Bacchus. When, later, they came to know the vine and to learn to drink wine, they thought even better of him. His functions in promoting fertility in general became somewhat subordinate to his functions in relation to the grape and the divine madness produced by wine.

Russell clearly explains the two forms of Bacchus-Dionysus, one savage and evolving and the other, serene, spiritual and influencing and its relationship with the original sect of the 'Orphics':

The worship of Bacchus in its original form was savage, and in many ways repulsive. It was not in this form that it influenced the philosophers, but in the spiritualized form attributed to Orpheus, which was ascetic, and substituted mental for physical intoxication. .....The Orphics were an ascetic sect; wine, to them, was only a symbol, as, later, in the Christian sacrament. The intoxication that they sought was that of "enthusiasm," of union with the god. They believed themselves, in this way, to acquire mystic knowledge not obtainable by ordinary means. This mystical element entered into Greek philosophy with Pythagoras, who was a reformer of Orphism, as Orpheus was a reformer of the religion of Bacchus. From Pythagoras Orphic elements entered into the philosophy of Plato, and from Plato into later philosophy that was in any degree religious.

4.1.3 Contacts with India: The Indo-European elements

Russell finally brings to light the salient features of the 'cult of Bacchus-Dionysiac' elements, and its formative impact on the genesis of early Greek Thought and later, Christianity itself. Russell however quotes John Burnet, a great scholar of Greek philosophy, who goes on to state that there is a striking similarity between Orphic beliefs and those prevalent in India at about the same time, but is not clear about any geographical contact:

The influence of religion, more particularly of non-Olympian religion, on Greek thought was not adequately recognized until recent times. A revolutionary book, Jane Harrison Prolegomena to the Study of Greek Religion, emphasized both the primitive and the Dionysiac elements in the religion of ordinary Greeks; F. M. Cornford's 'From Religion to Philosophy' tried to make students of Greek philosophy aware of the influence of religion on the philosophers, but cannot be wholly accepted as trustworthy in many of its interpretations, or, for that matter, in its anthropology. The most balanced statement known is in John Burnet's Early Greek Philosophy, especially Chapter II, "Science and Religion." A conflict between science and religion arose, he says, out of "the religious revival which swept over Hellas in the sixth century B.C.," together with the shifting of the scene from Ionia to the West. "The religion of continental Hellas," he says, "had developed in a very different way from that of Ionia. In particular, the worship of Dionysus, which came from Thrace, and is barely mentioned in Homer, contained in germ a wholly new way of looking at man's relation to the world. It would certainly be wrong to credit the Thracians themselves with any very exalted views; but there can be no doubt that, to the Greeks, the phenomenon of ecstasy suggested that the soul was something more than a feeble double of the self, and that it was only when 'out of the body' that it could show its true nature....

"It looked as if Greek religion were about to enter on the same stage as that already reached by the religions of the East... John Burnet (Early Greek Philosophy, especially Chapter II, "Science and Religion") goes on to state that there is a striking similarity between Orphic beliefs and those prevalent in India at about the same time, though he holds that there cannot have been any contact. He then comes on to the original meaning of the word "orgy," which was used by the Orphics to mean "sacrament," and was intended to purify the believer's soul and enable it to escape from the wheel of birth. The Orphics, unlike the priests of Olympian cults, founded what we may call "churches," i.e. religious communities to which anybody, without distinction of race or sex, could be admitted by initiation, and from their influence arose the conception of philosophy as a way of life."

4.1.4 The Dorians and the Milesians: Traces of the second westbound movement

Russell however mentions that the third of the Greeks, the Dorians, retained their original Indo-European character:

The Greeks came to Greece in three successive waves, first the Ionians, then the Achaeans, and last the Dorians. The Ionians appear, though conquerors, to have adopted the Cretan civilization pretty completely, as, later, the Romans adopted the civilization of Greece. But the Ionians were disturbed, and largely dispossessed, by their successors the Achaeans. The Achaeans are known, from the Hittite tablets found at Boghaz-Keui, to have had a large organized empire in the fourteenth century B.C. The Mycenaean civilization, which had been weakened by the warfare of the Ionians and Achaeans, was practically destroyed by the Dorians, the last Greek invaders. Whereas previous invaders had largely adopted the Minoan religion, the Dorians retained the original Indo-European religion of their ancestors.

Thrace the intermediate origin of the Dionysian element was however centred on the modern borders of Bulgaria, Greece, and Turkey. Much of that is an extension of Asia Minor, the ancient belt of the speaker of the Indo-European language, the Hittites, and their colonies in Lydia, Lycia, Phrygia and many other places, an area that condensed to form the bases of earliest Asiatic Greek civilization, the Milesians, whose principal city was Miletus in 1500 BCE or earlier.

The characteristics of Milesian philosophy

The essential spiritual part of the Bacchic-Dionysiac element, more characteristic of the Orphic religion, having its origin in Thrace, in Asia Minor – with the Milesians and Dorians, having roots in the Asiatic mystery, and more so in the recovery of the ascetic and ecstatic elements of a reformed Indian metaphysical objective is alien to later developments in western Greece. The clarity is evident in the following words:

It is interesting to follow the evolution of Western science along its spiral path, starting from the mystical philosophies of the early Greeks, rising and unfolding in an impressive development of intellectual thought that increasingly turned away from its mystical origins to develop a world view which is in sharp contrast to that of the Far East. In its most recent stages, Western science is finally overcoming this view and coming back to those of the early Greek and the Eastern philosophies. This time, however, it is not only based on intuition, but also on experiments of great precision and sophistication, and on a rigorous and consistent mathematical formalism. The roots of physics, as of all Western science, are to be found in the first period of Greek philosophy in the sixth century B.C., in a culture where science, philosophy and religion were not separated. The sages of the Milesian school in Ionia were not concerned with such distinctions. Their aim was to discover the essential nature, or real constitution, of things which they called 'physis'. The term 'physics' is derived from this Greek word and meant therefore, originally, the endeavour of seeing the essential nature of all things. This, of course, is also the central aim of all mystics, and the philosophy of the Milesian school did indeed have a strong mystical flavour. The Milesians were called 'hylozoists', or 'those who think matter is alive', by the later Greeks, because they saw no distinction between animate and inanimate, spirit and matter. In fact, they did not even have a word for matter, since they saw all forms of existence as manifestations of the 'physis', endowed with life and spirituality. Thus Thales declared all things to be full of gods and Anaximander saw the universe as a kind of organism which was supported by 'pneuma', the cosmic breath, in the same way as the human body is supported by air. The monistic and organic view of the Milesians was very close to that of ancient Indian and Chinese philosophy, and the parallels to Eastern thought are even stronger in the philosophy of Heraclitus of Ephesus. Heraclitus believed in a world of perpetual change, of eternal 'Becoming'. For him, all static Being was based on deception and his universal principle was fire, a symbol for the continuous flow and change of all things. Heraclitus taught that all changes in the world arise from the dynamic and cyclic interplay of opposites and he saw any pair of opposites as a unity. This unity, which contains and transcends all opposing forces, he called the Logos. The split of this unity began with the Eleatic school, which assumed a Divine Principle standing above all gods and men.

Modern Physics: Chapter one
The Tao of Physics

The reformed Indian metaphysical objective, which is alien to later developments in western Greece, is Buddhism, whose influence became global under the impact of Indian King Ashoka. In the present chapter, it will be worthwhile to chart out the second system's framework based on the transformation that took place in India in relationship with times after Alexander the Great.

4.1.5 The system's framework

In the words of Bertrand Russell, the third wave of Greeks, the Dorians, having an unknown eastern and Indo-European origin, swept the Mediterranean world; and they revolutionized a new face of the European civilization. The question still remains; who were the Dorians? What was characteristic in Dorians containing a more ascetic and puritan version of the earlier revelry-driven and ecstatic Bacchic-Dionysian element? The question still remains that who were they? And in what way were they associated with a rapid spread of ascetic monastic and mostly rock-cut settlements found all along the shores of the Eastern Mediterranean (Lower Greece; Coastal Anatolia; and Egypt)? (see Template 4.1)

Figure 4.1 explains the evolution and ramification of these Phase II developments.

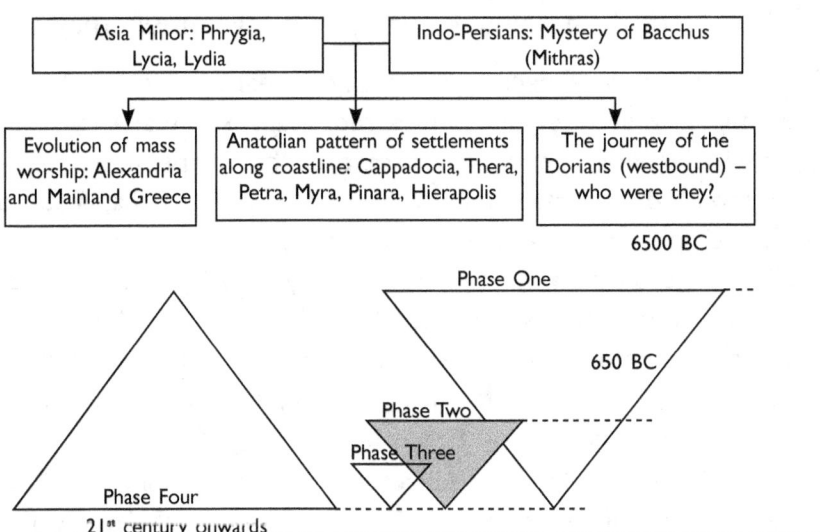

Figure 4.1 System of Phase II: evolution in the Eastern Mediterranean

'After the invasion of Alexander the great, these two great waterfalls (Indian and Greek principles) colliding with each other, deluged nearly half of the globe with spiritual tides, such as Christianity.'

Swami Vivekananda
Problem of India and Its Solution

'.... For Priyadarsi, the beloved of Gods, desires safety, self-control, justice, and happiness for all beings. The beloved of Gods considers that the greatest of all victories is the victory of righteousness, and that victory the Beloved of Gods has already won, here and on all his borders, even 600 leagues away in the realm of the Greek king Antiyoka, and beyond Antiyoka among the four kings Turamaya, Antikini, Maga and Alikasudara, and in the south among the Cholas and Pandyas and as far as Ceylon'.

Les Inscription d'Asoka, Paris
On *'Buddhist Missions to the Eastern Mediterranean'*

4.2 Part one: The imagery of the 'Year Sempiternal (*Sana*)' and *AGNUS DEI*

4.2.1 The first signs: The physical and inner imageries

The discussion may begin with a key research clue – which is predominantly architectural and symbolically spiritual – a binary approach of iconography-driven researches that the previous chapter has attempted. The clue holds both the origin and manifestation of the temple form evident in the entire Western world – the Basilica and the Abbey, which was gradually transformed to a more popularly known expression, the 'Church'. In Old French or Celtic: it is Kirk; in Latin: Cirice; Greek: Circe or Kyrakion and it is the symbolism of an abstract geometry that lay hidden in that imaging of the Temple of Christ or the 'Kingdom of god'!

The discussion has to begin with a set of very significant imageries (key abstraction) of the new Temple of God carved out in the Eastern Mediterranean world. The abstraction triggered both a distinct shape grammar behind the physical built form, which was executed and erected at the material plane and also symbolizes an inner layers of experiences based on the journey the soul aspiring for a communion with the supreme – the soul of the Universe. Aspiration is defined in terms of an inner fire – an inner urge – an inner spark conceived as a principle that evolves (in a lifetime) and rotates (transmigration) the path of a long journey of psychic evolution before it reaches its destination. The journey is represented by a circle with seasonal, astral and zodiac implications. An important point is the point of Aries, the Passover point – the symbol of a Ram (a sheep) – that marks 'Easter' or more celestially, spring equinox (see Template 4.2). Here, the sun, the soul of the aspirant, the seat of fire, crosses winter and heads forth (spring).

4.2.2 The root of the abstraction: 'Personified' and 'Impersonal'

Any abstraction is simultaneously anthropomorphic (based on human imagery) and a-morphic (formless or at least devoid of human imagery). The various imageries of this abstraction carry through them a message of guidance for the human spirit and that is reflected by the physical spaces that would stand to convey the rhythm of guiding movements and the chants of inner celebrations. In effect, the imagery at its very root was the symbolical cult of the 'Shepherd and the guidance offered to the Lambs that were helpless without him'. The Shepherd and the Lamb (the Sheep) was the connection between divine providence and human submission. This abstraction is the ancient cult of the Igneous principle called the Agnus or Agnes Dei (see Figure 4.2). It is said:

> "He tends his flock like a shepherd: He gathers the lambs in his arms and carries them close to his heart; he gently leads those that have young."

Isaiah 40:11
The Old Testament

The abstraction was a key feature of Orphism, and the different shades of Mithraic mysteries associated with Egyptian and Babylonian lore. The image of the sacred Lamb was in cause an image of sacrificial life – representing an upward inner fire – a passion for the divine that Passover and in effect a continuity to a point of renewal and resurrection till the first fruits of the sacrifice are realized.

Figure 4.2 Agnes Dei – the Shepherd and the Lamb; the chosen or sacrificial Lamb

Note: The symbolism of the Agnus Dei is the same as that of the Paschal Candle; the wax is the pure flesh of Christ – the wax been the basis of the Lamp – the fire; lower images are from ancient Greece and Rome culminating to the key Figure of the New Testament: 'Jesus as Good Shepherd'

The image of the sacrificial Lamb or Agnes Dei perhaps has an origin in the Vedas. The culmination of the inner fire at the highest plane is also of innermost contemplation, for the life that is 'truly universal' – meaning 'catholic or divine', a cosmic plane beyond description – but open to experience, rapture and realization. Seen from a lesser plane, the imagery is closely related to the sacred Lamb of Aries. In the circle of things, the Lamb makes the movement. Lamb becomes 'Tauras', the basis of the Mithraic mystery. The circle or the year sempiternal provides the necessary geometry or mandala or the 'Circle' of movements and cosmic frameworks that we have discussed in the subsequent section.

4.2.3 The imagery and the built form: Movement in the Cosmic Wheel

In expression and tangible substance, it is the circuit of the sun and its assumable impact on human life – much of which is partly astral (non-corporeal) and human (corporeal). This is the concept of the double that we have discussed in the preceding chapter. At the astral plane or the Ram or full-grown Lamb stands for Aries ear-marking the point of Spring equinox. Dually, as just pointed out, it has both astral significance in the macrocosm and the connections of an inner significance of the upward human journey in the inner container of human body termed as the microcosm. In the language of St. Paul (Chapter 10 of Corinthians: 1, the New Testament) – it is the body of Christ and also that of the universe – with all of us in it. That is why, with the sacrifice of Christ on the Cross – we are all sacrificed. That is why, too, with the resurrection of Christ, we are all resurrected. In Buddhism, such an equivalent Catholic concept of universal spirit is the 'Bodhisattva'.

In the Vedas, the 'sacrificial Lamb' is both the first point of the Aries, which is solar as it signifies the circuitous movement of the Sun in 360 degrees and also lunar as the constellation of *Aswinis* (constellation of the two riders of the Horse, as the lunar sign or *naksatra*) exactly matches with the solar and therefore it is the starting point of the solar leap (spirit) in matter and mind (lunar) determining the renewed trip of human journey again and again. This is signified by the renewed 'Circle' – the *Mandala* and that point of renewal is the tropical turn of the Sun moving upwards. It is also the symbolism of the inner journey of a sacrificial human mind. In the Vedas this double symbolism is represented by *Agni* through its double sense – one in the vast and one in the small:

- The vast is the journey of sun upwards in the tropics called Uttarayana and this we have discussed in previous chapters.
- In the small, we carry out the reflected plan of an inner journey.
- The plan of the Temple dedicated to the Lamb who connects the vast and the small, and therefore it is the two-way bridge between the corporeal and the non-corporeal.

'Therefore the Son of God is also the Son of Man'.

The image of the church therefore stands in between:

Outer journey (macrocosm) = Plan of the Church = Inner journey (microcosm)

At Aries or Spring Equinox (around March–April) the Sun takes the new turning. It marks the point of 'Easter'. In Indian mythology and in the Indian calendar system this is the New Year or *Vaisakhi* (refer Figure 4.3) – just born after sacrifice at the month prior to that called *'Chaitra'* (in Sanskrit) – or 'Chaitya' in Pali or common Indian dialect. The figure provides the geometry of the plan – the movements and the circuits. It has to be noted that the circular-ambulatory path of the Sun centers the Nave (Nabhi) or Boss as the Kendra (Sanskrit) or the Centre and the circuit is the very rim or aisle (alley) all around. It forms the basis of the Vedic cruciform that had shaped the inner plan of later Indian Temples – the first Chaitya Hall designs venerated by the ancient Buddhists and the Greco-Roman 'Kirke' (Circe).

The Circuit, the inner movements, the apsidal ends, the inner and outer aisles and the naves are the built definitions of the higher abstractions of human mind. Etymologically, it is the basis or the root of the word 'Church'. The spark of fire – the 'inner divinity' in the corporeal framework of man is the Jataveda Agni (in the Vedic esoteric tradition).

- In the Western ancient pre-Christian world it was called Agnes Dei
- In the Eastern ancient world that spark, which is the potent seed of consciousness in the living form – is called the Chaitya Purusha.

Thus the ancient image of the cult of *Agnes Dei*, resurrected from the subterranean gloom (the *Erebus* of Orphism or *Karakula* in Sumerian mythology) for a renewed movement, is the circuit of the inner sun – the *Chaitya Purusha*. It is an innermost truth, hidden in the outer, known only to the inner-seeker. But its recovery, the hidden lost sun in the human form, is a necessity to unlock the understanding forwarded by this chapter. It was in its imagery, the *Garbha-griha* or the inner sanctum of the late Vedic grammar was carved out to be developed into the Chaitya Hall of the ancient worshippers of the Buddha and later the ancient worshippers of the Christ – both in the impersonal (the Cup-like Stupa or the Vajra as the Cross) and personal (the image of Buddha or Christ as personal savior) senses. Template 4.3 furnishes a glimpse of the iconography of the 'Cross' attached with the ancient world like the Mithraic Mysteries of Veda in Persia, of Avesta in Persia and in ancient Rome.

4.2.4 The ancient Vedic image of Agnus Dei: The circuitous journey (Sana) of the Chaitya Purusha

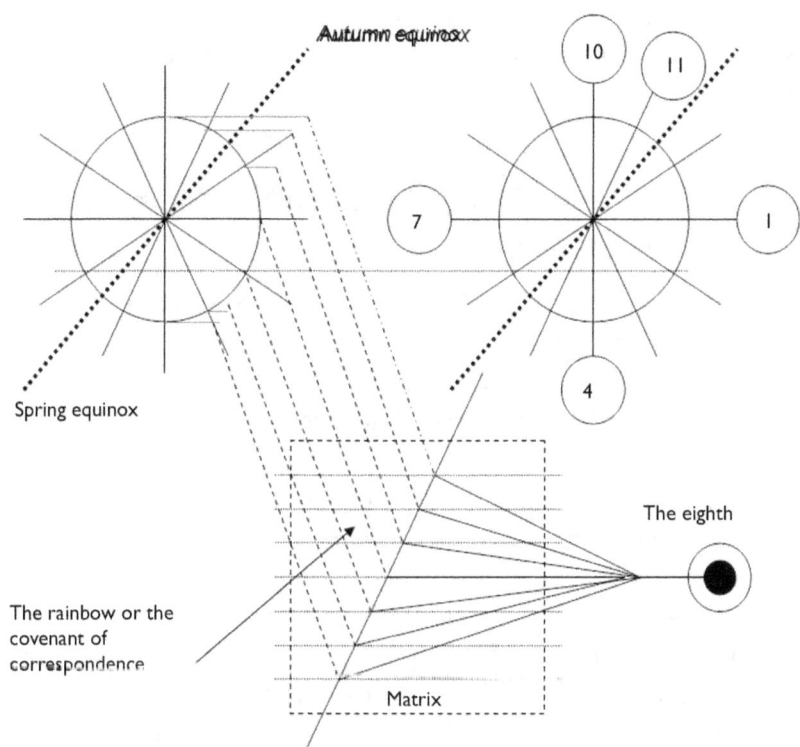

Figure 4.3 The Vedic symbolism of the Circe (Kirk) based on the Circuit of the Sun or year sempiternal (called 'Sana' or Aditya mandala)

The textual sources of the image of Agnes Dei

A discussion on the textual sources of the Agnes Dei can be many and prove beneficial to decipher its universality. Only a few major ones have been briefly highlighted to best forward the ancient imagery in the present historical time-line. We begin with the Old Testament, followed by the more ancient Vedic, the Egyptian and the subsequent Buddhist sources.

4.2.5 The Old Testament

The symbolism of the lamb also has its ancient roots in the Old Testament. This is a dream at Bethel (a well venerated by Prophet Ibrahim or Abraham, the early Patriarch) found in the Old Testament. This has been discussed in the previous chapter and the symbolical story talks about the image of the seven lambs and the symbolical bloody sacrifice that connects 'Abraham' and one who follows him (his son or Ishmael).

4.2.6 The Vedic foundations and the Alexandrian Theraputtas

The Vedic parallel is found in the birth of seven *marutis* (seen as differentiated life-powers or *Vayu*) and their further 7 × 7 divisions (or 49 *Marutis*). References may be drawn from the Vedic (Rig Veda: 5.52.17; 8.28.5) and later Upanishadic foundations (like *Mundaka*: 2.1.8).

The ancient tradition of a sect called 'Theraputtas' connected with the beginnings of Christianity and ancient Alexandrian or Egyptian monasticism is intimately connected with this principle of 7 × 7 = 49 and the 50th principle as the terminal, when the full-grown white and effulgent Solar spiritual achievements are celebrated following 50 lunar days (after seven weeks) after the Easter (spring Equinox) on a Sunday. Hence is the term 'Whitsunday', also known as the 'Pentecoste' (meaning the 50th day or resurrection marking the full ascent achieved by the true descent of the divine support or 'Holy spirit'). It is thus the meeting ground of the ascent of the divine spark and the transfiguration of the body (soma) to accommodate the 'Holy spirit' in union with the 'Chaitya purusha' or the 'Lamb (Lamp) in the body'.

'The City does not need the sun or the moon to shine on it, for the glory of God gives it light, and the LAMB is its LAMP' (Revelations: 21.23)

The day of 'White-sun' or resurrection is symbolically mentioned in the Book of Revelations (the parable of the Seven Churches/ the Seven bowls and Trumpets – the Seven lambs and the Eighth King), the New Testament. The Choir and the Songs that this ancient sect had practiced bears close resemblance with such inner foundations of songs and mantic vibrations. Observations on the are found in works on 'Therapeutes' in Encyclopedia of Religion and Ethics, edited by James Hastings, Volume 12, Edinburgh (CSS), pp. 315–319 (based on the works of Philo of Alexandria around 1 AD):

"..........They are the Jewish recluses who reside in simple huts, at a short and suitable distance from one another. Each hut has a sacred chamber reserved for their sacred books by means of which religion and sound knowledge grow together into a perfect whole. After praying at dawn, they devote the day to meditation upon the Scriptures; these include writing or commentaries drawn up by the ancient founder of their sect...Prayers at sunset close the day. Such is the life in each hut. On the seventh day the various members meet for common worship; they arrange themselves according to age, sitting on the ground with the right hand between the chest and the chin, but the left tucked down along the flank.

...The seventh day is their day for relaxation. On the other days no one eats before sunset, and some go fasting almost entirely for three or even six days, in their contemplative raptures. But all use oil and on the seventh day all propitiate the mistresses hunger and thirst, which nature has set over mortal creatures; the diet is simply water and cheap bread, flavored with salt, and occasionally supplemented by hyssop.

...Once every seven weeks they assemble for their supreme festival, which the number 50 has had assigned to it, robed in white and with looks of serious joy.

...The final act of the festival is the famous 'all-night celebration' of a sacred singing dance by men and women in two choruses each headed by a chosen leader. Each of the choirs, the male and the female, begins by singing and dancing apart, partly in unison, partly in antiphonal measures of various metres, as if it were a Bacchic festival in which they had drunk deep of the divine love. Then, both unite to imitate the choral songs of Moses and Miriam at the Red Sea...It is a thrilling performance, this choric dance and exulting symphony: but the end and aim of it all is holiness...

Such says Philo, the Alexandrian philosopher, is the method of life practiced by these true citizens of heaven and of the universe (from 'Therapeutae' in Hasting's Encyclopedia).

Nazarenes in Palestine likewise observed these Jubilee times. The imperfect Biblical Book of Acts, Chapter 2, records a day of Pentecost, or a '50th' day, when special miracles occurred. This reflects true traditions in vogue among true Nazoreans. This day is also called 'The Birthday of the CHURCH' marking the descent of Holy Spirit on the chosen (Act of the Apostles). The Pentecostal traditions are widely observed even today – the largest churches being the Assemblies of God, the United Pentecostal Church and the Pentecostal Church of God in the Americas (The Wordsworth Encyclopedia of World Religions).

4.2.7 In Epic Ramayana and the Tantras

A more ancient story is found through a symbolical interaction between Sage named *Goutama* and the representative Godhead Indra and this is as encoded in the Vedas (and probably later in Epic *Ramayana* (*Adi kanda*). The story symbolizes the agents of transfiguration of 'Indra as the Lamb' as 7×7 life principles or '*Marutas*', which are the agents of divinization of the corporeal senses and the thought-mind for accommodating the descent of Godhead in the corporeal.

This idea, rooted in the Vedas (Rig Veda: 5.52.17; 8.28.5), is ramified and extended as the basis of 'Tantra' – a complete system of Indian spirituality emphasizing the role of power (Shakti) in the making of the corporeal world and its possible transfiguration. The 7×7 Marutas or life principles are the matrix of the seven rows (levels) of consciousness and the columns (axis) of functioning. The

closest explanation of this is found in the seven inner plexus of the root nervous system of the human body:
1. The coccygeal plexus (base of spine) having 4 principles – place of terrestrial functions.
2. The sacral plexus (base of procreation) having 6 principles – place of watery functions.
3. The solar plexus (connecting point of central and autonomous nervous systems and root called the 'Manipura') having 10 principles – place of fiery functions.
4. The dorsal plexus (heart point) having 10 principles – place of biotic functions.
5. The cervical plexus (terminal point of human torso or living forms) having 16 principles and all the principles accumulate and Passover as the sum of 4 + 6 + 10 + 12 + 16 principles = 48, which is the 49th principle. This is the ascendant.
6. The sinusoidal point between the eyebrows (matching the pineal gland) having the meeting point of the two (called dwi-dala) – the meeting point of the ascending 49th principle and the descending 50th principle. Here the bush burns – the inner fire or the Lamb becomes the 'Lamp of God'. This is the beginning of the inner celebration of the human form leading to its very transfiguration and acceptance of the Holy Spirit as a transfiguring agent. This is the beginning of the Pentecost.
7. The Crown or fontanel, where the two meets and becomes one – 51st or the infinite principle of the Divine. Reaching this plane and sustaining there in the highest one becomes 'one with the supreme' and all pervading. This is the completeness – the *'Sukla'* or the White-sun-tide – called the *'Madhya-nindan'* Aditya in the Vedas – the complete belonging to the Noon-tide (Rig Veda, 8th Mandala or Sukla-Yadjur Veda).

These are the seven circuits or the seven inner 'Churches' in the inner well – the inner axis of the corporeal. One may therefore carefully study the parable of 'this Well of Seven' at 'Beer-Sheba' in Book of Genesis, the Old Testament in this light. This has been discussed in the earlier chapter.

The ancient parable of the Lamb has also found its ways through the depiction of the 'Shepherd' – from Judeo-Christian tales and the 'Shepherd's wool' represented in esoteric Islam, which is Sufism.

4.2.8 Explanations of Vedic imagery of the Lamb by Shri Aurobindo

The earliest roots are evident in the Vedas, mainly in the Sama Veda and the 9th *Mandala (Soma or Amrita Angirasi Mandala)* of the Rig Veda, where the Lamb is seen as the seat of fire in the inner solar-plexus (the *Manipur* of Tantras) which provides the upward strainer, the sieve, through which soma or amrita – the juice of immortality descends.

On this Sri Aurobindo explains what the strainer actually stands for:

'The physical system of the human being is imaged as the jar of Soma-wine (the bowl of Supper) and the strainer through which it is purified is said to spread out in the seat of Heaven, deva spade.

.....The strainer or purifying instrument (pavitra)...the mind enlightened by knowledge.

....The strainer or purifying instrument (Pavitra) spread out in the seat of Heaven seems to be the mind enlightened by knowledge (cetas); the human system is the jar. Pavitram te vitatan brahmanaspate, the strainer is spread wide for thee, O Master of the Soul; Prabhur gatrani paryesi visvatah becoming manifest thou pervadest or goest about the limbs everywhere....The strainer in which the Soma (elixir) is purified is made of the fleece of the Ewe. Indra is the Ram; the Ewe must be an energy of Indra, probably the divinized sense-mind, indriyam.'

On the Vedas

Sri Aurobindo further explains the role of the divinity within that guides our psychic being, which is the Chaitya Purusha:

'I wanted to know if the word has a fixed connotation. If it has not, then one can use the word "Chaitya Purusha" for the "Psychic being". It has the advantage of carrying both the functions of the

Psychic being: it is the direct portion of the Divine in the human and it is also the being that is behind the Chitta (mind expanse or stuff).

(Evening Talks)

4.2.9 The New Testament – Book of Revelations

The evidences can be best quoted from the Book of Revelations, New Testament:

'Then I saw a Lamb, looking as if it had been slain, standing in the center of the Throne, encircled by the four....had seven horns and eyes, which are the seven spirits and took the scroll of God by his right hand..' (Rev: 5.8-9).

'The beast, who once was, and now is not, is an eighth king. He belongs to the seven and is going to his own destruction (transformation)' (Rev: 17.9-11, New Testament)

'The City does not need the sun or the moon to shine on it, for the glory of God gives it light, and the LAMB is its LAMP' (Rev: 21.23)

'I, Jesus, am the Root and the Offspring of David and the Bright Morning star.....The Spirit and the Bride say 'Come!' (Rev: 22.16-17 and John: 4.27-29)

The symbolisms definitely carry forward the following meaning:
- The sacrificial Ram – the Lamb of God, the Passover;
- The symbolism of the Seven and the Eighth represents the WORD itself;
- The assimilation of the Beast as an element of evil and the beast that was no more an element of evil achieving its original divinity;
- The convergence of the root and the offspring meaning the zenith and the nadir or the beginning and an end of the cycle of creation; and
- The parable of Matrimony talking about an eternal unity of the WORD – the Bride and her Groom (the supreme reality).

They are all endorsements to a complete truth, which is the Christ principle. This is the secret encoded in the Bible.

On this the Penguin Dictionary of Symbols (1996) provides the striking explanation both in terms of parallels or connections and the historical distortion that was used to avoid the original connections of this symbolism:

'In the Book of Revelation, the Lamb stands on Mount Zion in the centre of the Heavenly Jerusalem. Basing himself upon a description of the Brahmapura in the Bhagavad Gita (15:6) almost identical with that of the Heavenly Jerusalem, R. Guenon suggests a kinship – purely phonetic – between the Lamb (Latin Agnus) and Vedic Agni (connected to Latin Ignis that means fire, which leads to common English word Igneous), the God who rode on the back of a ram. The similarity is more than a piece of pure chance since, apart from Agni's sacrificial character, both are seen as the light at the center of existence, the goal of the quest of supreme knowledge. This comparison of the Lamb with the Vedic fire-God emphasizes the solar, virile and luminous aspects of the Lamb.....

.....it was doubtless to avoid all confusion in worship and belief which could arise from the similarity of symbols which led the Council held in Constantinople in AD 692 to give orders that Christian art should depict Christ upon the Cross in human form and no longer in the shape of a lamb, nor flanked by Sun and moon.'

(p. 586).

A similar departure perhaps was also taking place in India at around the same time. It was when the earlier image of Buddha identified with Vedic image of Indra as the Ram or Ewe. The solar symbolism of an upward Vedic journey of the Sages was classified in Buddhist literature as gradations of Indra and Maha-Indra (identified with Brahma and Maha-Brahma) and also with the cross-like thunderbolt. Later the image was made to drift from 'Indra identified as the Lamb' to a 'separate Figurehead seated on the cruci-form' or Vajra-asana. That was the beginning of separation of Buddhism from its Vedic roots of the Lamb and its symbolic wool or the strainer (Rig Veda: 9.61.4; 9.26.1).

4.2.10 In Esoteric Islam or Sufism

The parable of the 'great shepherd', his Lamb and the sacrificial lamb's wool (refer *Rig Veda* entire 9th *Mandala*) are the various keys to the esoteric doctrine of the Sufis. A Sufi is a man wrapped in pure *Cashmere* – the Lamb's wool (the suph), which is the sieve, the strainer to the elixir (*sura* or *madiera*) of immortality. They represent a non-conformist lineage of Islamic Mystics who is more interested in:

- The allegorical interpretation of the Koran
- Spirituality as a way of life and
- A serious underplaying of a popular mode of organized religious movements aiming at proselytizing and mass conversions.

Their way of life is comparable to the non-conformist: like the most ancient school of Indian bards or *fakirs* (either called the Sais or the *Abadhutas*); the Celtic minstrels; and the ancient Druids of Gauls or Galatians (the celebration of Ewe and Beltane, an ancient Celtic Festival symbolizing the lactation of the Lamb); and finally even among the Turkish Dervishes.

Sufis are probably found everywhere. As believers of truth and caring little for what country or race one initially belongs, they finally represent a scientific basis of a universal religion of humanity.

Even non-believers round the world who are essentially morally good human beings and have a lot of sympathy and love for others can explicitly and implicitly lead a 'Sufi way of life'.

4.2.11 In Egypt and in Tibetan Buddhism

In the earliest History of the Roman Catholic Church, it is called the Symbol of fire, often typified by a wax or a wax candle, called the *Agnes Dei* in Latin *(Igneous Deva)*. In Egypt, particularly, the ancient cult of Ammon-Re had depicted this solar cult as the 'Ram' (the matured Lamb). The research clue which is needed to be explored is:

- Ram = Lam(b) = Lamb = Lam = Mim (Wax) = Rama (or Lama, which is Central Asian)

195

The Shepherd Cult of the Vedas was also the heart of Ancient Buddhism, where the Buddha is described as the lineage of living Shepherd of God, guiding the wandering lambs in the dark meadows of life – and hence its innermost association with the *'Manipura'* Chakra is the whole contemplative idea of raising the inner fire hidden in the solar plexus. Hence the mantra: *Om – Manipadme Hum!*

These ancient connections are largely evident in the whole course and expression of Buddhism. More than a divine point or a divine spark, the entire flux or evolutionary journey of the soul, represented by the circuitous path, is the mystery of the *Chaitya Purusha*. The architecture of Buddhism was guided by this cardinal principle, and it also affected the ways of another great religious movement that had surged: Christianity! After the invasion of Alexander the Great, the ancient connection was renewed and the renewed spiritual tide of India had met the Greek mind and life again producing the greatest of spiritual tide in the West. The name of this tide is Christianity. The renewed spiritual tide that moved from India was Buddhism. And the most important proponent of this mission was Emperor Ashoka of India.

But today they were lost in distant obscure past – under the layers of a hidden history. So it is important to review the missionaries of Dhamma that reached the Mediterranean. The missionaries were sent by Priyadarshi – the Belover of Gods. In history he is better known as Ashoka.

4.3 Part two: The missionaries of 'Dhamma' to the Mediterranean

4.3.1 Introduction

Ashoka had changed from a tyrant power-mongering king to a great man – to an Emperor with a mission – that of universal love and peace. This happened within years of his growing adherence to the lineage of Indian spirituality, preached earlier by the Vedic sages and then fulfilled by Lord Buddha. Ashoka had started sending 'missionaries of peace' preaching the brotherhood of nations to the world. A part of these missionaries left for South-east Asia. The other part left for the West. The discussion concentrates on the second part. It is extremely important for any student of Indian architecture to be aware of this great event – of which much seems to have been lost. The contributions of these missions to the historic beginnings of the Western world – in terms of art, culture, architecture, sciences and religion – are paramount. In this chapter we give both the historical and the undeniable architectural evidences of this mission.

4.3.2 The Indian history of sending missionaries to the West

In Ashoka's own words:

'.... For Priyadarsi, the beloved of Gods, desires safety, self-control, justice, and happiness for all beings. The beloved of Gods considers that the greatest of all victories is the victory of righteousness, and that victory the Beloved of Gods has already won, here and on all his borders, even 600 leagues away in the realm of the Greek king Antiyoka, and beyond Antiyoka among the four kings Turamaya, Antikini, Maga and Alikasudara, and in the south among the Cholas and Pandyas and as far as Ceylon' (Bloch, 1950).

These are inscriptions from an Ashokan rock-cut Edict bearing the engraved letters on stone. Here Ashoka claims to have won greater victories, to which the mundane victory of a tyrant king is of the lesser kind. Ashoka mentions sending these missionaries to five Hellenic kings, whose name nearly match with the historic figures of Antiochus II Theos of Syria, Ptolemy (Tul(r)amaya) II of Egypt and Alexandria, Antigonus Gonatas of Macedonia, Magas of Cyrene (Libya) and Alexander II of Epirus (Basham, 1967).

Sir Bertrand Russell (1946) in his book named 'A History of Western Philosophy' admits that Buddhism at that time (250 BC) was a vigorous proselytizing religion. Russell refers to these missionaries by quoting from Bevan – House of Seleucus, Vol I but regrets that no Western accounts of these missionaries have survived. The historic connections between the extreme western borders of India and the Mediterranean world are not a matter of speculation. A number of evidences can be cited that precede the missionaries of Ashoka by a few hundred years or more:

1. Archaeologists have substantiated trade connections between the ancient Indus valley and Mediterranean Crete via Kish, Mesopotamia and the Persian Gulf (Edwards, 2000; Possehl, 2002).
2. The Achaemenid Empire of Cyrus and Darius was probably world's largest urban empire stretching from the shores of Anatolia (modern Turkey) to Bacteria and historic Gandhara (modern Kandahara) way back in 700 BC. Two things are important in this connection:
   - India and Persia then had shared in common philological and spiritual root called the Indo-Iranian lineage (Hinnels, 1973; Renfrew, 1987).
   - Gandhara (modern Kandahara) and Kamboja were already powerful confederations (sixteen Mahajanapadas of India around 600 BC) of India by that time (Majumdar, 1952). It was from Kamboja the architecture of north-western Indian front, via the 'Pallavas' of Deccan India (similar to 'Pehlevis' of Persia) had reached the shores of Myanmar (Burma), Siam (Thailand) and finally another Kamboja or Cambodia. Hinduism–Buddhism was then an original synergetic one and that integrity had reached Southeast Asia to build the wonders of 'Ankor-dham', 'Ankor-Beth' (the Temple of Omkara), and 'Boro-Budur' (the thousand Buddhas). They are the eastern connections vide the legacy of kings having a suffix 'Varman' (akin to Persian Bahram or the Vedic Brahman). But our recent concern is the Western connection. This has been discussed in the previous chapter.

In addition, a few later cross-evidences may be cited. Three hundred years later, Christian missionary activities are seen in south of India. This is corroborated by an adventurous Alexandrian Monk of later 6th century AD, who mentions St. Thomas (Didymus), a direct disciple of Christ and one of the Apostles, coming to India and spending his last days of missionary activities till he is entombed at a place called Mailapuram near Chennai (Madras) (Basham, 1967).

Additionally, the Romans persecuted the Jews around 100 AD or so and then the Jews sought their first resort in the Malabar Coast, South India. Thus long-lasting ethnic and reliable connections between the ancient Near East (The Fertile Crescent) and India are evident. Corroborating such evidences, following the historic march of Emperor Alexander to India the subsequent descriptions of India by Megasthenes and Arrian highlight even earlier Indo-Greek connections (prior to Alexander) (McCrindle, 2000). Within such cross-cultural set-up of India and the Mediterranean, the missionaries of Ashoka sent to Anatolia, Lebanon, Libya and Egypt definitely secured a historic root and left a lasting built or architectural expression in the entire region (see Figure 4.4 and Templates 4.4 and 4.5).

Figure 4.4 The Stupa or Tumulus form of Urnfield (burial urn containing the incinerated ash of a 'revered deceased') in Sanchi, India and in Cerveteri, Italy

4.3.3 Extended Indian architectural history: Evidences in the Eastern Mediterranean

Professor A.L. Basham of Australian National University, Canberra (1967), goes a little beyond. He points out similarities between the teachings of Greek philosophers from Pythagoras, Plato, Stoics and Plotinus and those of the Indian Upanishads and particularly the preaching of Buddha. He says:

'...We can only say that there was always some contact between the Hellenic world and India, mediated first by the Achaemenid Empire, then that of the Seleucids, and finally, under the Romans, by the traders of the Indian Ocean. Christianity began to spread at the time when this contact was the closest. We know that

Indian ascetics occasionally visited the West, and that there was a colony of Indian merchants at Alexandria. The possibility of Indian influence on Neo-Platonism and early Christianity cannot be ruled out.'

Prior to Basham, many other scholars had agreed upon such evidences. The preliminary evidences provided by Sir Percy Brown, James Fergusson, and E. B. Havell are to name a few. Fortunately, all of them are art-architectural historians and critics. Thus factual evidences drawn by them are essentially tangible as they are physical and 'architectural'.

Evaluating the splendid rock-cut monastic architecture of Buddhism, mainly during the Mauryan period and particularly during the times of Ashoka (230 BC), Brown comments:

'This development of the art of working in stone, therefore, which Ashoka introduced into this country represents an Indian offshoot of that forceful Graeco-Persian culture, which flourished with such vigor in Western Asia some centuries before the Christian era.'

Brown further adds:

'The building activities in the neighborhood of Sanchi immediately previous to the Christian era were not entirely confined to the Stupa and its accessories.... elsewhere in Besnagar, were found the divinity of Vasudeva (of Orissa) and in the form of Garuda pillar raised in the honour of the God Vasudeva by Heliodorus, son of dion, who was a resident of Taxila (near Kashmii Gandhara) and had come to the court of the local prince as an envoy from the Indo-Bactrian king Antialkidas (Antioch)...whose name gives 140 BC, the approximate date of its erection'.

Brown finally adds:

'...Rock-sculpture and rock architecture have been practiced in many countries in the past, particularly in Egypt and Assyria, by the Greeks in Lycia, and the Romans in Petra, while in Persia under the Achaemenids, and later by the Sasanids as seen at Naksh-I-Rustam.... but in none of these instances did the art of the rock-cutter show so wide a range or such audacity and imaginative power as in India, where some of the most original examples of architecture produced in this manner may be seen.... but the most striking fact in connection with the plan and the general design of the Buddhist Chaitya hall is its undeniable resemblance to the Graeco-Roman basilica, a type of structure, which was being evolved in Europe about the same time'.

Fergusson (1910) makes a more specific observation while studying the rock-cut caves at Karli, between Mumbai and Pune, and cites it as the finest example of series of caves built around the earliest Christian era. He commented:

'...It resembles an early Christian Church in its arrangements; consisting of a nave and side-aisles terminating in an apse or semi-dome, round which the aisle is carried'.

The most important evidence comes in as one observes a striking similarity between the construction styles (wooden form in stone) in a rock-cut cave known as the 'Lomash Rishi cave' at Barabar Hills near Gaya in northern-eastern India (place where Buddha attained his Nirvana and built by Emperor Ashoka) and that at Pinara, Xanthos and many other places at Coastal Turkey (near Antakaya or later Antiochus) (see Templates 4.6, 4.7 and 4.8). Additionally are the striking similarities of the reclining or meditative pose of Buddha holding a lotus in his hand (found amongst Ajanta paintings and many other places in India) and those found in the rock-cut sculptures sarcophagi at Letoon, Turkey (refer Template 4.8). Finally, there are evidences of numerous Buddhist stupa-like structure built all over coastal Anatolia and Etruscan Italy in the Villanovan era (National Geographic, June, 1968) (refer Template 4.4 and particularly, Template 4.5). These are a part of the greater Urn-field Complex found in ancient Europe, particularly the lower Eastern Mediterranean Europe. The Urnfield culture (c. 1300 BC to 750 BC) was a late Bronze-Age culture of central Europe. The name comes from the custom of cremating the dead and placing their ashes in urns which were then buried in fields. The Urnfield culture followed the Tumulus or 'Stupa like built form culture' and was finally succeeded by the Hallstatt culture. They are all part of the broader Dorian Bronze-Age culture in the Mediterranean world.

These direct archaeological evidences reinforce more and more the presence and the impact of the Buddhist–Therapeutic missionaries on the ancient Mediterranean world.

But it is now important to look at the last phase of our search.

4.3.4 Reorganizing the timeline of architecture

The predominant nature of Buddhism that was preached during the time of Ashoka was called 'Thera-vedas' meaning the 'preaching of the Elders' (Sthavira in Vedic Sanskrit or Thera in Sinhalese/Pali). The story of the Ashoka and his missionaries fit into the legacy of the legendary sects, the Therapeutes and the Essenes, existing or possibly preceding the beginnings of Christianity (Sen, 2003).

It was under the influence of the two sects, Egypt and Judea (parts of Anatolia, Jordan and present day Israel) were spotted with rock-cut monastic establishments, rock-cut basilicas and underground rock-cut catacombs. From these monastic and austere establishments, the early Christians were preaching silently as they were facing persecution by the Romans. But such silent conditions changed later when Roman diplomacy took over the mandate and formed the new Gospel and started using it as a state policy. Then the ancient linkages were probably broken. It will be a matter of great delight for any future researcher of Indian architectural history to look into the full details of these evidences.

The evidences are important for any true human being who would appreciate the great ideals that Ashoka stood for a few thousand years ago. They are cherished only recently by the humanitarian charter of the United Nations. The book entitled 'The Argumentative Indian' by Nobel Laureate and economist Amartya Sen has forwarded this argument in favor of an Indian cultural originality. It was Ashoka who had sent these earliest missionaries to the West.

The high ideals of a 'better way of life' that these missionaries preached were not properly understood by many in the Mediterranean world. But the Buddhist rock-cut marvels definitely shaped and nurtured the earliest Greco-Roman Basilicas and a distant 'echo-like message of the new Gospel' that was preached from these Temples of God.

4.3.5 The archaeology of the Phaistos Disc and other rock-cut architectural evidences: Evidence from Crete

The recent works of archaeologist Sir Arthur Evans are of paramount importance in this context. Particularly among them is a later discovery of a disc coming from Pre-Christian times. This disc comes from a location in Crete called Phaistos and hence the name 'The Phaistos Disc'. This disc provides evidences of the Dorian age. It has strange evidences of near similarities with symbols that had been used then in ancient Indian spirituality and particularly Buddhism (refer Templates 4.9, 4.10, and 4.11).

- The disc depicts a spiral meditative movement where a Greek soldier wearing a helmet is depicted spiraling to the center having a lotus spread. There in that center the soldier achieves his final conversion to be a monk (shown as having a tonsure).
- The journey shows others symbols that match the allegories of archery in Indian spirituality; the icon of divine footsteps (used by Ancient Buddhism symbolizing Buddha as an incarnation of Vishnu at Gaya, a place that was the headquarters of Buddhism and Shaivism and the steps of the Buddha in the temple of Gaya called the chanka-ramana).
- The symbol of a river-current (an allegory of the inner current and the inner fish known as the term srotapatti of Buddhism and associated Tantric lore of India), a symbol of Indian palanquin – Rahu-gana – the clan of Gautama of the Rig Vedas (first mandala) – the forerunners of Madhu Vidya (the wisdom of ambrosia or immortal honey of the Vedas).
- A definite plan of a rock-cut monastery, a rhythmic instrument called the sistrum used for mass-songs and hymns (like Bhajana of India practiced even today).

- Symbols of the archetype cosmic or the 'Bodhi-tree' that is found in the shape of a cross-like object like the Vajra.
- A forest-dove used in Theravada and found as an engraved symbol on the railings of temples built in India during Ashokan Buddhism as a symbol of good or Holy spirit; and many others.

(Refer National Geographic, February 1978)

4.3.6 Evidences of rock-cut monastic establishments in Anatolia

Additionally, rock-cut tombs and rock-cut caves used for monastic traditions (a style similarly used by Buddhist and other ascetic traditions of India) have been found all along the western and southern coastline of Turkey and northern Syria. These areas are also known as the ancient Damascus Line – where St. Paul was probably converted from a revolting man to a great man of faith.

The rock-cut tombs of Myra and Sura: that of Telmessos, Fethiye and Amyntyas, that of Letoon, Caunos and Cappadocia (referred in the Acts of the Apostles: 2.9) in Turkey and Lalibela in Ethiopia supply ample evidences of these unique earliest Christian traditions that were primarily monastic-hermetic and characteristically very close to original Buddhist establishments found in India (see Templates 4.12 and 4.13).

4.4 Part Three: Architectural Parallels – Ancient Buddhism and early Christianity

4.4.1 Buddhist Chaitya halls and the earliest basilicas of the Greco-Roman world

The final evidences may be drawn from comparing two figures – one, the plan of an early Buddhist Church and that of an early Greco-Roman Pagan Basilica – the forerunner of Christian Church. It can be assumed that the etymological root of the Greco-Roman 'Basilica' lies in the much older ancient Near Eastern traditions of the Hittite establishments in Anatolia – mainly the temple forms of 'Yasili-kaya' – akin to – Basilica!

In the early Syro-Hittite Temple, the following note may provide an insight:

"The Asian expedition of Alexander the Great marks the beginnings of the Hellenistic period in Asia Minor. Although at first it had little impact on Central Anatolia, in the first half of the 3rd century BC Celtic Galatian emigrants from central Europe settled here. The site of Tavium near the village Büyük Nefesköy some 20 km south of Boğazköy became the seat of the Trokmer clan, who took the land around Hattusha/Boğazköy under their control. Büyükkale once again became a fortified citadel, and a small village occupied part of what had been the Lower City. The painted pottery characteristic of the Galatians was recovered here, as well as vessels imported from the Hellenistic cities along the west coast.

...............The most noticeable is the apse of a church cut into the rock called Mihraplikaya (= rock with a prayer-niche)"

The Hittites, their forerunners and their followers
A brief history of Hattusha/Boğazköy over the millennia
http://www.hattuscha.de/English/cityhistory2.htm

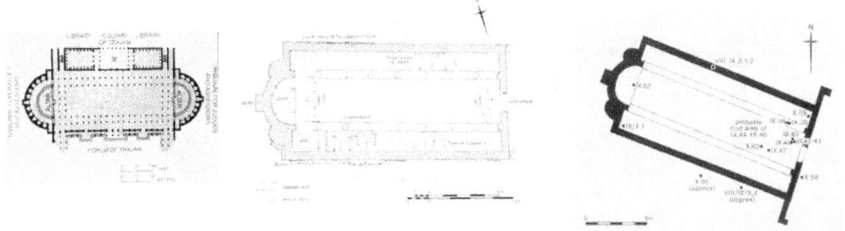

Figure 4.5 Intermediate forms of Roman Forum and Apsidal Mithraeum in Wallbrook

The origins of a Basilica, which is also a predominant Greco-Roman form, is grafted from an ancient shape grammar of the site of a Mithraeum, which may also be identified by its singular entrance or vestibule, which stands opposite from an apse-shaped wall in which a pedestal altar at the back stood, often in a recess. The name Mithras, in whose name is the ancient form of a Mithraeum, is a form of Mithra, the name of an Indo-Iranian god, a deity whose names are related Indo-European languages. The content includes Mitra, found in Rig Vedic hymns in Sanskrit, «mitra», which means «friend» or «friendship» and a more contemporary 'Maitreya' in Buddhism, which is analogous to the Vedic word 'Viswamitra' or 'Friend or Saviour of the Universe', an idea that is intertwined with 'Bodhisattva' in Buddhism and 'Christ' in Christianity.

According to historian John R. Hinnells: 'The god is unique in being worshipped in four distinct religions: in Hinduism as Mitra; in Iranian Zoroastrianism and Manicheism, as Mithra; and in the Roman Empire, as Mithras. In the inscribed peace treaty of 1400 BCE between Hittites and the Hurrian kingdom of the Mitanni in the area southeast of Lake Van in Asia Minor, the form *mi-it-ra-* appears as the name of a god invoked together with four other divinities as witnesses and keepers of the pact, an earliest evidence of Mithras in Asia Minor. M.J. Vermaseren in his book 'The Excavations in the Mithraeum of the Church of Santa Pricsa in Rome' (2011) says that:

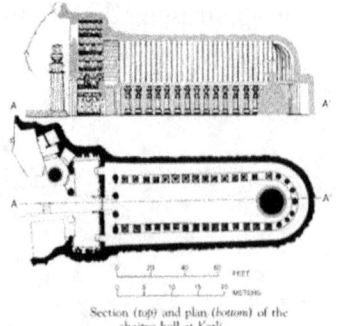

Section (top) and plan (bottom) of the chaitya hall at Karli.

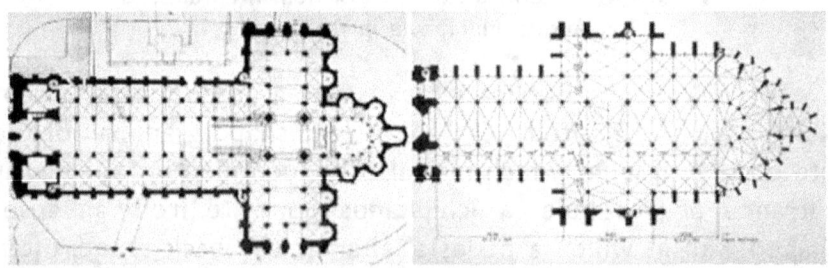

Figure 4.6 Similar Apsidal forms, Naves and Aisles of Buddhist and Christian Churches

The ground-plan ... shows clearly that the presbytery of the Church lies over the ante-Room V of the Mithraeum and that the apse covers the first part of the main hall W, including the niches of Cautes and Cautopates. One cannot fail to see the symbolism of this arrangement, which expresses in concrete terms that Christ keeps Mithras "under". The same also applies at S. Clemente Church, which is an older form of Basilica or a Mithraeum."

The variety and spread of an Indo-Iranian deity 'Mithra' in ancient Europe is a matter of great enigma. Scholars like Franciz Cumont have traced more than 150 archaeological finds, including meeting places, monuments, and artifacts; throughout the Roman Empire, centuries before Christianity had begun. The Apse (bulbous and semi-circular) end of the Mithraeum is a matter of a shape grammar investigation. The idea of circum-ambulatory and the turning around is a pattern that recurs in the ancient religious spaces of India including the Buddhist Chaitya halls and some later temple tradition of India that grew out of it (see Figures 4.5 and 4.6; and Templates 4.14, 4.15 and 4.16).

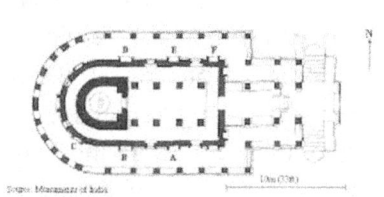 

Figure 4.7 Similar Apsidal forms continued in later Temple traditions in India at Aihole

Six important observations can be safely drawn with regard to the striking similarity of the temple traditions – one practiced in North Indian Buddhism (Taxila, Gandhara, Kashmir and Tibet) and other in Europe, in the earliest Christian cult of the Agnes Dei. With an initial description, they are listed below. The first is with regard to the Blessed Sacrament and the practice of holy ablution (baptism). The second is based on the logic of mass structures and the evidence of pictures (wall paintings that are common to both early Buddhist and Christian Temples) showing Monasticism in orange robes and tonsure. The third point is the presentation of the elements of design. The fourth and the fifth points are on the two systems of Mandala – symmetrical and asymmetrical particularly based the Cross, the Greek Version of the Asian Vajra and the later argument of the half-mandala leading to the predominance of the spiritual over the material as signified by the Latin cross and also the striking overlaps of the cross-plan, the nave, the aisle, the circular ambulatory path and the apsidal (semi-circular end), where stood the inverted Cup (the Stupa and/ the Cross with the cult of *Agnes Dei*). The last point is the most significant one emphasizing the deeper ecology of the architecture of the mansions of God and human and the symbiotic relationship between the two:

1. *The commonality of rituals:* First the Blessed Sacrament appeared to have strong connections with Vedic prasadam. Agni and Soma were the chosen Lambs of universal sacrifice and the Holy Spirit of divine intoxication – thus linking it to intermediate astral symmetry of the Sun and the Moon of Mithraism of Persia and Europe.

2. *The revival of mass structures for collective worship and Institutional Monasticism:* The priestly tonsure (shaved head) reminded him of the shaven head of the Indian monastic tradition. Buddhism inherited this and Prophet Adi Sankaracharya in India revived it later. It is a reminder of someone who is just not withdrawing from the world but of someone taking a detached viewpoint from his previous ego-centric viewpoint of the world. This led to ideal of 'Bodhisattva' in Buddhism and 'universal Catholicism' in Christianity where the spirit of one's own salvation is for the resurrection of the whole world. The picture of Emperor Justinian receiving 'the Law' from two shaven monks is a reminder of such early eastern traditions in Christianity, much of which came from via Egyptian Seraphic Thebes or Alexandrian Monasticism of the Therapeutes.

3. *The play of Light and Forms:* The nature of paintings, lights, the incense and the allied ritual music and the sign of the

cross referring to different parts of the body constituted another analogy to Asiatic and particularly Indian traditions. The reversibility of light and shades of light – the grey scales are the very foundations of Indian spiritual traditions and the journey between the two is expressed through the edifices that represent such traditions (see Templates 4.15 and 4.16).

4. *The architectural framework and symbolism (The Eastern group of Churches – the symmetric Greek cross or Vajra):* Studying the earliest of European Cathedrals, one can easily notice similarities in content, arrangement of chairs and nature of collective worship. Particular similarities were observed in forms of apsidal (semi-circular) ends and circuits of worships (aisles and naves) seen in the earliest Buddhist rock-cut caves in India (200 BCE or earlier) and those in later Greco-Roman Basilicas following Greek Cruciform Vajra-shaped Cross-plan. This is perfectly symmetrical and following a pure circle or Mandala. As a common noun, KIRK is the Celtic or Scottish English word for 'church', attested as a noun from the 14th century onwards, but as an element in place names much earlier. Both words, KIRK and church, derive from the Koine Greek κυριακόν (δωμα) (kyriakon – meaning the circle or dōma – meaning Lord›s house), which was borrowed into the Germanic languages in late antiquity, possibly in the course of the Gothic missions. Whereas church displays Old English palatalisation, KIRK is likely to be a loanword from Old Norse and thus has the original mainland Germanic consonants. Compare cognates: Icelandic & Faroese Kirkja; Swedish Kyrka; Norwegian & Danish Kirke; German Kirche; Dutch Kerk; West Frisian tsjerke; and borrowed into non-Germanic languages: Estonian Kirik and Finnish Kirkko. The English word 'church' developed from Old English Cirice, from West Germanic Kirika, from Greek Kyriake is 'Lord›s house', from kyrios 'ruler, lord of quarters.' The basic derivations of the word are related to the sect of ancient Alexandrian healers – the Therapeutes through connections like:

- Circle (Late Vedic or Buddhist Charka or Charkee or Circa – an important symbol showing the wheel of Indian loom and weaving in Gandhi's philosophy and approach to traditional Indian industries = Greek. *Kyriakon* (West Asian Gypsy word Circassion = Cherkes).
- Vedic *Dharmma* = Late Vedic or Buddhist *Dhamma* = basis of Buddhist *Dhamma-nikaya* = Christian *Dominican* = with the word Doma (Greek) as an intermediary (Alexandrian connection).

5. *The architectural framework and symbolism (The Western group of Churches – the asymmetric Latin Cross or Apsidal Mandala):* Most Western European churches say the Gothic churches, also, unless they are entitled chapels, are of the Latin Cross plan, with a long nave making the body of the church, a transverse arm called the transept and beyond it, an extension which may be called the choir, chancel or presbytery. There are several regional variations on this plan. Here, there is one-way asymmetry, leading to evolution of one-way apse or apsidal ends.

6. *The system's deep ecological approach and design significance:* Both Buddhist and Christian churches are reformation of the later ancient world religious traditions – one following a later ossified Brahminical phase of the Puranic Age in India and the other a similar response to later Judaism under the ossified priestly Rabbinical tradition. Accessibility to greater domain of people and nature and systems was revived in both – thus bringing the universal catholic idea of an Assembly of God – unifying the 'Temple of God and ordinary man' as one. This was the original Deep Ecological or a system's approach of the Vedic times, when more ancient forest-laid or semi-monastic Vedic style of mass worship and mass initiates were drawn in for a Catholic approach to the contemplation of human–nature dynamics culminating in the realization of the Absolute 'Brahman'. Hinduism is only a later mainstream derivative of this original Vedic religious idealism. The history of Gautama Buddha is a response to that derivation and deviation in later times. So are the

various phases of Christianity followed by ones reforming and counter-reforming the preceding? And this process is a continuous one in the history of humankind. Mass monasticism or worship can be traced in the interim history like followers of Orpheus (the non-Olympian religious beliefs that emphasized the doctrine of transmigration of souls and principles of karmic reincarnation like Indian religions). Orphism was practiced in the ancient Cyclades and Anatolia and found its way into later European thought through the earliest Milesian sages of Greece and subsequently Pythagoras, Plato, Plotinus and Spinoza.

4.5 Part Four: The legend of Therapeutes – Who were they?

– 'Physicians, heal thyself' (Therapeutic purgation, Catharsis and Lutheran ideals)

4.5.1 Universal resurrection through the Cross and the ideal of Bodhisattva

The legacies of the greatest of saints have treaded the greater book of human history. The ideal of 'that one truth is but a hierarchy minds and the possibilities of both evolution and involution containing all the levels' is in essence the ideal of 'One Body and Many Parts' and it is also the foundation of the Bodhisattva. In ancient Nath Yoga, it is called the perfect reciprocity of the individual (microcosm or pinda) and collective (macrocosm or Brahmanada) body of the spiritual aspirant. In the Vedas it is described as the balance between the path of going in (Antardhana) and the path of going out (Habirdhana) (RV: 10.1–17). The principle of reciprocity has been discussed in Chapter 13, 'Gorakshanath and the Kanphatta Yogis' by George Western Briggs (1989). This gospel of 'One Body and Many Parts' has been the foundation of another great world religion – Christianity. In the words of St. Paul:

"....Now you are the body of Christ and each one of you is a part of it" (Corinthians 1: 12.27)

And in the words of St. John:

"...Don't you believe that I am in the father and that the father is in me" (John: 14.10)

The greatest oneness is the unity of the many and one. But over time the ideas shifted, and there were unfortunate departures and disarrays. The realization of Christ, as realized originally by St. Paul and by St. John, had changed hands and gone far away. The concept of original divinity of humanity was founded on the greatest gospel of 'One Body and Many Parts' (one *Bodhi* (body of the Christ or the *Buddha*) and many Buddhas) was replaced by a principle of weakness and disjointedness. It incited a movement that suppressed the spirit of completeness and replaced it with partiality. This weakness is the concept of Original Sin – a growing problem of later Semitic religious movements and particularly historic Christianity. In Buddhism the idea of latent divinity in all, the idea of the *Chaitya Purusha*, was also suppressed, and the whole religion degraded to one of nihilism and agnosticism.

4.5.2 Problem of Original Sin: A global perspective

The concept of *abhava* (the shortcoming of partiality) takes man to an incomplete truth and makes realization one-legged. Original sin is probably one of the greatest shortcomings in the history of religion. It is probably the greatest of all shortcomings. The concept takes away the linkage and even the hopes of that linkage to a natural religious growth of the human mind. It de-links the individual (microcosm) and the universal plan (macrocosm). Instead it offers damnation, a gloom of doomsday, a distant apocalypse and a state of despair. This departure has been characterized by the entire history of all world religions. In ancient India such departures took place characterizing the closing of the Vedic ages. Such dark times had recurred again and again in India. They are evident in the opening verses of the forth chapter of the Hindu scripture called the Gita (the Divine words that are sung) (Gita 4: 1–4).

In these verses we find Krishna, the mentor and the chariot-driver of warrior Arjuna reminding him of a lost age, a lost tradition, a glorious tradition of the lineage of the *Rajarishis* (the Sage-kings).

Krishna recovers this great lineage and forwards the synthesis of Knowledge and action based on devotion (Bhakti). That becomes 'the Gita'.

Later such times recur during the Buddha and even more after him. Tendencies in later Buddhism failed to keep up with the early universal ideal of a *Bodhisattva*. Instead came in the new meaning of the word *Maya*. The concept of *Maya* changed hands, changed meanings and the world viewpoint of quality *(Guna)*, emotion *(Bhava)* and beauty *(Shri)* was reduced to zero *(Sunya)*. Spirituality was de-linked from the material living styles. Asceticism became an abstruse goal for many and materialism devoid of value and morality slowly turned to hedonism.

The new concept of *Maya* de-linked the two. Much of Hinduism following the days of Acharya Shankara is derivative of a disjointed Mayavada. A dualistic viewpoint an absolute *Nirguna* Brahman (without any qualities and lacking any creative surges) was separated from all life (or *prana*) in this universe and all life was seen as illusionary and therefore zero. This is akin to the dualistic concept of a good God and an evil Satan in Semitic religions. We had discussed this earlier at the beginning of Chapter 2.

Similar departures are seen in China after the great days of Confucius. Later Chinese ways of life turned more to materialism and lost the completeness of a universal Taoist viewpoint. Later Pehlevis transformed Zoroastrianism thus moving away from the original preaching of the Prophet.

Thus 'Original Sin' became a universal phenomenon and a determinant. It was applied to re-interpret the Old Testament allegories of Lilith – the sacred primordial feminine seen prior to Eve; a further role of Eve reviewed then as an agent of the fall and the cause of the original sin; and the role of women seen as problematic and sinful agents of creation in general society. Thus religion appeared to create and serve a one-legged society – an age of the orthodox 'male chauvinist'! The idea and the expression are evident in the following words:

"That morning the river was broad and shallow and clear, and two of us walked with the Swami across the fields and along the banks about three miles. He began by talking of the sense of sin, how it was Egyptian, Semitic and Aryan. It appears in the Vedas, but quickly passes out. The devil is recognized there as the Lord of Anger. Then, with the Buddhists he became Mara, the Lord of Lust, and one of the most loved of the Lord Buddha's titles was "Conqueror of Mara" (Vide the Sanskrit lexicon Amarkosha that Swami learnt to patter as a child of four!). But while Satan is the Hamlet of the Bible, in the Hindu scriptures the Lord of Anger never divides creation. He always represents defilement, never duality.

Zoroaster was a reformer of some old religion. Even Ormuzd and Ahriman with him were not supreme; they were only manifestations of the Supreme. That older religion must have been Vedantic. So the Egyptians and Semites cling to the theory of sin while the Aryans, as Indians and Greeks, quickly lose it. In India righteousness and sin become Vidyâ and Avidyâ — both to be transcended. Amongst the Aryans, Persians and Europeans become Semitized by religious ideas; hence the sense of sin.

And then the talk drifted...."

WALKS AND TALKS BESIDE THE JHELUM
Complete Works of Swami Vivekananda

Creation was seen as a fall and a de-linking of the microcosm from the vast — macrocosm and its underlying divinity. Humanity was then seen as a fallen existence. The continuity between the highest and lowest was lost. This cause was 'Original sin'. The problem of Original sin has been equally damaging in almost all world religions. For one of them, the damage possibly has been so far the greatest. This is the case of historic Christianity. They are evident in the historic words of St. Paul.

4.5.3 Evidences from the Epistles of St. Paul

Events around the ancient place of Galilee dates back to a remote time — almost two thousand years back. At that time serious gaps and deviations were already emerging between the original preaching of a small group of realized souls and other groups, which were growing larger — politically and diplomatically. Evidences of departures come from the original Pauline Epistles. These Epistles are probably the only direct historic records of the times then. A majority of these evidences are from a letter that St. Paul addressed to the local men of Galilee – called the 'Galatians'. Historical researches have shown that the Galatians (or local people of Galilee) are also same as the Gaul of Europe (seen in France, Iberia and Ireland). It is now believed that the historicity of the Christ is rooted to this Indo-European chain. This we shall discuss more in the following chapter. Paul mentions a deeper commitment to the great apostolic mission and points out an emerging problem. This was a growing tendency of other powerful groups damaging the earliest preaching of the Christ and that of the original groups that were rooted in those preaching (of which he was definitely one):

'I am astonished that you are so quickly deserting the one who called you by the grace of Christ and are turning to a different gospel – which is really no gospel at all (1.6)...I want you to know that the gospel I preached is not something that man made up. I did not receive it from any man, nor was I taught it; rather I received it by revelation from Christ (1.11).....

....Yet not even Titus, who was with me, was compelled to be circumcised, even though he was a Greek. This matter arose, because some false brothers had infiltrated our ranks to spy on the freedom we have in Christ Jesus and to make us slaves (2.3-4)....

..........when Peter came to Antioch, I opposed him to his face, because he was in the wrong. Before certain men came from James, he used to eat with the Gentiles. But when they arrived, he began to draw back and separate himself from the gentiles because he was afraid of those who belonged to the circumcision group. The other Jews joined him in his hypocrisy, so that by their hypocrisy even Barnabas was led astray.

When I saw that they were not acting in line with the truth of the Gospel, I said to Peter in front of them all: 'You are a Jew, yet you live like a gentile and not like a Jew. How is it, then, that you force Gentiles to follow Jewish customs?

We who are Jews by birth and not Gentile sinners know that a man is not justified by observing the law, but by faith in Christ.... (2.11-15)...

...If, while we seek to be justified in Christ, it becomes evident that we ourselves are sinners, does that mean Christ promotes sin? Absolutely not!

If I rebuild what I destroyed, I prove that I am a lawbreaker. For through the law I died to the law so that I might live for God. I have been crucified with Christ and I no longer live, but Christ lives in me. The life I live in the body, I live by faith in the Son of God, who loved me and gave himself for me. I do not set aside the grace of God, for if righteousness could be gained through law, Christ died for nothing! (2.17-21)....

.... What I am saying is that as long as the heir is a child, he is no different from a slave, although he owns the whole estate. He is subject to guardians and trustees until the time set by his father. So also, when we are children, we were enslaved by the basic principles of the world. But when the time had fully come, God sent his son, born of a woman, born under law, to redeem those under law, that we might receive the full rights of son. Because you are sons, God sent the spirit of his son into our hearts, the Spirit who calls out, 'ABBA' - Father (4.1-7)...

....And by him we cry, 'ABBA' - father. The Spirit himself testifies with our spirit that we are God's Children. Now if we are children, then we are heirs – heirs of God and co-heirs with Christ, if indeed we share in his sufferings in order that we may all also share in his glory (Romans: 8.15-17).....

Formerly, when you did not know God, you were slaves...but now that you know God – or rather are known by God – how is it that you are turning back to those weak and miserable principles?

(Galatians: 4.8-9).

- Two issues are evident here:
- One, needless to say, there were gaps emerging between the preaching of an original divinity (Ephesians 4:17–32) and the new tendencies. This is evident from the Pauline Epistles.
- Two, it is further evident that some other groups, growing large in number and power had other interests for what they were doing.

The questions then are:
- What could have been the real story behind these new tendencies?
- Who were these later groups?
- And what could have been the nature of the earliest groups?

Perhaps in the New Testament we still find the answers.

4.5.4 Evidences of a 'Group' in St. Paul's letter to Timothy

The hints are everywhere in the Pauline epistles. But a significant and convincing one comes from a letter that he addressed to Timothy. Here Paul speaks of an early prophetic group, which is known for their direct spiritual authority. And this authority as he highlights is not by law or institutional power but by faith and the power of realization. In the New Testament they are known by a special name. They are called *the body of Elders*.

The Concept of Eldership (Alderman) is a position of seniority. It signifies a higher point in realization as compared to a lower one. Thus Eldership is not defined in terms of ordinary power. The earliest traditions of Elders are seen as a prophetic group carrying that inner spiritual touch to impart the spirit of the faith that would eventually lay the foundations of Christianity. Earliest Christianity still found in desert and monastic Egypt, Iberia (lower France and upper Spain), Ireland and Celtic Scotland, and particularly in the desert plains of Cappadocia (Central Anatolia) and also perhaps in Southern India is still based on this ancient tradition of Elders. Later United Reform Movements of Calvinism and the Presbyterian Church movements are still broadly founded on this ancient system of Eldership.

The body of Elders finds a very special mention in this letter:

'...Until I come, devote yourself to the public reading of scripture, to preaching and to teaching. Do not neglect your gift, which was given you through a prophetic message when the body of Elders laid their hands on you' (Timothy: 4.13–14).

In the Old Testament, there is special mention about such a tradition where Moses appoints a body of elders as intermediaries between himself and the ordinary common man (Numbers 11.16). They are also mentioned to have existed in the early Old Testament times as governing bodies of tribes and this was prior to the monarchical times of Judea. In the Vedas there is a similar idea known by the word *'Sthavira'*.

The question is who are these elders? Where do they come from? Why do they posit a prophetic approach as against later trends?

4.5.5 The dream and events at Galilee: Clues from ancient Mediterranean

The experience of Saints and Yogis are not within the purview of subjective experiences. If the world of realization is true, then dream of a realized soul is not a common human dream and the explanations based on such a dream are also beyond the questionable subconscious domains of a layman's explanation.

The topic that we are about to discuss is based on the dream and explanation of a fully realized soul who had a spirit of no compromise with anything but truth. Swami Vivekananda was a personality of this stature. When it had come to the slightest variations – be it religion or philosophy or science, in India or in other lands – he had no hesitation to point out the fallacies or shortcomings. With the crystal clarity of the powers of mind founded and guided by the original light of truth-realization, he had spoken and pointed out, both as large and as small, the goodness and the gaps in any stream of thought and dissemination.

One of such pointers was that of the origins of Christianity. On that there have been many debates and conflicting researches starting with the first group of people in Galilee of those days accepting Jesus of Nazareth as their personal savior. His pointers were not the questioning of the origins. That he said will be the hypothesis of later secular scholarship. They were to review and explore in depth a historic spectacle of the meeting of Indian and Egyptian elements in places and areas that were close to the geographical origins of Christianity. In a nutshell the Swami had pointed out the meeting ground at the opening of the Nile

– abutting the ancient port city of Alexandria. Alexandria was the famous maritime port in the northern coastlines of Egypt, where ancient mariners converged and co-existed from different corners of the world namely Phoenicia, Iberia, Anatolia, Arabia, Persia, India and of course from all the Mediterranean Islands. Near to Alexandria, in the eastern Mediterranean, he talked about a few places. Primary among them were the Islands of Crete and others in the Cyclades near Turkey.

Swami Vivekananda's experiences centered Crete and Turkey, though his pointer was on Alexandria and the islands between them. There was perhaps a specific pointer to that region – the Cyclades – the many dotted islands laded sea region between coastal Turkey and Eastern Crete.

4.5.6 The vision of historic reformulation

The description is as follows in the words of Sister Nivedita who heard it directly from the Swami:

'...it was night, and the ship on which he (Swamiji) embarked at Naples, was still on her way to Port Said, when he had this dream. An old and bearded man appeared before him, saying 'Observe well this place that I show you. You are now in the island of Crete. This is the land which Christianity began'. In support of this origin of Christianity, the speaker gave two words – one of which was Therapeute and showed both to be derived direct from Sanskrit roots. The Swami frequently spoke of this dream in after years, and always gave the two etymologies; but the other seems nevertheless, to be lost beyond recovery'.

What is very important here is the reference to Swamiji's frequent mention of a subjective experience of his which is in contrast to his otherwise external objective, analytical and scientific personality. This possibly proves the importance of the dream he had in the ship sailing the Mediterranean. The other important fact is that of the two words he mentioned. One is Therapeutes. The other is lost. But in the words of Nivedita:

'...It is my own belief that the second word was Essene. But alas, I cannot remember the Sanskritic derivation!'

Of Therapeutes, the meaning she recollects is sons of Theras – which means an Elder amongst the Buddhist monks, and putra, the Sanskrit word for son. The original word is Sthavira i.e. the older or 'Elder' (one who is advanced in spiritual enlightenment). There is an unexplained tradition of elders in the Presbyterian (Scotland) hierarchy and also in the original body of elders mentioned in Pauline letters and epistles. Theravada is the Doctrine of Elders mostly found in Southeast Asia and often believed to have been preached by the emissaries of Emperor Ashoka.

4.5.7 The archaeological implications of the dream

There is an additional part of Swami Vivekananda's vision. Nivedita adds:

'...the proofs are all here (in Crete), added the old man, pointing to the ground. 'Dig !.... and you will find!'.......The Swami woke, feeling that he had had no common dream and tumbled out on deck, to take the air. As he did so, he met a ship's officer, turning in from his watch. 'What is the Time?' he asked him.

'Midnight', was the answer.

'And where are we?' (The answer was): 'Just fifty miles off Crete!'

Nivedita further adds:

'.....This unexpected coincidence startled the Swami, lending inevitable emphasis to the dream itself.....he confessed afterwards that up to this time it had never occurred to him to doubt the historic personality of Christ, and after this, he could never rely upon it'..

The pointers of old bearded man in the dream thus led to significant archaeological implications of the island of Crete. In addition to the descriptions left with Sister Nivedita, we get another one from a man named Surendranath Sen. The account left by Surendranath is equally important because it re-clarifies the spatial pointers.

4.5.8 Descriptions by Surendranath Sen: Pointers to Cyclades

This is from the private diary of Sri Sen. He meets the Swami on January 22, 23, and the 24th of 1898. On the second day he meets the Swami for the whole day – in the morning and in the afternoon. In the afternoon, in the later half (after 4.00 PM), the larger gathering and the general conversation was coming to a close. There were only a very few left including the note-taker. In the course of conversation the Swami had said:

Figure 4.8 Tumulus 'Urn-field' mounds (like Stupas) in Hierapolis, Turkey (upper row) And in Cerveteri, Italy

'I had a curious dream on my return voyage from England. While our ship was passing through the Mediterranean Sea, in my sleep, a very old and venerable looking person, Rishi-like in appearance, stood behind me and said – 'Do ye come and effect our restoration. I am one of those ancient orders of Theraputtas (Therapeutes), which had its origin in the teachings of Indian Rishis. The truths and ideals preached by us have been given out by Christians as taught by Jesus; but for the matter of that, there was no such personality by the name of Jesus was born. Various evidences testifying to this fact will be brought to light by excavating here'. 'By excavating which place can those proofs and relics you speak of be found?' I asked. The hoary-headed one, pointing to a locality in the vicinity of Turkey, said: 'See here.' Immediately after, I woke up, and at once rushed to the upper deck and asked the Captain, 'what neighborhood is the ship in just now?' 'Look yonder', the Captain replied, 'there is Turkey and the island of Crete'.

A slightly enlarged picture emerges that includes a greater spread from the eastern end of the island of Crete and the western shores of Turkey (Anatolia or mainland Asia) (refer Templates 4.18, 4.19, and 4.20).

The necropolis in Hierapolis, near Thera in Turkey, extends from the Northern to the Eastern and Southern sections of the old city. Most of the tombs have been excavated. This necropolis ("city of the dead") consists of about 1200 tombs were constructed with local varieties of limestone. The extent of this necropolis attest again to the importance Hierapolis had in the Antiquity (see Template 4.21 and Figure 4.8).

Figure 4.9 Tumulus 'Urn-field' mounds or Stupas in Kushinagar, India

The ancient city of Thera has been localised in the recent researches at the rocky hill called as Okkataş or Taşyenice between Ula and Yerkesik in Muğla. The history of the site starts in the 4th century BC according to the evidence but the early settlement form. The eastern and western sides of the settlement used as necropolis. The rock-cut chamber tombs in eastern necropolis and monumental tomb complex in western necropolis are the remarkable ones of the burial structures. Such Tumulus (Urn-field or 'Kurgan') found amongst the entire coastal stretch of south-western Turkey (seat of later Eastern Roman Church) and Cerveteri, Italy (seat of later

Western Roman Church) bears strong resemblance with similar 'Urn-field' complexes called *'Stupas'* (Cup or chalice like structures) in India, like the ones of Kushinagar in India, where the immortal ashes of the Buddha were stored in urns/caskets and put inside the mound or stupa (a term which is derived from Hiranyastupa of the Vedas).

4.5.9 The other pointers of Swami Vivekananda

The Swami had a few other supporting observations. They can be listed as follows:

- The Swami felt at once that it was St. Paul alone of whom one could be sure in the Bible. Swamiji saw the meaning of the fact that the Acts of the Apostles was an older record than the gospels.
- The Swami then saw the origins of the teaching of Jesus with Judaic Rabbi Hillel, while the ancient sect of Nazarene contributed the name and the person or in the words of Nivedita: '……*the 'beautiful sayings of Jesus' might really have been uttered by Buddha and the tale told in the Gospels, opening thus only another vista for the seeing of Him'*. The important fact in here is the synonymy of Jesus with traditions of Prophet Isaiah or several of them by the same name (whose traditional sayings are mentioned as doxologies in the New Testament).
- The root of the word Jesus comes from 'Yeshua' or 'Isaiah' (which is later Semitic Joshua) of the proto-Judaic tradition. Now it is known that much of these traditions were in Aramaic that bear strong parallels with the North Indian Brahmi or Kharosthi script spoken at large in the pre-Christian and Greco-Bactrian times. Aramaic was a language commonly spoken in Western Asian region namely the belt near the Dead Sea and Judea. This was also the language commonly used during the times of Indian Emperor Ashoka. We know that Ashoka had send Buddhist missionaries that reached the Mediterranean more than two hundred years prior to the beginning of Christianity. The missionaries

carried with them the 'gospel of healing' to the eastern Mediterranean (see Template 4.22 and Figure 4.10).

Figure 4.10 Cults of 'Healing' (catharsis and emotive palliative care) in Smyrna Tablet, Anatolia

- Emotional expressions on Greek tombstones from the Hellenistic period (323–331 BC) help increase our understanding of social communication and cultural values. This is the conclusion of a doctoral thesis in Classical Archaeology and Ancient History from the University of Gothenburg has studied ancient grave reliefs from the Greek city-states Smyrna and Kyzikos in present Turkey. The reliefs display both figurative motifs and inscriptions. 'The tombstones served not only as a commemorative marker but also as "visual therapy" for the bereaved. For example, the dead could be portrayed as standing next to their grave markers. The choice of location reveals that the deceased are believed to exist happily in the underworld, while, at the same time, the tomb site was a place of interaction between the living and the dead.' The tomb as evident in

Anatolia portrayed both:

(a) A practice of incineration (cremation) as ash kept in urns and finally entombed (Tumulus/ Stupa/ Kurgan)

(b) An idea of transmigration and afterlife both of which are evidences of oriental influences.

- Swami Vivekananda observed an important similarity between the original method of intoning Sanskrit and the Gregorian plainsong of the early Christian tradition. These musical cadences had much in common with those in ancient Anatolia (or later Byzantium in the regions of Lycia and Caria, where the earliest rock-cut monastic Christian traditions were found). Most of the Christian Carol traditions are founded in the seven historic (or symbolic) churches mentioned in St. John's Revelation. Much of these traditions have strong bearings with the iambic verses (syllable-based) of ancient Mediterranean tradition. Closest were the hymns of Bacchus (Dionysus-Sabazius or the Greek god of Wine or Holy Spirit). The idea was synonymous with Mithraism Mysteries. The hymn was called 'Thriambus' from which the meaning of ecstasy and victory coined the later Christian word 'Triumph' (sound of trumpets) or the notes of the Archangels. Revelation of the New Testament is a later derivative of this. The origins are considered pagan today. But secular scholarship knows that they were ancient Orphic beliefs that influenced a generation of important men from Pythagoras to Plotinus and his neo-Platonism that shaped later Christian Philosophy. Sir Bertrand Russell points out the fact that he and other scholars like John Burnet had gone ahead to state the striking similarity between these beliefs and those prevalent in India at about the same time. The ancient Orphism (the Doctrine of Erebus or Hell and transmigration of soul was close to Indian religions) founded community worship that was precursor to Churches, i.e. religious communities to which anybody, without distinction of race or sex, could be admitted by initiation. They are identical with the records on Therapeutic hymns (care for 1 Corinthian: 14.15–16) by Philo of Alexandria. Recent studies have shown that there is one-to-one similarity between the earliest Greek modes and the Indian Ragas:

Ancient Greek Modes (Hittites/ Proto-Milesian or Pythagoreans)		Indian Ragas
Ionian	=	Bilawal
Dorian	=	Kafi
Phrygian	=	Bhairavi
Lydian	=	Kalyan
Myxolydian	=	Khamaj
Aeolian	=	Asavari

- During the Swami's travel to Catholic Europe, he had been startled, like others before him, to find the identity of Christianity with Indian religions in a thousand points of familiar details.
  1. First the Blessed Sacrament appeared to have strong connections with Vedic prasadam.
  2. The priestly tonsure (shaved head) reminded him of the shaven head of the Indian monastic tradition. Buddhism inherited this and Shankaracharya in India revived it later. The Swami referred to the picture of Emperor Justinian receiving 'the Law' from two shaven monks. The Swami also referred to connections with Thebaid (Boetian Thebes of ancient Greco-Egyptian times where similar tonsure traditions were found in Alexandria observing the therapist rites of the followers of Seraphic (or Isis) cult).
  3. The lights, the incense and the allied ritual music and the sign of the cross referring to different parts of the body constituted another analogy to Asiatic and particularly Indian traditions.
  4. Finally, when the Swami (during his European tour) had entered some Cathedrals, he saw strange similarities in content, arrangement of chairs and nature of collective worship. Particular similarities were observed in forms of apsidal (semi-circular) ends and circuits of worships

(aisles and naves) seen in the earliest Buddhist rock-cut caves in India (200 BC or earlier) and those in later Graeco-Roman Basilicas. Such traditions of mass worship and mass initiates were also a central theme amongst the followers of Orpheus (non-Olympian religious beliefs that emphasized the doctrine of transmigration of souls and principles of karmic reincarnation like Indian religions). Orphism was practiced in the ancient Cyclades and Anatolia and found its way into later European thought through the earliest Milesian sages of Greece and subsequently Pythagoras, Plato, Plotinus and Spinoza.

It can be broadly said that the origins of Christianity has significant bearings with Asiatic religions particularly early Buddhism. Additionally there are the critical names of the two sects that had been mentioned in that dream. They are the Essenes and the Therapeutes on whom we shall focus now.

4.5.10 The sect of Essenes

In this century, a locality (QUMRAN), north-west of the Dead Sea caves had been discovered in 1947, and they were possibly homes of an ascetic community in the 2nd century BC. This ascetic community had some form of relationship with another historic sect called the Essenes, who existed in this area and the Nile Delta around a time around Christ.

The application of laws, simplicity of rituals, celibacy, water initiation and remnants of 500 books that survive till date (called the Dead Sea Scrolls) have some relevant bearings with the Christian gospels and also the Buddhist way of living. Prominent among these scroll writings is the repetitive mention of lineages of prophets (or messianic legacies) foretelling the coming of a 'teacher of righteousness' to make preparations for the Day of Judgment and the wonders (like those described in the later revelations of St. John).

In fact, the life of St. John and his earlier workings based on water sprinkling (Baptism) and rites of 'Ash Wednesday and Lent' (concerning the tonsured head of the penitent) have strong bearings with Asiatic ascetic religions, particularly the ascetic movements of India and specifically *Shaivism*.

4.5.11   The sect of Therapeutes

Scholars have discovered another sect in and around Alexandria having similar features that of the Essenes. They are the Therapeutes. In Part I, Section 8 of a book entitled 'The Messianic Legacy' (1989, A Dell book), the authors namely Michael Baigent, Richard Leigh and Henry Lincoln have mentioned about this ascetic sect of Alexandria and Egypt, whose attitudes and spiritual practices are near identical with the Essenes or Zadokites in the holy land and identical also with those of Jesus and his subsequent following.

The sect of Therapeutes had historic bearings with the missions of St. Paul and St. James, and they also have archaeological bearings with other ascetic sects found in Lower Egypt (Nile Delta) that were predominantly Gnostic. A Gnostic sect called the Nag Hammadi sect has been discovered in Egyptian caves with cave paintings, scrolls and parts of Christian gospels giving different versions of St. James in relation to the Messiah. Their publication has been entrusted to an international team of scholars.

On the whole, the rock-cut caves and the way of life of these sects had undoubtedly an Asiatic ascetic tradition primarily Buddhism. Also at the heart of early Christian Gnosticism in Nag Hammadi was another sect called the Naassenes (close to the Essenes), who took their name from the serpent (Hebrew Nahash). In the recent days, there has been a discovery of other non-synoptic or non-orthodox gospels like that of Judas, Philip, and Thomas and of Mary of Magdala. These gospels talk about other traditions (or say different versions) of Christianity right from the very first days. How is this possible given a definite historic Jesus? Or is it so there were others like him who became what he had also achieved – by being 'Christ-like'? It is to be noted that group of Naassenes with another in Asia is that of the Mandeans. They come from the Zagros hills of Iran and Iraq (the probable origins of Old Testament) claiming a descent from St. John and preaching a religion that was Gnostic and of the Indo-Iranian order.

The greatest mention of the Therapeutes comes from the work of Philo of Alexandria. In his work entitled 'De vita Contemplative', he refers explicitly to this historic sect existing from times that pre-date Christianity by a hundred year. They are further mentioned (probably the earliest works of the Orthodox Church) by Bishop Eusebius of Caesarea, as a group of early (or earliest) Christians. Following the years of Bishop Eusebius writings on early Christianity and the original role of the Therapeutes, the Council of Nicea (AD 325), guided by the interest of the powerful Roman Empire and other Alexandrian Popes suppressed the monastic prescriptions of Eusebius and other ancient church traditions (that of Arian and others). Instead the Nicene Council supplied the following:

- A re-definition emphasizing the absolute divinity of Christ (a schism) that had compounded further after the Council of Chalcedon, Turkey in AD 451 when the Monophysites (emphasizing an absoluteness or one nature of Trinity) of Egypt was victorious and they fully vetted against the original ideas of Asiatic Christianity of Syria, Anatolia, Persia (Assyria) propagated through the 'Nestorians' of Byzantium (emphasizing a divided idea of Trinity and also accepting son of the mortal man, who is elevated to a state of divinity through asceticism, purity and contemplation).
- Establishment of a 'personal savior myth' (restoration of images in churches) based on an absolute (fully other worldly) divinity and a contrasting opposite of a 'this-worldly' concept of original sin.
- Reorganization of gospels by carefully selecting parts or pieces from a chosen few that befitted the interests of the Roman emperors.

4.5.12 Etymological evidences

If the legacy of the Therapeute is true, then in all later Christian tradition the original impacts of this historic sect can be made evident. There are many but here are three of the most convincing ones. The evidences have strong etymological foundations, i.e. the logic carried by the root and the meaning of the word over time.

Each of these evidences is provided as a research question, and they are subjected to further investigation, inquiry:

1. In the famous book by I. Wilson entitled 'Jesus: The Evidence' (London, 1984), there is a unique reference to several records in Rabbinical literature quoting person(s) known by the name *Yeshua* Ben Panthera, (also found as 'Pantera' or 'Pandera' where t = d) whose life and story are near similar to that found on Jesus of the New Testament. These literatures (mainly in *Baraitha* and Tosefta) supplementary to the Hebrew *Mishnah* – based on later research works of American Rabbi Morris Goldenstein) – are from 200 AD (or even earlier), and they claim a legacy of Yeshua (Jesus) born of a lady known Miriam (or Mary) and a Roman soldier (or an archer) known as Panthera. Here is a story of a Semitic Yeshua connected to the word Thera. The symbolism of Archery (Herrigel, 1971) is common to Japanese Zen Buddhism; mainstream Buddhism; and an even of Upanishadic traditions namely the ancient Mundaka (2.2.3) Upanishad. The name of Mary on the other hand suggests her importance in the story. Is it then that the conception of Mary is an allegorical event and her secret marriage with a senior monk named Panthera provides us a different interpretation of the Biblical story?

2. The *'Thera'* tradition continued through other Christian traditions. The names of Saint Eleuthera (and the traditions of a later movement called the 'Eleutheri' (or a probable later *Lu-thera?*) – a Greek word meaning freedom from material bondage) are the first evidences. Other important evidences are found in matriarchal traditions through the names of Saint Kythera (or Catherine) and similar others like Saint Catherine of Bologna (AD 1413–1463); of Siena (AD 1347–1380); and of Genoa (AD 1147–1510). How a suffix of 'thera' did got intertwined with so many major names and histories of early and medieval Christianity?

3. In other traditions of the Gospel of Mary of Magdala, the lineage of the sacred Feminine is still an important component. They were made available through the historic sect of 'the

Catheri' (or Cathars), who suffered the biggest persecution in the history of the Church called the Spanish Inquisition. The root of the word 'healing' used for all Christian apostolic traditions and miracles come from the way of 'The Cathars', i.e. Catharsis. The original word is 'therapy' and that comes from the ancient word 'Therapeutes'.

4. The associations of the earliest Egyptian Therapeutes, the medieval Cathars, are associated with another heroic group whom the Church of Rome had once patronized for reasons unknown. They are the historic Knight Templars, who were the Guardians of a great Secret and eventually what they uphold had become unacceptable to the Orthodox Church. Their doctrine became that of a confirmed *'Advaitic Vedantists'* and their history ended through ridiculous Crusades that were finally set against their Knighthood (The East and the West, Swami Vivekananda (1994), page 99). Is there any connection with what the Templars had hold and the reasons behind the inquisition that led to the brutal extermination of thousands of Cathars, associated female worshippers (Catherines) and near similar people all over Europe and particularly in specific regions of ancient Gaul and Iberia (southern France and the Basque Region)?

5. A particular research concern here is that of the mythical story of a Basque Mother Goddess named *Mari* and her son. The two are intertwined with the ancient tales of death and resurrection, commonly available in all over the pre-Christian world. Is it against this myth of an ancient Sacred Feminine in the Iberian region, the medieval patriarchic agenda had launched the agenda of harsh persecution and discrimination?

6. Finally here is the third and last research clue. Etymologically, there can be a simple research on words that are closely related to 'Thera'. First is the term 'Eleuthera' which is 'Free' and that also means 'El-tera' or a higher position of a man significantly known as the 'altar' (high above or free from lower positions). The position is that of an Altar-man, who is higher morally and spiritually and hence free

from lower standpoints. He is also called the 'Alderman' in the Presbyterian Protestant traditions. The tradition of the 'Elders' as found in the New Testament is possibly a closer version to 'El-thera' or 'El-dera'. It is quite possible as we get evidences of such interchanges of t=d in words like 'Thorn' (in Old English) which in Old German is 'Dorn' meaning sharp leaf; or words like 'Thursday' (or Thunresdaeg) in Old English which is 'Donnerstag' in Old German. The more important consonant exchanges comes in the pairs of other ancient words like Greek 'Thyra' and English 'Door' (meaning an opening or a way); the Greek 'Thare' and the English 'Dare' meaning penetrating and positive aggressiveness; and the pair 'old' in old English and 'alt' in German meaning the same. What these connections suggest?

There can be a set of further deductive questions:

- One, Can we suggest that the Body of Elders is the historic Body of El-Theras?
- Two, is it then that another historic word representing a particular group of Greeks known for their relatively austere, Spartan and simplistic mode of life called the 'Dorian' (as against the more ornate Ionic or Corinthian modes) is actually the word 'Therian'?
- Three, if that is so, do we get a further connection between earliest church music styles which is actually based on the known simple Dorian (Do-Re / The-re) Mode and the historic hymns of the El-'Theras' (or Therapeutes) and their Seraphic traditions?

Incidentally, the Dorian Mode is real close to the Indian system of music based on direct and simple melody (which is monotones and monochords). It contrasts the Western system of variations and compounded harmony based on multiple chords. The essence of monotone-based octaves is used in the Indian spiritual music based on systems of Yoga and Tantra. In fact, a whole body of Syro-Hittite music is of the Indo-European order which has been pointed out before.

On the *'Theras'*, there are probably further evidences. Strangely and more convincingly, the current body of interconnected evidences is mainly archaeological-iconographic-epigraphic and etymological. That is what makes the whole body strong and almost undeniable. The evidences have opened up a wider and deeper approach of evaluating the evolution of settlement systems and architecture in the ancient eastern Mediterranean. The system's approach is established as a two phase venture, of which is the second one is established in the present chapter. The phase can be traced from the times of remote antiquity to times constituting what is marked as the 'Dorian migration' and an allied pattern of the 'urn field' culture based on the 'Kurgan' (funerary/ cremated urn containing tumulus) hypothesis.

4.6 Conclusions

A system's approach to Phase II has been earmarked. To best establish the dynamics of the system, a set of four evaluations have been conducted:

1. *Shape grammar and Iconography based:* An assessment of the origin and manifestation of the Basilica and the Abbey, which was gradually transformed to a more popularly known expression, the 'Church'. It is evident that the shape grammar of the 'Church' and its semiotic dimensions owe its origin to a major religious movement of the Orient – and particularly directly, of the Indo-Iranian order of the Vedic episteme. The name of that movement is called 'Mithras', which swept the ancient Near East in times of remote antiquity and became a characteristic feature of the Syro-Anatolian or Mittani-Hittite confederation of the Indo-European or specifically, the Indo-Aryan order. A specific feature of divine revelation called the 'Agnus Dei' or the 'Shepherd's Lamb' has been used as a key to unlock the mystery of the shape grammar. Its foundations lay in the Cosmogony of the Vedas and the movement of the sun, which is both astral-celestial and aspirational-psychic. In Vedas, the double intender of the sun, the solar white sun tide is called the 'Adityas', the seat of undifferentiated universal consciousness. 'Mithra' is one of the Aditya, one of the twelve movements, which is

circuitous and non-linear. Its spirit is that of a benefactor, an agent of universal resurrection after death and Passover at Aries or Easter equinox, of which the 'Lamb' is the symbol of an aspirant. A cross-religious and interconnected pool of constructs have been forwarded to best establish the inner dynamism and its material revelation, in form of a 'Chaitya Hall', or a 'basilica', or a 'Church', of which the half-circle of the apse, represents the upper crown, the turning after Passover or Easter. It is the Brahma-Chakra, the year sempiternal called 'sana' in the universal sense and 'samvatsara' in the temporal sense. In the words of Sri Aurobindo, describing the cyclic movement of the Cosmic wheel, holding in itself the Lord, the 'Isha' or 'Ishaiah', the Sana, the impersonal universal being, which you may call the 'Son of God', is the integration of one containing the many (being) and the many reaching that one (becoming). The dynamics of Vedic ontology is evident in his words:

"It is He that has gone abroad – That which is bright, bodiless, without scar of imperfection, without sinews, pure, unpierced by evil. The Seer, the Thinker, the One who becomes everywhere, the Self existent has ordered objects perfectly according to their nature from years sempiternal."

2. *Review of the missionaries of 'Dhamma' (or Domos) sent by Priyadarshi:* Ashoka missionaries to five Hellenic kings, whose name nearly match with the historic figures of Antiochus II Theos of Syria, Ptolemy (Tul(r)amaya) II of Egypt and Alexandria, Antigonus Gonatas of Macedonia, Magas of Cyrene (Libya) and Alexander II of Epirus that made a greater difference in the Eastern Mediterranean. The primary concentrations and dissipations of these missionaries are mostly lost in the plethora of many successive events and departures. Part II of this chapter has however tried best to forward a pool of evidence – epigraphic, archaeological, inscriptional, textual and finally, cultural-anthropological. How the 'Dhamma-nikaya' (the embodiment of Dhamma) of these missionaries gradually became the 'Dominicans' of a new order of Eastern Europe is a great question? Part II

has attempted to deal with it comprehensively and come close to conclusion that they are the same.

3. *Architectural parallels and details:* The similarities in approaches, texts, rituals, composition or hymns, symbols and semantics, and how all of that is one body of evidence are explicit both in ancient Buddhism and earliest Christianity. It is a matter of more explorative and in-situ research by field art-historians, anthropologists accompanied by architects–engineers with an archaeological orientation.

4. *Finally, it is the legend of the sect of 'Therapeutae':* Whom Philo of Alexandra around 10 AD, and even later, Bishop Eusebius of Caesarea around 3rd century AD, 4th-century Christian Epiphanius of Salamis, and 5th-century Christian writer Pseudo-Dionysius have identified as the 'first Christians'. A whole body of international scholars like Robert Linssen, Elmar R. Gruber and Holger Kersten, Zacharias P. Thundy has placed the sect as a significant transfer point of spiritual knowledge from ancient Buddhism to the earliest and formative Christian orders in the Eastern Mediterranean. To create an argumentative approach, the present chapter has dared to induct a premise, a vision, something more than a late night dream of an Indian Yogi of our own times, Swami Vivekananda. Scholastic researches have argued and debated much on the interpretation of this dream. The chapter however has tried to conclude in favour of the interpretation by drawing cues from a certain significant feature/aspect of the sect, which is the art and science of 'Therapeutics' meaning 'Catharsis', or 'healing or Therapy', various words which are believed to have originated from the name standing for the vision, mission and activities of the sect. The concluding part forwards a system of evidences based on the vital cue, that is a key to understand the purpose of any great Sainthood generally, and specifically, both the reforming religion, 'Buddhism' and 'Christianity'. 'The gospel of healing' stands for a deeper revelation of something which is both an original spiritual essence and mostly lost, and also of another thing, which is 'new' and

'socially' more all-embracing is the idea of imparting that to all, 'gentiles', the 'marginalized', and the 'deprived, who are the children of lesser God'. Both the Buddha and the Christ, at least as a living idea, are the epitome of that ideal!

Additionally, noted historians such as, Will Durant, Jerry H. Bentley and Elaine Pagels have suggested that there is a real possibility that Buddhism influenced the early development of Christianity. Early Church fathers like Saint Jerome (4th century CE) has mentioned the birth of the Buddha, who he says «was born from the side of a virgin;» it has been suggested that this virgin birth legend of Buddhism influenced Christianity; and even earlier, Church father Clement of Alexandria (died 215 AD) was also aware of Buddha, writing in his Stromata (Bk I, Ch XV). And these are a few of many proofs and evidences that are available and need to be more powerfully stitched. The present book has initiated a system's recovery of the deeper truth.

The present chapter streamlines what has been initiated by the previous chapter. It forwards the second system's approach to the evaluation of a successive order of Indian architecture in relationship to the world. And there it can be well said, as a second and successive premise that, *'After the invasion of Alexander the great, these two great waterfalls (Indian and Greek principles) colliding with each other, deluged nearly half of the globe with spiritual tides, such as Christianity.'*

System framework two: Phase II of global history of architecture

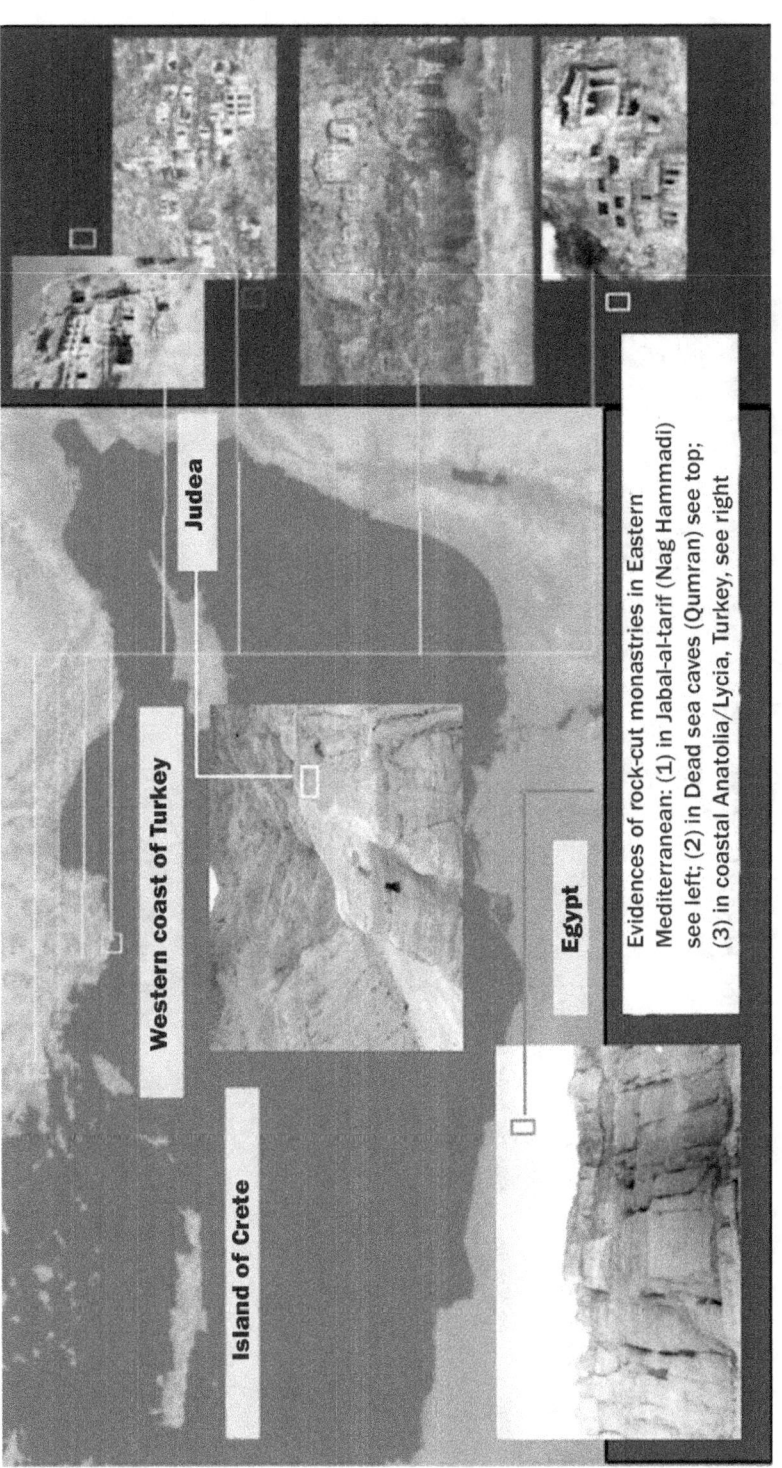

Template 4.1 Rock-cut monasteries in the Asia Minor and Egypt

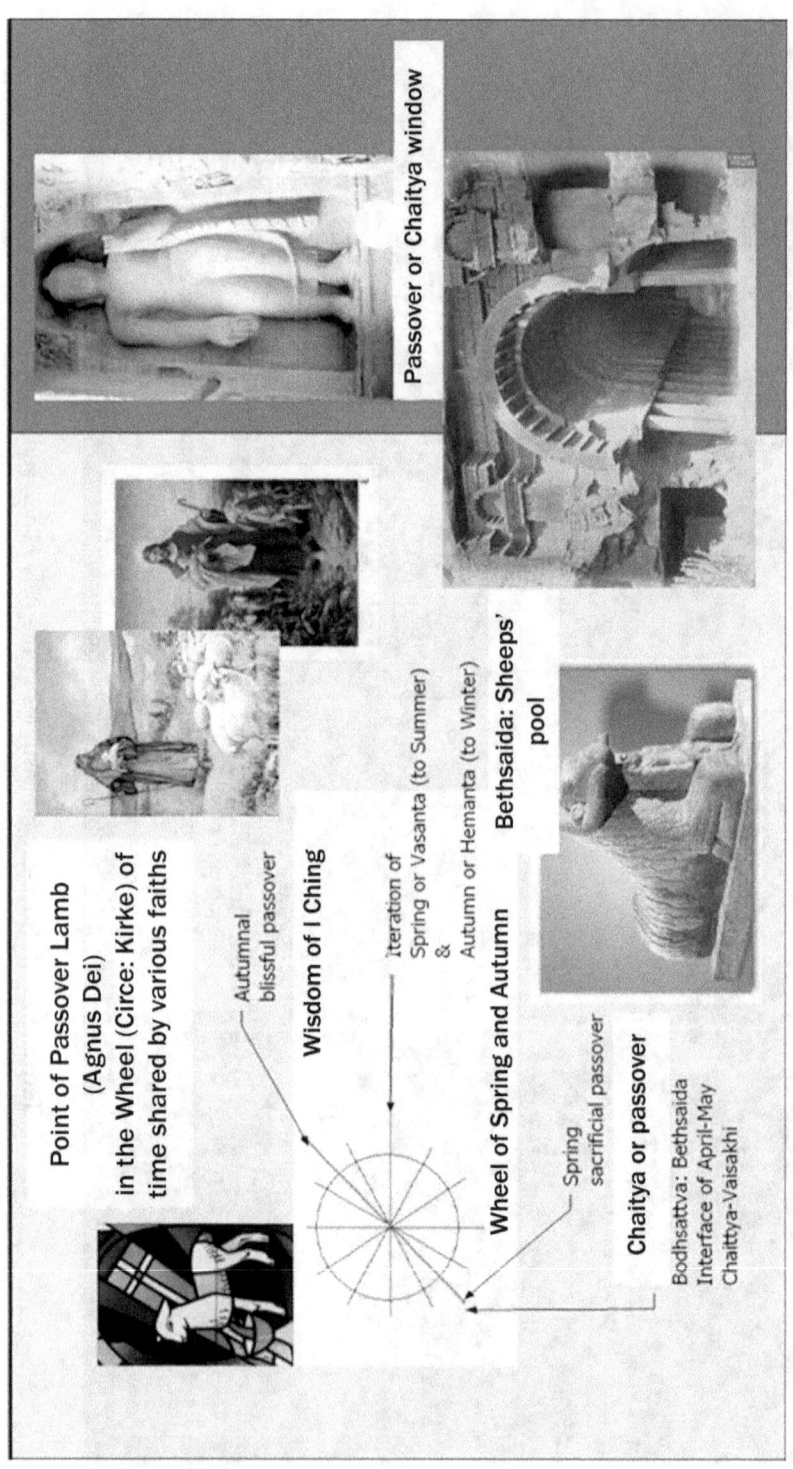

Template 4.2 The imagery of the Agnus Dei

System framework two: Phase II of global history of architecture

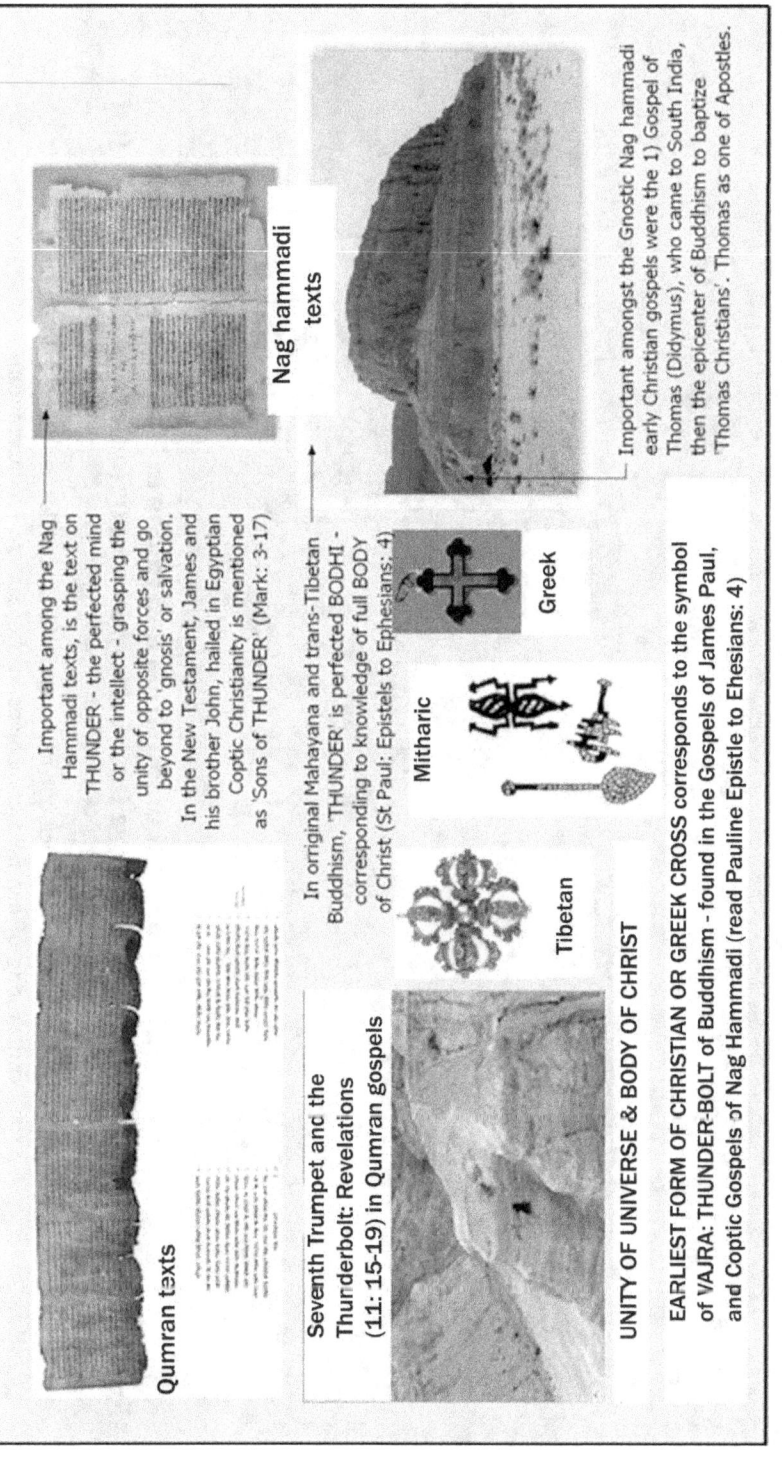

Qumran texts

Nag hammadi texts

Important among the Nag Hammadi texts, is the text on THUNDER - the perfected mind or the intellect - grasping the unity of opposite forces and go beyond to 'gnosis' or salvation. In the New Testament, James and his brother John, hailed in Egyptian Coptic Christianity is mentioned as 'Sons of THUNDER' (Mark: 3-17)

Important amongst the Gnostic Nag hammadi early Christian gospels were the 1) Gospel of Thomas (Didymus), who came to South India, then the epicenter of Buddhism to baptize 'Thomas Christians'. Thomas as one of Apostles.

Seventh Trumpet and the Thunderbolt: Revelations (11: 15-19) in Qumran gospels

In orriginal Mahayana and trans-Tibetan Buddhism, 'THUNDER' is perfected BODHI - corresponding to knowledge of full BODY of Christ (St Paul: Epistels to Ephesians: 4)

Tibetan

Mitharic

Greek

UNITY OF UNIVERSE & BODY OF CHRIST

EARLIEST FORM OF CHRISTIAN OR GREEK CROSS corresponds to the symbol of VAJRA: THUNDER-BOLT of Buddhism - found in the Gospels of James Paul, and Coptic Gospels of Nag Hammadi (read Pauline Epistle to Ehesians: 4)

Template 4.3 The imagery of the Cross and the Vajra

Templates 4.4 Evidence of rock-cut monasteries and tumulus type (or, Stupa type) constituting of urn-field complexes in the eastern Mediterranean

Templates 4.5 Evidence of rock-cut monasteries and tumulus type (or, Stupa type) constituting of urn-field complexes in the eastern Mediterranean

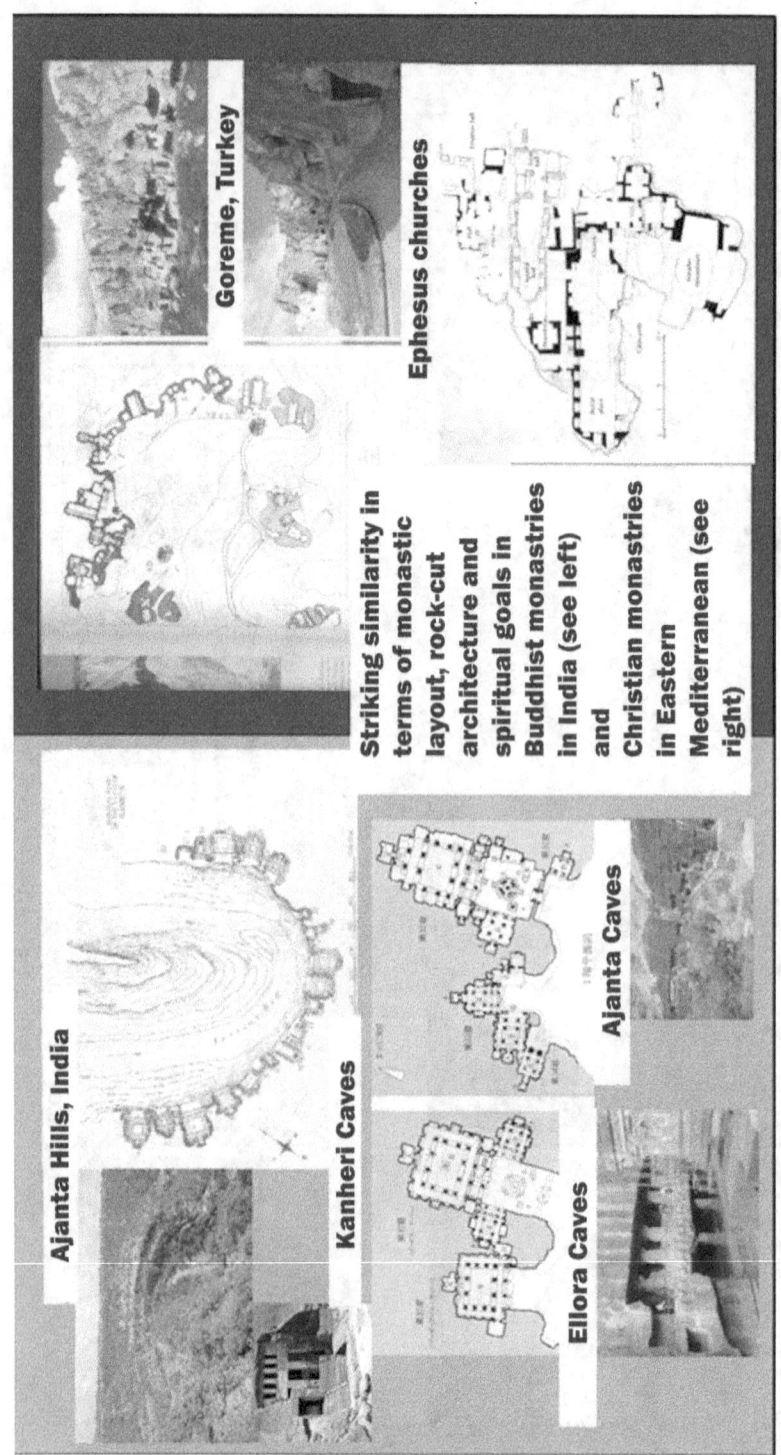

Template 4.6 Patterns of rock-cut monasteries: Eastern Mediterranean and India

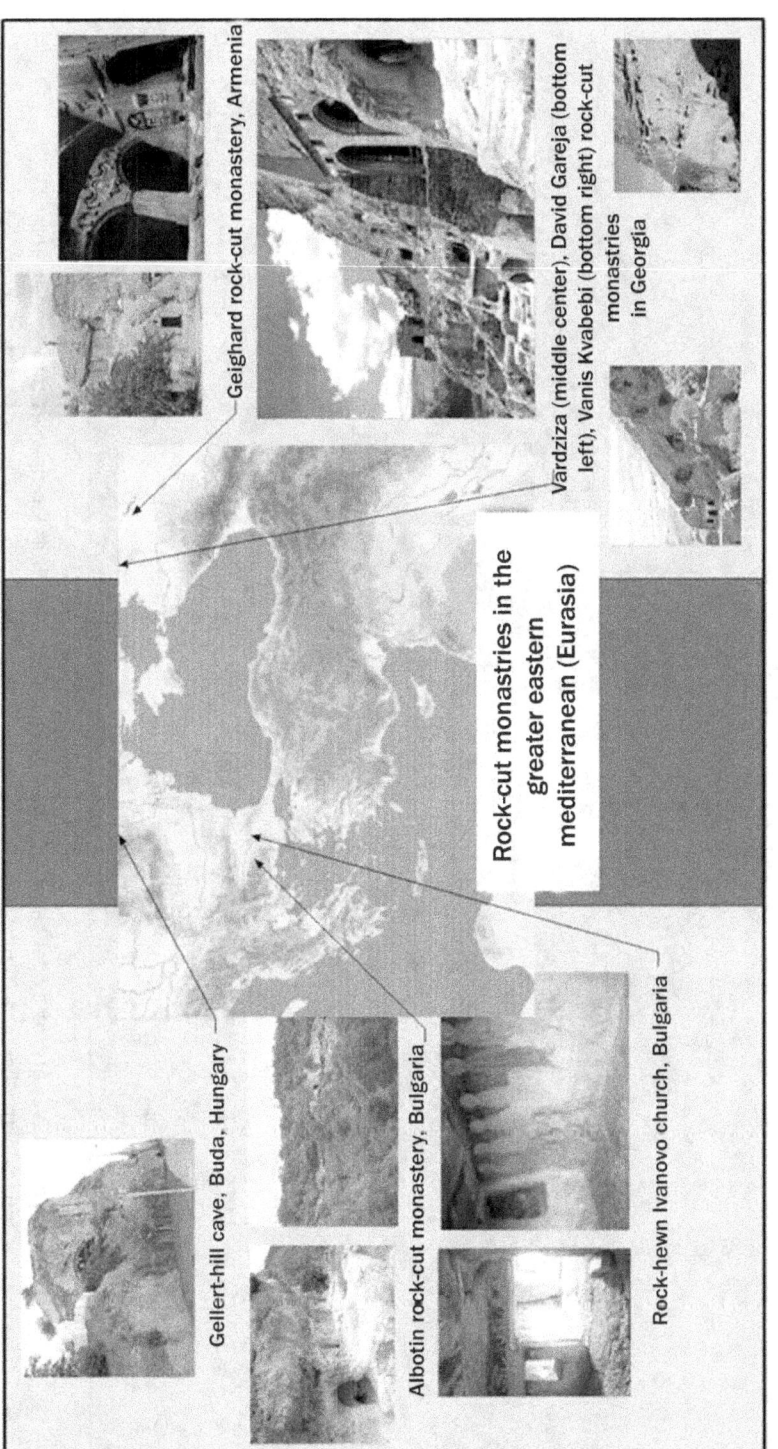

Template 4.7 Variety of evidence of rock-cut monasteries in Western Asia or Eurasia (Bulgaria to Georgia)

Template 4.8 Variety of evidence on similarities between Monastic Complexes and Iconography as found in the Eastern Mediterranean (Letoon, Turkey) with those in India (Ajanta Caves)

System framework two: Phase II of global history of architecture

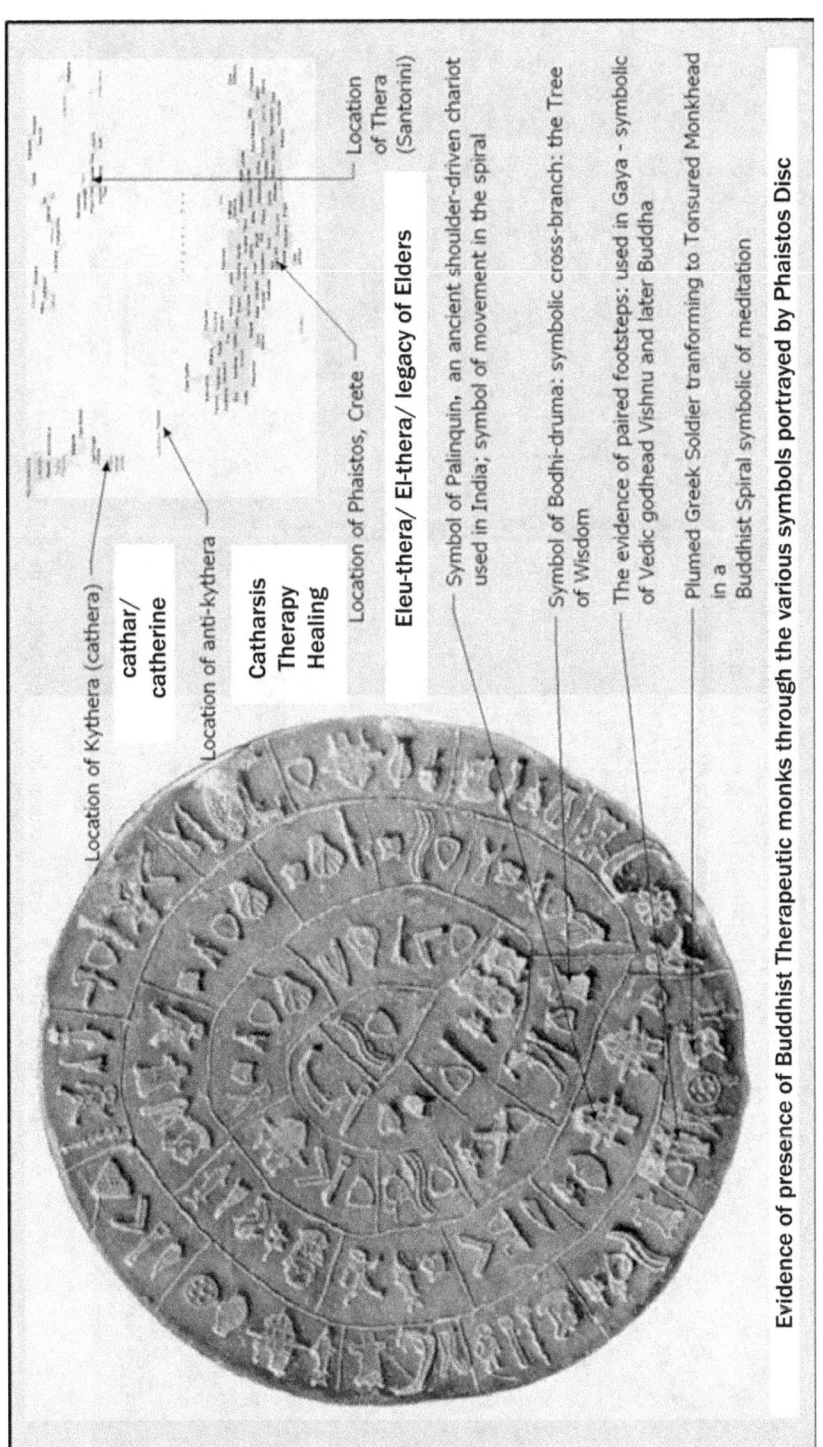

Template 4.9 Evidence of a range of iconographic elements in the Phaistos disc

Evidence of presence of Buddhist Therapeutic monks through the various symbols portrayed by Phaistos Disc

Templates 4.10 Architectural iconic evidences in the Phaistos Disc

System framework two: Phase II of global history of architecture

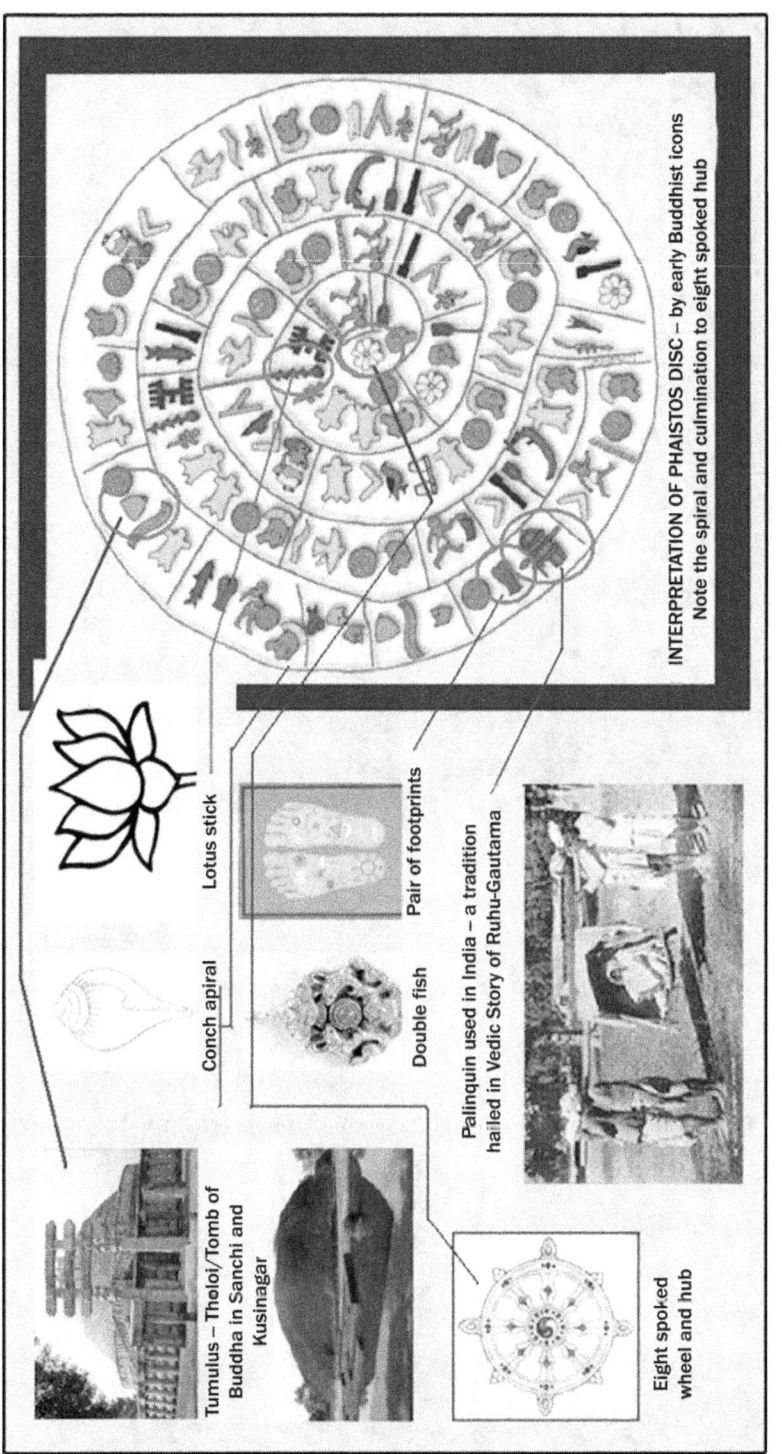

Templates 4.11 Architectural iconic evidences in the Phaistos Disc

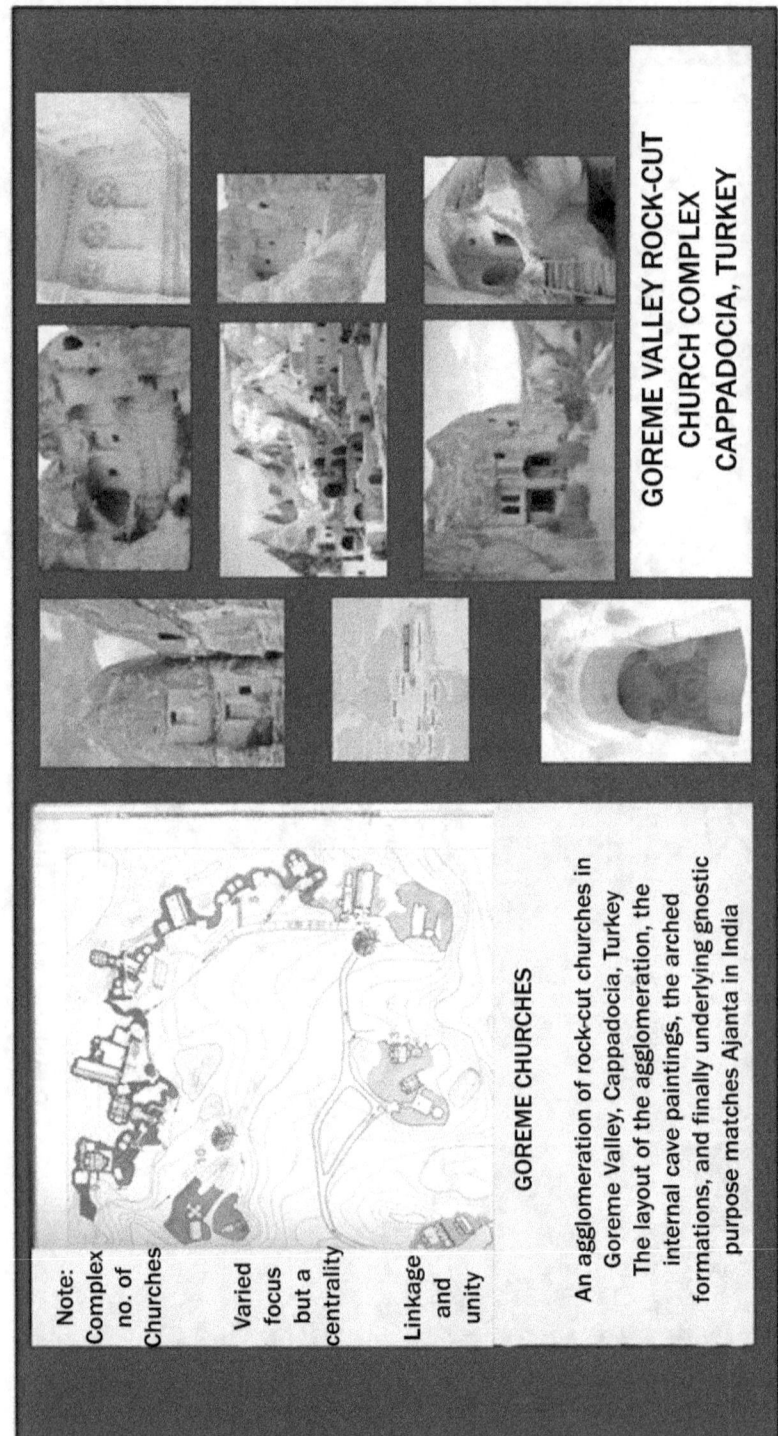

Template 4.12 Monastic establishments in Cappadocia

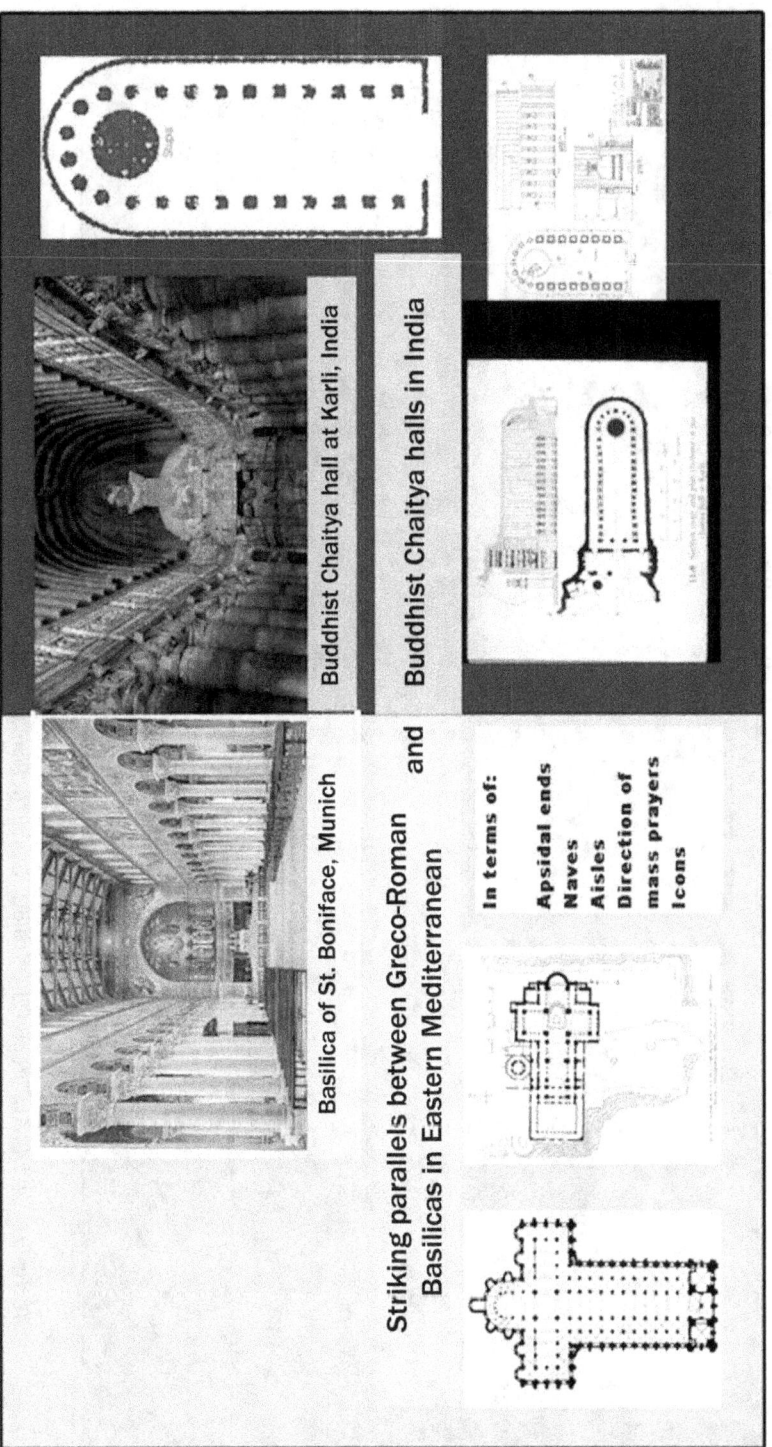

Template 4.13 Monastic establishments in Buddhism and Christianity

Template 4.14 Architectural parallels: Construction techniques and design semiotics – Anatolia and India

Template 4.15 Art parallels: Cave paintings and art styles and techniques

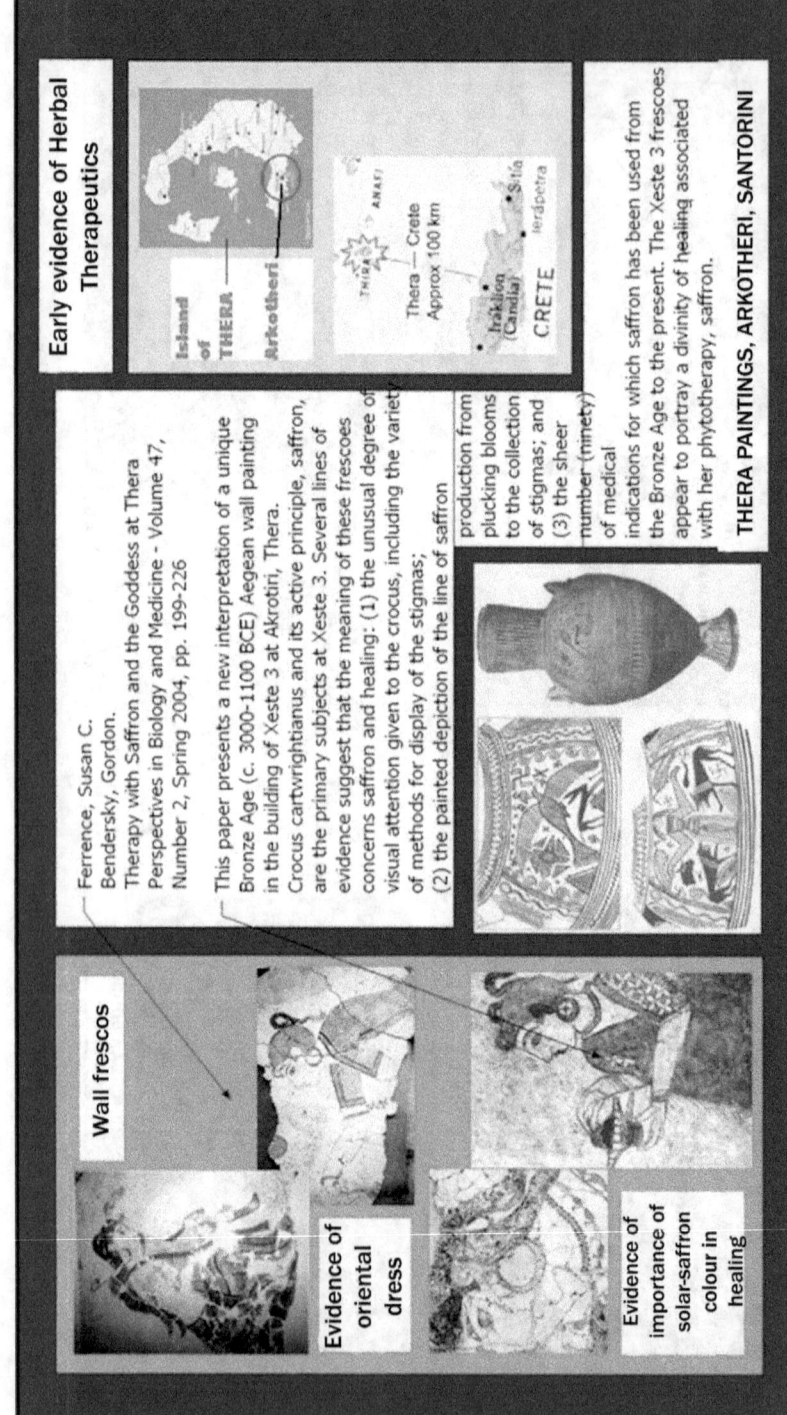

Template 4.16 Art parallels: Paintings in the larger Eastern Mediterranean

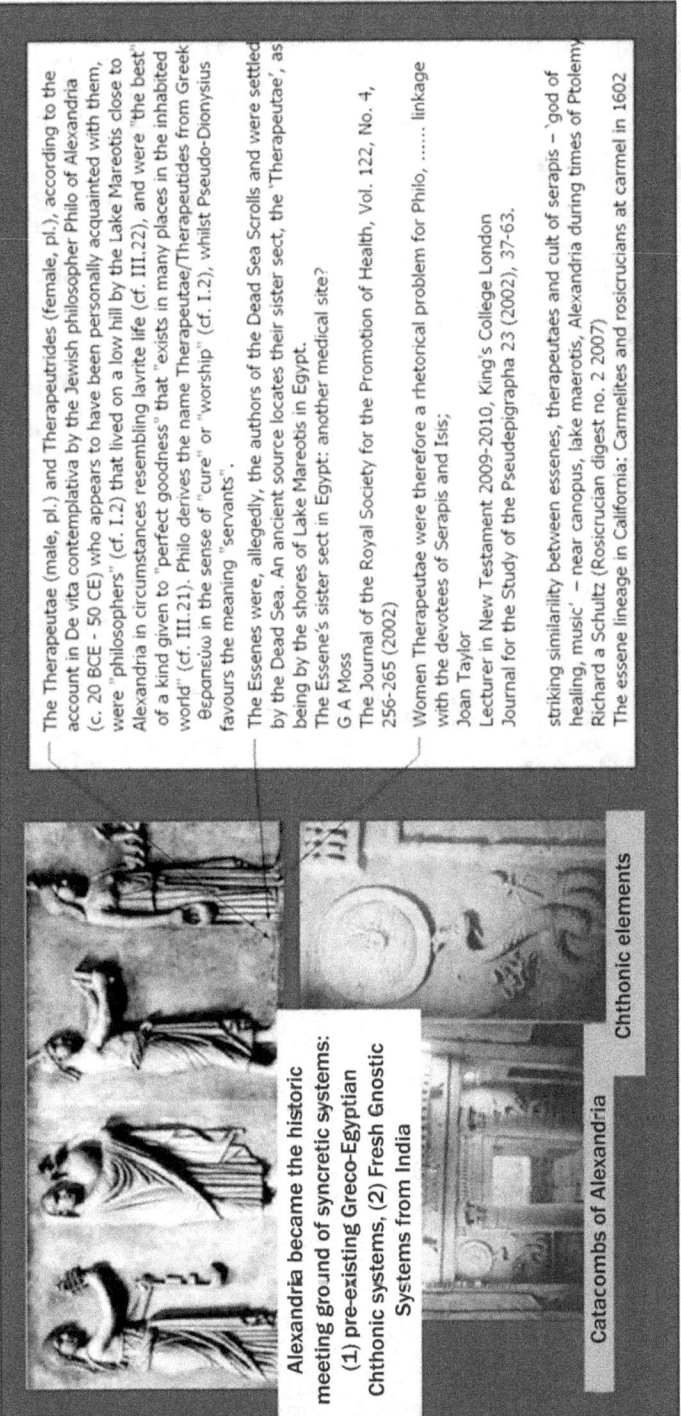

Templates 4.17 Evidence of a Gnostic and Ascetic group in Alexandria

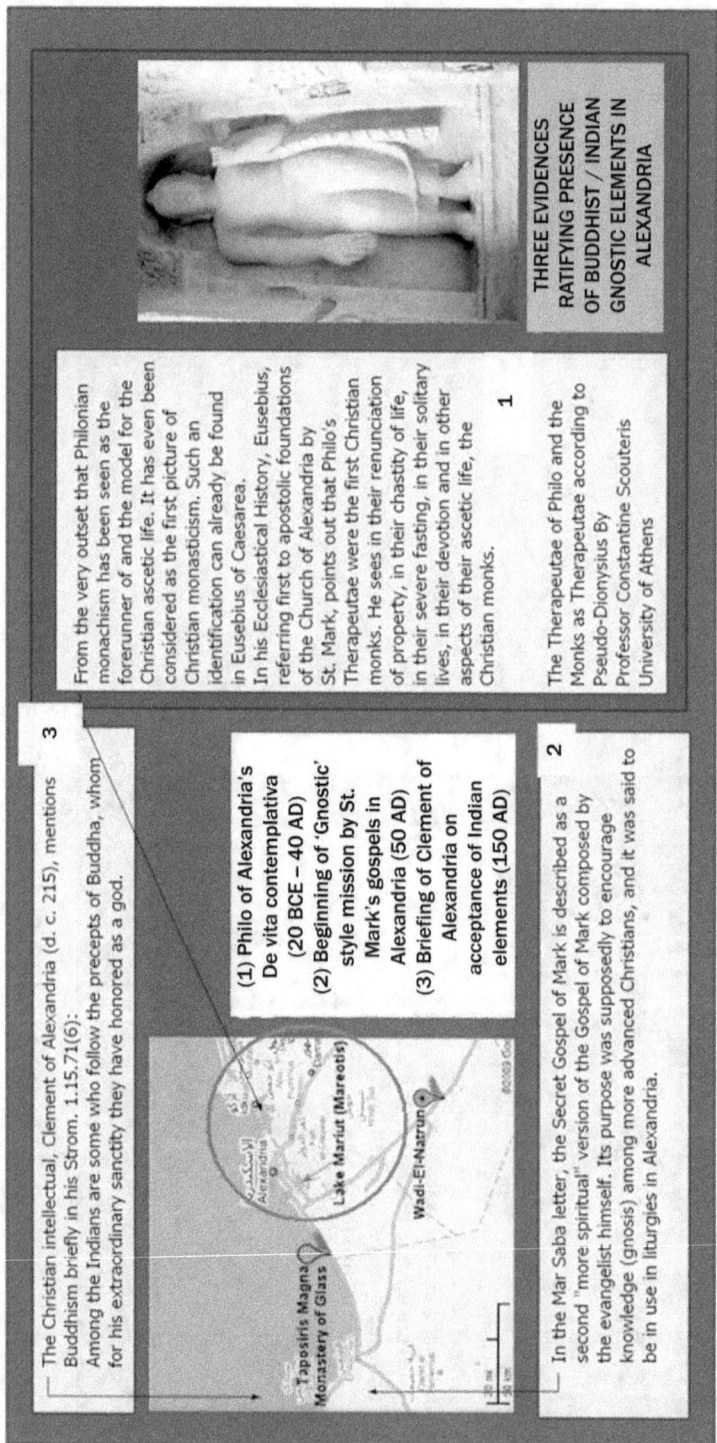

Templates 4.18 Evidence of a Gnostic and Ascetic group in Alexandria

System framework two: Phase II of global history of architecture

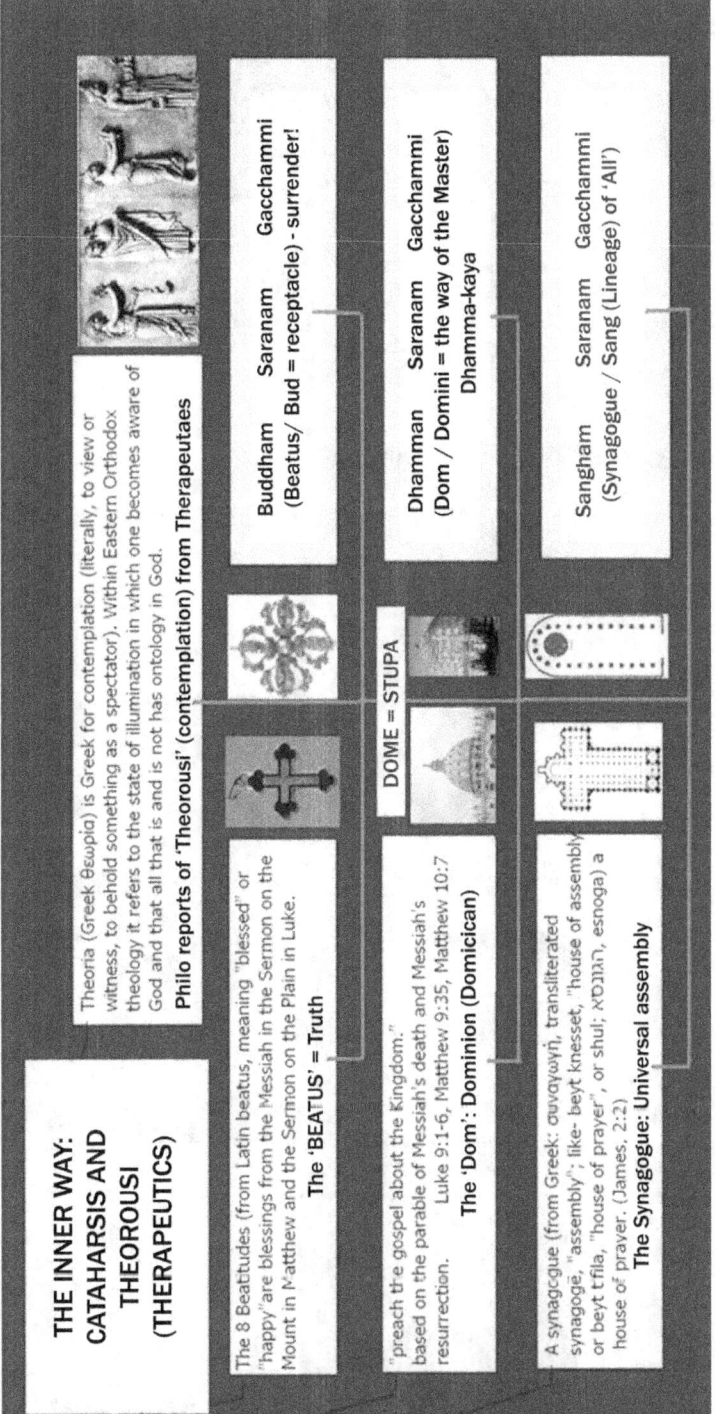

Template 4.19 Various oriental features of the group of Therapeutaes

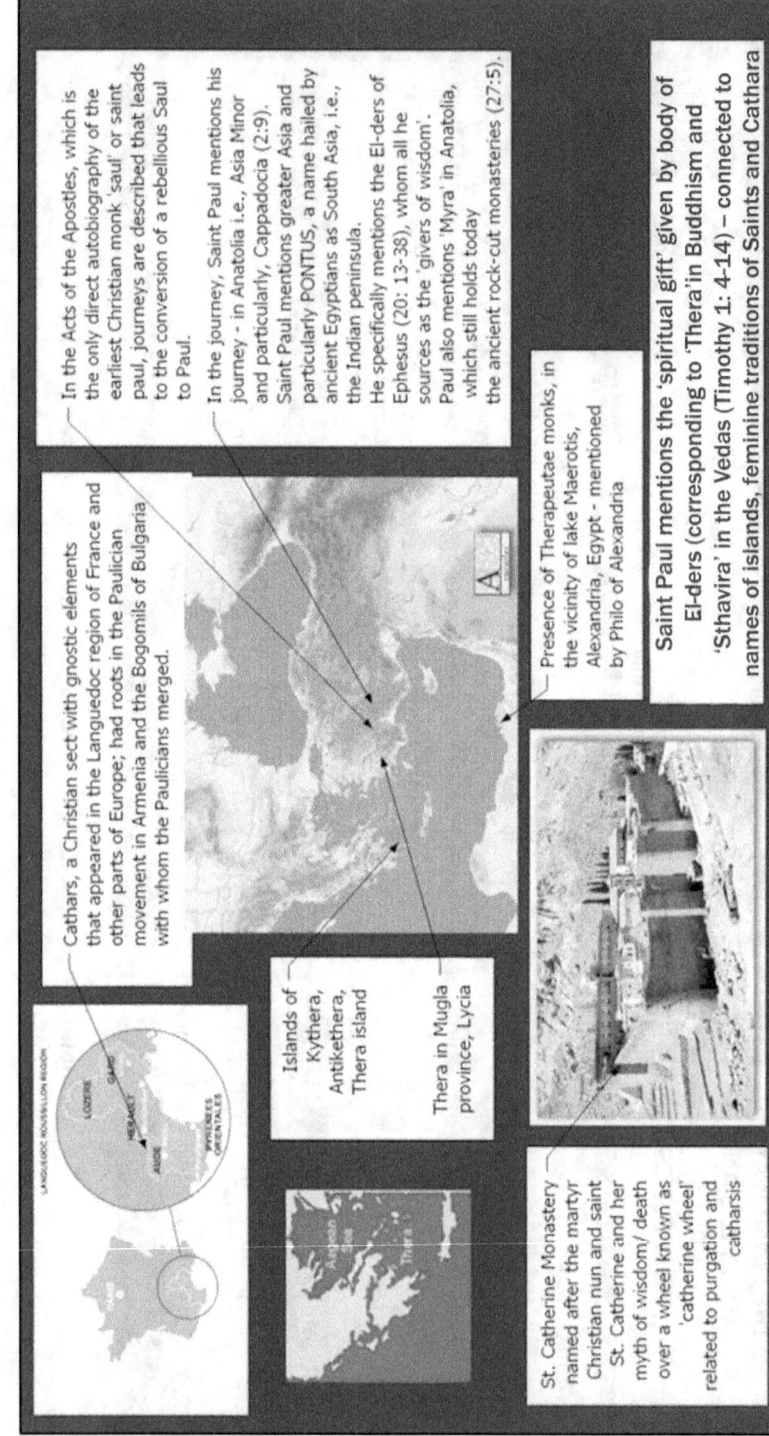

Template 4.20 Various locations in Santorini and in Turkey associated with 'Thera'

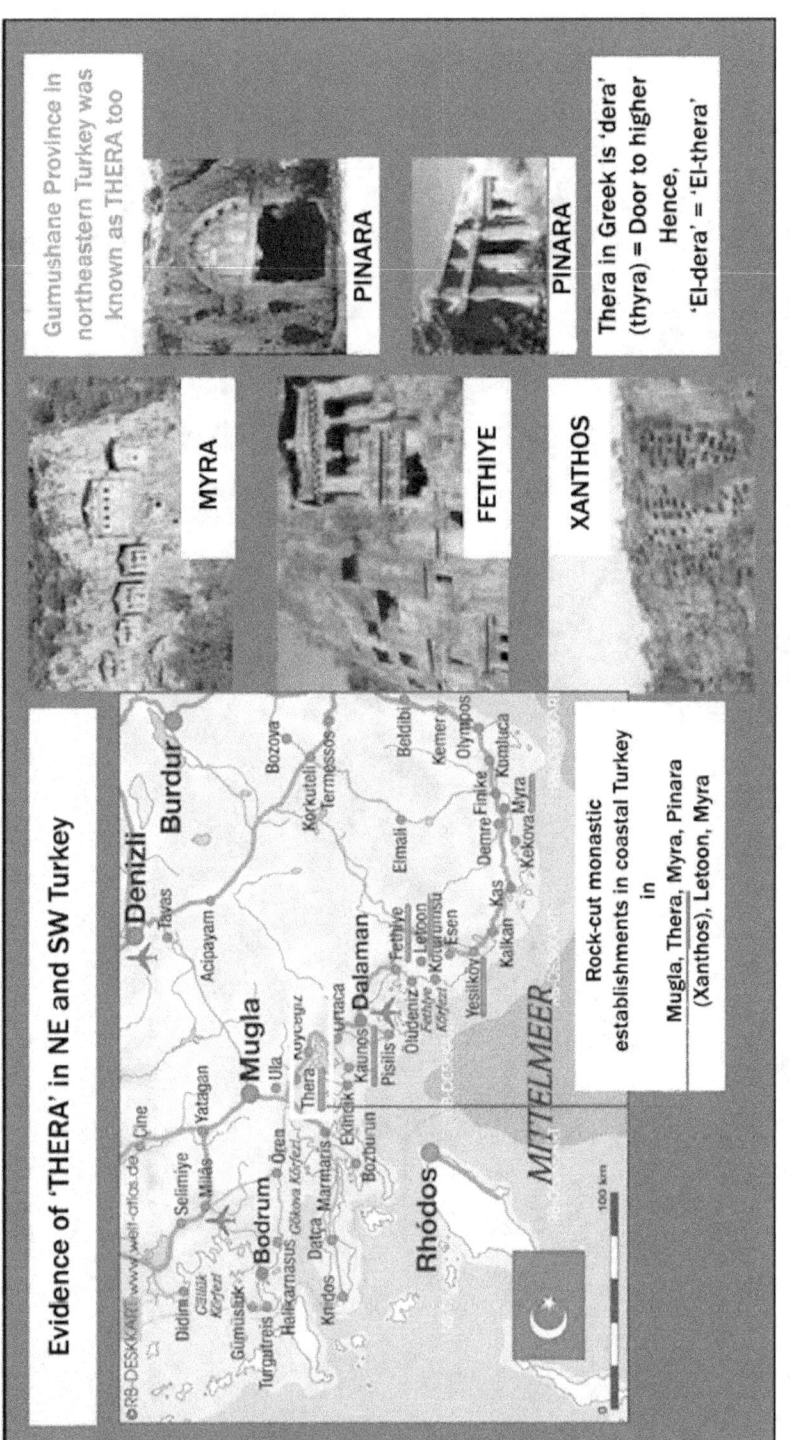

Template 4.21 Specific location called 'Thera' near Hierapolis in Mugla, Lycia, Turkey

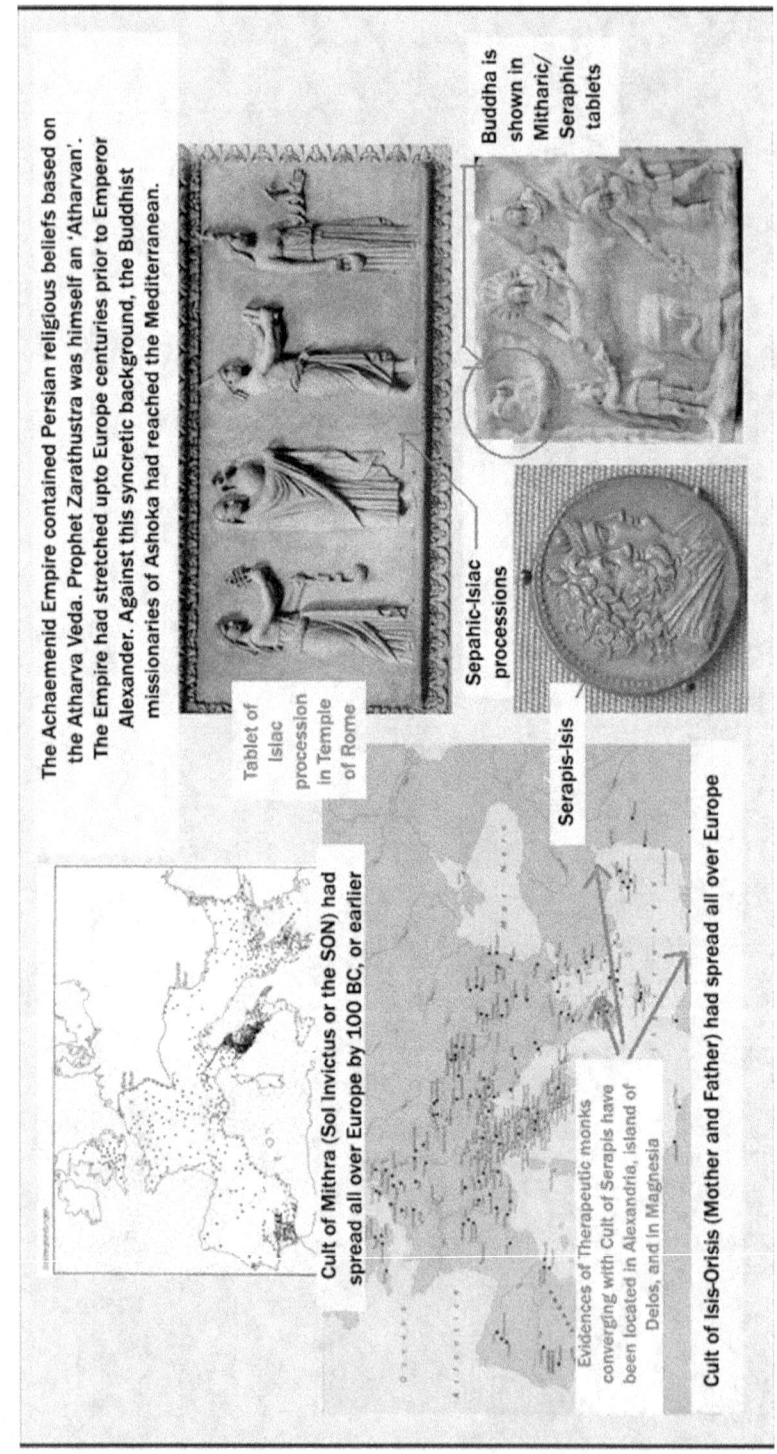

Template 4.22 Cults of Mithra (root of Maitreya) and its associated symbols of 'healing'

5

System framework three: Phase III of global history of architecture

5.1 Systems' framework three: Introduction

The third phase of Indo-Greco interactions took place in the deeper interfaces of Western Mediterranean, in lands what we had called 'the Land of the 'Ibri' (based on an ancient root of 'Apri'/ Euphri or [H]brew), which is now called Iberia. The interactions consolidated westbound, as the gravity shifted from the lower eastern Mediterranean to the lower western Mediterranean. It was occurring for the third time, out of a commingling of the two forces, laying first, the foundation of Arabia; and eventually laying the foundation of modern European civilization'. Sir Bertrand Russell, outlining the making of the great event in his seminal work 'The History of Western Philosophy' says and acknowledges the paramount contributions of the Orient in the making of Europe:

'...To us, it seems that West-European civilization is civilization, but this is a narrow view. Most of the cultural content of our civilization comes from the Eastern Mediterranean, from Greeks and Jews......I think that, if we are to feel at home in the world after the present war, we shall have to admit Asia to equality in our thoughts, not only politically, but culturally'

A similar acknowledgement comes from another seminal work by Will and Ariel Durant called 'The Story of Civilization'. While outlining the sequel of the West, they initiate the story with a title called 'Our Oriental Heritage' and not just 'Oriental heritage'. The word 'Our' makes a vast difference underscoring the origins and westbound movement of civilization from Asia to Europe and finally to the new world. In the chronology and the movement, the intervening Dark Ages, which loomed Europe from late 4th to early 14th century (almost 1000 years), can be seen both as a deterrent and a catalyst of future changes. It was in and through these times, Christianity evolved and consolidated first as a continental religion. It shaped 'the European Renaissance', the most popular and recent one that we know, and labelled as 'The Third one' in the context of the present book, and eventually led to the rise of Western–European civilization order.

An exploration of the chronology and the movement has been initiated in the following sequence:
1. Christianity during the Dark Ages
2. Barbaric invasions shaping the Dark Ages
3. Continuity of trade between Asia and the lower Mediterranean (while the dark ages continued)

5.1.1 Christianity during the Dark Ages

The earliest Christians, who were once persecuted by the Greco-Romans, changed generations and hands of transformation; and they gradually acquired political power. During these times of transformation and an early rise to power, there was a schism between many. The principal fighting groups were the Monophysites of Egypt and the concentration of Nestorians in Syria and Byzantium in West Asia. The then powerful and rich urban and mercantile centers of Alexandria and Constantinople (previously Byzantium) became the hearing centers of three most controversial Councils (Chalcedon, Constantinople, Nicea) of Christianity.

The Monophysites believed in an undivided Trinity of Heavenly Father, the Son and the Holy Ghost as opposed to the Nestorians in the Eastern world. The Nestorians emphasized a 'Corporeal' nature of the Word of God, and believed not in the incarnation but the 'idea of a Messiah', in the status of an earthly prophet. The Monophysites emphasized the heavenly non-corporeal nature. The East and the West therefore remain divided. The Old Testament, at the root of the Semitic branch, was fulfilled by an idea of a heavenly incarnation of the 'Word of God' that satisfied the West only. The East was still awaiting a counter response. In other words, the line of 'Isaac' (son of Abraham) and his free spouse 'Sarah' had provided a response. The other line of Abraham, that of Ishmael and his slave wife (Hagar), was yet to yield results (see Template 5.1).

Till about AD 378, the Roman emperors inclined to 'Arianism' preached by Arius. Arius was an Alexandrian priest, maintaining that the Son is not the equal of the Father but created by him. Constantinople and Asia inclined to Arianism; Egypt adhered to the other view known as Athanasian. The Western world soon adhered to Athanasian viewpoint and the decrees of Council of Nicea. Finally, Emperor Theodosius (AD 379) exterminated the Arian viewpoint thereby de-linking the Eastern and Western Christian worlds. The image of Christ was transformed to an isolated 'Personal Savior' imagery to an extent denying all major elements that was inherited from pre-Christian times. One major was that of *Agnes Dei*, which has been discussed before.

5.1.2   Barbaric invasion shaping the Dark Ages

The religious and political times in the West soon changed, mainly in the West, by the invasions of barbaric tribes from the north. They were mainly the Goths and the Lombard. Three factors were imminent:

1. The impact of the heresies to begin with
2. The split of the two worlds of Christians
3. The barbaric invasions consequentially impaired the unity of the Eastern Empire

These factors weakened the Roman–Christian confederation in the lands east of the Eastern Roman Empire (Byzantium) and actually facilitated the Mohammedan conquest from the further East. By 5th century AD, the Germanic Goths plundered Western and Southern Europe. On the east, the Huns came in with equal impact. Soon the Vandals established themselves in the Mediterranean world including the devastation in several old Roman trade outposts in Africa. The outrages matched the Visigoths in south of France and the Franks in the north and north-west. It was a phase of de-urbanization and the devastation of ancient Italy (Italia) (see Template 5.2).

Over time, the principal urban centers of Europe were vandalized; life and activity shrank to insecurity and doom;

population was dispersed in the less insecure and more inaccessible hilly countryside. Old cities decayed and were replaced by these new forms of hill-top moated settlements and fort-towns. De-urbanization was an overarching phenomenon. In AD 568, three years after Emperor Justinian's death, the Lombards invaded and plundered the seat of culture and religion in Europe – Italy. The Eastern Byzantines slowly lost control over the West as from the South; they had to face the invading Saracens too.

With the collapse of the Italian civilization, the Dark Ages fully descended in Europe. The Western empire broke up into numerous barbaric kingdoms and Christianity fell into their hands. The original ideas and scriptures were severely subjected to misinterpretation, forces of bigotry and forced mass-proselytization.

During the successive centuries, the Church performed very imperfectly as superstition prevailed, secular learning was discouraged and fanaticism grew through horrifying times of 'Inquisition' in the subsequent centuries of the Dark Ages. The most noted among them are the extermination of the 'Knight Templars', the 'Inquisition' around 'Albi' in France on a large following called the 'Catharsis'.

This became the foundation of the Western Foundation on which the events of successive wars were built stretching up to the French and German Revolution by Robespierre and Garibaldi, respectively.

Referring to the true nature and impact of these times on defining a 'Western civilization', Sir Bertrand Russell presents his comments:

'...To us, it seems that West-European civilization is civilization, but this is a narrow view. Most of the cultural content of our civilization comes from the Eastern Mediterranean, from Greeks and Jews......I think that, if we are to feel at home in the world after the present war, we shall have to admit Asia to equality in our thoughts, not only politically, but culturally.'

(Chapter VII: Papacy in the Dark Ages, page 395, A History of Western Philosophy)

5.1.3 Continuity of trade between Asia and the Mediterranean: A phenomenon superseding the European Dark Ages

Despite the Dark Ages in the West, the connections in the lower Mediterranean had always continued. Mercantile commerce was highly developed since the ancient times of Phoenicians.

The Cambridge Medieval History, Book IV, forwards the real strengths of these hidden linkages; always well beyond the scope of the Dark Ages. These point out to just not the political-economic linkages but the real forces that facilitated the Mohammedan conquest of the West:

'...not only did the possessions of enormous wealth create a demand for costly articles, such as silk from China, and fur from Northern Europe, but trade was promoted under special conditions, such as the vast extent of the Muslim Empire, the spread of Arabic as a world language, and the exalted status assigned to the merchant in the Muslim system of ethics; it was remembered that the Prophet (Mohammed) himself had been a merchant and had commended trading during the pilgrimage to Mecca.'

One has to remember this ancient mercantile linkage. One has to further underscore the military cohesion behind it. Even deeper one has to look at the religious zeal of a new wave. The trade linkages were ancient from Phase One. The linkages were mainly through sea and partly through land, which the Arabs inherited from the ancient Persian Empire (Phase I) and later Greco-Roman Empire (Phase II). The Arabs utilized these as a successive network through which the great intermingling of the East and the West was in the offing.

5.1.4 Rise of Moors and the message of the Prophet of Arabia

The linkages networked the meeting of elements hidden in Spain and North Africa (the ancient Celto-Hellenic order) with Persian civilization and Indian principles. This was right through and more from a time in AD 622 (the Arabian Hegira), 10 years from which the Prophet of Arabia had passed away. Immediately after his death, the Arab conquest had begun and proceeded at a fast speed.

Several reasons facilitated this great Mohammedan conquest:
- The exhaustion of Persian and eastern empire after great wars
- The separation of Nestorians of Syria and East Asia, who suffered persecutions under the Western Roman Christian world. They received tolerations from the Arabian conquest by default and in return for the payment of tribute. They believed in a 'Christ in Jesus' – only as the Son of Man. This the Mohammedans accepted.
- In the North African coast, the Arabs allied with the Berbers and older Phoenician stock and merged to form the broad group of people called the 'Moors'. Finally, they invaded Spain and being helped by the pre-existing Jewish and Eastern European population there. These pre-existing people, by default, were the enemies of the West and North European stock – the Barbaric invaders in whose hands lay the decrees of Christianity. In Iberia, such barbarians were mainly Visigoths.
- The simple monotheism of the new religion of the Prophet served the minds of the gentiles and the oppressed. Islam inherited the Judaic roots of Ishmael, son of First Patriarch Ibrahim (Abraham) and reformed the old Jewish customs that had been constricted over the ages and forwarded simple principles of an open-ended liberal social acceptance 'once you are a Muslim'. Much of this idea in common the 'Celto-Hellenic' principles nurtured the humane principles of 'French Revolution'. Today we know that they are great ideas of 'Fraternity and Democracy'.

5.1.5 Rise of Arabs and the resurrection of the ancient Persian civilization

The role of the Arabians, who was under the Caliph (a successor of the Prophet), had facilitated the marine power. This led to the rise of Umayyads (750 AD). In Spain, in particular, the Cordovan capital lasted from 735 to 1031 AD, when it became the most cultivated part of Europe. On this we get a brief but essential narrative:

'...At this time the Moslem Empire extended from Spain to the Middle East. It included several cities such as Alexandria, which had formerly been great centers of learning in Greek times, and other cities, such as Baghdad, which were go-ahead centers of new Knowledge. Thus the Moslems were able to make far great advances in science and in particular arts than were the Christian countries of that time.

For more than two centuries Spain was in the very forefront of progress. At the great Moslem universities, mathematics, astronomy, medicine and the science of navigation flourished. New navigational and time-keeping instruments, such as the astrolabe, were used in Spain long before they found their way to the rest of Europe. Spanish Architecture took on a new and somewhat oriental look; and Spain felt the full benefit of better irrigation schemes, better trade, better craftsmanship, better standards of hygiene.'

(Man's Past and Progress (1961); page 76; Colourama, Odhams Press Ltd., London)

The whole repository of knowledge and material advances that Moslem Spain had excelled was later downloaded by Christian Europe. By the end of Dark Ages and actually through the intermixing and inter-mingling with this Asiatic treasure-house, the seeds of Renaissance and a later navigational Industrial Revolution were sprouting. It was finally from here, in AD 1492, Spain, then Christian, funded Christopher Columbus for his 'the search for India' via the Western Route, which Vasco da Gama (from Basque Spain) had already reached earlier (AD 1497 via the ancient sea-route rounding Africa).

On the other hand were the resurrection of the ancient Persians and the successive role of Abbasids. They best represented the extended domains of an Indo-Persian culture. They played a pivotal role in the removal of the primacy of civilization in the Eastern world from Syria (Damascus) to Baghdad (Mesopotamia or modern-day Iraq). Finally the contacts with the 'Paradise' – the land east of Persia were then fully established.

5.1.6 Role of Baghdad: Rise of Arts and Sciences – re-contact with India

The seat at Baghdad facilitated the greatest of all linkages – the renewed contact with India. The climax reached a point when Harun-al-Rashid (AD 809) furnished a court which became an epicenter of oriental luxury, poetry, art-architecture and learning. His empire had stretched from the Mediterranean Straits of Gibraltar to the banks of Indus (see Template 5.3). That brought the Celto-Hellenic Element again at the heart of Asia – 'India'. This is evident in the following words of Russell, where a significant connection has been highlighted – an event that has influenced the best of Western scientific world – the knowledge of numbers, computational mathematics, logic and information sciences – the basis of modern Western Science and later technology:

'...Meanwhile, in Persia, Muslims came in contact with India. It was from Sanskrit writings that they acquired, during the 8th century, their first knowledge of astronomy.

About 830 AD, Muhammad ibn Musa al-Khwarizmi, a translator of mathematical and astronomical books from the Sanskrit, published a book which was translated into Latin in the 12th Century, under the title 'Algoritmi de numero Indorum'. It was from this book that the West first learnt of what we call 'Arabic numerals, which ought to be called 'Indian'. The same author wrote a book on Al-gebra which was used in the West as a text book until 16th century.'

(Page 416, Chapter X, Mohammedan culture and philosophy, A History of Western Philosophy)

Just not sciences and technology, but the entire spirit of the built environmental culture and way of life exploded across two continents – Western Europe and the other in India (see Templates 5.4 and 5.5). It is a story the present chapter has unfolded. But what is that underlying power that has led to the genesis and the ramification of the explosion in Arabia.

1. What has been the basis of the power?
2. How did it shape a third ramification of the Semitic order with its location in Arabia?
3. What are its true depths in the fathoms of history?

A great intermingling had begun in the release of an immense energy from Arabia leading to the third system's framework. It is this great intermingling facilitated by the improvement and prosperity of Arabia that laid the foundation of Arabia and also the foundation of Modern European civilization.

The ancient Semitic order that was formatted in the Cradle of Western civilization, i.e. in Western Persia (the Hill countries) and the land between the two rivers, branched off from the Mother Faith Judaism. They were two. First, it came as a fulfillment of the Old Testament in the lands of the Levant and the Fertile Crescent, once grafted as the earliest Phoenician colonies. The fulfillment came as a 'New Word of God', who was identified as the Star of Bethlehem by the three Magis, one from Egypt, the other from Persia and the last, perhaps from further east, India. Europe was shaped by that. But reformation of the ancient wisdom of Isaac, David, Solomon and Isaiah could not satisfy people who remained in the eastern part, in Arabia. As a response to that, Arabia produced a third wave, from the line of Ishmael, Solomon and the Queen of Sheba. An exploration of the third wave is thereby provided in three sections:

1. Section one: The legacy of the Korahites
2. Section two: Contribution of the Kores

The two sections lead to the system's framework three, the foundation of the present chapter, based on which the three subsequent sections reviewing a making of the European civilization, and the features and elements of Iberian architecture have been finally forwarded.

5.2 Section one: The legacy of the Korahites (Quraysh)

The strength of the intermingling of the two forces – the Greek and the Indian forces facilitated by the improvement and prosperity of Arabia – laid the foundation of Arabia and the foundation of Modern European civilization, which can be traced back to an ancient lifeline *of civilization* that holds the clue to the basis of the present chapter – the system network three (see Figure 5.1).

And that basis can be found in a 'chain of event-patterns-parts' of an ancient powerful thought, sometimes a race, sometimes a movement and sometimes an etymological foundation of a large scheme of histories underlying the system's network.

As a race, it is that of the 'Korahites'. As a movement, it is a forerunning legacy in the history of human settlements – the 'Divine Gatekeepers of truth' – the 'Kore'. And as an etymological foundation, it is linked to 'Kara' or 'Karya' (the basis of creation or creative zeal or seed) or Core (the essence of anything) or 'Cura/Care', which holds the secrets of healing, purgation and human evolution. In some sense or other, whether it is a race or a thought movement of a race, or a dive into the etymological foundations of the word expressing either the race or the thought – the key idea is that of the 'ray' (Kara) of the Sun. Traditionally, the words in ancient Sanskrit are 'Prabhakara', 'Divakara', or 'Kara-rashi', which are all connected to the 'Core' of the Universe, seeking its life, the first principle, the Ark, the seed of the cosmos – which is the 'Sun'.

The legacy of the 'Kores' is found across the history of human civilization, and the description can be forwarded in five parts, beginning with the most antique one, perhaps, which originates in India:

1. *The Indian part:* In ancient Indian history, they are mentioned as the "Karush' tribe – a major offshoot of the solar race, the same race from where the entire lineage of 'Rama' has descended. Vaivasvat Manu and his wife Shradha had other sons also. They were Sudyumna, Drishta, Nrig, Nabhag, Prishdhar, Vrishah, *Karush*, Vasumant, Shrayati and Narishyant. It is mentioned and highlighted that from the son of Manu, Karush, was there a dynasty of Kshatriyas called the Karushas who as kings of the northern realm (or the upper stratum of Yoga and Tantra) were highly religious protectors and gatekeepers of the original Vedantic teachings. It is mentioned in all ancient sacred literature that this particular son of Manu (earliest Man) produced a great son – Karush, an exceptionally strong Kshatriya. It is a matter of separate research to explore in depth the legacy of 'Karush' in times

dating back to the solar race, the beginning of creation or the array of the divine solar world (Kora-mandalam).

2. *The Greek part:* In Greece, the kouros (Ancient Greek: plural kouroi) is the modern term given to free-standing ancient Greek sculptures which first appear in the Archaic period in Greece and represent great male youthful archaic figures. In ancient Greek, kouros means "youth, boy, especially of noble rank". The female sculptural counterpart of the kouros is the kore. Even in the later Greek times, one of the more accomplished products of the time is the Thera kouros (NAMA 8), softer and less muscular in modeling, which is more Ionian than Dorian though Thera was a Dorian colony (a term known has Orchomenos–Thera group) [Around 500 BCE]. But its history can be broadly traced in three steps:

(a) According to the Greek mythology, the Korybantes were the armed and crested dancers who worshipped the Phrygian Mother goddess Cybele (Principal KORE) with drumming and dancing. They are also called the Kurbantes in Phrygia. The conventional English equivalent is "Corybants". The Korybantes were the offspring of Thalia and Apollo.

(b) The 'Kores' were intimately connected with the 'Sibyls'. The Sibyls were oracular women believed to possess prophetic powers in ancient Greece. The earliest Sibyls, 'who admittedly are known only through legend,' prophesied at certain holy sites, under the divine influence of a deity, originally – at Delphi and Pessinos – one of the chthonic deities. Later in antiquity, a number of Sibyls are attested in various writers, in Greece and Italy, but also in the Levant and Asia Minor (from Syria to Upper Arabia). Incidentally, mother of Alexander the Great was also a Sibyl and a Kore. So was Ayesha, one of the wives of the Prophet of Arabia.

(c) There is a story Sibyl the VIRGIN KORE – who bears a child in the Old Testament that cuts an ancient story centuries prior to the New Testament (Isaiah, Chapter 7).

Lilith is a Sumerian or Babylonian demon Goddess, who is perhaps better known for her role as the Kore in the Jewish legend. She is depicted on a Babylonian clay plaque from 2000 BCE to 1600 BCE as beautiful winged woman with bird's feet and claws. The historical Queen of Sheba, portrayed in some legends as a seductive temptress or sorceress, is associated with Lilith in Jewish tradition; and she bears connect between the Semitic tradition in the Levant (Solomon and David and their prophet NATHAN) and that of development and histories in the Arabia. It bears a direct relationship with the Sheba or the Sabean kingdom of Arabia, which is the evolutionary core of the tribes of Karush (Quraysh) in Arabia.

3. *The Semitic Counterpart:* The story of the sons of Korah in the Old Testament is truly a tale of two fathers and two destinies. The story begins with the Israelites of Moses' time as they journeyed through the wilderness just after leaving Egypt. In Numbers 3, God set aside the Levites, out of the tribes of Israel, for full time service to Him. They were ordained to take care of the tabernacle and all of its implements, as well as the Ark of the Covenant. Only the descendants of Aaron, however, were allowed to serve as priests, the high priests of the ARK (solar 'Arka'), who were intimately connected with similar tribes in Saba or Sheba in Arabia. Sheba is believed to be biblical Sheba and was the most prominent federation. The Sabaeans or Sabeans were an ancient people speaking an Old South Arabian language who lived in what is today Yemen, in the south west of the Arabian Peninsula. Sabeans inhabited the Biblical land of Sheba, a trading state that flourished for over a thousand years in modern-day Yemen. Modern archaeological studies support the view that the biblical kingdom of Sheba was the ancient Semitic civilization of Sabaeans in Yemen, between 1200 BC until 275 AD with its capital Marib. The Kingdom is mentioned in the biblical books of Job, Joel, Ezekiel, and Isaiah in the Old Testament, and in sura 2:62 of the Koran. The important features are:

(a) *The important center of 'Yathrib' (Atharba):* The 'Sabean' civilization stretched as far as Aqaba with small colonies to protect the trade routes; these colonies included Yathrib and the central Arabian kingdom of Kindah and northern Ethiopia where archaeologists found an ancient temple dedicated to the Sabaean chief god El-Maqah (Michah). The study of the history and culture of this kingdom is still patchy, especially the chronology of historical events and kings. (Y)Athrib came to be known as 'Medinah' in the later times.

(b) *The ancient ethnographic linkage:* A late Arabic writer wrote of the Sabaeans that they had seven temples dedicated to the seven planets, which they considered as intermediaries employed in their relation to God. Each of these temples had a characteristic geometric shape, a characteristic color, and an image made of one of the seven metals. They had two sects, star and idol worshippers, and the former doctrine was similar to one that come from Hermes Trismegistus (KORE – Korykea – Hermes Caduceus). The Greek counterpart is exactly known by the same name: Korykea or an ancient tribal name of 'Koryka' in India (legendary KORAs).

(c) *The Greco-Romanic Kore-Bacchic-Dionysiac-Sabazius element:* Almaqah or Ilmuqah was a moon god of the ancient Yemeni kingdom of Saba' and the kingdoms of D'mt and Aksum in Eritrea and Northern Ethiopia. On Almaqah being the sun god, scholar Jacques Ryckmans states 'Almaqah' is considered a moon god, but scholars have shown that the bull's head and the vine motif associated with him may have solar and Dionysiac attributes. He was therefore a sun god, the male counterpart of the sun goddess Šams, who was also venerated in Saba, but as a tutelary goddess of the royal dynasty. The ruling dynasty of Saba' regarded themselves as his children. Almaqah is represented on monuments by a cluster of lightning bolts surrounding a curved, sickle-like weapon. Bulls were sacred to him.

4. The mention of Kore as a symbol – in the recent stories of H. Rider Haggard: The connections did not escape the

minds of many. One of them is a writer of the early 20th century – H. Rider Haggard. Haggard became famous for his sequels namely: (a) Ayesha – SHE – Caves of Kor, and (b) The King Solomon's Mines. Haggard dedicated the novel to his friend Andrew Lang. He sets the books context in Tibet and in Coptic Africa and Arabia. It is first set in Tibet, reincarnation being a familiar tenet of Tibetan Buddhism; however, the back story is set in the ancient Mediterranean of Egypt, Arabia, and others. Haggard's daughter, Lilias (from Lolita or LILITH) in her biography, explained the origin of the names: 'She-Who-Must-Be-Obeyed' was a doll in the author's nursery. Ayesha was borrowed from Arabic, being traditionally one of Mohammed's wives' names; a note by Haggard indicates that it should be pronounced "Assha"; it is an alternative name for Isis (the bases of Dionysiac-Sabazius-Mithraoc mysteries of the ancient Greco-Roman and Persian world based on the Vedic Godhead Mithras). She stands for the 'lady of the deep waters, of the sea and the stars' – called Mari or Maryam in the Arabic folk-lore, a concern taken up later in this chapter.

5. *The tradition of the Prophet of Arabia:* Finally, according to this tradition, the prophet descends from the Quraysh is Nadhr ibn (son of) Kinanah ibn Khuzaimah ibn Madrakah ibn Ilyas (Elijah) ibn Mudhar ibn Nazar ibn Ma'ad ibn Adnan ibn Add ibn Sind ibn Qedar ibn Ishmael ibn Abraham. From the roots of the Semitic tradition of the Kore (in Greece), Karish (in India) and Quraysh (in Arabia), the various suras of the Koran are derived like 'Surat Saba' (Arabic "Saba, Sheba") is the 34th sura of the Qur'an with 54 ayat. It focuses on the lives of Solomon and David, and the promises related to the Day of Judgment. Here the 'Star tradition of Arabia' (the Sabeans on the 'Host of Heavens') makes a direct complementarity with the Magen (Persian) Star of David or the Seal of Solomon, which is incidentally, the Star of Mother Goddess Lolita/ Lalita / Lilith Tripura Sundari in India, called the Sri Chakra.

We begin to start reaching the heart of the matter – the genesis and the ramification of the explosion in Arabia and find

answers to the most intriguing answers to the three aforesaid questions of the explosion in Arabia:
- What inspired that?
- Was it just a response of the third branch of the Semitic order, which is Islam to the two others?
- Or, was it something deeper in the fathoms of history?

George Stanley Faber (1816) in his path-setting book entitled 'The Origin of Pagan Idolatry: Ascertained from Historical Testimony and Circumstantial Evidence' makes the most powerful statement (p. 292):

"Considering then as Noah [the Indo-European Naiah = Semitic Noah meaning the Navy chief presiding over the Old Ship (Ark or seed of Creative Matrix) in Deluge] we find Jupiter both esteemed the Father of the three most ancient Caberois (= Kores), and himself also reckoned as the more primitive of the two primitive Caberoi, Bacchus being associated with him as the younger. This however is a mere reduplication, where Jupiter and Bacchus is the same person: and they seemed to have been joined together in the Samothracian orgies (as One – of the two Dionysius), much in the same manner as Horus and Osiris are connected in the mysteries of Isis (In Egypt). Hence Jupiter (Idean Jove or Bromius) bore the title of Sabazius as well as Bacchus : a word, not derived from the Hebrew Sabaoth as some have imagined, but from Siva or Seba which is the Indian name of [Isha (Ishaiah) or] Ishwara"

Thus a relationship between the Indian and counter parts (in Greece, Persia or Arabia) can be best presented as follows:
- Shiva = Sabazius = The idea of supreme transcendence / father in the Heaven = Rest (Sabaoth) = Later Bromius (Bromius becoming Bromius) = Brahman
- Vak = Bacchus = Al-Book (the Koran)
- Dio-naza/nascre (born twice) = the twice born (Dwija in India) = Father / son (Shiva and Kumara) – 'The SON of God' (rooted in the etymos of the word Nascent/ First born = First Fruits = Afri/ Apri of the Vedas)
- Maenos = Menas (in Indian tradition) = Maeneds or KORE in Elesusinian/ Phrygian tradition in Anatolia

And hopefully the rest falls out from these basic relationships echoing the aforesaid observation of George Stanley Faber. The ancient foundations of the Celto-Hellenic race was also the original foundation of the ancient Semitic Faith, i.e. Judaism in Arabia and the changes that were coming in later Europe with the fight between the Nestorians of Syria and the Monophysites of Egypt over the 'idea of the Word of God' in Christianity. It led to an explosion in Arabia, the power of which unleashed a new transformation of the Semitic order in intensities, never seen before. It was as if a response of the East to the West, and a revival of the remnants of the Celto-Hellenic foundations of ancient Judaism in Arabia. The result was the birth of Islam, as a third ramification of an ancient race.

5.3 Section two: The contribution of the Kores

5.3.1 The system's network based on 'the Kore'

A system's network can be accordingly drawn:

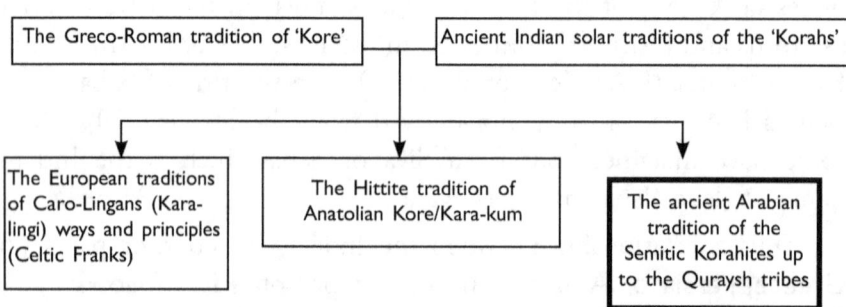

Figure 5.1 The Kore in the extended trans-continental Indo-European link – ' the Celto-Hellenic framework'

5.3.2 From the Kore to the Carolingian: The impact of Persia and the rise of Franks

The turning point has been the upper Iberian Peninsula, where the civilized Islamic dominion in Andalusia was slowly exposed to barbaric Europe gradually rising from its dark ages. From ancient times, France through a conflict of many races, and after the destruction of the Roman Empire, was led by the Franks, the Carolingian (Core) race of the Celto-Hellenic order and they gradually obtained absolute dominion over Europe. Their King, Charlemagne, forced Christianity into Europe, by the power of the sword. Europe was re-exposed to Asia by the Franks, and hence, around the earliest colonial times, the Europeans broadly were known as the Franki, or the Feringi.

Ancient Greece had degraded from its past and the vast empire of Rome was broken into pieces by the dashing waves of the barbarian invaders, and it was at this time that another barbarous race rose out of obscurity in Asia – the Arabs. With extraordinary rapidity, that Arabian tide began to spread over the different parts of the world, and the predominant portion of which was Iberia (Spain and Portugal) begin to express, the cultural power of Persia shaped the tide and the new religion of the Arabs and the civilisation of Persia became intermingled. With the sword of the Arabs, the Persian civilisation began to disseminate in all directions, and it had been borrowed from ancient Greece and India.

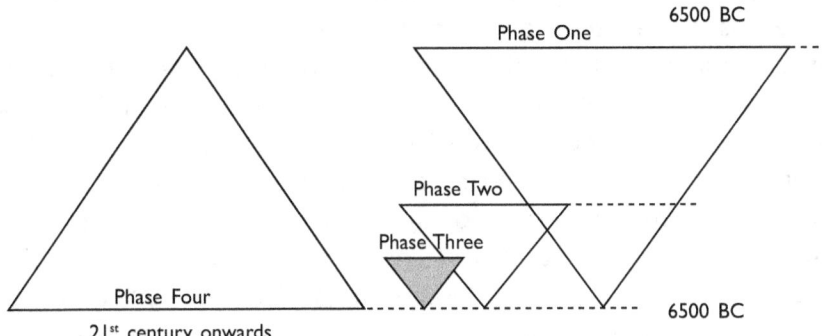

Figure 5.2 Systems of Phase III – Rise of Europe

From the East and the West, the Islamic invaders charged Europe and the light of wisdom and civilisation began dispersing the darkness of blind and barbarous Europe. The pulsation of this new life took a strong and formidable shape in the city of Florence – old Italy began showing signs of new life. This is called Renaissance, the new birth. But this new birth was for Italy only a rebirth; while for the rest of Europe, it was the first birth. Europe was born in the 16th century AD, i.e. about the time when Akbar,

Jahangir, Shahjahan, and other Moghul Emperors firmly established their mighty empire in India. Again, France is the home of liberty. From here, the city of Paris, travelled with tremendous energy the power of the people, and shook the very foundations of Europe. From that time the face of Europe has completely changed and a new Europe has collie into existence. "Liberté, Equalité, Fraternité" is no more heard in France; she is now pursuing other ideas and other purposes, while the spirit of title French Revolution is still working among the other nations of Europe.

5.3.3 Fall of Granada and rise of France vide the Spanish Inquisition

The Emirate of Granada had been the sole Muslim state in Al-Andalus. It stood for the Arab name for Iberia – for more than a century by the time of the Granada War in the late 1490s. The frontier between Granada and the Castilian lands of Andalusia was in a constant state of a large number of war wages by an increasing Christian dominion of the Franks and Spain. Soon the surrender of Granada was seen as a great blow to Islam and a triumph of Christianity and the rising confederations of Christian nations offered their sincere congratulations to Ferdinand and Isabella, the two spear headers of the Granada wars. Soon many Muslims in Iberia were being forced to choose between baptism, exile, or execution. Tensions remained high, and a large military force in Granada under Isabella also strengthened the Spanish Inquisition, and Ferdinand brought the Inquisition gradually to entire Europe.

It was in the year 1478, the Tribunal of the Holy Office of the Inquisition (Spanish: Tribunal del Santo Oficio de la Inquisición), commonly known as the Spanish Inquisition (Inquisición española), was established by Catholic Monarchs Ferdinand II of Aragon and Isabella I of Castile. It was intended to maintain Catholic orthodoxy in their kingdoms and to replace the Medieval Inquisition, which was under Papal control with predominance through the tribunal in Iberia. The Spanish Inquisition is perhaps the closing and the darkest phase in Middle-Ages literature and history and an inhumane example of Catholic intolerance and repression. There are unrecorded events about the Inquisition; and although records are incomplete, estimates of the number of persons charged with crimes by the Inquisition range up to 150,000, with over thousands being executed in Iberia alone.

5.3.4 Albigensian Crusade and the Cathars: Linkages with Therapeutaes and the symbol of 'Mari'

The Albigensian Crusade or more innately known was the Cathar Crusade (1209–1229) was a 20-year military campaign initiated by Pope Innocent III to eliminate Catharism in Languedoc, in the south of France marking the beginning of Spanish Inquisition. The Cathars were known as Albigensians because of their association with the city of Albi. Because the 1176 Church Council which declared the Cathar doctrine heretical was held near Albi and their later association with the Knight Templars and the Islamic dominion in Iberia in the 11th century was the greatest of all 'heretical alliances' spotted by the Roman Catholic Church.

The medieval Christian sect of the Cathars, whose name suggest a connection with Catherine of Egypt and the ancient Christian movement that might have triggered in Kythera or Cathera in the Mediterranean may bear an underlying connection with the ancient sect of the Thera or the therapeutes. It was against these connections and a different interpretation of the New Testament, the Catholic crusade was directed. There are historic connections with the Bogomil churches in Bulgaria calling for a return to the original Christian message of perfection and Catharsis' that was the bone of content in the earliest inquisition crusades.

The Cathars claimed to possess a secret Book of Love (Mari or TARA), which was a mysterious manuscript attributed to Jesus in a female or Gnostic form (attributed to Mari the Magdalene) who gave it to John the Divine. It was transmitted through many Gnostic sects and the Knights Templar and the Cathars finally in upper Iberia and France adopted it. The Book of Love was the foundation of the Cathar Church of Love or Amor (the reverse of Roma). The existence of the Gnostic gospel was revealed when the Catholic Church subjected the Cathars and Templar in around 1308 onward to great torture. Its contents were a secret, symbolized by the Templar skull, which was the basis of an older form of Gnosis found in Indian and Orphic religion in the Asiatic mainland Greece, and it is said to grant one the ability to control the forces of nature and to transform ordinary human blood based on what is known as Alchemy. It is equated with the Holy Grail.

The most important objection from a patriarchal foundation of the Roman Church was towards the role of women that were accused of being heretics in early medieval Christianity included those labeled Gnostics, Cathars and Beguines. The Cathars, like the Gnostics who preceded them, assigned more importance to the role of Mary Magdalene in the spread of early Christianity than the Church previously did. Her vital role as a teacher contributed to the Cathar belief that women could serve as spiritual leaders. Having reverence for the Gospel of John, the Cathars saw Mary Magdalene as perhaps even more important than Saint Peter, the founder of the Church.

The most important aspects are the legends of Martha and the Tarasque (Mari and Tara of earth and water foundations – similar to the UNICORN), and the foundation of a teaching school marked by the sign of Aradia or the Lady of the Snakes' grace, the ability to change water into wine. This legacy leaves the researcher wondering about the beginnings of Christianity in Iberia, France in relationship to the ancient Near East and Egypt. Perhaps at the very core of the movement in France in the 1st century CE was the direct absorption of these traditions into the making of a "Christianity" that was originally a Goddess religion, perhaps even with a female, Aradia-like messiah figure, would have been a powerful secret to have in the medieval era. The polarities are conjoint – one in the Semitic origin of the Ancient Arabia – the Kore Mari (tablets in the ancient Near East and Sumeria) and the other in Basque Iberia connecting the legendary cult of Mari and Atharba:

1. *The Semitic origin:* To the Egyptians, Bronze Age Cyprus was known as Ay-mari or the land of Mari, because of the island's devotion to the ancient goddess; as the name Mari appears in the most unexpected places. Ma-ri in Sumerian means fruitful mother. There is a city of Mari on the Euphrates and the Hebrew name Miryam, which is the origin of Maria, is a

contraction of Marat-Hayam – Lady of the Sea – leading to the idea of the Unicorn. Why these names appear among the Basques, of all people, is anyone's guess. It points perhaps to a very old connection; those Phoenician traders again, coming originally from the Persian Gulf and India, had maintained connections among all the people around the Mediterranean. It might also explain why the name Maria occupies a prominent position in Christian mythology, and why St. Jerome called the Virgin Stella Maris – Star of the Sea.

2. *Mary, or Mari of Iberia:* The last of the ancient Neolithic Celtic / Gaulish Indo-European people were migrants from distant eastern cultures; in this case in Rome in the late 3rd century, were the Basques of the southwestern coast of France and northern Spain. In the Basque folklore, there had survived prominent traces of the sky as a kind of thunder god, Ortzia, and the earth was a mother goddess known as Mari.

3. The connections are broadly explained in Figure 5.3, where the deeper connection among the earliest versions of Mari can be best traced.

Figure 5.3 Ancient depiction of Mari of Anboto (Iberia); (Ish-tara) or Mari helmets of the Knight Templar/Cathar; Metamorphosis into Mari – the Virgin Mary as the Unicorn (Chi-lin).

The divine Lady, 'Mari' (Mare: Marine), is the Star of the Sea and is an ancient title for the Virgin Mary, mother of Jesus Christ. The words Star of the Sea are a translation of the Latin title Stella Maris. The unicorn, the horned-Horse, normally, is associated with strength, represented Christ make poisonous waters safe, coverts into wine or Holy spirit, as the unicorn placing is horn in a poisoned stream and purifying the waters before its capture. The poisoned stream represented sin, overcome by the power of Christ, and the capture of the unicorn represented Christ's arrest, trial and crucifixion. The virgin stood for Mary's participation in the sufferings of her Son.

Two more important events may be cited – one at the prior beginnings of Christianity, before the times of Hannibal (200 BCE), and another later.

1. Way across the Rhone nearby, a small town of boatmen and marsh dwellers had been formed. Known as the Ernaginum by the Romans, a name that reflects a Celtic or Indo-European origin derived from, perhaps, *ur-naga*, or primeval serpent, the locality seems, from early on, to have had a connection to dragons. This suggests that the local cult was the Lady of the Serpents, common to both the Neolithic Ligurians and the later Celtic tribes. Examples have been found in various places from La Tene in Switzerland to southern France, so we are on safe ground supposing that the dragon of Ernaginum was of this type. It was the formal historical beginnings of the Cathar movement, perhaps.

2. In this connection statues are in the Musee Borely in Marseille and were found in the 1920s and 1930s in the caves near Salon-de-Provence, in the hills north of Marseille. Otto Rahn, in his 1933 *Kreuzzug gegen den Gral* (published in Freiburg), reports the find in 1930 of a Ligurian-Greek Buddhaís head in a burial chamber near Nimes. For a discussion of the possible Buddhist influences on early Christianity, one may read – Elmar R. Gruber and Holger Kerstenís *The Original Jesus: The Buddhist Sources of Christianity*, Elements Books, London, 1995.

It is recorded in the annals of Basque or lower Andalusian history that a new influx of ideas and philosophies had come from the East. The history talks about the late 3rd century BCE, when the Buddhist missionaries arrived, dispatched by King Asoka in the entire Mediterranean. In these connections, small enclaves of Buddhist hermits could be found living in the ancient grottoes and caves of the Iberian region. Hellenized statues of the Buddha have been unearthed in the caves near Lamanon, and strangely, there is at least the case of one grotto reportedly used by Mary Magdalene, north of Nimes. The ongoing Jewish messianic cult along the lines of a multitude of Prophet Isaiah (Semitic Joshua or European Jesus); the compassionate techniques of the early Buddhists laid an emphasis on the Mother Goddess in Iberia and the older Ligurian mystery cults was most completely transformed into a matriarchal version of the new "Christianity". The Ligurian cult emerged in the vicinity of ancient Etruscan world bearing a long time connection between Italia (Italy) and Ana-talia (Turkey). It forms the foundation of the ancient Indo-European Çelti-Hellenic order of Gnosticism and closely inter-linked orphic mysteries. It is an area that needs to be re-explored.

According to an ancient French legend, Mary Magdalene or the Mari landed in a small boat around 42 CE, along with a number of early Christians, including a young, dark-skinned servant named Sarah, patron saint of the gypsies and often equated with the black Madonna statues in the churches of France. They had braved a dangerous passage from the Holy Land, without sails and oars, to spread Jesus' teachings after his Crucifixion. Purportedly a great preacher in Palestine who even wrote her own Gospel (among the more recently discovered esoteric Gnostic texts being studied by scholars), Magdalene is said to have preached to the locals in Saintes-Maries, converting many. Their legacy with a female Messiah of Christianity was transmitted to the Catherine sect in France – the Cathars. At the 13th-century ruins of the Montsegur and Queribus castles, one may still be connected with the great tragedy of the Cathars who found refuge here. Thousands were burned at the stake during the Inquisition for refusing to renounce their beliefs, rooted in direct mystical contact with the Divine. Yet their teachings, like those of Mary Magdalene, remain with us, founded upon the true understanding of the power of love. She remained as the CORE, the Virgin Maiden, the Gnostic witness to the inner resurrection of Christ, an event that is yet to be explored, realized and then understood.

5.3.5 Mari and her metamorphosis into the black unicorn

The idea of 'Çhi-lin' (the Unicorn of the East), which the earliest Christians metamorphosed into Virgin Mary may have four major zones of exploration:

1. The Matriarchal version of "Christianity" drew heavily on the ancient traditions of the Lady Underground or the Goddess of the Springs, with a lot to be downloaded from the Neolithic Mother-Goddess and her successors.
2. The tradition of the Mother-Goddess remained as the 'Matrix" of animating spirit through sacred wells or springs or the vast waters (Marine). The Lady Underground, under the stars in the heaven, was a common label given to the Black Madonnas, a derivative from the ancient Mother-Goddess traditions that pervaded the ancient world from Euphrates to Hebrides.
3. In the eastern Andalusian region, at an ancient period, the Ligurians of Provence worshipped a deeper version of the Lady Underground, which merged during the early Christian era into the Virgin Mary.
4. The earliest eastern sources could be drawn from the city of Mari on the Euphrates and also from the Hebrew name Miryam, which is the origin of Maria, which is a contraction of Marat-Hayam – Lady of the Sea. Finally, she became the Black Madonna to which the newborn was the cult of the White resurrection – the star of Bethlehem (see Template 6 and 7).

This special version of an universal and impersonal Gnostic approach to Christianity, as derived from the original oriental sources, soon became an unacceptable éthos to the 'personal savior' myth of the Catholic cult, where 'salvation' could be only sought through the church and organized religious submission. As a result, from 1208 to 1244, the first European holocaust was conducted. The Church of Rome savagely attacked the Cathars, the peaceful 'heretics of the Languedoc' of Southern France, with a viciousness and detestable arrogance paralleled only by the Nazi atrocities during WW II. The matter regarding the Cathars is a subject of inquiry and perhaps a key to a redrafting of Christian history of Europe before and after the Fall of Granada. The journey from the days of Inquisition to the rise of the French civilian power is the most important one. It resonates with the rise of a reformation, i.e. Protestant Christianity, that finally moves out of Europe to the new world, the Americas. During the reign of Charles IV of Spain, in spite of the fears that the French Revolution provoked, several events took place that accelerated the decline of the Inquisition. It is to be remembered that the French Revolution was an influential period of social and political upheaval in France that lasted from 1789 until 1799 and through the revolutionary wars, it unleashed a wave of global conflicts that extended from the Caribbean to the Middle East, bringing about a great change to the face of European history, the third Renaissance or the third phase, which is the concern of this chapter.

The essence of the present Section two is evident in the following words of Swami Vivekananda, quoted from 'The East and the West: The Progress of Civilization". The following lines also throw light on the two sides of the tide – the Spanish Inquisition and the events just before the Fall of Granada that begun to shape Europe:

"Here the result was the same, as usually happens in a war between barbarians and civilised men. Jerusalem and other places could not be conquered. But Europe began to be civilised. The English, French, German, and other savage nations, who dressed themselves in hides and ate raw flesh, came in contact with Asian civilisation.

An order of Christian soldiers of Italy and other countries, corresponding to our Nâgâs, began to learn philosophy; and one of their sects, the Knights Templars, became confirmed Advaita Vedantists, and ended by holding Christianity up to ridicule. Moreover, as they had amassed enormous riches, the kings of Europe, at the orders of the Pope, and under the pretext of saving religion, robbed and exterminated them.

On the other side, a tribe of Mohammedans, called the Moors, established a civilised kingdom in Spain, cultivated various branches of knowledge, and founded the first university in Europe. Students flocked from all parts, from Italy, France, and even from far-off England. The sons of royal families came to learn manners, etiquette civilisation, and the art of war. Houses, temples, edifices, and other architectural buildings began to be built after a new style".

5.4 Section three: The making of European civilization

5.4.1 The first signs

We have provided so far with a synoptic backdrop – a set of timeline observations. Given this backdrop one may begin to understand the making of the third phase. It earmarks a Moorish invasion of southwestern Europe – not just that of politics and commerce, but also of tolerance, values, ethics, arts and sciences – that founded the European civilization and inspired its beginning. This is based on the key observation of Swami Vivekananda:

'Again, a similar commingling, resulting in the improvement and prosperity of Arabia, laid the foundation of Arabia, laid the foundation[1] of modern European civilization'.

In a different work entitled 'The East and the West', the Swami underpins the highlights of this phase and forwards the dual roles played by the Arabs and the Persians.

- First, it is the roles that they had played in shaping European civilization and her architecture.
- Second, it was the impact that had been created in Moorish Iberia to spark of the era of global exploration. Within the early 15th century, explorers left Europe to trace that ancient land of the 'Indies' – the mariners and ship builders,

---

[1] The Alexandrian Jews in Spain preserved the light of knowledge under the Muslim patronage after the eclipse of Roman Papacy. Bertrand Russell says '... (From 11th to 13th Century), between ancient and modern European civilization, the dark ages intervened. The Mohammedans and the Byzantines (Eastern Roman civilization in Anatolia, Turkey), while lacking the intellectual energy required for innovation, preserved the apparatus of civilization – education, books and learned leisure. Both stimulated the West when it emerged from barbarism – the Mohammedans chiefly in the 13th century, the Byzantines chiefly in the 15th. In each case the stimulus produced new thought better than any produced by the transmitters-in one case scholasticism, in the other the Renaissance' (page 420, Chapter X, A History of western Philosophy, Unwin paperbacks (1987).

the Basques of Iberia began to inspire persons like Vasco and Columbus – that comes out in the subsequent comment by the Swami:

'..........Ancient Greece, the fountainhead of western civilization, sank into oblivion from the pinnacle of her glory, the vast empire of Rome was broken into pieces by the dashing waves of the Barbarian invaders - the light of Europe went out; (this were the dark ages beginning with the fourth century) it was at this time another barbarian race rose out of obscurity in Asia - the Arabs. With extraordinary rapidity, that Arab tide began to spread over the different parts of the world. Powerful Persia had to Kiss the ground before the Arabs adopt the Mohammedan Religion, with the result that the Mussulman religion took quite a new shape; the religion of the Arabs and the civilization of ancient Persia became intermingled...with the sword of the Arabs, the Persian civilization began to disseminate in all directions.

That Persian civilization had been borrowed from ancient Greece and India (the result of the intermingling of the first phase).... The wisdom, learning, and arts of ancient Greece entered into Italy, overpowered the northern invading barbarians of Europe and with their quickening impulse, life began to re-pulsate in the dead body of the world-capital of Rome ....the pulsation of this new life took a strong and formidable shape in the City of Florence - old Italy (of the Etruscans) began showing signs of new life. This is called the Renaissance, the new birth. But this new birth was for Italy only (born before during the two earlier waves); while for the rest of Europe, it was the first birth. Europe was born in the sixteenth century (after 1200 years of Dark Age in eastern and eastern Mediterranean Europe or Eurasia) A.D. i.e. about the same time when Akbar, Jahangir, Shahjahan and the other Mughal emperors firmly established their mighty empire in India.'

The search for that ancient land became a fascination of the new Europe. Why?

Swami Vivekananda forwards the answers to such questions and the reasons why Columbus and others sailed for India and reached different destinations – bringing about the discovery of the Americas:

'As I look back upon the history of my country, I do not find in the whole world another country, which has done quite so much for the improvement of human mind.........the same holds good with respect to sciences. India has given to antiquity the earliest scientific physician......even more it has done in mathematics, for algebra, geometry, astronomy, and the triumph of modern science – mixed mathematics – were invented in India, just so much as the ten numerals, the very cornerstone of all present civilization, were discovered in India, and are in reality, Sanskrit words.........In philosophy, we are even now head and shoulders above any other nation......In music India gave to the world her system of notation, with the even cardinal notes and the diatonic scale......In philology, our Sanskrit Language is now universally acknowledged to be the foundation of all European languages......In literature, our epics and poems and dramas rank as high as those any language......In manufacture, India was the first to make cotton and purple (dye), it was proficient in all works of jewelry, and the very word 'sugar', as well as the article itself, is the product of India. Lastly, she has invented the game of chess and the cards and the dice. So great, in fact, was the superiority of India in every respect that it drew to her borders the hungry cohorts of Europe, and thereby indirectly brought about the discovery of America'.[2]

5.4.2 Liberalizing performing arts and architecture: European Renaissance

The first contribution came from the Seljuk Turks, who drove further westwards, and brought the culture of the Orient – Mughals (Mongolians), India (Vedic and Buddhism), Persia (Achaemenes and Sasanian) to the eastern doors of Europe – the Byzantines, from where it was transshipped to Iberian Peninsula (Spain, Portugal and Southern France). The presence of Seljuks was a major factor to trigger Crusades. The Seljuk Empire extended from Indus Valley (Gandhara) through Byzantium and coasts of North Africa to Iberia. The first centers of learning 'Madrasas' were introduced all over leading to the first leading educational institutions of Iberian

---

[2] Complete Works (1963), page 195 and pages 511–512, Volume 2.

peninsula – the rise of Cordova and Zaragoza. The great al-Nizamiyya Madrasa of Baghdad was one such.

The great Mosques of Isfahan inspired great construction styles and technology that continued to draw in inspirations from the Mughals in India on the one hand and the pre-existing Celto-Hellenic style hiding in the lower Mediterranean world since the earlier Phases.

One important architectural achievement in addition to Mughal Architecture in India was the development of *Muqarnas* – complex system of structural vaulting integrated with floral patterns and fixture details (doors, windows, jaffris). Great examples are Al-Barubiyin in Marrakesh (Morocco), Al-Azhar Mosque (Cairo) and similar innovation in many Byzantine Mosques. These great sciences and art of building gradually penetrated Western Iberia and inspired the greatest of European Christian Architecture – the Gothic Cathedrals and their attractiveness at a continental level. The later 11th to 12th century was the beginning of an end of the Dark Ages in Western Europe. Pilgrimage churches were built linking various parts of the Continent (from Jerusalem to Toulouse in France). The famous adventures of the 'Knight Templars' are built on these routes.

By 1260, the Mongols plundered Syria and de-linked the Mediterranean route a great extent with the Arabian heartland in turmoil. But the linkages between the two extreme stable most outposts – one in India and the other in Spain – were maintained. The great centers in the South of Spain were Malaga, Granada, Cordoba and Seville where the greatest of Moorish building designs were executed under the Nasrid Sultanate. The best of the many examples found here are the palaces, courts, gardens, forts of Alhambra. The major evidence of the classical Char-bagh is that of the Court of Lions, Hall of the Kings, Court of Myrtles in Alhambra. In these were laid the first seeds (1260 AD) of emerging art and building sciences of an emerging age – the European Renaissance.

In the architecture of the Moors, we see the classical admixture of the ancient quadrangular and symmetrical garden and building principles of Eden following the ancient cardinal principles of the Vedic cruciform – the *Vajra* and the interlaced patterns of symmetry and asymmetry – the floral and Florentine vegetation pattern showing infinite mazes and laces of creative powers of the Supreme. All these were complemented by stone engraving, calligraphic embossing of 'suras' of the Al-Koran.

5.5 Section four: The birth of Iberian architecture

5.5.1 The revival of Cardinal Principles of Architecture: Indo-Persian roots

Beyond the infinite laces of creation, God's (Al-ilah's) eternal omnipotence stood as absolute. The secret encoded in these deeper understanding lay in the heart of Islam's sacred book, much of which comes from an ancient background – the Indo-Persian roots mainly from the sacred texts of the Priests of City of Ashur (Assyria) and its extended practices in Sumeria, that is later coded as the Old Testament. This is a vast topic. Only a major area is highlighted here to draw attention. Part of that area has been discussed in Chapter 4 to explain the imagery of the sacrificial Lamb – *Agnes Dei*. In that section, the inner doctrine of phonetics associated with the Lamb (the inner fire) was introduced.

5.5.2 Music of Creation *(Sura)* and the pattern language system of Arabic numerals and Indo-European scripts

Spiritual phonetics, as per the Vedic foundation, is based on two groups: the vowels and the consonants. Overall it may be said that:
- The vowels are independent being produced by unimpeded passage of inner breadth. This is formed at and above the 'Adam's apple' (cervical plexus).
- The consonants are dependent on body-influences found in levels below the cervical (throat point) plexus. This is the lower Torso or Microcosm.

The combination of the two creates all words and language systems. Thus meaning is formed and 'thought-vibration' is affected. Creation is forwarded. Very broadly, it can be therefore said:

- The lower influence of consonants in making of words makes them subtler and closer *(sukshma)* to the inner realms of existence.
- The higher influence of consonants, on the contrary, makes words and meaning grosser and mundane *(sthula)*.

In the words of Etymologist-Linguist Norm Chomsky, it may be said that the two above are broadly the 'deep structures' and the 'surface structures', respectively.

These structures actually can be divided broadly into four levels (four types of Vaka or Vag – Rig Veda: 1.164.45) based on the stages of transitions of outward expression (construction) and inward contemplative de-expression (de-construction):

1. *Para* – formed at the subtlest and most hidden of language systems
2. *Pasyanti* – the first principles experienced (or seen) from the hidden depths
3. *Madhyama* – the derived principles that are first registered – say the vowels
4. *Vaikhari* – the more tangible forms of articulation

5.5.3 Indian philosophy in the Judeo-Islamic order and Iberia

The *Tantras* point out a fifth layer hidden at the other end – in the human torso – called the coiled pattern of potent language-energy system or *Kundalini*. This layer is the circuit of the immanent function of human language evolution – as 'Response to stimulus'. This is the microcosm. *Natha Yoga* and systems formulated by Bhartihari include this aspect too to make the system of macro-micro correspondences complete. But the top four are often seen as a whole. The whole represent the macrocosmic aspect of the Divine – the formless transcendental aspect of the Supreme which makes this creation. The later Persian and Islamic traditions had emphasized this transcendental side only. Sufism is a link between the two as the Sufis interpret the Koran allegorically and draws in from the tradition of *Tantras* in India. The overall tradition of Bauls of Bengal, the Bards of Western India, the Dervishes of West

Asia, the Shamanistic Druids of the Celto-Hellenic world conform to such holistic belief systems.

The concept of universal creation experienced by Vedic Seers is called 'Char-Vak': the circuit of quadrangular formation of the Word. There are three basic cardinal principles, which are based on the pattern language system of the 'Divine Word' – both as an agent of manifestation *(apara)* and deconstruction or reconciliation (para):

1. In Ancient Arabia the practice of creative lores was called 'Al-Vaka' (The expression of the Word of creation in form of the Book).
2. The emphasis on the reciprocity or the inversion of 'Al-Vaka' thus became the 'Ki-bala' (Ka-Ba-la) – the direction or the arrow of re-tracing the steps of creation in the reverse order. In Judaism, Kabalah forms a distinct class of esoteric doctrine and a path of atonement, which means a state rapture or oneness with God, which is Gnosis. This matches directly with the state of *'Samadhi'* in Indian *Yogic* and *Tantra* traditions. One has to therefore see these imageries of spiritual achievements in this light of cooperative cross-civilization studies.

The entire pattern language of the architecture of Ancient Arabia is based on the combination of the two – the double intender. They explain the latent and the potent systems – allegorically the double lines of Ishmael and Isaac – the two sons of Ibrahim.

The structure of the Mosque and its Miharb, Mimber, Sahn and the Qiblah in relationship to the *'Ka-ba'* (the mirror inversion of *Va-ka*) is inter-related and independent.

In Chapter 3 (Phase four), we had touched the principles of the 'Ka' and the 'Ba' in explaining the belief system and the tomb-architecture of Egypt. This is the sacred basis and the great secret encoded in the Cardinal principles of the Architecture that had disseminated from Arabia. The inner music that is encoded in the syllabic progression (Mantra of Vedas or the Sura of Koran) is the unfrozen version of the material expression made out of the building units and the pattern of building. A detailed concept of the KA-BA-LA (Cybele) is beyond the scope of the present book and this chapter. Yet it remains as a deep basis of what and how behind the shaping of the late 14th century European orders. The branch of Sephardi Jews, who were mainly concentrated in the Iberian Peninsula established communities throughout Spain and Portugal. They underwent massive internal and external mass conversions and executions during the Inquisition, but they continued to pour in the esoteric and deep knowledge of the 'Sepharial' and the oriental basis of alchemy, i.e. 'Ka-ba-la' as the basis of its expression in the ideas of 'pardes' or paradise. The branch of Islam in Iberia had a hidden agenda closely working with the Cathar and other Gnostic sects; and finally discharging it into the womb of Reformation and Protestant Christianity. The idea of paradise, the sacred Garden of Eden, ultimately shaped France, shaped Gothic Christianity and shaped the whole course of the its highest built environmental expression, Renaissance Architecture.

5.6 Section five: Redepiction of the Garden of Eden: The Char-bagh

5.6.1 The first sources

The earliest sources of the Garden of Eden can be drawn from the cult of ADONIS, a central figure in various mystery religions in ancient Near east, from Sumeria to the Land of Hittites. The cult and associated religion of Adonis belonged to women: the dying of Adonis was fully developed in the circle of young virgin girls and his resurrection was the most coveted goal. Adonis is an annually renewed, ever-youthful vegetation god, a life-death-rebirth deity whose nature is tied to the calendar. The near eastern parallel is 'Sabazius' or a later 'Dionysus' (twice-nasci or born).

'The Story of Adonis' finds a special place in the description made by C. Kerenyi, in the 'The Gods of the Greeks', where it is said – the ancient tale of the father and the daughter off his body, were married to each other to produce Ádonis', an occurrence, as the author points out, is also found in the Biblical tale, the Book of Genesis, analogous to the garden of Eden. Adonis gets involved with Aphrodite in the cycles of 'Death' and 'hopes of resurrection', and as a seasonal cycle, an ancient pattern of 'Spring' and 'Áutumn', women down the ages brought him – the memory of fresh seeds, the first fruits, the pardes – the symbol of 'little gardens'. Hence, it is Adonis and his Garden, the primordial source of 'The Eden'.

5.6.2 The Indian sources

The etymons of the word Ádonis and Éden' can be traced to an ancient word – meaning the pure seed, born in the waters – Odona. The term is found in the Atharva Veda and later used in the Upanishadic literature like the Katha. It remained a popular term till the birth of Gautama the Buddha. Hence, we get the name 'Suddha odona', the father of Siddhartha, of the Gautama Kshatriya (warrior) clan of the Vedic tradition.

The death and resurrection of a chthonic god, a vegetarian god, symbolized in form of a seed, a 'Vija" (a Vege-table) form, runs through the entire chronology of oriental religions, from the Vedas to the Hittites, and provided the necessary, so called 'pagan' background to a similar chthonic cult of Osiris in Egypt and finally, the 'Word' of God, dying and resurrecting as the Star of Bethlehem.

The mysteries and the linkages of a dying and resurrecting God can be best summarized in Table 5.1:

Table 5.1 The couplets of Death and Resurrection around the world

No.	Cult name: Son–Mother Early Oriental versions	Origin
First	Brahma-ODONA and Brahma-jyaya	Atharva Veda
1	CHI-LIN or unity of Yin and Yang	Chinese (the symbol of unicorn)
2	Shiva or Kumar (Vishak/ Scanda) – Kumarika (Kanya or Virgin) Mundaka Upanishad** KA-LI	Indian
3	Attis-Cybele	Asia Minor
4	Sebazius (Oriental Zeus) – Demeter (Cybele) [Double serpent or Caduceus]	Asiatic Greece (Pre-Miletus / Hittites)

5	Dionysus-Demeter/Persephone (Greek Zeus)	Eleusinian (earlier Greek)
6	Osiris/ Horus-Isis (Chthonian father/ son iteration)	Egyptian
7	Tammuz (or Dammuzi) – Astarte (Ishtar or Ashtoreth)	Ancient Near East (Phoenician origin)
8	Mari-Sugar (Sukra) – parents of Atarrabi (The Sage)	Basque symbolism/Cathar or Iberian sources (Mundaka Village,** Iberia)
9	Adonis-Aphrodite	Greek
	Semitic Versions:	
10	Adam (Adim) – Eve (Havvah)	Judaic symbolism
11	Christ-Mary Magdalene	Christian symbolism
12	Y(Athrib) – Mari	Arabian or Yemenite symbolism

In Table 5.1, she, 'Mari', is seen again and again in different names, Kali, Isis, Rhea, Demeter, Astarte, Diana, Athena, 'Mari' and the 'Kore' are to name a few. Finally, she became our beloved 'Madonna' – The Virgin Mary – the mother of the Christ principle. The interesting points are:

1. The departure of this ancient couplet "Mari-Atharva' from India to Iberia, as a part of the Basque mythology
2. The intermediate transitions of Odona to Adonis and finally to the Cult of Eden and its expression as a Garden of eternal resurrection or Indo-European Gypsy driven word: pardes/ paradise based on which the 'Lordship of Four Quarters' or the Four Vedas are derived.

5.6.3 The ancient sources: The mysteries of Ka-Ba and El-Ilah

The KA is a symbol of the reception of the life powers from each man from the gods, it is the source of these powers, and it is the spiritual double that resides with every human. The word BA is usually translated as 'soul' or 'spirit'. However, BA is probably better translated as 'spiritual manifestation'. The BA is one of the specific components of the human being as understood in Egyptian thought. In the New Kingdom, the BA was a spiritual aspect of the human being which survived – or came into being – at death. The chief Canaanite god is 'EL, which means simply 'God,' familiar as one of the names of the single god of the Bible. The linguistic root may mean 'That' or 'the One.' He is called 'Creator of all Created Things,' as well as 'Father of Humanity.' 'EL is therefore the prime creator god of the pantheon, although we do not currently have a Canaanite creation story. 'EL is also the king and head of the divine assembly, the council of the gods, although He is not necessarily 'biological' father of all the deities.

5.6.4   El-KA-BA (El KAB) in pre-dynastic (3500 BC) Egypt (Mishrah or Magara)

In general, this area is called El Kab but it is really the two ancient cities of Nekheb El Kab on the east bank of the Nile River and the older Nekhen, now known as Kom el Ahmar (the Red Mound) on the opposite bank. Both cities were religious centers that date from the pre-Dynastic period. In those times, Egypt was known as Mizrah = Magara, perhaps an ancient name of the Indian Crocodile, Makara, standing for the eastern version of the astral Capricorn.

The Pyramid Texts inform the gods that the deceased *'is a 'BA' among you'* and assure the deceased that *'your Ba is within you.'* Later, during the First Intermediate Period and Middle Kingdom, the deceased appears as the BA of various gods but also as his own Ba, with the physical powers of a living body. The second view is also demonstrated in the destiny described in the 18th Dynasty tomb of Paheri at El Kaba: *'Becoming a living BA having control of bread, water, and air.'*

5.6.5   The evolution of Char-bagh (see Figure 5.4)

Evolution of European Architecture

Gardens are symbols, icons of the cosmic archetype – the macrocosmic whole engrafted on the microcosm, the earth. To the heavenly paradise, it is a pre-figuration and a preparatory set-up for upward resurrection of the 'First dead' (Aspirant souls) to those spiritual levels in the heaven. The great Sufi thinker Abu Yakub Sejeshani observes that the word Jannit in ancient Persia stood for Paradise, which means a state beyond filled with fruition; of fecundity in expression and fullness; of immortal juvenile expression represented by scented plants with flowers drawing 'elixir' from the streams of running water representing ambrosia or Amrita. In that sense, the mystic Islamic tradition calls the supreme, Al-ilahas, a perfect gardener. Another part of the Semitic tradition, Christianity labels God himself as the divine Garden. Particularly, St. John of the Cross had earmarked the City of god based on the cardinals of the cross, the garden or God himself (Guenon, 1931).

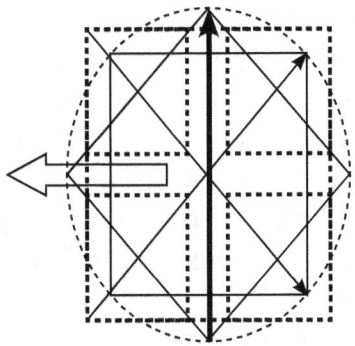

Figures 5.4 Imposition of the four quadrangles [Char-Vaka (Bag)] on the two: Brahma sutras (West-East), Yama sutra (South-north or North-south) and Karna sutras (resultant vector or diagonals). The Westward arrow is the reversal of the Ki-bala (Qiblah), explaining the Arabic language system

In the origins of the Semitic tradition, mainly in Judaism, there is a deeper esoteric line of thought-realization called the Kabalistic tradition. The tradition calls the garden, Parades. Parades, as per the Indo-European language tradition, means garden and often, a state, a domain or a distant land that is revered as a higher realm of knowledge and bliss. Pardes is the domain of higher knowledge and the four consonants in the word (P,R,D,S) correspond to the four rivers, which flowed from the Garden of Eden described in the first chapter of the old Testament, the Book of Genesis (2: 10ff) or creation itself (Corbin, 1961).

Gardens and its four quarters

In addition to the birth of the tradition of garden in the Semitic tradition, one has to look to lands further East, namely Persia or

Iran, i.e. ancient Airyan – the celebrated Land of the Aryans. It was in Persia, the garden embraced metaphysical and socio-physical attributes also. Love for gardens became the pleasure of great Achaemenid emperors like Cyrus (Kurus) and Darius (Darayush) in times as early as 700 BCE. Of the two, Cyrus had built his famous garden of Pasargadae, which is till date, the seat of his sepulcher, the tomb awaiting divine resurrection from earth, for the heavens. Till today, Persian carpets are embroidered on the 'checkers' (square patterns) of these ancient gardens called the 'space of four divine quarters' or simply, the 'Char-bagh'. The word 'Char' means 'four' in the eastern or 'Satem' stream of Indo-European language system that covers both ancient Indian and Persian sub-language systems. And 'bagh' means garden, which metaphysically represents 'Bak' or 'vak', the word of God in India. Thus Par-deus meant a distant land often signifying a 'celebrated divine' realm of the east, an idea that the Gypsies had cherished as they travelled westbound. In ancient Egypt, the famous 'Book of the Dead' contains the word several times. The term Egypt, incidentally, is derived from '(A)gypsia' meaning the land where the Gypsies had finally settled.

History tells that Cyrus and his son, Darius, had built an intercontinental road from Susa in Western Persia (close to the Tigris and Euphrates valley) to Sardis in Anatolia (Turkey). Travellers from the ancient Near East (Western Asia: the Fertile Crescent) and Asiatic Greece (Caria, Lydia, Lycia, and Phrygia) used to come to these gardens of Persia in the ancient times thus making the road as world's first international highway and attributing the ancient Persian empire as world's first gigantic urban empire that stretched from the western banks of the Indus to the eastern shores of Danube. Emperor Alexander had treaded this route to reach India a few centuries later. It is evident in Figures 5.5 to 5.7.

Now, what is contained in these gardens as a cultural landscape, as a mosaic of mystic treasure? The squares or 'checkered' patterns are themselves filled up with heavenly flowers and green shrubs – that more than a millennium later became the basis of the sacred 'Ishmaeli diagram' portraying the infinite lace of creation by the Supreme, i.e. Al-ilah in Islamic tradition (Corbin, 1964). More than two thousand years later, these patterns inspired the great works of AIA Gold-medal winner American Architect Sir Christopher Alexander (1979), who worked out his famous 'pattern language systems' for the built environment. In between, these patterns continued to evolve through the advent of Moorish Islamic architecture in Iberia (Spain and Portugal), mainly by the Nasrid sultanate. From Iberia, it continued to inspire the rest of Europe and, mainly, Gothic architecture in France throughout the entire course of early dark ages (7th to 13th century AD). The westward journey of the 'symbol' of the Lordship of four quarters is evident in Figures 5.5 to 5.7, as it traces its earliest origins in the Vedic quadrant to the use of swastika in Buddhist architecture and Iconography and earliest Persian architecture, say in the gardens of Pasargadae (700 BCE).

Centuries later in Persia, the typical Sassanid park was arranged in the form of a cross (200 BCE). The features were the four arms meeting at right angles, with the palace in the center. The quadrangular pattern corresponded to the cosmological notion of the universe divided into four quarters and watered by four rivers flowing from the representative earthly paradise. Finally, the pattern became the heart of Islamic tradition, mainly in the form of 'Char-bagh' representing many of the Moghul gardens in India, of which the Humayun's tomb and its later representative in marble, the famous 'Taj Complex', are just the two of many. The Koran (18:55) particularly forwards the divine implications of death and resurrection in a garden, which is the prototype of paradise holding the entombment, a link between the two.

However, in traditions that are perhaps pre-historic, gardens were famous in the entire ancient Near East including Anatolia or oldest Asiatic Greek settlements. They are evident amongst the gardens of the 'Ancient Gods' (James, 2004), who were somehow pagan to the more formalized and institutionalized order of Semitic traditions. One of these ancient gods was 'Adonis', who lamented, died and was resurrected in a garden. Thus the garden of 'Adonis', who was a mysterious pagan corn-god, still stands as a possible source to the origins of the Garden of 'Eden'. From 'Adonis' to 'Eden', there are enough evidence and a trace of a long journey of religious and iconic evolution and this is however not the scope of the present chapter. But what this chapter seeks is to highlight the celebration of life and death contained in the deeper cycle of renewal and sustainability, implied in the deep ecological patterns of these ancient gardens of Adonis. Adonis symbolized as the 'corn god' (vija) re-sprouted (spring forth) after it was reaped following a Passover festival (after winter). The journey from 'reaping' to 're-sprouting' represented the cycles of agriculture and the changing seasons in a year, and the return of the next year, the next spring. These cycles actually portrayed the deeper mysteries of death and resurrection, and they were often portrayed by a lot of ancient religions in Egypt, Greece and Anatolia. From one spring, through summer, to autumn, and from there through winter to the next spring is an eternal journey of the four seasons, the four quarters, the four cardinals in a cross-like form delineated as a landscape, an icon of perfection. This landscape of perfection is 'the Garden of Eden'. The pattern and the mystery contained in the icon are best evident in the following words:

"In course of time the slow advance of knowledge, which has dispelled so many cherished illusions, convinced the more thoughtful portion of mankind that the alternation of summer and winter, of spring and autumn, were not merely the result of their own magical rites, but that some deeper cause, some mightier power, was at work behind the shifting scenes of nature......and as they now explained the fluctuations of growth and decay, of reproduction and dissolution, by the marriage, the death, and the rebirth or revival of the Gods, their religious or magical dramas turned in 'great measures' of these themes. They set forth the fruitful union of the powers of fertility, the sad 'Death' of one at least of the divine partners, and his joyful 'Resurrection'...the resemblance of these ceremonies to the Indian and European ceremonies which I have described elsewhere is obvious......His affinity with vegetation comes out at once in the common story of his birth.......the story that Adonis spent half, or according to others a third, of the year in the lower world and the rest of it in the upper world, is explained most simply and naturally by supposing that he represented vegetation (the corn) which lies buried in the earth (the tomb) one half (or one-third the year) and reappears above ground the other half (or two-third). Adonis has been taken for the Sun (or Mithras)...... moreover, the explanation is countenanced by a considerable body of opinion amongst the ancients themselves, who again and again interpreted the dying and reviving God as the reaped (separated from body or earth) and sprouting (conjoined again to rain-fertilized body or earth) grain.

Sir James G. Frazer

'*Adonis Attis Osiris: A Study in the History of Oriental Religions*'

But to unlock the deeper truths lying behind the secret of gardens, one has to come finally to another land, lying further east of Airyan (Persia or Iran). That land from the very ancient time was called 'Arya-barta', meaning 'the circle or quarters of the Aryans'. For the Greeks, it was the land east of the 'Quetta-Pishon' Valley, the Indus, called 'Indica' or India.

5.6.6 Basics of the Lordship of four quarters: Origins in the Vedas

In the Vedic lore, the concept of altar comes out best through the establishment of the Sarvatati. The instrumentation is procreation of the original universal being. This is represented by Savita. Savita is the highest point – the creative luminance of noontide (madhyanindan Surya). The entire eighth Mandala of the Rig Veda is dedicated to this highest stride of realization.

The term Savita originates from Pra-sabita, which means the all-producing womb – the Matrix of things (represented by the word Matarishwan, which is the first procreative principle of life or Vayu in the summits of transcendence and re-immanence or resurgence of the universe as evident in the Rig Veda: 1.141.3; 1.71.4. Here are some references:

'*Savita paschatyat Savita purastatSavito-uttaratwat Savita dharatat Savita nasubatoSarvatatim*'

[*Rig Veda: 10.36.14*]

'*Savita Yantra-I prithvim-bana-shambane Savita dwamdyung-hat*'

[*Rig Veda: 10.141.1*]

Savita, the luminous spirit of self-manifestation, produces the manifested (array of things) from the un-manifested (from the limits that are beyond to manifestation) and by doing so embraces all the worlds and the lordship over all four quarters and beyond. Savita thus becomes the con-joint – Yantra – the universal framework of things in all directions (mainly ten). The directions are:
- East – which is a priori and followed by the rest (purva)
- North – which follows in a later phase (uttara)
- West – which is following as the linkage (paschat-paschima)
- South – which is sacrificed (dakshina) and that is from below or outside for the sake of higher or inner openings (dakshin) and
- The four corners (diagonals) – Agni, Nairit, Vayu and Issan.
- Up–Down – everything that is beyond – the origin (Up) and from the origin or the original (Down)
- In effect, the cardinals are established and the cross and the four quarters are consequentially established.

5.6.7 Array of four quarters and the seats of the four representatives

The four quarters are established by the impersonal seat – personified by the four cardinal realizations. The four realizations, as per the first principles, are personified by four Sages representing the four Vedas. The four are a con-joint – 'Yantra' – an orchestrated sequential action of sacrificial ascent. The sequential action is as follows:
- East – the Rishihood of Rik-mantra – Hota (Precedent)
- North – the Rishihood of Yggna (Sutra-Yaddju-dharaka) – the sacrificial configuration – Adhwarju (Antecedent)
- West – the Rishihood of the culmination of the Rik-mantra to chants of Poetry – Udgata, who establishes the rhythm of things in centrality – Devatati (Sama)
- South – the Rishihood of the completion of the circuit or movements of things – from centrality (Devatati) to the all-embracing rim (Sarvatati) – this is the principal Ritwik or Brahma (Atharvan) and thus going beyond the four quarters

(four faces) to beyond (fifth and sixth). This is the later part (Descending phase).

'Richang twang poshamastepapubangyatrang two gayatisakkarishu Brahma two badatijatavidyangyaggyashomatrang bi mimita u twa'
[Rig Veda: 10.71.11]

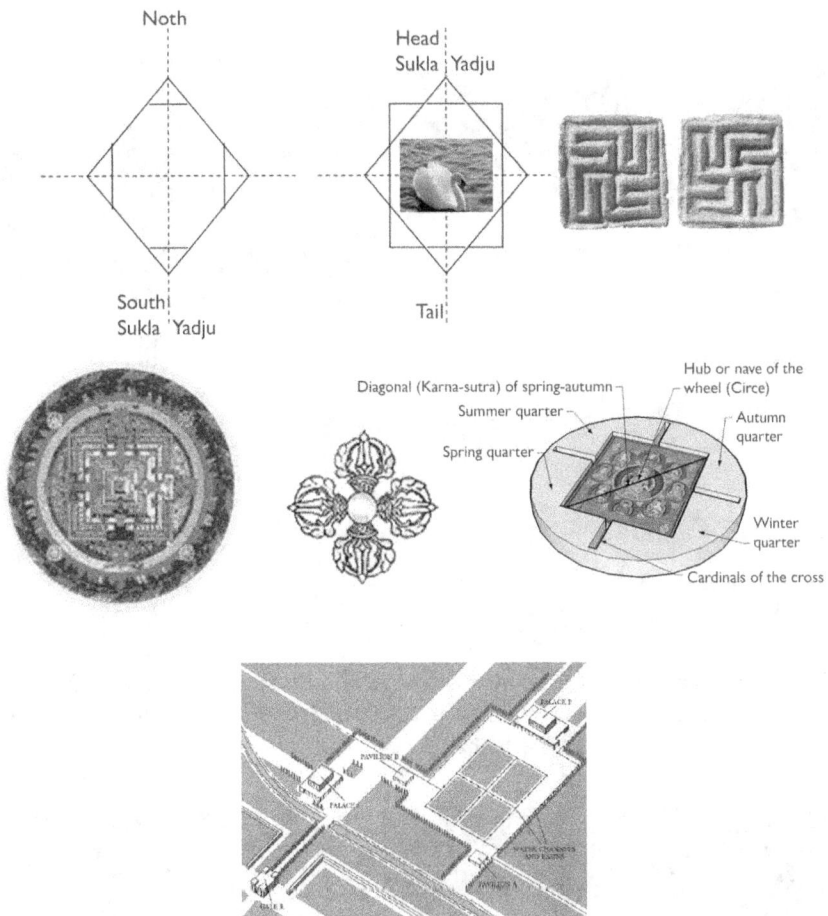

Figure 5.5 Lordship of four quarters in: (a) the four Vedas forming a Fire-Ceremony Quadrant (Ritwik, Yadju, Hotar and Brahmana) and Swastika in the Indus valley (2500 BCE); (b) Thunderbolt (Vajra) and Tibetan Mandala; and (c) Ancient Persian sources at Pasargadae (600 BCE)

In summary, the plan or pattern of the garden is also a yantra or an imagery of sacrifice and resurrection of the primordial purusha, which echoes those evident in the ancient pagan traditions of the ancient Near East, Greece (Eleusinian mysteries) and Egypt (the Cult of Osiris). The Garden of Adonis was one of many. The Garden of Eden, evident from a more formal tradition, is perhaps, just continuity with minor adaptation and modification – in place and time. Figures 5.5–5.7 are a living testimony of that tradition.

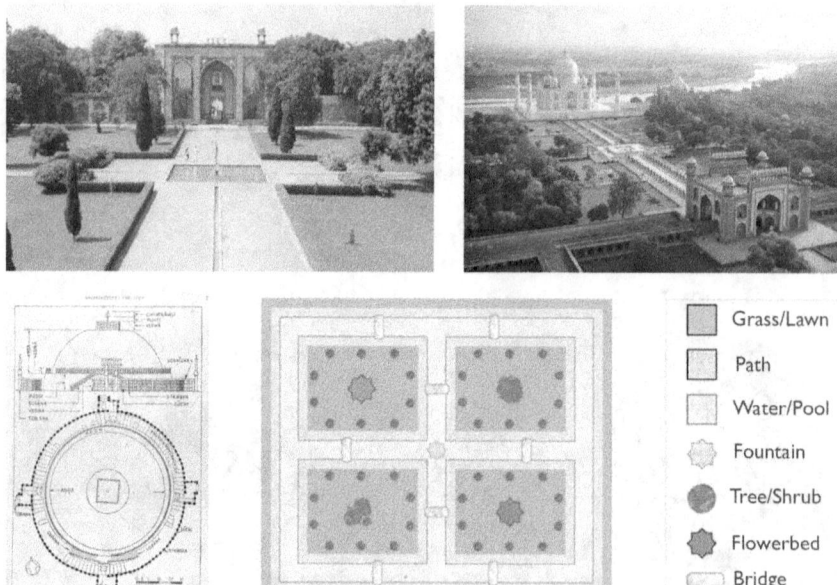

Figure 5.6 Lordship of four quarters in (a) Buddhist (Sanchi Stupa, 300 BCE); (b) Islamic and Moorish architecture (India and Iberia): 10–15th century AD (Humayun's Tomb; and (c) Taj Mahal

Figure 5.7 Lordship of Four quarters in Andalusian Spain and the Chateau of Versailles, France (The transfer of Architectural principles from Moorish Iberia to Gothic France)

5.6.8 Four quarters in Buddhist Iconography

The idea of four quarters continued even during the Buddhist times. The idea of circum-ambulatory path having four quarters, say in the Sanchi Stupa, or in the various sections of the four lions or four cardinals of the Pillar of Asoka are iconographic evidences. A lot of research needs to be activated to establish the continuity of the four cardinals (Swastika) or cross-like order in Buddhist iconography. Research in isolation may be ideally kept aside and replaced by researches that are orchestrated chronologically with fixities and flexibilities, both.

Idea of historic continuity explicit in the story of evolution of an icon is evident in the following words of Sri Anirvan (2001):

> It may be debatable whether material history is the expression of an original idea, but it is an indubitable fact that spiritual history is always so. 'It is of the One existence that yearning hearts speak in diverse ways' – has said a Vedic seer (RV: 1.164.46); and this is true not only in an abstract way, but in a concrete form also.
>
> Like the mystic Asswattha tree of the Upanishad, [the Bodhi Tree] 'with its roots above and the branches below', the Vedic tradition, in a broad sense, it stands at the very source of almost all forms of spiritual cults. And the interpretation of this tradition can be attempted with best results if we do not place the Vedas on the isolated heights of the past, but with a total (complete) vision of the present retrace our steps to the roots discovering, with a penetrating insight, the links at every steps.
>
> Vedic Exegesis
> 'The Cultural Heritage of India',
> Volume one,
> RMIC, Kolkata (2001)

The mystical Asswattha tree has always found a place in the ancient garden of India called the panchavati or a field of five trees – where 1 +4 trees represent the cardinal and the quadrangle. The idea continued through the Buddhist period as the central Bodhi tree of a Vana/ Vithi/ Brahm-Vihara or a Buddhist monastic garden. The ancient tradition of the Green paradise of the rishis or sages called Rishipatanna in Saranganath (Sarnath), adjunct to

Varanasi, is an ancient imagery between the two periods. Gautama the Buddha began his first sermon from this ancient paradise of India.

Thus to trace origins of an icon as important as the Garden of Eden, one has to take an inter-continental, trans-cultural and cross-religious perspective. Such a viewpoint will certify how different cultures and religions, either related or not related to each other, arrive at a commonality of cosmic truth and truth-realization. This is what we mean by the 'impersonal universal' often termed as the 'sanatana' – a lore that finds a special place in the ancient Vedic lore and then up to Buddhism; and also from pagan West Asian or East European religions to the later big three of the Semitic group: Judaism, Christianity and Islam. Even in the ancient Meso-American religions, it has a place, for instance, in the quadrangular Mayan calendar. In all of them, the iconography of the Garden and the Lordship of the four quarters persists, and has secured a central place or hope called the idea of Pardes or Paradise. A proper interpretation of the immortal tradition of Paradise as a garden can be best attempted if we do not place the more ancient traditions on an isolated realm of the past having no continuity, but try and establish a holistic vision of tracing its evolution at every steps and niche of history – to which a later religious belief is perhaps another additional step added to the larger ladder of time and human history heading for the future. And there can be more in store for the ramification of the iconography of the Garden of Eden, in the distant future.

5.7   Conclusions

The journey and the triumph of the European civilization with the fall of Granada and the absorption of all design, art and cultural elements vide the Iberian Moorish or Nasrid Sultanate to France have been made evident in the present chapter. The following words of Sir Bertrand Russell simply outlines a marking of the departure and the subsequent triumph called the European Renaissance and perhaps, the third one in the making, to which the systems frameworks one and two in the two preceding chapters have abided by:

'...During the 15th century, various other causes were added to the decline of the papacy to produce a very rapid change, both political and cultural. Gunpowder strengthened central governments at the expense of feudal nobility. In France and England, Louis XI and Edward IV allied themselves with rich middle class, who helped themselves to quell aristocratic anarchy.'

'...the new culture was essentially pagan, admiring Greece and Rome, and despising the Middle Ages. Architecture and Literary styles were adapted to ancient models. When Constantinople, the last survival of antiquity, was captured by the Turks, Greek refugees in Italy were welcomed by humanists. Vasco Da Gama and Columbus enlarged the world, and Copernicus enlarged the Heavens. The Donation of Constantine was rejected as a fable, and overwhelmed with scholarly derision. By the help of the Byzantines, Plato came to be known, not only in Neo-Platonic and Augustinian versions, but at first hand......the long centuries of asceticism (and denial) were forgotten in a riot of art and poetry and pleasure......the intoxication could not last, but for the moment it shut out fear (the medieval sense of fear). In this moment of joyful liberation the modern (Western) world was born.'

(The Eclipse of Papacy, page 475)

But the last lines by Russell in his seminal work 'The History of Western Philosophy' end with a note of apprehension and incompleteness, in spite of the joyful liberation of the spirit of Renaissance that swept the Western mind process:

'.........the intoxication could not last, but for the moment it shut out fear (the medieval sense of fear)......at least, for human sake, in that moment of joyful liberation the modern (western) world was born.'

Therefore, questions that still remain are:
1. Why the spirit of free aesthetics, pleasure, art, poetry, music and architecture could not sustain the priorities of a new emergent Europe?
2. Why European Renaissance at the broad humane–cultural level and other associated movements of Reformation at

the theological or organized religious level failed under the new advents of a Counter-Reformation and the mechanized order of the Industrial Revolution?
3. Why the joy of freedom in art and poetry and pleasure, which was unleashed at around 15–16th century, was soon replaced by processes of machines, materials production and mercantile trade that gave way to an absolutely different order of competitiveness and mass exploitation of the labor, perhaps exceeding in scale and atrocities of even the Feudal order of the Middle Ages? The consequences culminating up to the 19th century Europe in terms of the number of ethnic wars and war years are a testimony to that.
4. Why the true spirit of democracy and joyful liberty of the Masses in France succumbed to a formal western imperial and mercantile model of development since the early18th century?
5. Can we call this third Renaissance partial? And then, why was this so?

Many answers can be forwarded. But the more important of these answers perhaps remain in the understanding of a deeper foundation of progress and civilization. It is the respect of the Feminine. It is the raise and the elevation of that as the 'sacred Feminine', in the highest realms of purity and acceptance. A part of that foundation has remained underlying the whole course of the book and mainly the present chapter. A clue to that finally emerges from the following words of Swami Vivekananda, of which the first three paras are the deeper cognitive constructs and the last is the movement and application in history, particularly in the transition that took place in Iberia at a crucial point of European history:

"The Tantrika religion is very mysterious, inscrutable even to the Yogis". It is this worship of Shakti that is openly and universally practiced. The idea of motherhood, i.e. the relation of a son to his mother, is also noticed in great measure. Protestantism as a force is not very significant in Europe, where the religion is, in fact, Roman Catholic. In the religion, Jehovah, Jesus, and the Trinity are secondary; there, the worship is for the Mother—She, the Mother, with the Child Jesus in her arms. The emperor cries "Mother", the field-marshal cries "Mother", the soldier with the flag in his hand cries "Mother", the seaman at the helm cries "Mother", the fisherman in his rags cries "Mother", the beggar in the street cries "Mother"! A million voices in a million ways, from a million places—from the palace, from the cottage, from the church, cry "Mother", "Mother", "Mother"! Everywhere is the cry "Ave Maria"; day and night, "Ave Maria", "Ave Maria"!

Next is the worship of the woman. This worship of Shakti is not lust, but is that Shakti-Pujâ, that worship of the Kumâri (virgin) and the Sadhavâ (the married woman whose husband is living), which is done in Varanasi, Kalighat, and other holy places (still in India).

It is the worship of the Shakti, not in mere thought, not in imagination, but in actual, visible form. Our Shakti-worship is only in the holy places, and at certain times only is it performed; but theirs is in every place and always, for days, weeks, months, and years. Foremost is the woman's state, foremost is her dress, her seat, her food, her wants, and her comforts; the first honours in all respects are accorded to her. Not to speak of the noble-born, not to speak of the young and the fair, it is the worship of any and every woman, be she an acquaintance or a stranger.

This Shakti-worship the Moors, the mixed Arab race, Mohammedan in religion, first introduced into Europe when they conquered Spain and ruled her for eight centuries. It was the Moors who first sowed in Europe the seeds of Western civilisation and Shakti-worship. In course of time, the Moors forgot this Shakti-Worship and fell from their position of strength, culture and glory, to live scattered and unrecognised in an unnoticed corner of Africa, and their power and civilisation passed over to Europe. The Mother, leaving the Moors, smiled Her loving blessings on the Christians and illumined their homes".

The idea of the softer principle of life, of 'the principle of the emotive YIN', and the co-existence of holism along with reductionism are now a new wave of science. The idea of the womb, the cosmic matrix, the cyclic and non-linear thinking to science may be a latest word of the Western mind; but with the Orientals it was always there with the constructs called 'Kali-Lilith-

Innana-Ishtar-Cybele (Matar Kubele)-Demeter and Diana'. It is this very strength that shaped Asia, as it had later shaped the Moors and finally shaped the Europeans, in the context and scope of the System's framework three.

The coming together of the two forces, that of India and that of Greece, of the internal and external pursuits of liberty, is the basis of the making of the Whole, the totality of human civilization. Architecture is perhaps, a material expression of that, as one of many.

The symbol of the 'Çhar-bagh' represents that matrix, the complete array of civilization. European Renaissance recovered that from the ancient Greco-Roma wisdom, a gift from so-called Pagan world of the Orient and forwarded to the shaping of the Americas – through the Matrix of Liberty and Democracy covering both – men and women, equally.

Far from the horrors of inquisition and bigotry, the Great American melting point has been a response to that holism and the expression of the whole. There are mainly names who initiated that – Brunelleschi, Bramante and Michelangelo; Leonardo Vinci and Isaac Newton; Rapheal and Alberti; Kepler and Copernicus are just to name a few. But the non-linear thinking which was initially absorbed by the Celto-Hellenic order from Asia before the Dark Ages and re-expressed by High Renaissance after the Dark Ages slowly succumbed to the incoming advent of an Imperial-machine order. The reversal takes the reader back to the concluding question. Therefore, the stages of interaction that the third system's framework has forwarded are still not complete and the shift and departure of the European civilization crossing the Atlantic to the new world cannot be explained covering the full depths of civilization if we just remain within the thresholds of the first three frameworks. The answers are inclusively beyond, which has been attempted by a set of reviews in the sixth and concluding chapter.

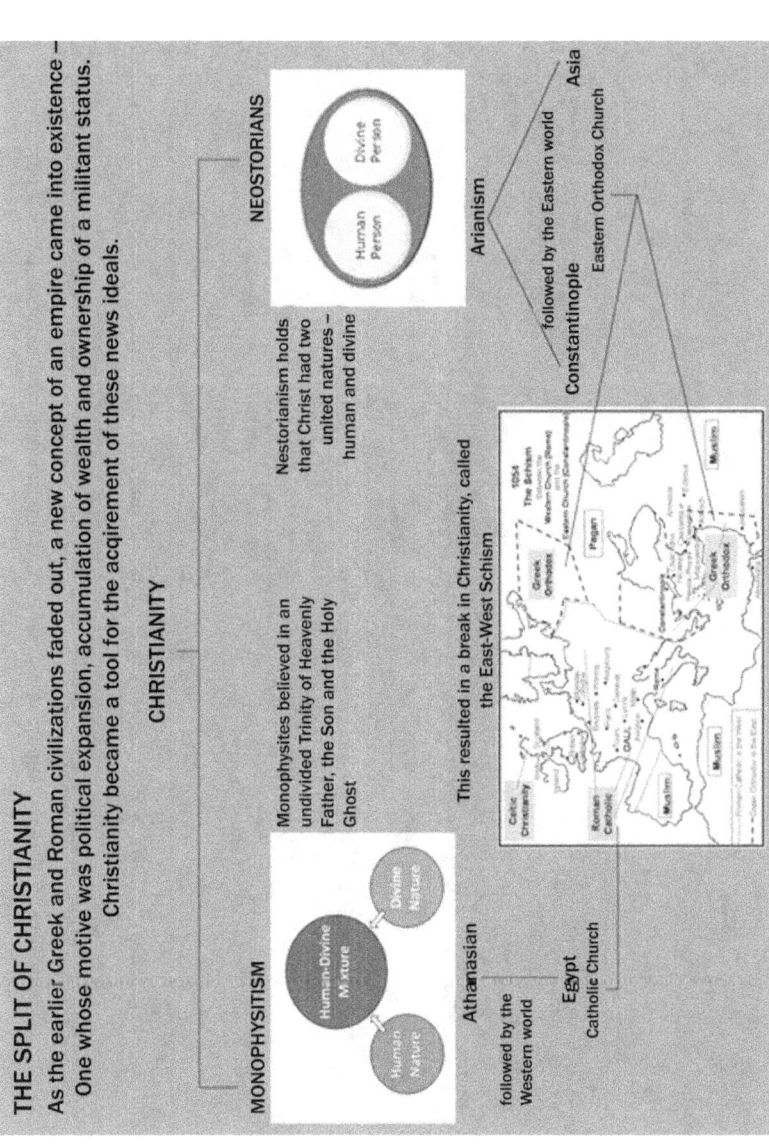

Template 5.1 The Line of Isaac (see left) and the Line of Ishmael (see right)
Locations: Italia (Western Roman Empire) and Ana-Italia/Anatolia (Eastern Roman Empire)

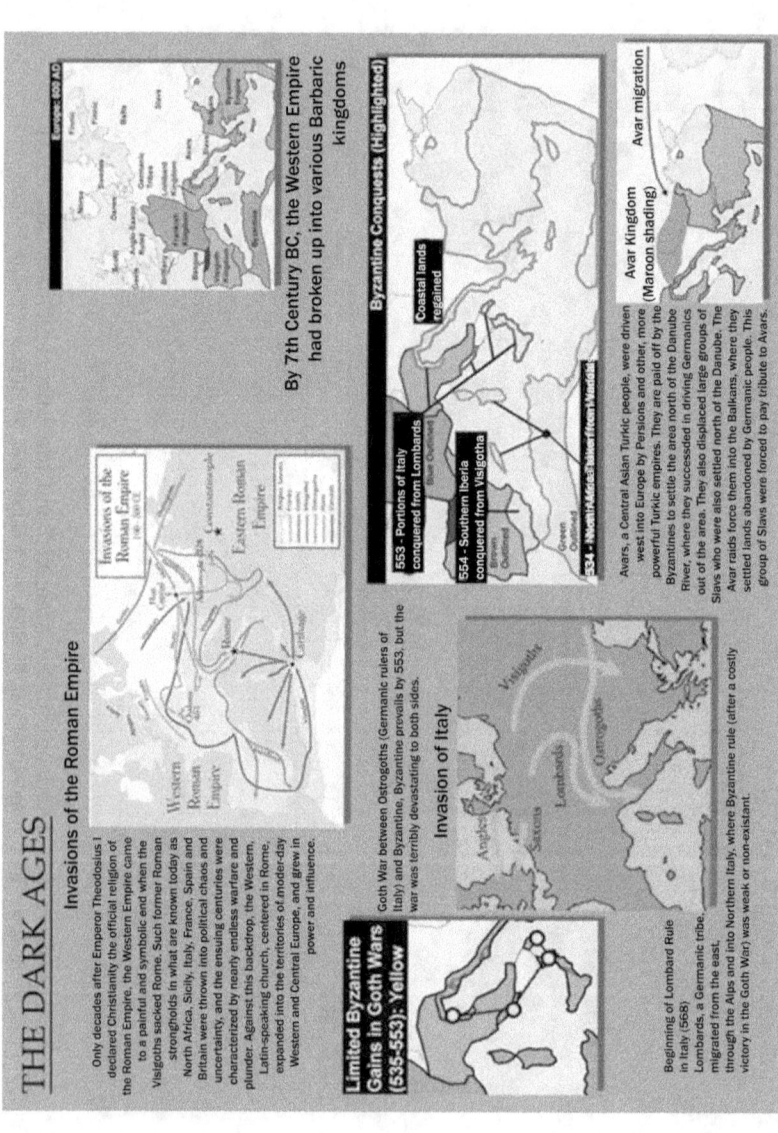

Template 5.2 The beginning of barbaric invasion and consequent Dark Ages

Note: The origins of barbaric tribes are mainly in North and West Europe

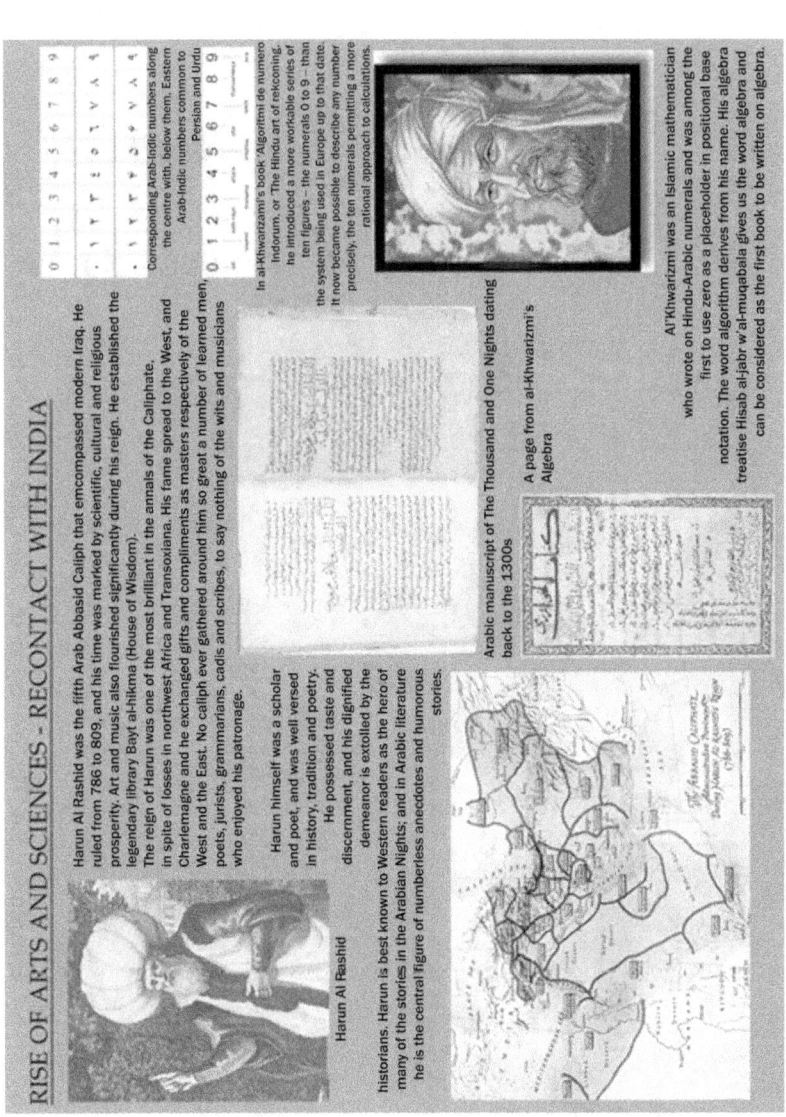

Template 5.3 The advent of the Islamic-Moorish civilization and the exchanges between India and Iberia via Baghdad

Templates 5.4 The explosion of Indian and Iberian Islamic Architecture

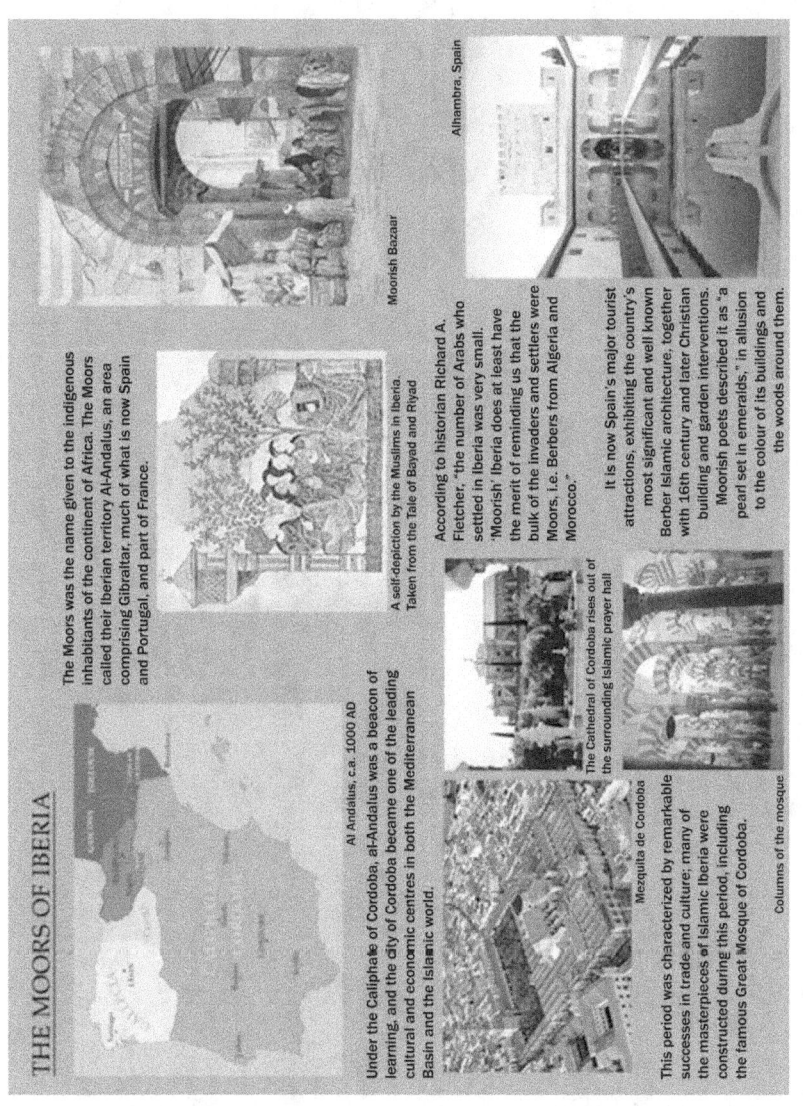

Templates 5.5 The explosion of Indian and Iberian Islamic Architecture

System framework three: Phase III of global history of architecture

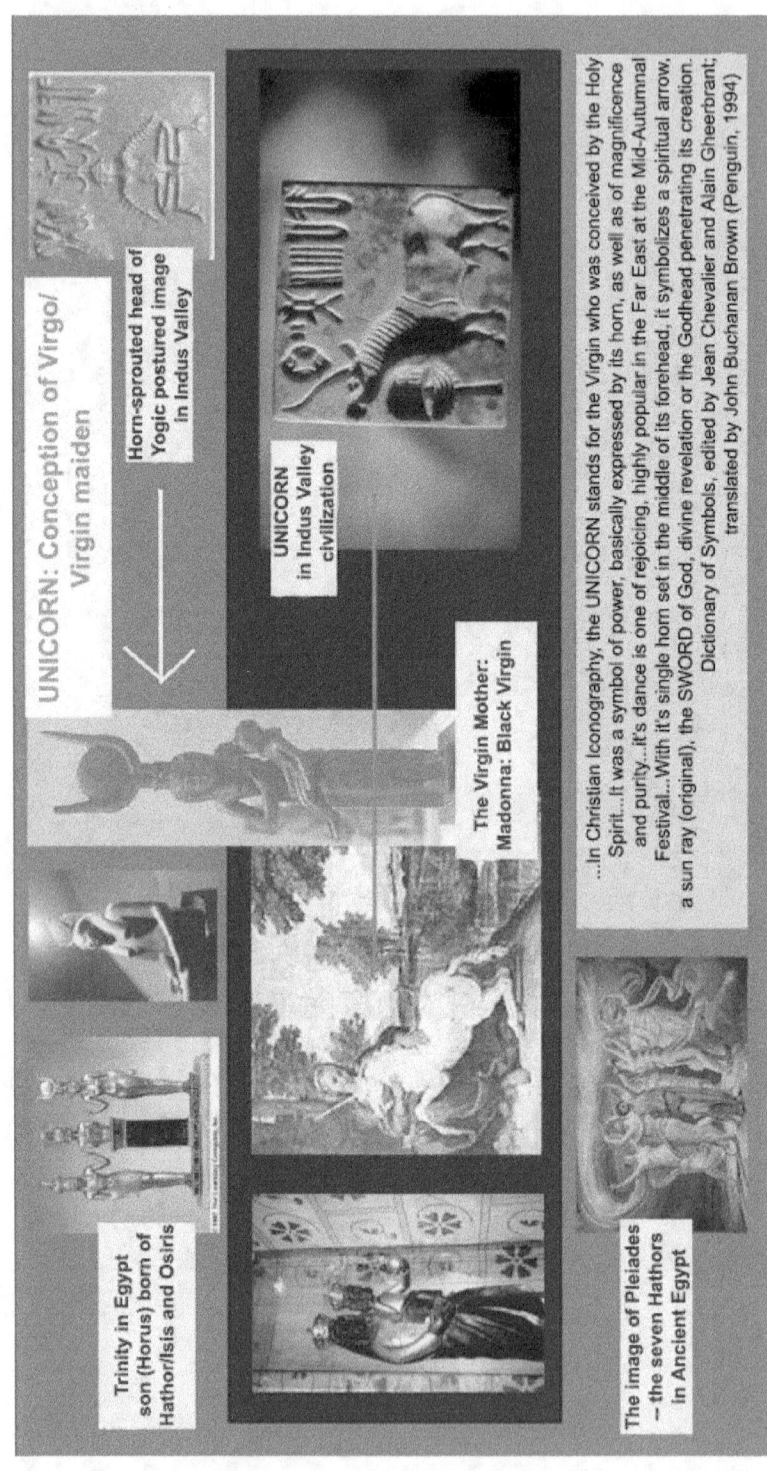

Template 5.6 The iconic form of Virgin Mari – A concept of Mother Goddess

System framework three: Phase III of global history of architecture

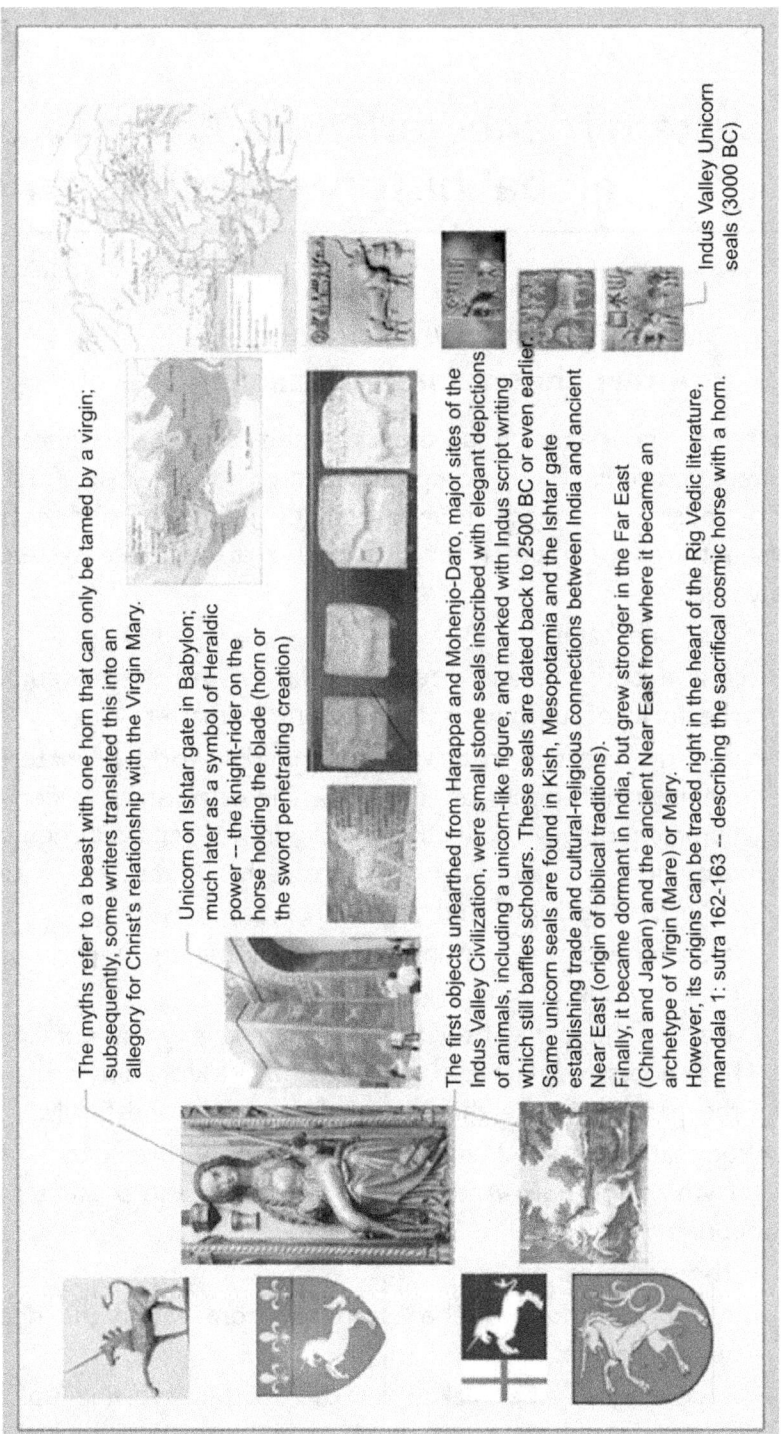

Template 5.7 Virgin Mari – her oriental sources

6
System framework four: Phase IV of global history of architecture

6.1 Systems' framework four: Interpenetration and turning

A system's understanding of the evolution of global civilization and architecture is a deep comprehension of how the twin forces, that of India and Greece, have constantly interacted and finally interpenetrated each other for the making of complete system's architecture:

- On the one hand:
  - it is a constant and deep interplay of the descendent in the form of an inner spirit working in matter;
  - it is the run and in-delving here in the world of material manifestation having an aim is to fully establish an order of humanity through collective social mindset and a subsequent evolutionary maturity in terms of ethics, presence of the collective decisions and philanthropy;
  - it is a force that is working here and making the preparations for a turning around;
  - it is also the force of social and cultural liberty that humanity has successively achieved through many twists and turns in the passage of the three preceding phases; and finally,

In summary, it is a culmination of the ancient Greek thought-force of which the Euro-American civilization of the present age is the updated maturity.

- On the other hand:
  - it is the working of the ascendant from within the deep human nature;
  - it constitutes the making of the matter evolving up to a domain of free spirit reaching and bridging the higher

intuitive, and the overarching ambit of the universal and beyond to the transcendental;

– it is also the other force, the inner force that has constantly surged above, crossing the limits of the material, and reached the sense of freedom and liberty imparted in the undifferentiated transcendental universal light of humanity here.

And correspondingly, it is the force of spiritual liberty that has been constantly sculptured by the deep Indian civilization ethos for ages after ages; and perhaps, aeons that the book has attempted to unfold.

The interpenetration constitutes a thought-force of an undivided and integral creation, and an eternal network and synonymy between the force of creation and creation itself. Such integrity integrates creation and the creator and therefore evolves to a matured level of a master unity that transcends the idea of sin and duality. Sin splits creation based on dialecticism of good and bad, transcending which and both one may reach the universal foundation of undifferentiated-ness. The foundation is a grand unification of all forces.

Every time, the Indian and the Greek forces have come together, the force of unification has been re-invigorated rendering and assuring the progress of unification of the material and spiritual liberties and furnishing a further leap towards a more progressive and open-ended civilization. The sequence has been portrayed so far in and through the preceding chapters of the book. The sequence is essentially the basis of the *systems architecture* constituting the step-by-step leap progress. It is this deep architectural process that can be termed as *the systems approach*.

The understanding of the systems approach, as traced by the present book, has been relayed in the first two introductory Chapters 1 and 2; and particularly, the surges and an intermingling that have occurred in the first three phases have been explained in Chapters 3, 4 and 5. Chapters 3, 4 and 5 have shown how the initial preparations have been accomplished by the turning of civilization and the interpenetration of the Indian and Greek thought-forces, which is in a stage approaching a full bloom, a maturity and perhaps, a climax and a turning. It is the outline of Phase IV.

As a culmination, the fourth and final phase of Indo-Greco interactions is constantly unleashing its highest glory. The two forces are going through a higher to higher order of interpenetrations, a rapture of parts of each other and a grand interpenetration symbolizing both the equilibrium and dynamism of the whole. The interpenetration is constantly occurring and maturing in our own times. The important questions are:

1. What are the interpenetrations that we see are maturing collectively as a matured Phase IV representing the climax of the intermingling?
2. How they are taking place over long time periods?
3. And how are they sustainably operational in the contemporary world?

The answers have been provided by the sequence of discussions carried out in the present book. But an answer to the last question in particular is the climax; hence, the final chapter.

Accordingly, the conclusive discussion of the book in the form of the present chapter is forwarded in three parts. Part one (6.1) recapitulates the cumulative causation of the four phases. It forwards how one phase is embedded on the other. Part two (6.2) forwards the pattern of transition reaching a matured level of the 4-phased systems process. It highlights the pattern of changes that has constantly occurred at the end of Phase 3 and how all that is collectively transiting to Phase 4. Finally, part three (6.3) forwards the first features of the turning. The features are broadly seven, which the chapter introduces. The features will go a long way to mature and evolve assuring a true blooming and turning of human progress. Perhaps, it is a return to where the last cycle started. But definitely the return shall recur in the present cycle in a more evolved way, which is the golden conclusion.

6.2   The cumulative causation of four phases

6.2.1   Succession in systems framework

Over the ages, the Indian spirit had travelled westwards. Indian philosophy had gone beyond its geographical borders to embrace larger frontiers of humanity based on a humanitarian approach founded on a deep spiritual realization of an essential unity and its outward universal embrace constantly assimilating the diverse and the heterogeneous. Chapters 3, 4 and 5 have shown how the dissemination had happened in three distinct phases. The principal recipient has been the Greek mind. The outcome of the exchanges had been taking place in three distinct broad phases, and now they have collectively forwarded a systems change which is still maturing and evolving.

We have seen that in times of extreme remote antiquity, such an intermingling founded the basis of world's first civilizations mostly concentrated in the West Asia. The forefathers of the Persian Achaemenes and Sumerian empires, the Etruscans, the Sabians and the Egyptians constituted the first cradles of expressions, when the two thought-forces had first met, in the present cycle of civilization. In the context of the present book, meeting earmarks *Phase I* of the system. That time, the forefathers of the Greeks were mainly concentrated in their earliest Asiatic abode, which is ancient Anatolia, the Land of the Hittites, whose names recur in the very beginning of the Semitic foundations in the Book of Genesis, the Old Testament.

The progress of civilization had made its first preparations to travel further west. At that point of time, the Indian Vedic religion had exuded out of communities residing east of the river Sindhu: (H) Indu: Indus, and the ancient Persian religion of Avesta/Gathas belonged to the communities on the west and both had shared a common root – an undifferentiated foundation of creation. It is an important point belonging to Phase I that we need to understand while we explore Phase IV in the present chapter. The essence of the point is made evident in an excerpt entitled 'Walks and Talks Beside the Jhelum', where Swami Vivekananda and a party of Europeans and disciples were discussing on the important issue (Kashmir, July 20, 1898):

"That morning the river was broad and shallow and clear, and two of us walked with the Swami across the fields and along the banks about three miles. He began by talking of the sense of sin, how it was Egyptian, Semitic and Aryan. It appears in the Vedas, but quickly passes out. The devil is recognized there as the Lord of Anger. Then, with the Buddhists he became Mara, the Lord of Lust, and one of the most loved of the Lord Buddha's titles was "Conqueror of Mara". (Vide the Sanskrit lexicon Amarkosha that Swami learnt to patter as a child of four!) But while Satan is the Hamlet of the Bible, in the Hindu scriptures the Lord of Anger never divides creation. He always represents defilement, never duality.

Zoroaster was a reformer of some old religion. Even Ormuzd and Ahriman with him were not supreme; they were only manifestations of the Supreme. That older religion must have been Vedantic. So the Egyptians and Semites cling to the theory of sin while the Aryans, as Indians and Greeks, quickly lose it. In India righteousness and sin become Vidyâ and Avidyâ – both to be transcended. Amongst the Aryans, Persians and Europeans become Semitized by religious ideas; hence the sense of sin.

And then the talk drifted..."

A set of dimensions or questions emerge as we begin to ponder and conclude:

1. What has been the motive power of the whole universe/ can the creation be divided?
2. Can there be a twin concept of a Good God and an evil Satan (Mara of the Buddhist)? Or, is there a Grand Unification lying higher and as greater, which is more acceptable?
3. Can there be a systems framework where the lesser good (evil) can be transformed and absorbed in the system itself after becoming greater good? It is evolution itself with flexibility, openness and experimentation.
4. And finally, to what extent, the interpenetration of the Greek and the Indian thought-forces have represented the grand unification?

To do that we may revert to another quote from a lecture note by Swami Vivekananda, entitled "Practical Vedanta, Part IV", delivered in London, 18th November 1896:

'What right has any section of the community to base the whole work and evolution of the universe upon one of these two factors alone, upon competition and struggle? What right has it to base the whole working of the universe upon passion and fight, upon competition and struggle? That these exist we do not deny; but what right has anyone to deny the working of the other force? Can any man deny that love, this "not I", this renunciation is the only positive power in the universe? That other is only the misguided employment of the power of love; the power of love brings competition, the real genesis of competition is in love. The real genesis of evil is in unselfishness. The creator of evil is good, and the end is also good. It is only misdirection of the power of good. A man who murders another is, perhaps, moved to do so by the love of his own child. His love has become limited to that one little baby, to the exclusion of the millions of other human beings in the universe. Yet, limited or unlimited, it is the same love.

Thus the motive power of the whole universe, in whatever way it manifests itself, is that one wonderful thing, unselfishness, renunciation, love, the real, the only living force in existence. Therefore the Vedantist insists upon that oneness. We insist upon this explanation because we cannot admit two causes of the universe. If we simply hold that by limitation the same beautiful, wonderful love appears to be evil or vile, we find the whole universe explained by the one force of love. If not, two causes of the universe have to be taken for granted, one good and the other evil, one love and the other hatred.

Which is more logical? Certainly the one-force theory.'

As said before, the Egyptians and Semites had cling to the theory of sin while the Aryans, i.e., the Indians and the Greeks, quickly lose it. The Indians and the Greeks quickly reached the 'One Force' system. In Egypt, there was an initial theme of Palin-genesis and transmigration of souls that the Greeks inherited. But eventually, later Egyptians degraded from that open-ended temporal order of evolutionary cosmology and accepted the dualistic base that even affected the once liberal schools of Alexandria and Greco-Romans.

- *Systems Phase I question I: Thus there is a need to trace the older networking between Zoroastrianism and Vedanta and its impact on archaic Judaism; and how it differed from a later version?*

In India righteousness and sin soon became Vidyâ and Avidyâ – and both are to be transcended. As the Indian mind evolved, the ancient Vedanta was reached as the cornerstone of the India mind, as it has always inspired the path of assimilation through exploration and experimentation. Thus said a Sage from an ancient Upanishad:

'Those who knew both as the same, as they found ways to cross death by virtue of the lesser truth or Avidya and also bring down immortality by the power of greater good, which is Vidya ' (Isha Upanishad).

But, amongst the other branch of Aryans, the Persians and the Europeans, who gradually become semitized by the later dialectical religious ideas, fell into the dualistic framework of the Judeo-Christian tradition; hence, evolved the sense of sin and gradually, original sin, that permanently operated the system into two parts – good and evil:

- *Systems Phase II questions: Thus there is a further need to re-trace the origin of Judeo-Christian tradition with regard to archaic Judaism.*

Subsequently, with further decay and degeneration of the West Asian civilization, the wave of integrity could be not anymore being contained there. It had to proceed further westbound. The new epicenter of civilization, the fresh cradle of Aryan intermingling of the two forces, was further west, i.e. the lands in the Eastern Mediterranean. The Greeks had moved out of their older Asiatic abodes, i.e. Milesia, Lydia, Lycia, Caria and Phrygia, and now they were in the Olympian islands. The new cradle had begun to flourish with great thinkers. They were the last generations from the archaic Samo-Thracian Orphic thinkers to Heraclitus, Plato and Pythagoras, who forwarded a short-time revival of the unique thought and a quick resuscitation of the ancient truth. But the star of wisdom could not be retained for long in the Eastern Mediterranean and it had to shift further westbound. The revival of the Messianic Judeo-Christian tradition again disintegrated and Europe under the Western Churches entered the savagery and barbarism of the Dark Ages. Rome fell at 470 AD precisely. It is closure of what we may call Phase II. Dark Age for a period of 1000 years was initiated. But these were also the times of explorations and absorptions.

A thousand years later, before Western Europe could finally step out of the Dark Ages, around late 13th century AD, the Moors – the trading Muslim-Arabs (offshoots of Phoenicians) had settled along the North African borders and the lower Mediterranean coastline. They founded a Golden Age in Iberia with the help of Greco-Alexandrian Judaic scholars. The Greek and Indian minds were again brought together in Spain and Portugal, and consequently the Islamic civilization was liberated by the Liberal Court of Baghdad, through which the Moors grafted a materially and culturally more advanced civilization in the extreme Western Mediterranean compared to the barbarism of a Middle Ages Judeo-Christian Europe. The systems intermingling had by then entered the Phase III. Some of the greatest universities of liberal learning and social equity that represented that of ancient Persia in Phase I and Alexandria in Phase II were re-created in Iberia by the Nasrid Sultanate.

- *Systems Phase III question: Thus there is a third need to re-trace the origin of Judeo-Islamic tradition with regard to archaic Judaism.*

The star of wisdom again could not be retained for long in Europe and it had further shifted westbound. With the Fall of Granada in 1490s, the network of Judeo-Islamic tradition between Asia and Iberia was disrupted and was semiticized thoroughly. On the other hand, the Roman Catholic system of papacy had degraded and the Church of Europe was dissected between the Eastern and the Western viewpoints. As a result, the liberals, the Protestants in Iberia, and most important of all, the culture of High Renaissance in France, which had once absorbed all the sovereign ideas from Islamic Alhambra, Seville and Cordoba made migratory plans to transfer its base to the new world, the Americas. Of course, the transition took place over two centuries (1500–1700 AD). All that happened at the face of a new industrial order that once again separated the normative from the utilitarian. It is the beginning of Machine Age – Form (Art) follows Functions (Utility and Engineering). Renaissance took a back seat.

With the beginning of the 21st century, the primacies of Euro-American civilization seem to have exhausted its own powers. The great thoughts of the Protestants in the Euro-American civilization, which were born out of Phase III, nourished and fostered making of the Great American Melting Pot. But with time, the American liberalism and democracy (1870–2000 AD) had again succumbed to the narrowness of a Judeo-Christian order offering myopic ways of an imperial approach to ecological exploitation and colonial subjugation. The 18th century saw a separation of humanity from nature and a religious viewpoint also separating the Judeo-Christian from the Judeo-Islamic, and perhaps from others in the world. World became divided between the industrially advanced and the Third World, or sometimes, the White men (new Aryans) and the rest. As a result, the star of wisdom could not be retained for long in the Americas and it is now beginning to shift further westbound.

- *Systems Phase IV question 1: Thus there is a fourth need to retrace the original pattern of American civilization and its vision and the pattern that we have seen in the recent times.*

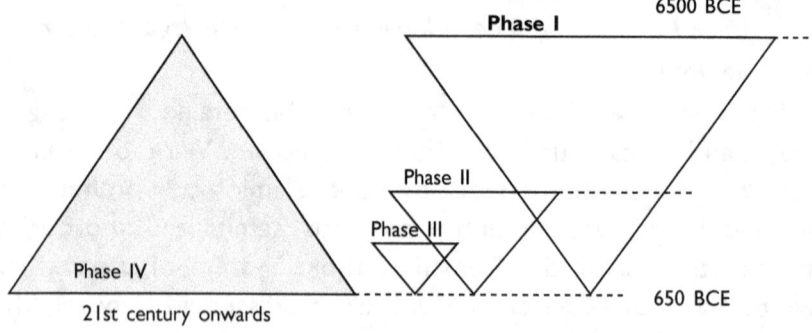

Asia Pacific < Americas < West Europe < East Europe < West Asia < Asia

Figure 6.1 System shift to Phase IV

Today, the star is well beyond the western coastlines of Americas and perhaps, also the Asia-Pacific. At the end of Phase III, what had been crossing the Atlantic and what had shaped a New York or a Chicago and placed it as more important than a Paris or a London is now shifting further to new geo-political domains. Today, Tokyo or Shanghai or perhaps, Singapore is beginning to outweigh the material advances of the West, while the star has been very recently concentrated after crossing the Pacific. The circuit of development has followed the movement of the sun and it has made one full transition, a whole circuit – to reach where it was from the preceding cycle, perhaps. The climax of the transition represents *Phase IV as depicted in Fig. 6.1. The transition is also represented in the form of semantics of systems integration and interpenetration in Fig. 6.2.*

It is important to understand the forward linkage of Time (Figure 6.2), which is shown backward from Phase I–III; accordingly, the earliest Phase I can be backtracked, recovered and repositioned for its appropriate interpenetration with current Phase IV to loop or cycle. Here the linear view of time-series within which Phases II and III are logically intertwined can be revisited.

From Phase I: 6500 BCE
'Once in far remote antiquity, the Indian philosophy, coming in contact with Greek .energy, led to the rise of the Persian, the Roman, and other great nations'.
To: Phase II: 650 BCE
'After the invasion of Alexander the Great, these two great waterfalls (Indian and Greek principles) colliding with each other, deluged nearly half of the globe with spiritual tides, such as Christianity'.
To: Phase III: 650 AD
'Again, a similar commingling (of Indian and Greek principles), resulting in the improvement and prosperity of Arabia, laid the foundation of Arabia, laid the foundation of modern European civilization'.
From Phase One: 6500 BCE
'Once in far remote antiquity, the Indian philosophy, coming in contact with Greek energy, led to the rise of the Persian, the Roman, and other great nations'.

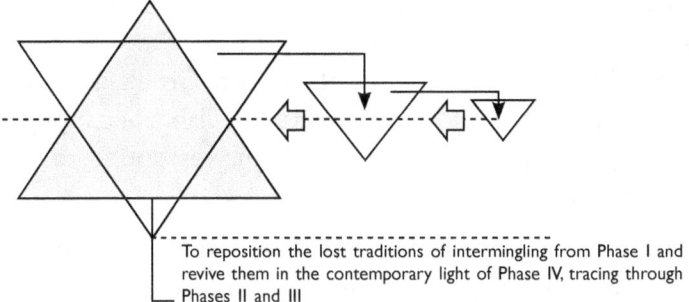

To reposition the lost traditions of intermingling from Phase I and revive them in the contemporary light of Phase IV, tracing through Phases II and III

Phase Four: 21st century onwards
'And perhaps, in our own day, such a time for the conjunction of these two gigantic forces (Indian and Greek principles) have presented itself again. This time their center is India'.

Figure 6.2 Interpenetration and systems integration as Phase IV

Note: The forward linkage of Time is shown backward from Phase I to III; Accordingly, the earliest Phase I is back-tracked, recovered and repositioned for its appropriate interpenetration with current Phase IV to loop or cycle the linear time-series within which Phases II and III are logically intertwined; therefore, there is a need to trace a more older networking between Zoroastrianism and Vedanta and its impact on archaic Judaism.

1. Phase I recovery: Older networking between Zoroastrianism and Indian Vedanta and its impact on archaic Judaism
2. Phase II recovery: Origin of Judeo-Christian tradition
3. Phase III recovery: Origin of Judeo-Islamic tradition

In Figure 6.2, it is also evident that the departure from one phase to the next represents the forward linkage of Time, following the normal course of time in history. But Figure 6.2 and more so in Figure 6.3, it is also shown as the backward linkage of time from Phase III to I, which points to time cycles and recurrence. The earliest of them, i.e. Phase I has to be back-tracked, so that the original movements from the previous cycle/ contained in that archaic phase can be recovered and repositioned for its appropriate interpenetration with current Phase IV, which can proceed to the next cycle. What Phase IV is trying to recover are the original movements from where Phase I from the current cycle had departed westbound in the making of earliest civilization in Western Asia. Hence, the statement has to be reviewed cyclically:

'Once in far remote antiquity, the Indian philosophy, coming in contact with Greek energy, led to the rise of the Persian, the Roman, and other great nations'.

Now we have to back track and make a system's feedback and recover the cycle of renewal. And that would be a Phase IV recovery which will trace the origins of the earliest Indian philosophy, which had come in contact with Greek energy in the same way a recovery of a more evolved Indian philosophy in the subsequent cycle will produce another run westbound to produce the next cycle of history.

Thus there is a great need to re-trace the pattern of an older networking between Zoroastrianism and Vedanta and its impact on archaic Judaism; and see what went westbound and what remained in India to re-assess the next cycle, so that it shall again have a re-start from India:

It is time to recollect the works of Max Muller, who speaks of the colonization of Persia by the ancient Indians in a time of remote antiquity. Discussing the word 'Arya', Muller said:

"But it was more faithfully preserved by the Zoroastrians, who migrated from India to the North-west and whose religion has been preserved to us in the Zind Avesta, though in fragments only.....The Zoroastrians were a colony from Northern India."

(Science of Language)

Phase IV: 21st century onwards – Heading for the next cycle
'And perhaps, in our own day (again), such a time for the conjunction of these two gigantic forces (Indian and Greek principles) have presented itself again (like previous cycles). This time their center is India'.

Phase I: 6500 BCE – Tailing from the previous cycle
'Once in far remote antiquity (after a long period since the closure of the previous or last cycle), the Indian philosophy (again), coming in contact with Greek energy, led to the rise of the Persian, the Roman, and other great nations'.

Figure 6.3 Systems integration as Aeon-based feedbacks and loops

Note: It is important to note that Swami Vivekananda has used the word again, hinting at cycles, repetitive and yet, evolutionary:
'And perhaps, in our own day, such a time for the conjunction of these two gigantic forces (Indian and Greek principles) have presented itself again. This time their center is India'.

Another scholar Arnold Hermann Ludwig Heeran also said:

"In point of fact that Zind is derived from the Sanskrit, and a passage to have descended from the Hindus of the second or warrior caste."

(Historical researches into the politics, intercourse, and trade of the Carthaginians, Ethiopians, and Egypt, Volume II, p. 220)

Sir William Jones, the founder of the Asiatic society also writes:

"I was not a little surprised to find that out of words in Du Perron's Zind Dictionary, six or seven were pure Sanskrit."

(Sir William Jones' Works Volume I)

A great scholar Jatindra Mohan Chatterjee in his seminal work funded by the Parsi Zoroastrian Association, Calcutta, and entitled 'The Hymns of Atharvan Zarathusthra' (1967) has traced that the *Atharva Veda* having two Samhitas namely the *Bhargava Samhita* and the *Angirasa Samhita*. As per Chatterjee, the *Atharva Veda* is the *Angirasa Samhita* and the Iranian *Avesta* is the *Bhargava Samhita*.

Chatterjee further identifies Bhrigu, as one of the primordial Seven Sages and his son Sukracharya (Kavya Ushana), the guru of the Asuras *(Ahura)* with the worship in Avesta; and he also connects *Anglrasa*, another branch of the Seven Sages and *Brihaspati* with the Deva worship that still remains in India. Incidentally, the ancient mythical tale of Sage Kuttcha of the clan of *Vrishaspati* and his wife *Debyani* of the *Bhargavi* Clan is a strong endorsement of the ancient relationship.

A complete assessment of the interconnection between Zoroastrianism and Vedanta and its impact on archaic Judaism, and positioning the findings in view of its westbound Persian and original eastbound traditions in India, remains as the vital task to conduct the systems loop proposed by the present chapter. From the sutra of the great *Kaushiki Prajapati Viswamitra* Sage of the Rig Veda, 3rd mandala, we get a glimpse of the grand intermingling – the making of the cosmic Godheads – the Great *Ahura Mahadeo*:

Mahadevana-asuratwa-mekwam (3:55)

[(Great is the unity of the Suras and the Asuras, who is the great Godhead (Mahadeo)]

It is not an either-or or a choice between the two paths – the ascendant and the descendent. It is interpenetration of the two; a rapture in the making; and a becoming of that one from two representing the many, all of which had once emanated from that one.

The Bhrigus followed the doctrine of the ancestors *(pitris)* or the older or *experienced descending gods* (Asura). The Supreme *Asura* the Father – *Varuna the Asura Mahat* (the mighty *Asura*) was highly venerated by the *Bhrigus*. The *Bhrigus*, also known as *Bhargavas*, are the descendants of the sage *Bhrigu*. The cult of the sage *Bhrigu*, whose name derives from the root bhrk meaning 'the blazing of the fire', happens to be intimately linked with the word 'Bharga' of the *Gayatri* tradition of the *Kaushikis* (Cushtics or Kazaks of the Semitic tradition) of the Vedas, which deserves a fresh research. Their tradition was mostly garnered on the west of the Sindhu stretching up to Persia. The descendent drops to the earthly tradition, as the *Bhrigus* bring down fire from the heavens to here, the terrestrial, and liberate life and living here (Rig Veda

1.24.7; 1.60.1; 1.131.3). A drop down from that derivative is the level of social and material liberty.

In contrast, the *Angirasas*, who represents the generic domain of the seven sages professed worship of *younger or fresh ascending gods (Deva)*, who were the preceptors of the Aryans, as the heroes of Rig Veda on the east of the Sindhu. The name *Angirasa* too is connected with fire as the 'glowing coal or the shouldering ember' *(Angara)*. The Angirasas, on the contrary, take fire up to the celestial to establish a greater liberty, as a first requirement or precedent before you descend. Here comes the first directive of spiritual liberty. Indian religion has always emphasized it as the first requirement, contrasting the specific clan of the seven sages, the *Bhargavas*, who represents a descending tradition.

The rift between the two aspects of life, the two liberties expanded over time. It was more or less formalized when the composite text *Atharva Veda*, also called *Bhrigu–Angirasa Samhita*, was split into two books along the lines of their affiliations: the *Bhargava Veda* (the Veda of the Bhrigus) and *Angirasa Veda* (the Veda of the *Angirasa*). It is believed that the *Atharva Veda*, which has come down to us in India is, in fact, only one-half of the original text – the Angirasa Veda part. The other half the Bhargava Veda is lost to us. It remained with the earliest Persians.

Jatindra Mohan Chatterjee argues that the *Bhrigus* whose improvisation on the divine notions and its working in the material plane and also of the moral order were not well accepted in the east of Indus that garnered the gradual transfer of sacred texts of the Bhargava Veda over to the west of the Sindhu River – to Gandhara and even beyond to further west to Khorasan. Chatterjee says that Zend Avesta is the Bhargava Veda text that was lost to India. He asserts that the Bhargava Veda, the missing book of the Bhrigu *Angirasa Samhita* is indeed the Zend Avesta (The Hymns of Atharvan Zarathustra – published by the Parsi Zoroastrian Association, Calcutta, 1967). The point has been explained by W. E. Hale (1986) in his book, *Asura in Early Vedic Religion*. In the book, Hale traces the earliest synonymous form of *Asura* in the Vedas almost equivalent and complementary to the younger flux of Suras, as an older and experienced one. The *Asuras*, considered to be more experienced spiritually, are the descending godheads in the ladder of creation to come down and carve out material liberty. The *Suras/Devas*, relatively younger, are busy in ascending and transcending the ladder of creation to achieve spiritual liberty as a first requirement. At some point of time there was a growing separation between the two complementary approaches and two groups bifurcated and separated. One moved to absolute Brahman in the ladder of the ascendant and the other descended to the dialectics of force and matter in the material world, eventually (see Figure 6.4).

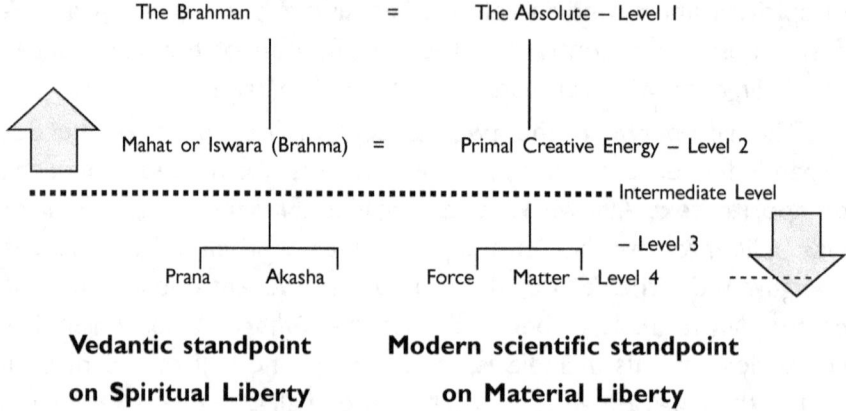

Vedantic standpoint on Spiritual Liberty   **Modern scientific standpoint on Material Liberty**

Figure 6.4 Systems integration (Ascending and Descending)

Note: (This diagram is discussed in the section under Akashic Records)
The Ascending arrow is in favour of Spiritual and Individual/ Cosmic Liberty. The descending arrow is in favour of Material and Social liberty. At one point of time, a higher form of Spirituality as encoded in the Shrutis had remained at the Apex and governed both, i.e., the twin and complementary approaches of the Suras (Ascending, levitating and aiming at the spiritual) and Asuras (descending, gravitating and heading for the material) having the foundations of both engrafted on a cosmic and universal-impersonal foundation.

But at some point of time, later, there was a growing separation between the two complementary approaches and two groups bifurcated and separated. Hence, there was a split in the Bhargavi and Angirasa Vidyas (Persia and India, respectively). From Persia, further westbound, the 2nd branch shaped the later ways of the Euro-American pattern of civilization.

But we know now that humanity needs both – both forms of liberty, material and the spiritual (see Figure 6.4). The reconciling point is Isha – or the Mahat.

As Swami Vivekananda had said:

'Three mountains stand as typical of progress – the Himalayas of the Indo-Aryan, Sinai of Hebrew ('ibri), and the Olympus of Greek civilization. When the Aryans reached India, they found the climate so hot that they could not work incessantly, so they began to think: thus they became introspective and developed religion. They discovered that there was no limit to the power of mind; they therefore sought to master that; and through it they learnt that there was something infinite coiled in the frame we called man, which was seeking to become kinetic. To evolve this became their chief aim.

Another branch of Aryans went into smaller and more picturesque country of Greece, where the climate and natural conditions were more favourable; so their activity turned outwards, and they developed external arts and outward liberty.

- The Greeks sought political liberty. The Hindu has always sought spiritual liberty. Both are one-sided.
- The Indian cares not enough for national protection or patriotism, he only defends the religion; while the Greek and in Europe (where the Greek civilization finds its continuation) the country comes first.

To care only for spiritual liberty and not for social liberty is a defect, but the opposite is still a greater defect. Liberty of both body and soul is to be striven for'.

Thus in and through the archaic complementarity of the two approaches, a greater and a complete form of Dharma is re-unfolded. That is the need of the hour! At one point of time, there definitely existed a much higher form of Spirituality as encoded in the Shrutis or the Vedas. That form was the Apex and as it governed both, i.e. the twin and complementary approaches of the *Suras* **(Ascending, levitating and aiming at the spiritual) and** *Asuras* **(descending, gravitating and heading for the material) having the foundations of both, which are engrafted on a more complete form. The complete form has a universal-impersonal sovereign foundation of religion and science. It is time now to recover that. They are evident in the three successive statements. The first one is by Sri Aurobindo:**

India of the ages is not dead nor has She spoken her last creative word; She lives and has still something to do for herself and the human peoples. And that which must seek now to awake is not an Anglicized oriental people, docile pupil of the West and doomed to repeat the cycle of the Occident's success and failure, but still the ancient immemorial Shakti recovering Her deepest self, lifting Her head higher toward the supreme source of light and strength and turning to discover the complete meaning and a vaster form of her Dharma.

It is probably true quite generally that in the history of human thinking the most fruitful developments frequently take place at those points where two different lines of thought meet.

– Werner Heisenberg

'The modern physicist experiences the world through an extreme specialization of the rational mind; the mystic through an extreme specialization of the intuitive mind......to paraphrase an old Chinese saying, mystics understand the roots of the Tao but not its branches; scientists understand its branches but not its roots. Science does not need mysticism and mysticism does not need science; but men and women need both'

– Fritjof Capra
'Epilogue: Tao of Physics'

6.2.2　Delineating Phase IV: A system's approach

We now begin to understand is that the Aeon-based (cyclic) movements of civilization and also realize what Swami Vivekananda, while delivering his final address on September 19, 1893, at the Parliament of World Religions, Chicago, meant while he pointed out the star of wisdom and its cycles of transition:

"The star arose in the East; it traveled steadily towards the West, sometimes dimmed and sometimes effulgent, till it made a circuit of the world; and now it is again rising on the very horizon of the East, the borders of San-po[1]

[Tibetan name of Brahmaputra, meaning 'po' (son) of Brahman (Sana)]

---

[1] Tibetan name of River Brahmaputra, meaning 'Po' (son) of Brahman or eternal time (Sana)

And perhaps it is evident and extremely important for Asia and particularly, India, as he says:

'In our own day, such a time for the conjunction of these two gigantic forces (Indian and Greek principles) have presented itself again.' 'This time their center is India.'

In the remaining portion of the present chapter, we begin to suggest the climax and continuity of the cycles and the maturity of a phase, where the cyclic viewpoint absorbs and exceeds the linear parts.

6.2.3 Restarting Phase IV: From the previous cycle

Here is a glimpse of such evidences. It is an excerpt from Chapter XIX, entitled 'The Swami's estimate of historic Christianity' written by Ms. Margaret Noble (later known was Sister Nivedita):

Some such train of thought is necessary, if one is to visualise no less than three striking subjective experiences, which exerted an undoubted influence over my Master's mind and thought. Chief of these probably, was that vision of an old man on the banks of the Indus, chanting Vedic Riks, from which he had learnt his own peculiar method of intoning Sanskrit—a method much closer to that of Gregorian plain-song than is the ordinary singing of the Vedas. In this, he always believed himself to have re-covered the musical cadences of the Aryan ancestors.

He found something remarkably sympathetic to this mode in the poetry of Shankaracharya, and this fact he expressed, by saying that Master must have had a vision like his own, in which he had caught "the rhythm of the Vedas."*

> "Om Ayahi Barade Devi Trakshare Brahamabadini,
> Gayatri Chhnadasang Mata Brahmayoni Namahstute"

*The Swami Saradananda says that this vision occurred about two years after Sri Ramakrishna had passed away, probably in January 1888. The passage which he heard was that Salutation to Gayatri which begins "O come, Thou Effulgent!"

When we juxtapose the two visions – one, on the borders of Brahmaputra (Sanpo) river, which is emanating from one of the glaciers of Mount Kailas; and the other, on the borders of Indus (Sindhu), which has exuded from another glacier lake of Mount Kailas – a pattern of transition is evident. It is a significant observation to be noted. The first one explains the starting point – the initiation of the next cycle; and the other is the closure of that climax at Indus, from where it has always proceeded further westbound to trigger the next cycle of westbound civilization diaspora (see Fig. 6.5). In his personal note, Swami Vivekananda forwarded a detailed note of that departure – the westbound diaspora.

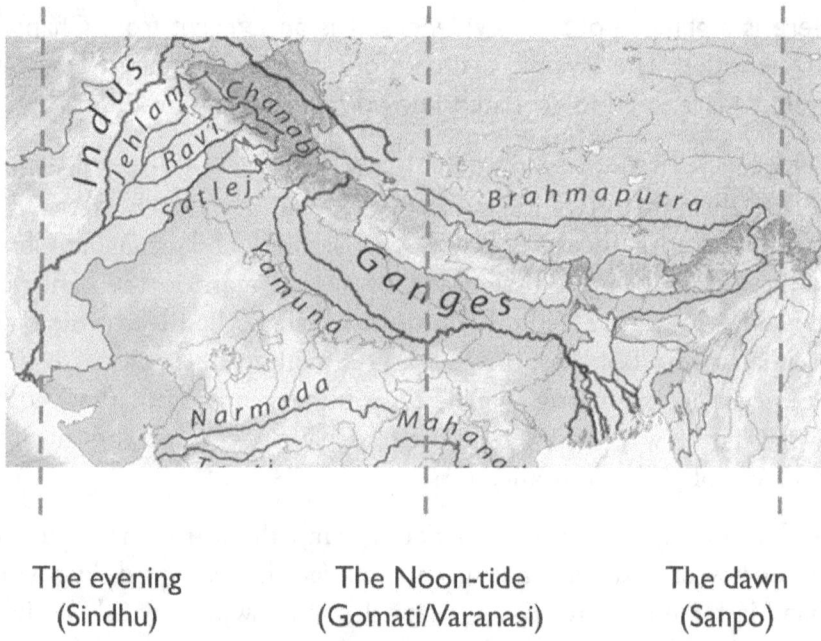

| The evening | The Noon-tide | The dawn |
| (Sindhu) | (Gomati/Varanasi) | (Sanpo) |

Figure 6.5 The bandwidth of the Indo-Aryan order

Dawn: The star arose ...again rising on the very horizon of the East, the borders of San-po (Brahmaputra) and **Evening:** It was evening in that age when the Aryans had only reached the Indus (Sindhu)

"It was evening in that age when the Aryans had only reached the Indus. I saw an old man seated on the bank of the great river. Wave upon wave of darkness was rolling in upon him, and he was chanting from the Rig Veda. Then I awoke, and went on chanting. They were the tones that we used long ago..."

"Shankaracharya had caught the rhythm of the Vedas, the national cadence. Indeed, I always imagine that he had some vision such as mine when he was young, and recovered the ancient music that way...his whole life's work is nothing but that, the throbbing of the beauty of the Vedas and the Upanishads."

The important feature of the bandwidth (as depicted in Fig 6.5) is the revival, spread and diaspora of the Aryan sages of *Aryabarta*, to which Gomati is the midpoint. It is to be noted that the midpoint of Gomati is a sacred branch of the Ganges in the upper Varanasi region. In Gomati (Rig Veda: 5.61.19; 8.2.8; 8.24.30; 8.32.8; 8.49 and 8.70), there is still the ancient citadel of Rishis, a forest resort called *Naimesaranya* (based on the semiotics or symbolism of the rim – the *Nemy* or the Felly of the wheel of cosmos). There are two important aspects of the Wheel or the turning, one – the Nabhi (the Nave) and the other, the Nemy (the distribution in the circle or the Nomy: refer suffix to words like Polynomial series; Economy; Nomination or assigning/earmarking and so on). Refer Rig Veda: 2nd Mandala: 5th sukta; 3rd sloka.

Naimesaranya is the ancient fountainhead of the noon-time tradition (Madhyanindan) of the Vedas – explained in the 8th Mandala of the Rig Veda. The tradition has been expanded as the *Sukla Yadjur* Vedic tradition. It means 'Whitsuntide', the highest summit in spiritual realization. Often hailed as the tradition of the Pentecost in Christianity, the imagery of the Christ principle is seen as the most resplendent noon-time White Sun!

The traditions of the Rig Vedic sages particularly that of Sage *Saunaka* of the tradition of Bhargabi and that of the *Atharvan Angirasa* Rishis are consolidated here. Rivers Gomati and Saraju are specifically mentioned in the Rig Veda. There has been some scholarly misrepresentation to identify these Indian rivers with ones in the West of Indus, in Afghanistan to continue with the errors of the Aryan invasion myth. On the contrary, it imparts the common basis of the Solar Dynasty – the epic Ramayana and its patron galaxy of Sages, who are also the key seers of the Rig Veda; the names from *Vasistha* to *Agysta* are just two of many.

At some ancient point of time, with western dispersals beyond the borders of Indus (Sindhu), the cycles of changes took another leap of westbound diaspora. It took a long way to reach France from Persia – from the land of *Pharisees* (Purushiya) to the land of *Parisees* – the citadel of a Celtic-Gaulic Indo-European order. The seeds of the ancient Asian wisdom were once recovered by the Greco-Romans (Phase 2) and one again by the men and women of High Renaissance centering Paris (Phase 3). From there, the star of wisdom has shifted further westbound leaving behind a growing pattern of critical lopsidedness in the Euro-American order. The discussion is forwarded herewith.

6.3 Forwarding the transition

6.3.1 Challenges in transition: Between Phase III and Phase IV

We have just crossed the first decade of the 21st century...

The pattern of current material civilization has a high rate of critical lopsidedness. A one-sided progress is evident in the pattern, which has brought the progress of civilization and humanity to the verge of a partial economic, environmental and ecological collapse. The pattern of civilization today is studded with shades of uncertainty in every sphere of material knowledge. The nature of progress that succeeds the European Renaissance (15th century till date) have had been a transitionary phase (see Figure 6.3) featuring an globally exploiting imperial-colonial order; rapid industrial exploitation by advanced or elite groups; detrimental impacts laid down by two major World Wars I and II; and a series of continental strife, a plethora of worldwide environmental disorders, booming and brewing ethnic and religious rivalries and a multitude of economic uncertainties shaking the very foundations of peaceful traditional communities. Uncertainty in global economies and interrelated issues of underdevelopment catering to gaps in wealth-related access to health, education and opportunities are on the rise. The material distribution of wealth is intertwined with alarming proportions of ethnic and racial issues; and more so, it is intertwined with critical imbalances in the patterns of collective and ecological ethics. Shades of material and the ethnic vulnerabilities of progress feature much of the 'developing world' today, and a sharp 'developed-underdeveloped' dividing line in terms of inequitable and unaffordable accesses to wealth and services forwards major hindrances to a possibility of a healthy human world order (refer Figure 6.6).

A predominant pattern of development is still guided by a post-colonial hangover. Majority of production in one country in terms of the establishment, exploitation, maintenance, acquisition, and expansion of an industrial colony in its territory is modulated by a superior political power from another territory. And much of that superiority is determined by the backdrop of material and arms wealth in the disguise of civilized discussions and distributions. The mercantile forces of the preceding 16th century to the mid-20th century colonialism still survives in the guise of a distinct neo-colonialism operated through a trans-national or multinational corporations (MNC)-driven exploitative policy-making and rigor. Science and technology, which have had evolved through 17th till early 20th century, had mainly catered that rigor taking into priority the superior advantages and pride of the industrially advanced Western economies. On the whole, the transition has been an expression of the superior advantage and pride.

Fundamentally, an advanced form of neo-Colonialism is powerful through its imperial outlook, thereby creating, through an empire, a distant colonialism and a mass-exploiter capitalism repressing local cultures, diversities and heterogeneity of traditional economies. As a result, a definitively shallow rendition of gaps between the urban and regional development patterns in developing countries has been patronized at the cost of inciting the shades of distrust, coups, local rebellions, and widening misunderstanding between the globalization forces and features of the local economies. For instance, much of these darker sides are evident in the ways and responses we have continued to witness in much of Asia in the last 100 years, and of late, North Africa, on the Balkans and in the Middle East, in the last 40 years since the Cold War era.

At the face of the negativism and in the name of development, much of the emerging scientific theories and technological proposals have begun to grope in their inability to cater and address holistic but heterogeneous needs of the human race. Much of science and technology today suffer by virtue of their inherent shortcoming or an inability to address the uncertainties of mechanisms of simulation, projections and accurate predictions. The science and technology of the advanced countries are often not applicable to the contexts of development in the traditionally advanced and culturally sensitive communities of the East. As a result, the transfer of development, though modern, is repressive, top-down and eventually anti-humanitarian not taking into accounts the variety, the diversity and the heterogeneity of development and its normative sides. Two uncertainties or shades of distrust have emerged:

- The industrial order has imparted a critical human interference with or destruction of the natural world, which poses a great threat therefore not only to humans but to all organisms constituting the natural order. *The first shade of crisis is predominantly at the ecological level.*
- The order has also created a sense of superiority syndrome on part of the industrially advanced economies and consequently resulted an unhealthy gap between the developed and the developing (once the 'Third') worlds based on human and trans-national trade, top-down economies and services exploitation. *The second shade of crisis is predominantly at the economic level.*

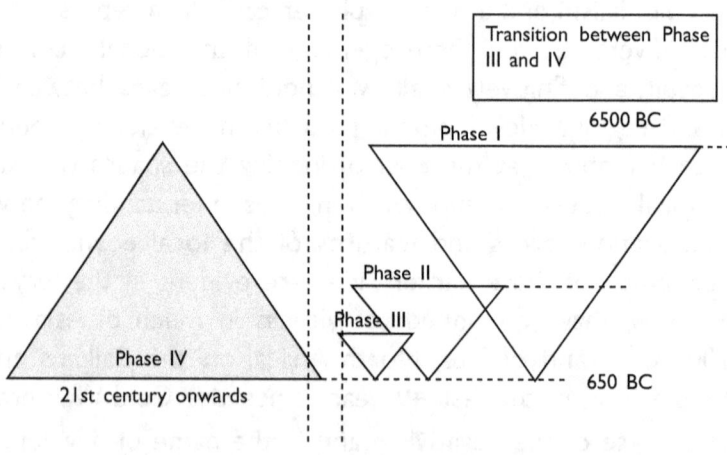

Figure 6.6 Transition: Current intermediate phase of Crisis

Different and major portions of the world order today are in a state of disorder, and all that disorder is happening at the face of scientific and technological advances that are increasingly questionable today. There is a great need for a new order seeking a shift from a materially shallow ecological perspective to that which will be governed by Deep Ecology, by more cooperative strands of trans-national capitalistic ethics and inter-continental and inter-regional Corporate Social Responsibility frameworks and environmental ethics, which are just to name a few only.

At the aggregate level of understanding today, there is now an emerging acceptance of the relevance of Chaos Theory and the Theory of Complexity in mainstream sciences. The acceptance have brought in the matter of unpredictability and energy imbalance at the very center stage of scientific research. It is evident in the following statement:

'...the predictability of science has been thoroughly questioned, and this has led to a more holistic approach to thinking about the world and about relationships and systems with it.'

A New Agenda – The Overview Effect:
Sol Power: The Evolution of Solar Architecture (1996),
Sophia and Stephen Behling, Prestel

The aforesaid observations by Behling echo that of Oswald Spengler. Also they echo that from another book on wealth of nations, which says wealth cannot be contained in a limited exploitive Western sense of one way flow, supremacy and subjugation. It is 'Cities and the Wealth of Nations' by Jane Jacobs. In the book 'The Decline of the West' (1923), Spengler proposes a more scientific and open-ended paradigm shift involving the rejection of the Eurocentric view of history, especially the Eurocentric division of history into the linear 'ancient-medieval-modern' rubric. Spengler brings to light the larger flows of meaningful units for history as whole culture recognizing the eight high cultures mainly Babylonian, Chinese, Indian, Meso-American, later Classical Greco-Roman, Arabian and the later addition the Euro-American flux. Spengler says that each of them has a lifespan of about a thousand years, and they are parts in a larger non-linear flow of returns to something exceeding them.

In 'Cities and the Wealth of Nations', Jane Jacobs has proposed similar shifts of wealth and cultures, which are not associated with countries but with cities and regions. Having an ancient beginning in Asia in times of remote antiquity and followed by the ones in North Africa and East Europe to the wealth had moved to ones in the Americas, she says. The shifts are still on, and very soon the largest share of wealth of nations will be concentrated in many urban nodes and regions in the Asia-Pacific rim and even beyond in deeper Asia in lands further east.

In the run of transition, the apparent supremacy of the industrially advanced West is only a passing phase and both Spengler and Jacobs say it is also a short one.

6.3.2   Evidences of the split

There had been a gap that was manipulated and the root causes behind the departure from that now needs to be understood and repaired. Since the days of archaic Western sciences, the departure was designed. To understand that let us go back to the beginnings of Greek science and its forerunners, the Milesian sages, who were the last successors of their Anatolian (Asian) forefathers. Dr. Fritjof Capra, the author of the book 'The Tao of Physics' makes an important observation by re-looking at these early beginnings of Western sciences, having its roots in Asia:

"The roots of physics, as of all Western science, are to be found in the first period of Greek philosophy in 600 BC, in a culture where science, philosophy and religion were not separated. The sages of the Milesian school in Ionia were not concerned with such distinctions. Their aim was to discover the essential nature, or real constitution; of things what they called 'physics'. The term 'physics' is derived from this Greek word and meant, therefore, originally, the endeavor of seeing the essential nature of things...

...the monistic and organic view of the Milesians was very close to that of ancient Indian and Chinese philosophy, and the parallels to eastern thought are even stronger in the philosophy of Heraclites of Ephesus. Heraclites believed in the world of perpetual change, of eternal 'becoming'. For him, all static Being was based on deception and his universal principle was fire, a symbol for the continuous flow and change of things. Heraclitus taught that all changes in the world arise from the dynamic and cyclic interplay of opposites and he saw any pair of opposites as unity. This unity, which contains and transcends all opposing forces, he called the Logos."

The Logos is the epitome of completeness preached by Heraclitus. The doctrine of a 'Couple' or *the unity of opposites* (External environment and internal human behavior) was the heart of the ancient Orphic school. The doctrine influenced all later Greek philosophers from Pythagoras to Plato (700–300 BC). But the split and the departure from the ancient wisdom began with Aristotle and particularly with the Eleatic school of Parmenides. On this Capra forwards further observations:

'...the split of this unity began with the Eleatic school, which assumed a divine principle standing above all gods and men. This principle was first identified with the unity of the universe, but was later seen as an intelligent and 'personal' god who stands above the world and directs it. Thus began a trend of thought which led, ultimately, to the separation of spirit and matter and to a dualism which has become characteristic of Western philosophy."

The separation of developments in the later Hellenic or Hellenistic world, a giving away to the rise of the militant imperial order of the Roman Empire transcending its earlier Celto-Hellenic and Etruscan features, and absorbing a continuous influx of the barbaric invasions (Vikings/ Visigoths/ Vandals/ Ostrogoths/ others) from the North of Europe were perhaps the root cause of the split. A later form of medieval Judeo-Christian tradition had evolved from the intermingling of these Teutonic and Anglo-Saxonic invasions. A male chauvinistic and an aggressive patriarchal side of human existence became a reigning feature of the new European tradition. Another important transformation was the gradual extermination of the Construct of God as the Mother, which almost disappeared in the European tradition. A further feature was a growing divide between humankind and Mother Nature imparted by a Judeo-Christian Monolith based only on a top-down Creator, who is always separate from its creation. The result is the idea of an Original Sin replacing the celestial networking and hierarchy with ordinary human life. It was a period of antiquity whose continuity was politically and religiously manipulated by the later Greco-Romanic rulers and the later Roman tradition of Christianity manipulated as a result. On this antiquity, the works of Robert Graves[2] and Charlene Spretnak[3] are of paramount importance, which is quoted in Capra's book 'The Turning Point':

"Throughout Greek antiquity healing was considered to be, essentially, a spiritual dimension and was associated with many deities. The most prominent among the early healing deities Hygieia, one of the many manifestations of the Cretan Goddess Athena who was associated with snake symbolism and she used the mistletoe as her all-heal. Her curative rites were a secret guarded by priestess. By the end of the 2nd millennium B.C., patriarchal religion and social order had been imposed on Greece by three waves of barbaric invaders, and most of the earlier Goddess myth were distorted and coopted into the new system, usually by portraying the goddess as the relative of a more powerful male god.

Thus Hygieia was made to be the daughter of Asclepius, who became the dominant healing God and was worshipped in temples all over Greece. In the cult of Asclepius, whose name is related etymologically to that of the mistletoe, snakes continued to play a prominent role, and the serpent (unfortunately a symbol of evil in later Patriarchal Judeo-Christian tradition) coiled around the Asclepian staff, has been the symbol of Western Medicine ever since."

The ancient school of Hippocrates and his wand called the Caduceus was an import from the ancient Orphic School. It was a construct of the two serpents, Zeus (or Sabazius) and Demeter (or Persephone), whose eternal union in the shape of the staff, was the key to the oldest concept of health and hygiene. In the words of Fritjof Capra:

"Hippocratic medicine emerged from an ancient Greek tradition of healing whose roots go back far into Pre-Hellenic times."

'Wholeness and Health'

'The Turning Point'

---

[2] 'The Greek Myth' (1975), 2 volumes, Harmondsworth: Penguin
[3] 'Lost Goddess of Early Greece' (1981), Boston: Beacon Press

6.3.3 Deepening of the crisis – The root cause

The dominant split in the Judeo-Christian tradition was operational at the helm of the 18th century modern mechanistic world-view. It shaped everything after the Renaissance, Sciences, Technology, Architecture, Medicine based on the suppression of the 'environment-behavior' approach of the ancient wisdom.

The limitations in the current Western World, since the end of Dark Ages and the beginning of Machine Ages, have accrued over time. First, it led to the foundations of the Western materialistic society and its attitudes that placed 'power of individual people' over 'nature' 'human collectivity' and 'warmth of place and land', rather than emphasizing humans in harmony with the physical environment (MacEwen[4], 1974; Brolin[5], 1976). It is evident in the following words:

"The view of man as dominating nature and woman, and the belief in the superior role of the rational mind, have been supported and encouraged by the Judeo-Christian tradition, which adheres to the image of a male god, personification of supreme reason and source of ultimate power, who rules the world from above by imposing his divine law on it. The laws of nature searched for by the scientists were seen as reflections of this divine law, originating in the mind of god."[6]

Richard C. Dorf (2001), University of California, Davis in his book 'Technology, Humans and the Society – Towards a Sustainable World' says the following words:

"The important sources of environmental thought are religious tradition, Malthusian economics and environmental planning. Many religious traditions identify humankind with nature (i.e. pointing out original divinity), whereas Judeo-Christian tradition is often seen as promoting exploitation or alternatively stewardship of nature."

Lewis W. Moncrief in his article 'The Cultural Basis for Our Environmental Crisis' of the department of recreation resources

---

[4] M. MacMewan, Crisis in Architecture, London: Royal Institute of British Architects publications.
[5] B. Brolin, The Failure of Modern Architecture, Van Ronstand Reinhold, New York.
[6] Chapter one, page 24, 'The Turning Point- Science, Society and the Rising Culture' – Flamingo (1990)

administration of the School of Forest Resources, Department of Sociology and Anthropology, North Carolina State University (in Science, 30 October 1970: Vol. 170. no. 3957, pp. 508–512) have argued that the forces of democracy, technology, urbanization, increasing individual wealth, and an aggressive attitude toward nature seem to be directly related to the environmental crisis now being confronted in the Western world. The Judeo-Christian tradition has probably influenced the character of each of these forces. However, as initial responses to a root shortcoming, the first remedies were pointed out. Here are some instances:

1. Peter J. Hill, Professor of Economics, Wheaton College, and Senior Associate, Political Economy Research Center in his article in favor of 'Environmental Theology: A Judeo-Christian Defense' in the Journal of Markets and Morality (Volume 3, no. 2, Fall 2000) cannot help but accept the various Western religious community's response to the increasing concern about the relationship between humans (microcosm) and nature (macrocosm). Examples are many.

2. In 1990 the Temple of Understanding; and officials of public affairs for the Cathedral of the Divine in New York City formed the National Religious Partnership for the Environment (NRPE), an alliance of the United States Catholic Conference, the National Council of Churches of Christ (NCC), the Evangelical Environmental Network (EEN), and the Coalition[7] on the Environment and Jewish Life (CEJL).

3. In other cases, the alterations to traditional theology have been substantial. Frontline management of the University of Creation Spirituality has argued for an end to dualism, in which humans and nature are seen as separate. He posits instead a 'creation-centered spirituality', which overturns the usual Christian emphasis on the 'fall' (based on Original Sin) and 'redemption'. In this humanity here is separated from original nature.

---

[7] The classic statement of that position is by Lynn White, Jr., "The Historical Roots of Our Ecological Crisis," Science 155 (1967): 120307.

4. The Episcopal Cathedral Church of Saint John the Divine in New York City, which is also the home of the NRPE, has led the way in the greening of Christian liturgy. In addition to sponsoring the Gaia Institute, whose purpose is to expand and explore the Gaia hypothesis (that the earth is a living, self-regulating entity), the church now blesses animals on the Feast of Saint Francis. James Lovelock, the originator of the Gaia hypothesis, represents one strand in that effort, while others have moved to a straightforward biocentrism, with its 'basic intuition ... that all organisms and entities in the ecosphere ... are equal in intrinsic worth.'[8]

A number of spiritual and philosophical traditions of the East are increasingly accepted by the modern Euro-American mind. In relation to the Judeo-Christian tradition, Deep Ecologist Arne Næss offers the following comment:

"The arrogance of stewardship [as found in the Bible] consists in the idea of superiority which underlies the thought that we exist to watch over nature like a highly respected middleman between the Creator and Creation."

The aforesaid conflict had also been expounded in Lynn Townsend White, Jr., 1967 article 'The Historical Roots of Our Ecological Crisis', in which however White also offered as an alternative Judeo-Christian view of human's relation to nature that of Saint Francis of Assisi, who spoke for the equality of all creatures, in place of the idea of man's domination over creation, which is the basis of reductionism that pervades the science and technology of today.

6.3.4 Crisis of reductionism

Reductionism has been the key feature of 17–20th century Western sciences. The expression of the Judeo-Christian view of human's

---

[8] Bill Devall and George Sessions, Deep Ecology: Living as if Nature Mattered (Salt Lake City: Peregrine Smith, 1985), 67. For a more complete discussion of the development of various religious positions on the environment, see Roderick Frazier Nash, The Rights of Nature: A History of Environmental Ethics (Madison: University of Wisconsin Press, 1989), chapters 4 and 5. For other statements of biocentrism, see many of the chapters in Michael E. Zimmerman, ed., Environmental Philosophy: From Animal Rights to Radical Ecology (Upper Saddle River, N.J.: Prentice Hall, 1998), esp. Part Two; George Sessions, ed., Deep Ecology for the Twenty-First Century (Boston: Shambala, 1995); Tom Hayden, The Lost Gospel of the Earth (San Francisco: Sierra Club Books, 1996).

relation to nature was finally shaped by three men – Rene Descartes, Charles Darwin and Sigmund Freud. A mechanistic view of science, human evolution and human psychology was imparted.

Rene Descartes is the founder of reductionism. Descartes' entire view of nature is based on the fundamental division between two important and separate realms called the 'mind' (res cognitas), which is the thinking being and 'matter' (res extensa), the extended being. To him, the material universe is a machine with no purpose, life and spirituality in matter sharply dividing an abiotic material realm from the 'biotic' mind. Nature worked according to the Cartesian division of mechanical laws, and everything could be explained in terms of the arrangement and movements of its parts. This mechanistic or reductionism's viewpoint of reality guided all scientific observations and shaped its very foundations – the mechanics and mathematics of *Isaac Newton*. This led to a drastic change in the image of nature from organism to a machine and this affected the people's attitude towards the natural environment – an effect that has accumulated to the building up of an inorganic machine style of built-environmental design at the expense of natural resources and passive design capabilities [Merchant, 1980[9]; Randal, 1976[10]].

Charles Darwin's Theory of Evolution was founded on the twin concepts of 'chance variation' and natural selection. It soon became apparent that chance variations, as conceived by Darwin, could not explain the emergence of new characteristics (like creativity) in the evolution of species. The solution to this greatest problem of the Darwinian viewpoint was discovered by Gregor Mendel and that gave away the 'reductionism' put forward by the 'genetic determinism or stability through adaptation' of Darwinian approach. Soon, the co-existence of the other dimension – 'mutability' (the ability to transform, change, create new changes) evolved.

Sigmund Freud's realm of the *sub-conscious* was limited to inferences drawn from experiments on a particular class of people conforming to retarded and animal-like instincts. From here, the

---

[9] 'The Death of Nature' (1980), New York: Harper and Row
[10] 'Making of the Modern mind' (1976), New York: Columbia University Press

three later works of Carl Gustav Jung[11], Abraham Maslow[12] and lately, Ken Wilber[13] have come a long way. All three of them have gone beyond the limited range of human functions and intelligence which was restricted to 'competitive animalism' and 'a survival instinct of the fittest'. The split between humanity and Mother Nature, unaddressed by the current framework of science and technology, has been put forward by Carolyn Merchant, a renowned Historian of Science at the University of Berkley, California:

'In investigating the roots of our current environmental dilemma and its connections to science, technology and the economy, we must re-examine the formation of a world-view and a science which, by re-conceptualizing reality as a machine rather than a living organism, sanctioned the domination of both man and woman. The contributions of such founding 'fathers' of modern science as Francis Bacon, William Harvey, Rene Descartes, Thomas Hobbes and Isaac Newton must be re-evaluated."[14]

Section 6.3 makes a system's approach for a re-evaluation. The re-evaluation contains the seeds of the system's recovery, and the whole essence and expression of the turning, the looping, which represents Phase IV:

'In our own day, such a time for the conjunction of these two gigantic forces (Indian and Greek principles) have presented itself again.'

'This time their center is India.'

6.4 Towards interpenetration: System's architecture

6.4.1 Post-Cartesian departure

The first break-way from the narrow viewpoint of reductionism had come through from the very world of fundamental Physics

---

[11] The Collected Works of Carl G. Jung', Princeton: Princeton University Press (1928)
[12] 'Towards a psychology of Being' by Abraham Maslow, Princeton – Van Nostrand Reinhold (1962)
[13] Ken Wilber's 'The Spectrum of Consciousness', Wheaton III: Theosophical Publishing House (1977)
[14] Page xvii, 'The Death of Nature', New York, Harper and Collins (1980)

– with the works of Werner Heisenberg (the dual wave-particle theory), Albert Einstein (the principles of relativity), Neils Bohr (the quantum theory) and the scientists of the EPR (Einstein-Podolsky-Rosen) experiment under the leadership of Einstein himself (Bohm, 1951[15]; 1980[16]). The resultant was the birth of the Quantum reality of nature recognizing non-local connections of energy systems and its interconnectedness amongst different parts in nature signifying a universal holism. We have discussed it in the concluding section.

6.4.2 Post-Darwinian shift

In the recent times, advances in genetic microbiology and evolutionary sciences have further shown that mutations are only one of the three avenues of evolutionary changes, the other two being the trading of genetic codes in the network of various organisms in the web of life and the process of sym-biogenesis that suggests *an element of creativity* – a creation of new living systems and approaches by merging of different species. These advances have led to a conceptual shift – from neo-Darwinian emphasis on 'chance and necessity' to a system's viewpoint that sees evolutionary change as a manifestation of the principle of life as a whole and its self-organization in the planetary and universal scale (Margulis, 1998[17]; 1997[18]). The point has been expanded later in the chapter.

On the system's viewpoint to human evolution and progress, its purpose and perfection, and returns to scale as a future teacher (what we call involution) Swami Vivekananda provides the clue to the turning point, in his seminal work, 'Raj Yoga'. It shows how Darwinian evolutionary scales based on competition and the limited gratification forwarded by Freud:

> Today the evolution theory of the ancient Yogis will be better understood in the light of modern research. And yet the theory of the Yogis is a better explanation. The two causes of evolution advanced by the moderns, viz. sexual selection and survival of the fittest, are

---

[15] 'Quantum Theory' (1951), New York: Prentice-Hall
[16] 'Wholeness and the Implicate Order' (1980), London: Routledge and Kegan Paul
[17] 'Symbiotic Planet' (1998), Basic Books, New York
[18] 'Microcosmos' (199), California Press, Berkley

inadequate. Suppose human knowledge to have advanced so much as to eliminate competition, both from the function of acquiring physical sustenance and of acquiring a mate. Then, according to the moderns, human progress will stop and the race will die. The result of this theory is to furnish every oppressor with an argument to calm the qualms of conscience. Men are not lacking, who, posing as philosophers, want to kill out all wicked and incompetent persons (they are, of course, the only judges of competency) and thus preserve the human race! But the great ancient evolutionist, Patanjali, declares that the true secret of evolution is the manifestation of the perfection which is already in every being; that this perfection has been barred and the infinite tide behind is struggling to express itself. These struggles and competitions are but the results of our ignorance, because we do not know the proper way to unlock the gate and let the water in. This infinite tide behind must express itself; it is the cause of all manifestation.

Competitions for life or sex-gratification are only momentary, unnecessary, extraneous effects, caused by ignorance. Even when all competition has ceased, this perfect nature behind will make us go forward until everyone has become perfect. Therefore there is no reason to believe that competition is necessary to progress. In the animal the man was suppressed, but as soon as the door was opened, out rushed man. So in man there is the potential god, kept in by the locks and bars of ignorance. When knowledge breaks these bars, the god becomes manifest.

It is important to understand the larger tide, the infinite tide that is behind our evolution and how it must express itself and how it is expressing itself; it is the cause of all manifestation.

From the limited subconscious of the animal, where the man was once suppressed, with evolution, as soon as the door was opened, out rushed the human conscious mind, more guided by reason and lesser and lesser by instinct. In the next rung of evolution, as in the human there is the potential godhead kept in by the inner locks and bars of higher ignorance, a larger and a greater policy of humanity is required as and when knowledge already potent will break these bars, the divinity will become manifest.

The changes which are happening now are in effect is a part of the making of that greater policy to unleash a system's evolution of what we call as Phase IV in this book. At this point, it will be extremely important to understand at least seven of these force-changes that are happening and bringing about the change itself. They are the recognition of the ancient wisdom (heritage) through a scientific view – that of:

1. *Akashic Records:* The science of the Collective Consciousness *(Mahat)* and passage of Individual *(Aham)* impressions through metempsychosis and transmigration *(Purva-pragna and Chaitya purisha)*
2. *Evolutionary Chemistry:* Inclusive doctrine of the non-linear dynamics, evolution in cyclic feedbacks and the pattern of self-organization in the universe *(Hamsah Vramyate Brahma-Chakra)*
3. *Deep Ecology:* Journey beyond just the material and transcending the shallow ecologies to reach the deepest self *(Guha hitam)*
4. *Cosmic Matrix:* The impersonal and yet universal Gaia's hypothesis *(Mahat-padam)*
5. *Co-evolutionary Biology:* Cybernetics and Cognitive scales – tracing roots and branches *(Urdhwwa mulam and addhwa sakham 1)*
6. *From Hierarchy of Minds to the Hierarchy of Needs:* Microcosm and macrocosm reflects the same plan – tracing roots and branches *(Urdhwwa mulam and addhwa sakham 2)*, and
7. *The Architecture of Interpenetration:* Parable of the double intender – the mirror of wave mechanics (Vajra) *(Viparit ratatura and samarasyam)*

Each has been portrayed as a system's dimension or architecture.

6.5 One: Cosmic Architecture

6.5.1 Recognition of Akashic Records: The Universe as Mahat (Collective Mind)

The science of the Collective Consciousness *(Mahat)* and Individual *(Aham)* metempsychosis and transmigration *(Purva-pragna and Chaitya purusha)*

Figure 6.7 The contemporary history of Akashic Records

Swami Vivekananda (see left) meets Nikola Tesla (see top order left) in 1893 after the City Beautiful Movement in Chicago; the knowledge on Akashic records travels to next generation: it reaches Ervin Lazlo and Erich Jantsch (see top order middle and right); philosophically it influences William James and Alfred North Whitehead (middle vertical order); partly influences Helena Blavatsky and Edgar Cayce (see lower right order) at some deeper normative level (through ideas of *Vasana* or *Samskara* (desire), *Chaitya* (the guiding flux) and *Pragna* (wisdom) in *Buddhism*.

Akasha is the enduring memory of the cosmos. The *Akashic* Records refer to a database of every word, thought or action that is stored energetically and encoded in a non-physical plane of existence. They are said to contain the information of every Soul or Being in the cosmos. The Records are continually updated, with each new thought, word or action that every Soul or entity makes. The *Akashic* Records therefore contain the energetic prints about the origination and journey of every Soul through its lifetimes.

They connect each of us to one another. Having in ancient origin in the Vedas and particularly, the Upanishads, *Akashic* forms the complementary basis of the universal (*Mahat* or collective or cosmic ego driven) consciousness and the discrete (*Aham* or individual ego driven) causations of the individual human mind and the interconnection between the two. In the book, 'The *Akashic* Experience: Science and the Cosmic Memory Field', Ervin Laszlo says:

...it is the "Akashic Record." In his classic Raja Yoga, Swami Vivekananda described the ancient concept of ... About a hundred years ago the maverick genius Nikola Tesla revived this idea.

Nikola Tesla used ancient Sanskrit terminology in his descriptions of natural phenomena. As early as 1891, Tesla had described the universe as a kinetic system filled with energy which could be harnessed at any location. His concepts were then greatly influenced by the teachings of Swami Vivekananda. Swami Vivekananda was the first of a succession of eastern yogis who brought Vedic philosophy and religion to the West. After meeting the Swami, Tesla began using the Sanskrit words *Akasha*, and *Prana*, and the concept of luminous ether to describe the source, existence and construction of matter. It was at a party given by Sarah Bernhardt in Chicago that Nikola Tesla had probably first met Swami Vivekananda. Sarah Bernhardt was playing the part of 'Iziel' in a play of the same name. It was a French version about the life of Buddha. The actress upon seeing Swami Vivekananda in the audience arranged a meeting which was also attended by Nikola Tesla (see Figure 6.8). In a letter to a friend, dated February 13th, 1896, Swami Vivekananda noted the following:

...Mr. Tesla was charmed to hear about the Vedantic Prana and Akasha and the Kalpas, which according to him are the only theories modern science can entertain......Mr Tesla thinks he can demonstrate that mathematically that force and matter are reducible to potential energy. I am to go see him next week to get this mathematical demonstration."

In deep theosophy and anthroposophy, where one explores the deeper connections between human thought currents and patterns of the universe and its variety, the *Akashic* Records are believed by

Theosophists to be encoded in a non-physical plane of existence known as the astral plane. *Akasha* as a Sanskrit word entered the language of theosophy through H. P. Blavatsky, who characterized it as a sort of life force; and she also referred to some "indestructible tablets of the astral light" at the cosmic or universal plane. According to Marshal McKusick, former professor of Anthropology at the University of Iowa, the term Akashic Record was augmented by Rudolf Steiner, who had probably inherited the doctrine from a preceding history in the Mid-West and particularly, the Illinois-Iowa region. Similarly, Edgar Cayce was no exception emphasizing a New Age Movement coming to late 21st century world based on the acceptance of reincarnation and *Akashic* Records.

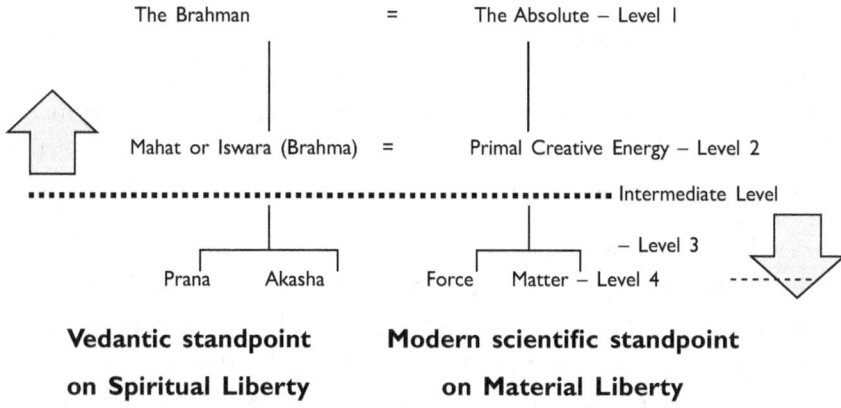

Figure 6.8 A normative and positive schema of Akashic Records

Note: There is a complementarity of Prana (elen vital) and Akasha (mind space) in the subtle human world to force and matter conjugate in the material or the gross phenomenal world

(Based on the letter dated February 13th, 1896, by Swami Vivekananda)

László's 2004 book entitled 'Science and the Akashic Field: An Integral Theory of Everything' posits a field of information as the substance of the cosmos. Using the Sanskrit and Vedic term for space, Akashic, he calls this information field at the level of the Universe, which is analogous to Kapila's *Mahat* from the ancient *Swetaswatara* Upanishad. László posits that the 'quantum vacuum' is the fundamental energy and information-carrying field that informs not just the current universe, but all universes past and present. This he calls 'Metaverse', which transcends a single universal theory.

László believes that such an informational field can explain why our universe appears to be fine-tuned so as to form galaxies and conscious life forms within it; and why evolution is an informed, not random, process, that is based on long-time-based or Aeon-based ranges of causation, its patterns and cycles. He believes that the hypothesis solves several problems that emerge from quantum physics, especially nonlocality and quantum entanglement.

Recently, trans-personal psychologist Stanislav Grof has compared László's work to that of Ken Wilber, saying 'Where Wilber outlined what an integral theory of everything should look like, László actually created one.' Jennifer Gidley, President of the World Futures Studies Federation has recently stated:

> A major distinction appears to be that László (2007) builds his general evolution theory in a more formal, systematic manner. He claims that he built significantly on the theoretical traditions of Alfred John Whitehead's process theory, Bertalanffy's general system theory and Prigogine's non-linearly bifurcating dissipative structures.

Wilber's process appears to have been much broader and more diverse – but perhaps less systematic – gathering together as many theorists in as many fields of knowledge as he could imagine, then arranging them according to the system that he developed – which he calls an integral operating system. Both Wilber's and particularly, Maslow's approach to an advanced transpersonal approach to human evolution had been influenced by Professor William James of the Harvard University, who had come in contact with Swami Vivekananda like electrical engineer and scientist Nikola Tesla. Akashic Records in the West are still at its nascent stage. With the works of Ervin Lazlo, Erich Jantcsh and others, one day, it will arrive at the science of the Collective Consciousness *(Mahat)*, which is the repository of the Individual *(Aham)* consciousness and holds the clue to all possibilities of causation. Hence, metempsychosis and transmigration of souls and their evolution based on the impact of the past patterns *(Purva-pragna)* of the lower immanent soul and the upper immanent or guiding soul from the cosmos *(Chaitya purusha)* may one day enter the contemporary realms of human sciences and realization.

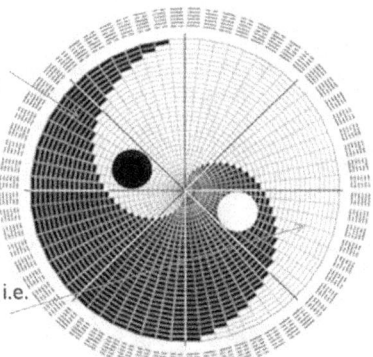

The individual merges with BLACK, i.e. the unmanifest and eternal Transcendent

The TAO / balance is restored by the Universal Flux which is the cosmic sum-total of souls, minds and bodies (Mahat)

The Transcendent re-emerges as WHITE, i.e. the manifest and impermanent individual

Figure 6.9 The cycle of changes (Brahma Chakra) is the Soul of Universe (Basis of Akashic records as a Universal Matrix or Vedic Matariswan)

The idea of immortality, signifying a connection between the individual (impermanent but manifest) and the transcendental (permanent but unmanifest), is restored through the *Mahat* – the universal plane. The *Mahat* constitutes the universal Matrix (Vedic *Matarishwan* or the Mother power-flow), which is the repository of arrays of deep electrical records of a cycle of creation that self-embeds impressions of all the individuals or parts. *Mahat* constitutes the epicenter of *Samkhya Darshana* and the works of Sri Aurobindo, where the individual, universal and transcendental are seen as the three layers of an interchanging truth (see Figure 6.9). The two-way iterations are like the ingoing Black *(Krishna)* and White *(Sukla)* threads of the cosmic wheel *(Brahma-Chakra)* as imaged in the Vedas, of which the *Mahat* is the two-way ladder.

6.6 Two: Architecture of Evolution

6.6.1 Recognition of evolutionary chemistry: Inclusive doctrine of non-linear dynamics and self-organization

Significant progress was made in Rasa-ayana (path of the essence of life) in alchemy (Al-Khemia) in Ancient India. Will Durant in his seminal work on the 'Story of Civilization' wrote in *Our Oriental Heritage:*

Figure 6.10 Brief history of thermodynamics (Agni) and entropy (Soma)

Note: Figure broadly traces the origins embedded in the ancient Near Eastern tales from the Orient that formatted the Orphic and Hittite foundations of the earliest Greco-Roman mythology; the tales of a dying and resurrecting sun-god (Vedic and Persian Mithras, as one of many) that swept Eastern Europe in very ancient times (see top left) prior to Christianity or Phase II. Great writer Jean de La Fontaine (see left middle) was the author of Adonis, the symbol of an ever-youthful vegetation god, a life-death-rebirth deity whose nature is tied to the calendar or time-cycles; it had a tremendous impact on Nicolas Léonard Sadi Carnot (see right middle), who pioneered a quantitative basis of Thermodynamics. Nobel Prize winning scientists Ilya Prigogine and Manfred Eigen (see right) have worked out the non-linear (cyclic) views of evolutionary thermodynamics.

"Something has been said about the chemical excellence of cast iron in ancient India, and about the high industrial development of the Gupta times, when India was looked to, even by Imperial Rome, as the most skilled of the nations in such chemical industries as dyeing, tanning, soap-making, glass and cement...By the sixth century the

Hindus were far ahead of Europe in industrial chemistry; they were masters of calcinations, distillation, sublimation, steaming, fixation, the production of light without heat, the mixing of anesthetic and soporific powders, and the preparation of metallic salts, compounds and alloys. The tempering of steel was brought in Ancient India to perfection unknown in Europe till our own times; King Porus is said to have selected, as an especially valuable gift from Alexander, not gold or silver, but thirty pounds of steel. The Moslems took much of this Hindu chemical science and industry to the Near East and Europe; the secret of manufacturing "Damascus" blades, for example, was taken by the Arabs from the Persians, and by the Persians from India."

But deeper achievements were evident in the evolutionary annals of Indian spiritual philosophy called Rasayana. In the words of Swami Vivekananda (Raj Yoga, Chapter IV Independence), it is an ancient neuro-physiological science of trans-mutation aiming to convert the base or lower functions of body-mind *(Dhatu-garbha)* to higher strands:

The Yogis claim that these powers can be gained by chemical means. All of you know that chemistry originally began as alchemy; men went in search of the philosopher's stone and elixirs of life, and so forth. In India there was a sect called the Rāsāyanas. Their idea was that ideality, knowledge, spirituality, and religion were all very right, but that the body was the only instrument by which to attain all these. If the body came to an end every now and again, it would take so much more time to attain to the goal. For instance, a man wants to practice Yoga, or wants to become spiritual. Before he has advanced very far he dies. Then he takes another body and begins again, then dies, and so on. In this way much time will be lost in dying and being born again. If the body could be made strong and perfect, so that it would get rid of birth and death, we should have so much more time to become spiritual. So these Rasayanas say, first make the body very strong. They claim that this body can be made immortal. Their idea is that if the mind manufactures the body, and if it be true that each mind is only one outlet to the infinite energy, there should be no limit to each outlet getting any amount of power from outside.

Why is it impossible to keep our bodies all the time? We have to manufacture all the bodies that we ever have. As soon as this body dies, we shall have to manufacture another. If we can do that, why cannot we do it just here and now, without getting out of the present body? The theory is perfectly correct. If it is possible that we live after death, and make other bodies, why is it impossible that we should have the power of making bodies here, without entirely dissolving this body, simply changing it continually? They also thought that in mercury and in sulphur was hidden the most wonderful power, and that by certain preparations of these a man could keep the body as long as he liked. Others believed that certain drugs could bring powers, such as flying through the air. Many of the most wonderful medicines of the present day we owe to the Rasayanas, notably the use of metals in medicine. Certain sects of Yogis claim that many of their principal teachers are still living in their old bodies.

Patanjali, the great authority on Yoga, does not deny this.

It may be also noted in Figure 6.10 that Adonis originally was a Phoenician god of fertility and analogous to Hurrian-Hittite God Kumarbi representing the spirit of vegetation. It is further speculated that he was an avatar of the version of Ba'al, worshipped in Ugarit, closest to Sabazius/Tammuz (later Plato's Timeus or Time) in Babylonia/Sumeria and archaic Greece. From the analytical development by Carnot, finally Ilya Prigogine (see right top in Figure 6.10) recovered the ancient truth as a basis of modern evolutionary bio-chemistry forwarding the principles of (a) non-linear dynamics, (b) dissipative structures and (c) self-organization; the other name is Manfred Eigen (see right bottom in Figure 6.10) who contributed to the theory of the chemical hyper cycle, the cyclic linkage of reaction cycles as an explanation for the self-organization of prebiotic systems. The whole idea (see Figure 6.10) is evident in the imagery of Nataraja, the dance of Eternal Time, Siva or Shiva, who holds the cup of both – enthalpy (Igneous surge/ Agni) and entropy (Somatic descent and subsequent decomposition), which is partly impersonated by the Water Lifecycle of modern science today.

There is important evidence in Figure 6.10, which can be researched later. It is that of the tale of *Gulistan* (The Persian – Gulaba or pink/'The Rose Garden'). The tale is a landmark of

Persian literature, perhaps its single most influential work of prose. Written in 13th century, it is one of two major works of the Persian poet Sa'di, considered one of the greatest medieval Persian poets. It is also one of his most popular books and has proved deeply influential in the West as well as the East. La Fontaine based his *'Le songe d'un habitant du Mogol'* on a story from Gulistan based on the ancient Moorish times (Phase III / System's framework III in previous chapter), when Christian Europe was in the Dark Ages. Much of the ancient transfers in the concept of death and resurrection from ancient Persian gardens (4 squares or the *Char-bagh*) can be traced to the deep ecological source of human transmutation/ immortality and the secrets of *Al-Khemia*. From there, through the times of Sadi Carnot, we come to the days of Ilya Prigogine.

Being a deep basis of the psycho-somatic (Agni and Soma of the Vedas/Evaporation and Condensation of Science), the most important turning point in Evolutionary Chemistry comes with Nobel Prize winning Ilya Prigogine who pointed out that the reductionist view of Newtonian physics has now been 'extended' three times:

- first with the use of the wave function in quantum mechanics,
- then with the introduction of space-time in general relativity and
- finally with the recognition of indeterminism in the study of unstable systems

Instances of cyclic evolutions of death and resurrection are evident in dissipative structures. And dissipative structures emerge in everyday life include convection, turbulent flow, cyclones, hurricanes and living organisms. Prigogine's formal concept of self-organization was used also as a 'complementary bridge' between General Systems Theory and Thermodynamics. An important essence of the cyclic rhythm is that of self-organization, which is the cycle itself; and it is realized in the physics of non-equilibrium processes, and in chemical reactions, where it is often described as self-assembly (as a system's approach). The concept of self-organization is central to the description of biological systems, from the subcellular to the ecosystem level self-organization usually relies on three basic ingredients:

1. Strong dynamical non-linearity, often though not necessarily involving positive and negative feedback
2. Balance of exploitation and exploration
3. Multiple interactions

Self-organization occurs in a variety of physical, chemical, biological, robotic, social, and cognitive systems. Examples of its realization can be found in crystallization, thermal convection of fluids, chemical oscillation, animal swarming, and neural networks. Self-organization occurs in a variety of physical, chemical, biological, robotic, social and cognitive systems.

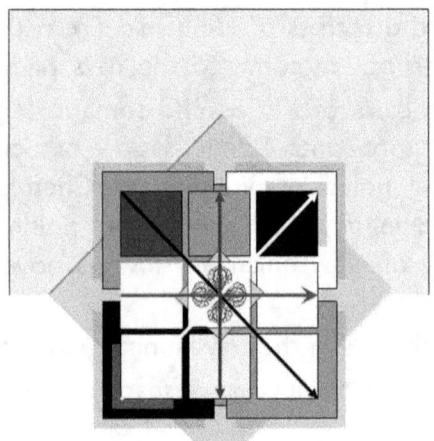

Figure 6.11 Deep architecture of Alchemy: The Vajra

Note: A combination of four quadrants; a turning of the cycle on the basis of the quadrants establishes equivalent in the cycle; spring, summer, autumn and winter and the symbolic shifts thermodynamically; from the winter or nescience of base metals, transmutation springs forth to full blaze or summer; but complete resurrection takes places as one proceeds to autumn, thereby completing the cycle and completing the four-way equivalence, which is Vajra, symbolized by the four-way cruciform in the center.
(Composed by the Author)

The idea of immortality signifying a connection between the individual and the transcendental can be again reviewed in light of the *Mahat* – the universal plane. The *Mahat* constitutes the universal Matrix, which is akin to the 'array of cosmic flows and arrangements', signified by the Vedic *Matarishwan* or Mother power-flow. The Mahat constitutes the epicenter of *Samkhya Darshana* and in the legacy left by Sage Kapil; it is *'Hiranyagarbha'*, which is the basis of the seat of Cosmogony and its impersonal lordship, which is Isha.

In the light of deep evolutionary chemistry, as encoded in the 'Secrets of the Vedas', the sages are greatest of elevated souls, who make the upward heavenly passage to the epicenter of Cosmos. They undergo the golden transmutation, becoming the egg of the Universe or 'Hiranyagarbha'. The base metals of isolated individuality (*pinda* or *dhatu-garbha*) are trans-mutated to universal principles (*Brahmanda*) or the Gold, which symbolizes truth.

Iron, Bronze, Silver and Gold are therefore the four ages, and the four steps to transmutation. A journey from Iron to Gold is the secret of alchemy. It is the retracing of truth, the unfolding of an enfolding order, which was concealed and now it is open to a recovery awaiting a return to origin, the full divine glory. For ages, this has been the secret, the way of the sages. From there, the sages move further to the transcendent, to the infinite – the all-immutable Thunderbolt, the *Vajra*. The black arrow to decomposition is cross-cancelled by the white arrow. It is evident in the following Fig. 6.11.

In Fig. 6.11, the four Quadrants of Truth are the cardinals, which are the time-movement of the Sun (Aditya); and the quadrants as a whole are undifferentiated space or the *Chid-Akasa*, or undifferentiated trans-mutated space, which is *Vajra* in the center. They are four Principles of Truth-realization – the four Vedas. They are the four expression of the word 'Vak'. Vak manifests herself in the circuit of four quadrants. It is Char-Vak. The four quadrants are the four faces of the truth-seer: Brahma-Odona. The Seer is *Brahmanaspati*. He is *Indra-Brihaspati* or *Brahma-Purusha*. The nave, the summit or the crest is the Purusha. The rim or the felly (Nemi) is Prakriti. The four quadrants are the four Buddhas. At the center is the immutable linkage between them. It is Vajra. The movements are navigation of cosmic Time – Kala-chakra-yana.

The cruciform of axes is 'Autumn and Spring' standing for the nodes of Death and Resurrection. It is the Garden of Adonis. The Circuit *(Mandala)* is the Circe or the Kirk – the Church. It is the Garden of Adonis, which is the Garden of Eden – that eternal

Paradise. One is eternal entombed in the core having resurrection in the periphery. It is Char-Bag. The integrity or the Circe is the Mandala. The *Mandala* is *Purusha* as Spirit and *Prakriti* as matter is the *Vastu*, which means the built environment or architecture. The upper and lower quadrants are Black and White – the alternations in the circuit with a centrality – Yellow *Vajra*. The two regulators or the diagonals are the two Karna-sutras. They 'regulate' the crisscrossing – the movement of the Sun *(Adityas)*. They are the complementarities of construction and deconstruction in the Mandala. The framework allowing the balance – the crossing is *Sama-karshana*. The field of the Vast is *Vasu-Deva*.

For thousands of years, from the ancient lore of the Vedas to the principles of Alchemy practiced in Egypt, Greece and other places, the secrets of transmutation from base-metals *(Dhatu-Garbha)* to Gold *(Hiranya-garbha)* and finally, beyond to Diamond *(Vajra)* had remained and shall remain. The principles of self-organization that Ilya Prigogine and his aftermath have hailed today are just a beginning of that return through the eyes of science. The essence of Figure 6.11 has been further expanded in light of fractals, shapes and interpenetrations in the last and seventh part in this concluding section (see Figure 6.27).

Given the twin discussions on evolutionary electrical sciences and evolutionary chemistry, we now move on to two subsequent discussions under evolutionary biology, which is best framed in the West under the guise of 'Deep Ecology' and an ancient construct of the Çosmic whole encoded in the form of the 'Gaia's hypothesis'.

6.7 Three: Architecture of Deep Ecology

6.7.1 Recognition of Deep Ecology: Journey beyond just material and shallow ecologies

Though the 'Deep Ecology' was first coined by the Norwegian philosopher Arne Næss in 1973, who stated that from an ecological point of view as the right of all forms of life to live is a universal right is there, is analogous to the *Mahat* of Samkhya and this cannot be quantified. In light of the universal plane, no single species of living being has a more right to live and unfold than any other species.

Deep ecology also offers a philosophical basis for environmental advocacy which may, in turn, guide human activity against perceived self-destruction through a shallow viewpoint which is through one-way modernization-industrialization-natural-exploitation. Deep ecology takes us through scientific viewpoint, to a deep ecological consciousness, to a cooperative platform of political consciousness, which matures as a collective or universal or the spiritual consciousness. The modern architects are poet Rabindranath Tagore, Mahatma Gandhi and Patrick Geddes, who have taken it closer to great contemporary thinkers and scientists like Rachel Carson, Aldo Leopold, John Livingston, and many others, inclusive of E. F. Schumacher. There are two principal dimensions that are to be noted:

Figure 6.12 Contemporary development of Deep Ecology

Note: Both Gandhi and Tagore's life, actions and living philosophy (see top left) were guided by the ancient Upanishadic teachings; that of Jainism and Buddhism, two principal offshoots of the same ancient thought; Patrick Geddes (see bottom left), the leading Environmentalist from Scotland, joined Tagore and other Green Creative souls to create a first basis of Green Environmentalism and Green Politics in the modern world; an important fallout is Rachel Carson (see middle below); from there the two scientists James Lovelock and Lynn Margulis (see right top) paved the modern holistic science of nature called the Gaia's hypothesis which provided and revived an ancient Pre-Christian or non-Semitic bases of cosmic, ecological and environmental interconnectedness; the final impact is provided by Arne Næss (see right bottom), who provided the deeper perspective of evolutionary eco-biology and its deepest interconnection with human growth, evolution and its purpose.

1. Transcending the limited Judeo-Christian or Semitic wisdom by embracing religions from the ancient wisdom, like Vedas, Upanishads, Buddhism, Jainism, and many others including Native American, Indo-Asian Shamanistic traditions that transcend the arrogance of stewardship encoded in the Semitic tradition separating Creator from Creation; carving an idea of superiority with chosen kinds as intermediary and a doctrine of original sin based on that separation.
2. The sacred feminine, important examples of which are the Gaia's Hypothesis and Eco-Feminism bringing back the latent and potent role of power as a Female Principle in the universe; as an agency of reconciliation, evolution and involution that presents Creator self-manifesting as the Creation itself. It brings back the deeper role and imagery of women and nature that are also united through their shared history of oppression by a patriarchal Western society.

Deep ecology takes us to the idea of the Collective, the Mahat, and the Matrix of the Universe. It offers the individual mind, which can evolve and contemplate the whole universe as the Collective matrix (Samasti) or the sum total of Mahat or mind. It appears as a Purusha, an abstract universal soul, yet not the Absolute, for still there is multiplicity. Both Akasha and Prana again are produced from the cosmic Mahat, the Universal Mind, the Brahmâ or Ishvara (Isha). It is pertinent to revert back to the idea that Swami Vivekananda and Nikola Tesla had shared (refer Figure 6.13):

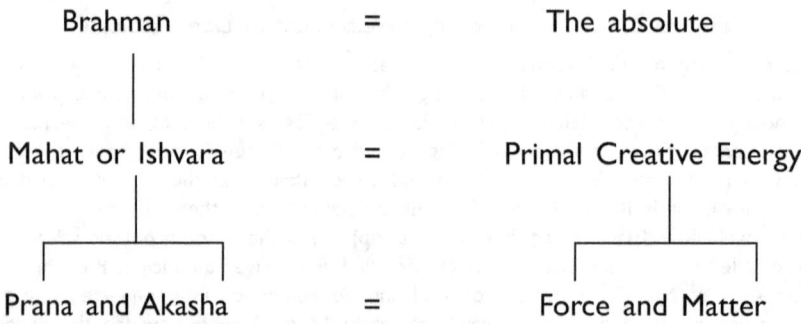

Figure 6.13 Deep Ecology and the idea of Mahat

6.8 Four: Architecture of the Cosmic Matrix

6.8.1 Recognition of an impersonal and the Universal Gaia

The ancient lore of a Pre-Hellenic or Orphic Gaia had shaped James Lovelock's initial hypothesis. Chemist James Lovelock and microbiologist Lynn Margulies defined Gaia as an array of all-inclusive entity involving the Earth's biosphere, atmosphere, oceans, and soil; the totality constituting a feedback or cybernetic system which seeks an optimal physical and chemical environment for life on this planet. The important feature is that it is a co-evolutionary Gaia: that life and the environment had evolved in a coupled way.

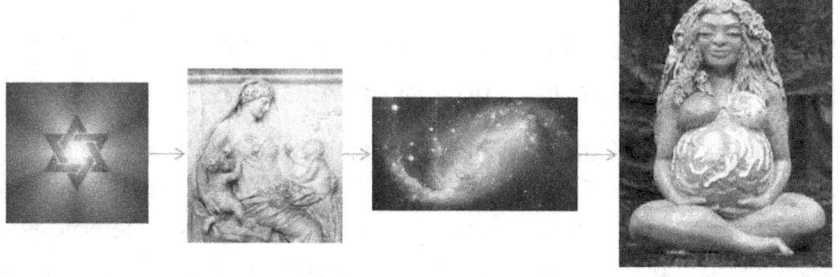

Figure 6.14 Gaia's Matrix and the idea of Mahat

6.8.2 Co-evolution: Cybernetics

In the archaic form of Gaia philosophy, all living forms are evolving and in addition with everything else in the universe, all of them considered part of one single living planetary being called Gaia. The important point is that the atmosphere, the seas and the terrestrial crust and many others are forwarding the involution of the macrocosm or the universal domain to which there is the coevolving diversity of living organisms. All are contained in her – everything is a part of her womb, the Matrix. Today the idea of Co-evolution, which is primarily a biological concept, is applicable to allied fields such as computer science, sociology, international political economy and astronomy. In the words of Sri Aurobindo, it is Matarisvan, as he explains in the Isha Upanishad (sutra 4):

Matarisvan ' seems to mean "he (Isha or the Lord) who extends himself in the Mother or the container" whether that be the containing mother element, Ether, or the material energy called Earth in the Veda and spoken of there as the Mother. It is a Vedic epithet of the God Vayu, who, representing the divine principle in the Life-energy, Prana, extends himself in Matter and vivifies its forms. Here, it signifies the divine Life-power that presides in all forms of cosmic activity.

Given the aforesaid understanding, an idea is to be revived; it is important to review the last two emerging domains on Co-evolutionary anthropology and transpersonal sciences.

6.9 Five: Architecture of Co-evolution

6.9.1 Recognition of Co-evolutionary Anthropology: Cybernetics and cognitive scales

The whole idea of the present premise is based on Deep Teleology which comes from Greek telos, "end"; logos, "discourse". Teleology explains the universe in terms of ends or final causes. Teleology is based on the proposition that the universe has design and purpose; and perhaps there is a Cosmic principle which is immanent or involved (involution) within the intermediate strata which is evolving. The idea comes close to the book 'The Self-organizing Universe', where Erich Jantsch attributed the entire evolution of the cosmos to coevolution. Also in astronomy, there is an emerging theory states that black holes and galaxies develop in an interdependent way analogous to biological coevolution.

Beginning with Pierre Teilhard de Chardin, a French philosopher and a neo-liberal Jesuit priest, who was also trained as a paleontologist and geologist conceived the idea of the Omega Point, which is a maximum level of complexity and consciousness towards which he believed the universe was evolving. Contemporary philosophers and scientists are still actively discussing on the applicability of teleological constructs where, in 2012, Thomas Nagel proposed a neo-Darwinian account of evolution that incorporates impersonal, natural teleological laws to explain the existence of life, consciousness, rationality, and objective value. Possibly, Teilherd is one of the first scientists to realize that the human and the universe are inseparable. The only universe we know about is a universe that brought forth the human.

Figure 6.15 Co-evolution and the Transpersonal Spectrum (Universal Mahat): The Cosmic Impersonal Anthropic Principle

Note: Beginning with the ancient ideas of Sambhuti (Evolution) and Asumbhuti (or Inclusive Evolution or Involution), the deep thought-currents of Sri Aurobindo (see extreme left) touched the triad Arnold Toynbee, Alan Watts and Abraham Maslow (see extreme top right) through Sri Haridas Chaudhuri (see middle) through the initial foundations of American Institute of Asian Studies and eventually through California Institute of Integral Studies and Esalen Institute at Big Sur, California; the idea percolated through the orders shaped by scientists David Bohm, Geoffrey Chew and to a certain extent, Stephen Hawking focusing on a anthropocentric view of the universe, as the universe. But in the top middle is the great evolutionist and Anthropologist Pierre Teilhard de Chardin who provided a deep view of cosmic and individual evolutions as a system of teleological completion (All in One and finally All in All as ONE).

Both Teilhard and Sri Aurobindo have seen evolution as a collective and teleological progression through particular levels: Matter, Life and Mind, or Inorganic Earth (material mind), Biosphere (human mind), and Noosphere (super-mind). These stages (see Figure 6.16) are almost exactly equivalent to the three evolutionary stages, or three codes, as described by scientific writers like Erich Jantsch and Rush W. Dozier.

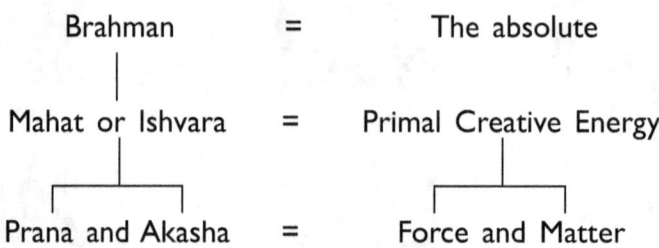

Figure 6.16 Three levels

Note: Lower: Matter to Biosphere; Middle: From Biosphere towards Noosphere; and Upper: Finally Noosphere where there is Super-mind, pervading all as ONE

It is evident from Teilhard and Aurobindo's works that the present state of evolution is not yet complete. And according to Shri Aurobindo, The stage of humankind cannot be the last term of this evolution. He is too imperfect an expression of the Spirit. The idea of evolution and involution emerging from the Vedic texts, particularly encoded in the Isha Upanishad had a deep impact on both Swami Vivekananda and Sri Aurobindo.

Swami Vivekananda had said in his lectures on 'Çosmology':

Out of what has this universe been produced then? From a preceding fine universe. Out of what has men been produced? The preceding fine form. Out of what has the tree been produced? Out of the seed; the whole of the tree was there in the seed. It comes out and becomes manifest. So, the whole of this universe has been created out of this very universe existing in a minute form. It has been made manifest now. It will go back to that minute form, and again will be made manifest. Now we find that the fine forms slowly come out and become grosser and grosser until they reach their limit, and when they reach their limit they go back further and further, becoming finer and finer again. This coming out of the fine and becoming gross, simply changing the arrangements of its parts, as it were, is what in modern times called evolution. This is very true, perfectly true; we see it in our lives. No rational man can possibly quarrel with these evolutionists. But we have to learn one thing more. We have to go one step further, and what is that? That every evolution is preceded by an involution. The seed is the father of the tree, but another tree was itself the father of the seed. The seed is the fine form out of which the big tree comes, and another big tree was the form which is involved in that seed. The whole of this universe was present in the cosmic fine universe. The little cell, which becomes afterwards the man, was simply the involved man and becomes evolved as a man. If this is clear, we have no quarrel with the evolutionists, for we see that if they admit this step, instead of their destroying religion, they will be the greatest supporters of it.

We see then, that nothing can be created out of nothing. Everything exists through eternity, and will exist through eternity. Only the movement is in succeeding waves and hollows, going back to fine forms, and coming out into gross manifestations. This involution and evolution is going on throughout the whole of nature. The whole series of evolution beginning with the lowest manifestation of life and reaching up to the highest, the most perfect man, must have been the involution of something else. The question is: The involution of what? What was involved? God.

Sri Aurobindo forwards the following observations while examining the ancient Upanishad:

Thus, the third movement of the Upanishad is a justification of life and works, which were enjoined upon the seeker of the Truth in its second verse. Works are the essence of Life. Life is a manifestation of the Brahman; in Brahman the Life Principle arranges a harmony of the seven principles of conscious being by which that manifestation works out its involution and evolution. In Brahman Matarishwan disposes the waters, the sevenfold movement of the divine Existence. That divine Existence is the Lord who has gone abroad in the movement and unrolled the universe in His three modes as All-Seer of the Truth of things, Thinker-out of their possibilities, Realiser of their actualities. He has determined all things sovereignty in their own nature, development and goal from years sempiternal...

But this evolution is the result and sign of a previous involution. Mind in the universe precedes, contains & constitutes life-action and material formation. Bhrigu Varuni, once more bidden by his father back to his austerity of thought, perceives a third and profounder formula of things. He sees Mind as that Sole Existence, Mano Brahma. "For from mind these existences are born, being born by mind they live, into mind they pass away & enter in."

From 1930–1931, Teilhard stayed in France and in the United States. During a conference in Paris, Teilhard stated:

For the observers of the Future, the greatest event will be the sudden appearance of a collective humane conscience and a human work to make.

6.9.2 The archaic evidences: The 1935 Yale–Cambridge expedition

Teilhard participated in the 1935 Yale–Cambridge expedition in northern and central India with the geologist Helmut de Terra and Patterson, who verified their assumptions on Indian Paleolithic civilizations in Kashmir and the Salt Range Valley.

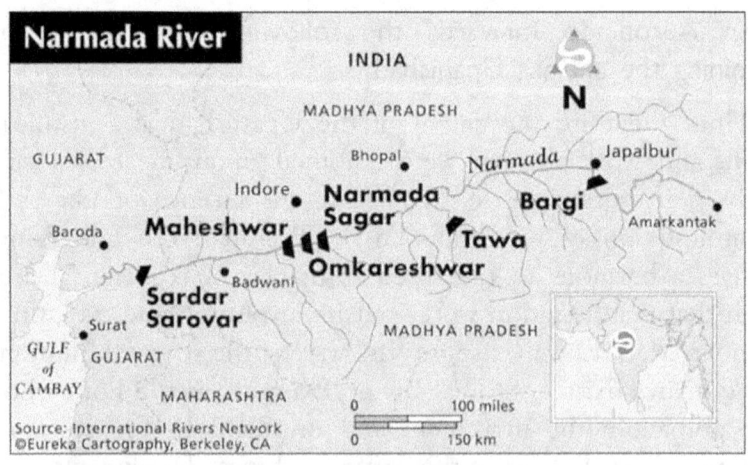

Figure 6.17 The current scape of the Narmada valley

The Yale-Cambridge team led by Dr Helmut de Terra together with Pere P. Teilhard de Chardin, a noted French paleontologist, and Dr T. T. Paterson to investigate the glacial cycles in Kashmir and the associated human remains in the periglacial area inclusive of the Narmada valley. As a result of all this he led the Yale-Cambridge expedition to investigate the problems of Stone Age and quaternary ice ages. And the areas he chose were the Kashmir valley across the range of Pir Panjal and Poonch region to the Salt range region between the Indus and the Jhelum.

6.9.3 Highlights in the Narmada valley: Traces of advanced or an older cycle of civilization

In view of an advanced chronology of Indian Paleolithic civilizations in India, some important features of the Chelles-Acheul culture of India were evident:

1. The main components of the complex are hand-axes, cleavers, scrapers-onflakes, obtuse angled flakes, cores, hammer-stones, choppers and chopping-tools.
2. The artifacts have been found in situ in bedded gravels, in many river valleys but it is only in the Narmada valley (Hoshangabad–Narsinghpur region) where hand-axes and cleavers and other components of this culture-complex are found in different stratigraphic horizons along with the Pleistocene mammalian fauna showing evolutionary trends from the crude pebble stage to the advanced Acheulian types.
3. Three evolutionary stages have been found so far in the Narmada valley, the basal-most stage consisting mostly of chopper-chopping tools made of pebbles. The stage has been named 'Mahadevian' and represents the Oldowan culture of India and may belong to the early part of the middle Pleistocene (50,0000 to 70,0000 years). The third stage is represented by the Late Acheulian hand-axes found in the yellow sandy layers of the upper group and probably belongs to the late Pleistocene. The second stage consists of early Acheulian tools, which were found in the cemented sandy gravel.

4. Raw materials generally used are grey sandstone, fine-grained hrematic red quartzite, olive coloured fine-grained quartzite, buff and yellow colour medium-grained quartzite, dolerite, trap, quartz, and jasper of various shades and flint too in the Narmada.

5. Instead of mixed industries in different horizons of the ancient alluvium, it appeared that there had been an evolution of hand-axe industry from the pebble pre-Chellian stage to the advanced Acheulian hand-axes. The basal-most horizon of the greasy red-clay-yielded chopper-chopping tools was made of heavy, massive pebbles of large size.

6. In the Narmada, the mammalian fossils of extinct Pleistocene fauna like Elephas namadicus, Bos namadicus, Hippopotamus namadicus, Equus namadicus, Bison, Bubalus, Sus, occur; and it is interesting to note that the sub-tropical forests along the bank of the Narmada still teem with the ancient wild life.

[Ref: A Century of Prehistoric Research in India A. P. KHATRI Council of Scientific and Industrial Research, Government of India, New Delhi Asian Perspectives 6.1 (Summer 1962): 169]

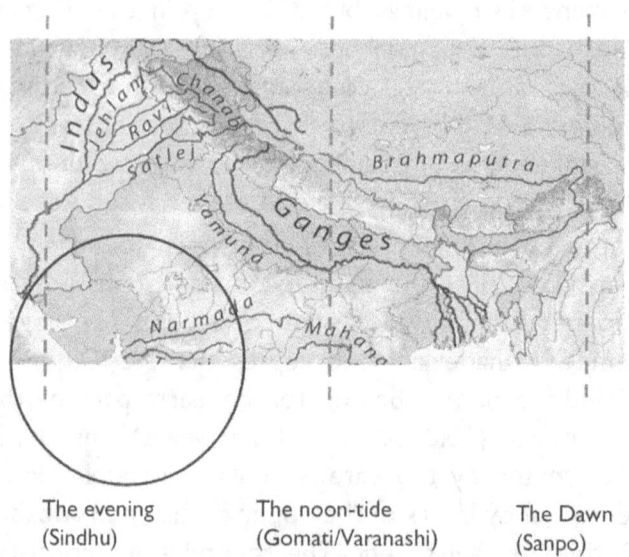

| The evening | The noon-tide | The Dawn |
| (Sindhu) | (Gomati/Varanashi) | (Sanpo) |

Figure 6.18 Westbound opening of Narmada valley and its proximity with the Indus Valley (see Figure 6.5)

It is evident that in the Narmada valley right from the stage which has been named *'Mahadevian,'* represents the Oldowan culture of India and may belong to the early part of the middle Pleistocene (50,0000 to 70,0000 years) showed evidences of advanced Paleolithic civilization. Perhaps, in the eastbound shift of the Vedic civilization, the Deccan played a more antique role (as evident in Figures 6.5 and 6.18). In that context, the position of Narmada valley and the Western Ghats (Sahyadri Mountains) are critically important.

According to the Skanda Purana, on the seven archaic Sages of the Vedas, Sage Bhrigu came to Bharuch *(Brigu Kaccha)* by sitting on an asana that symbolized the tortoise *(Kurma chakra)*. The tortoise is known as kachchha in Sanskrit. Hence the place was named 'Bhrigukachchha'. Sages like Shukra *(Kavya Ushana), Chyavana, Markendeya and Jamadagni* were from the lineage of *Bhrigu Rishi. Parshurama* (sixth incarnation of Lord *Vishnu*) was born in the seventh generation of Bhrigu. The 2nd mandala of the Rig Veda and particularly, the second offshoot of the *Atharva Veda*, the *Bhargabi Samhita* had contributed to the making of Zoroastrianism in Persia thereby belong to both the tradition and the place.

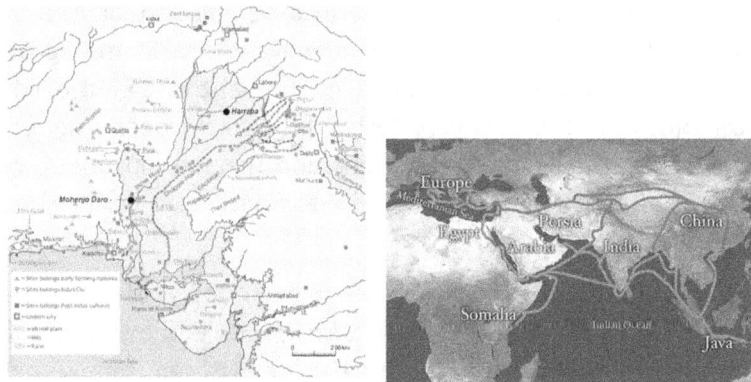

Figure 6.19 Inclusiveness of the Narmada valley in later Indus Valley, i.e. the Harappan civilization

Note: Its proximity to the ancient Near East as a point of westbound diaspora to Persia (Airyan) and Anatolia (the Land of Hittites)

Definitely in the larger domain of the Delta of the Indus and the west-facing mouth of the Narmada also exuding to the Arabian sea, the ancient mariners – the Phoenicians – must have knew of it, and they treaded further west from the Persian Gulf. From the distant upper Malabar Coast or Malay *(Meluha)*, ships had kept connections between Western India, Sumer (Mesopotamia), the entire Fertile Crescent and Abyssinia (Kush), which is part Ethiopia, Sudan and Egypt (somehow related to the tradition of first Pharaoh *Narmer Menes* of United Egypt). There is some relationship with Swami Vivekananda means by saying (in Memoirs of European Travel):

The borders of this Red Sea were a great centre of ancient civilisation. There, on the other side, are the deserts of Arabia, and on this – Egypt. This is that ancient Egypt. Thousands of years ago, these Egyptians starting from Punt (probably Malabar) crossed the Red Sea, and steadily extended their kingdom till they reached Egypt. Wonderful was the expansion of their power, their territory, and their civilisation. The Greeks were the disciples of these.

In the Vedas it is said again and again that the Isha, who represents the impersonal lordship of the Universe extends himself and his power (herself) in 'the Mother or the container', who is *Matariswan* or the cosmic matrix. *Matariswan* (Celtic *Matrice*) is the containing mother element, or the material energy called Earth in the Veda and labelled as the earliest designation of Mother in Srutis. It is *the Matrix*, who brings down the fire from the origin, the divine principle in the life-energy, Prana, through the lineage and teleology of the *Bhargabi Rishis*. In other words, *Matariswan* brought him down from the heavens and handed him over to the Bhrigus for keeping. Shri Aurobindo explains that in 'The Secret of the Vedas':

The Bhrigus in the Veda (Brij = to burn) are evidently burning powers of the Sun, the Lord of Knowledge...It is the powers of the revelatory knowledge, the powers of the seer-wisdom, represented by the Bhrigus, who make this great discovery of the spiritual will-force and make it available to every human creature.

That is how the transcendental extends or exudes itself and gets involved as the Universal immanent – the *Mahat*. Reciprocally, *the* individual ascends step by step in an evolutionary journey and expands to become that, by embracing that. That evolutionary journey today has been retraced by the trans-personal psychologists, and evolutionary planners of the West. Section 6.10 forwarded herewith discusses that journey.

6.10 Six: Architecture of the Mahat

6.10.1 From hierarchy of minds to the hierarchy of needs: *Microcosm and macrocosm reflect the same plan*

Figure 6.20 Contemporary development of Trans-personal hierarchy

Note: From William James the formative ideas moved on through Abraham Maslow and Ken Wilber, both drawing from the pioneering works of C. J. Jung; at the root, remained a vital impact of the twin waves of Swami Vivekananda (Cosmology) and Sri Aurobindo (Hierarchy of Minds), drawing in the vast reservoir of the wisdom of the Vedic sages.

6.10.2 Post-Freudian shifts: The trans-personal tide

Carl Gustav Jung proposed a theory of psychological types by identifying four characteristic functions or levels of human psychology, namely:

1. The level of sensation at the gross body level – the very level on which Freud mostly or only concentrated.
2. The level of thinking and intelligence from where mainly scientific and rational functions emerge.
3. The level of feeling and aesthetics that facilitates collective causes and value systems of larger humanity.
4. The level of intuition that goes further beyond to even larger ecological and natural understandings of human anthropology in relation to overall nature and the final purpose of human evolution.

Abraham Maslow's 'theory of trans-personation and self-actualization' followed Jung's view. Maslow had rejected Freud's view of human intelligence dominated by lower instincts or animalism. The reasons Maslow gave for this rejection was Freud's experimental and consequential inferential limitation based on the study of neurotic and psychotic individuals coming from a strained part of the society, which was afflicted by the perils of earliest industrial revolutions. Maslow and his colleagues stressed that human personality and intelligence could not be separated from the network of human relations in which it exists. He defined psychology as a discipline dedicated to the study of interpersonal relations and interactions – the key to social intelligence. From here, transpersonal psychology begins to recognize, understand and ultimately realize the 'wider or beyond the single individual' states of consciousness and consequential intelligent networks.

Subsequent works of Ken Wilber called 'spectrum psychology' has furthermore contributed to the evolutionary journey from personal to inter-personal, and from the inter-personal to the trans-personal states. Wilber's approach cohesively assimilates numerous models, both eastern and western, and presents a hierarchy of progressive bands or 'spectrums' of consciousness(s) like the seven colors of a rainbow (like the septuplet matrix discussed finally in the present and conclusive chapter – see Figure 6.24).

Each band or levels is characterized by a different state of identity, ranging from a supreme identity of cosmic consciousness and intelligence as a primal unity from where it steps down to the levels of the narrow identity of the ego-intelligence – called the weaker individual Anthropic principle. Through evolution in the context of *Akashic* records (transmigration and metempsychosis), the weak Anthropic finally becomes stronger and gets right reason and right vision, from where it trans-personates itself and reaches the *Samasti* (collective) called the *Mahat*.

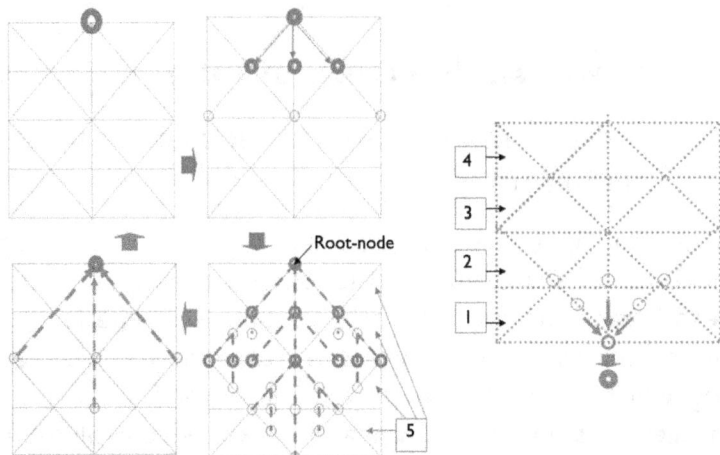

Figure 6.21 A four-stage cycle of evolution and involution stratified framework of the TREE Starting from bottom right – full TREE (5) with 4-depths or levels:

Bottom left – Traversal through the four levels and tracing back to root node of TREE (transcending the Universe via Mahat);

Top left – Reaping of all levels (or contraction to the trans-personal level or the root-node);

Top right – Sprouting or extension from the Transcendent root node (Brahman or the Absolute expands like the ear of the corn)

Individual intelligence that has traversed all four stages attains holistic intelligence by knowing the complete TREE.

Figure 6.21 explains a four-stage cycle of evolution and involution through a stratified framework of the Dendron-gram (a tree-like graph); if we start from bottom right – we see the full TREE (5) with 4-depths or levels (as explained in a rudimentary form by C. S. Jung and later by Abraham Maslow as the Hierarchy of Needs); if we look at the bottom left – we see a traversal through the four levels and tracing back to root node of TREE (transcending the Universe via *Mahat*). It is evolution; then at top left we can see the reaping of all levels (or contraction to the trans-personal level or the root-node); finally, at top right, there is sprouting or extension from the transcendent root node (Brahman or the Absolute expands like the ear of the corn). It signifies Death and Resurrection as encoded in the Vedas and Kumar-Sambhav (double birth of the Primordial Son); as used by Sadi Carnot as his famous Carnot Cycle; and also later used by the Christian parables of First Death (reaching Crucifix) and Resurrection.

6.11 Seven: Architecture of Interpenetration

6.11.1 Fractals and Holism: The double intender – the mirror *(Vajra)*

The *Spring and Autumn Annals* is an ancient Chinese chronicle that by the time of Confucius, in the 6th century BCE, had come to mean "year" and was probably becoming a generic term for 'annals' or 'scribal records'. Closest to these annals are the book I Ching, which is also known as the Classic of Changes or Book of Changes. It is an ancient divination text and the oldest of the Chinese classics.

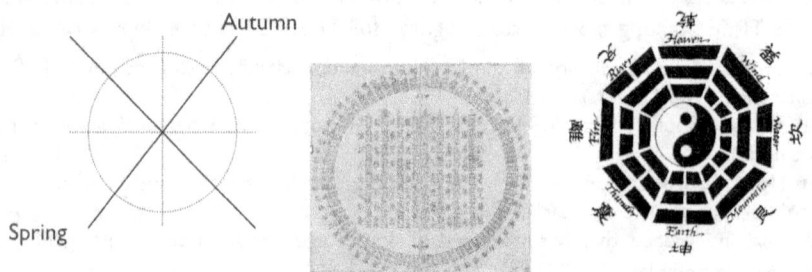

Figure 6.22 Cyclic changes: Spring and autumn and I-Ching Hexagram

Note: In the middle is the diagram of I-Ching hexagram, which was sent to Gottfried Wilhelm Leibniz from Joachim Bouvet. The Arabic numerals were added by Leibniz. Joachim Bouvet was a French Jesuit who had worked in China. Psychologist Carl Jung took interest in the possible universal nature of the imagery of the I-Ching, and he introduced an influential German translation by Richard Wilhelm by discussing his theories of archetypes and synchronicity.

Chinese writers often had offered parallels between the I-Ching and subjects such as linear algebra and logic in computer science. Much of their efforts aimed at demonstrating that ancient Chinese cosmology had influenced the Western discoveries. There is a possible connection which could have been disseminated to Europe prior to and during the Dark Ages through the upper Silk Route (Tartary) from East Asia to Anatolia (Turkmenistan). Biochemist Joseph Needham also referred to the Book of Changes.

6.11.2 Interpenetration: All in One and One in the All

The I Ching uses a type of divination, which produces apparently random numbers, and is turned into a hexagram. It is arranged in an order known as the King Wen sequence. The hexagrams themselves have often acquired cosmological significance and paralleled with many other traditional names for the processes of change such as yin and yang. The book often provides guidance for moral decision making as informed by Taoism and Confucianism. It is to be noted that:

1. The *I Ching* is essentially the fundamentals of Returning to the Unity and Balance of the Tao. It is not a system to be understood solely with the mind, but lived fully through the human experience. The Book of Changes describes the eternal dance of cycles occurring in our life as an evolution itself. For thousands of years, sages and mystics have used the binary code of this system to unlock deeper layers of profound wisdom.

2. The *I Ching* is also an intricate expression of the fundamental patterns of the universe, based on the principles of yin (feminine) and yang (masculine) energy. This binary pattern forms 8 Elemental Trigrams, the Ba Gua (akin to Vak or soul itself). An Elemental Trigram expresses a specific primary energy. A Hexagram is formed by combining two elemental trigrams, thus revealing the 64 possible combinations of yin and yang. Each Hexagram is a pictographic binary expression of two elements interacting with one another, the basis of all the phenomena of life. Finally, the turning and the return (tropics) is the Motion of the Tao, which explains the flux both as stability and change akin to the Dynamic Equilibrium of modern science. Thus Atman is Brahman, as the Vedas say, and the equivalence is both the dynamism (flux and changes) and also the equilibrium (order and fixity). Thus Soul is not a fixed identity but essentially a Circuit of Changes as the Universe itself; that is *Mahat*. In the center is the immutable which supports all changes and is beyond it. Seen in this light, all are contained in the Whole as parts, as the Whole

or Equilibrium itself is embedded in the chain of changes, i.e. all it parts. Here, the ancient conception of Soul and No-soul, both are transcended and truth emerges as an undifferentiated unbroken whole (Akhanda), which is the reality within everything and also the reality all pervading.

That is what Swami Vivekananda meant by saying in his seminal talk – 'The Mother Worship', while referring to Confucius, who touched the universal Mahat and the level of *Matariswan:*

The two conjoint facts of perception we can never get rid of are happiness and unhappiness—things which bring us pain also bring pleasure. Our world is made up of these two. We cannot get rid of them; with every pulsation of life they are present. The world is busy trying to reconcile these opposites, sages trying to find solution of this commingling of the opposites. The burning heat of pain is intermitted by flashes of rest, the gleam of light breaking the darkness in intermittent flashes only to make the gloom deeper.

... Confucius alone has expressed the one eternal idea of ethics. "Manu Deva" was transformed into Ahriman. In India, the mythological expression was suppressed; but the idea remained. In an old Veda is found the Mantra, "I am the empress of all that lives, the power in everything."

(Fragmentary notes taken on a Sunday afternoon in New York in June, 1900)

So it is said:
Returning is the motion of the Tao; going far is returning.

Lao Tzu

'Tao Te Ching'

'The seer-wisdom realizes that supreme solar world in the form of a Asswattha (pippal) tree, where the branching of rays carrying the immortalizing waters (the madhu) reverts back to its roots at night and resurges again to flood the universe with the day light – they know the truth who are one with their 'Father in the heaven'.

Seer Dirgha-tama

Rig Veda: mandala one, 164:20

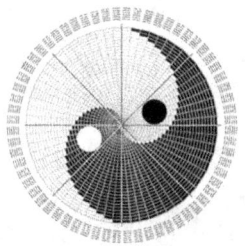

Figure 6.23 Cyclic changes: Spring and autumn and I-Ching hexagram

Note: As a whole, the book *I-Ching* forwards a perfect depiction of a unified field theory which includes the description of absolute as the integration of changes and equilibrium.

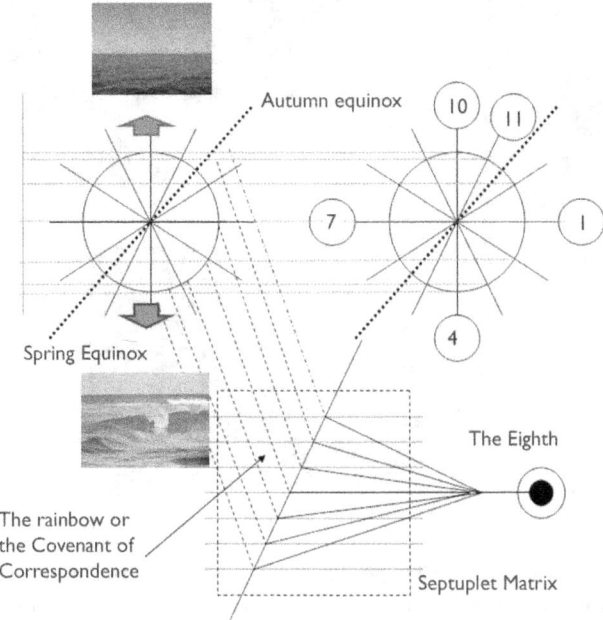

Figure 6.24A Cyclic changes as coded in the Vedas: Dasagwas and beyond [from sea with waves (position 4) to the sea without waves (position 10)]

Note: The Vedic sage (Mandala 1, sukta 164) realizes that 'the supreme solar world in the form of a Asswattha (pippal or Bodhi) tree (a framework of tree having branches below and roots above), where the branching of rays carrying the immortalizing waters (the madhu) reverts back to its roots at night and resurges again to flood the universe with the day light – they know the truth who are one with their transcendental realm symbolized as the 'Father in the heaven', to which the Sages are sons of the Original Divinity. The Septuplet Matrix is the web of creation, like a rainbow, to which the origin is the condensed word, the Eighth. The Seven Sages impersonally represent that impersonal web, to which the Eighth is both immanent and the transcendental.

Figure 6.24B Cyclic changes as the patterns of involution (return to multitude of waves) and evolution (collapse of the wave function)

Note: From sea with waves (position 4: Tree formation) to the sea without waves (position 10: back to seed) and returns to re-scaling (further evolutionary cycles) – see the relative grey scales that exceed any absolute.

The wheel of the Cosmos is also the wheel of seasons. Both are equated with the concept of an inner time – a psychological time of the earth *(Prithvi)* matched with the movement of time in the heavens *(Dyava)*. The matching happens in the inner world of the Sages *(Antarikswa)*. This matching can be interpreted at two levels:

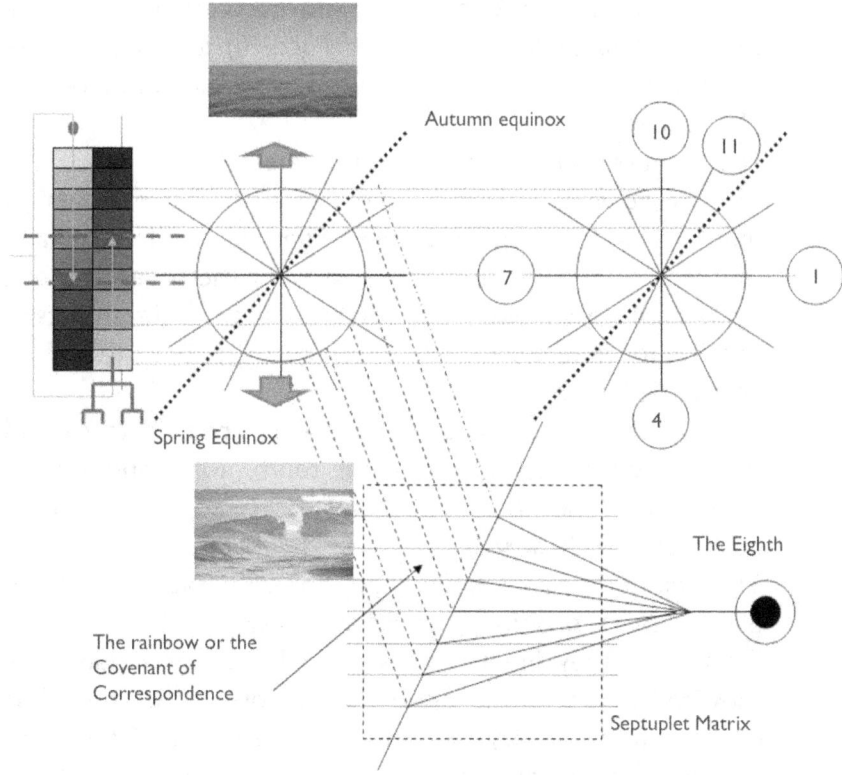

Figure 6.24C Cyclic changes are the ascending and descending steps as the patterns of involution (return to multitude of waves) and evolution (collapse of wave function) in the relative grey scales that exceed any absolute; in the grey scale are the TROPICS that represent the turning of the individual soul in the wheel of universal resolution and dissolution (Mahat) and beyond
[Based on the life-cycles of condensation and rarefaction]
The same plan of macrocosm (Dyava-prithvi) – microcosm (Antariskswa)

- *The first level* is based on the symbolism of the equinoxes (balance of day and night) and the solstices (day exceeding night and vice versa). These balances carry a deeper meaning of cosmological thermodynamics. Day and night are the internal representations of *Agni* and *Soma* – or of Sun and Moon, externally found in the universe itself. At spring equinox, there is a balance of day and night in the solar ascendant and from there the Sun makes a Passover to a phase of increasing heat till it reaches the next climax – the summer solstice (This is *uttarayana*).

This balance is also found in the internal world of a growing Sage-mind (*antariksha* or the Microcosm) and the scheme of events in the external world (The *Dyava-prithvi* or the Macrocosm).
The two are therefore built on the same plan.

- *The second level* is that of the degree of achievement in that turning (Tropic). Given the balance of the internal and the external worlds (the first Passover), the Sages proceed further to reach two different classes of achievements – called the *Navagwas* (The ninth) and the *Dasagwas* (The Tenth) (RV: 6.22).

The Dasagwas are supreme sages, who are able to extend their period of sacrifice up to the tenth month and achieve something higher than the Navagwas (who can extend it up to the ninth only[19]).

The *Dasagwas* can sustain their universal sacrifice till the highest tenth position (see Figure 6.24B).

From here they inherit the second Passover (at Libra) as they roll down to the eleventh position and beyond. This happens from the highest position or summit of the 10th. By doing so sustainability of completing another cycle of symbolic twelve months is attained.

This keeps the wheel of life and Cosmos rolling.

The sages transcend and encircle the whole circle – the circuit of creation and form the WORD (VAK or the Eighth) by their greatest sacrifices.

Figure 6.24A forwards the turning and the climax.

The idea has been described in the following line of Rig Veda:

'Agni surpasses the holding of the septuplet matrix and becomes that eighth by encircling the whole rim – the cycle itself and emerges as the supreme among all'

(RV: 2.5.1-3)

---

[19] The idea of the two levels is equivalent to the category of jivakotis and iswarkotis mentioned in various scriptures and of late, in the Gospel of Sri Ramakrishna. Jivakotis are human souls still ascending and trying to reach that summit. Iswarkotis are realized (inborn) human souls, who are currently ascending in the present life but had reached that state in previous incarnations thereby carrying the strength of that achievement, in subsequent births when they are both a true 'son of man' and the 'son of god', by virtue of realization.

Hence the Srutis (Vedas) say:

Agni, who has encompassed everything – all gods, is like the felly encompassing the spokes of a wheel.

Rig Veda: 5th Mandala: 13.6

6.11.3 The two-way ladder

The description in the turning of the Cosmic Wheel and its symbolic representation by the twelve months, of which the zenith is the tenth month, is forwarded in the following words:

These are the four eternal worlds hidden in the guha (the inner cave), the secret, unmanifest or superconscient parts of being which although in themselves eternally present states of existence (sana bhuvan ⁻a⁻) are for us non-existent and in the future; for us they have to be brought into being, they are yet to be created. Therefore the Veda sometimes speaks of Swar being made visible, as here (vyacaks.ayat svah.), or discovered and taken possession of, vidat, sanat, sometimes of its being created or made.

These secret eternal worlds have been closed to us, says the Rishi, by the movement of Time, by the months and years; therefore naturally they have to be discovered, revealed, conquered, and created in us by the movement of Time, yet in a sense against it.

This development in an inner or psychological Time is, it seems to me, that which is symbolised by the sacrificial year (samvatsara/sana) and by the ten months (dasagwas) that have to be spent before the revealing hymn of the soul (brahma) is able to discover the seven-headed, heaven conquering thought which finally carries us beyond the harms of Vritra and the Panis (darkness).

– Sri Aurobindo
The Secret of the Vedas

The Book of Changes, *I Ching*, explicitly denote the same turning of the wheel. The explanatory discussion is quoted from the two lectures on 'microcosm' and 'macrocosm' delivered in New York, USA, on 19th and 26th of February in 1896 by Swami Vivekananda:

- *Parable of the seed and the cyclic process:* What does man see around him? Take a little plant. He puts a seed in the ground, and later, he finds a plant peep out, lift itself slowly above the ground, and grows and grows, till it becomes a gigantic TREE. Then it dies, leaving only the seed. It completes a circle – it comes out of the seed, becomes the tree, and ends in the seed again.
- *Cycles or waves of cause and effect:* The universe with its stars and planets has come out of a nebulous state and must go back to it. What do we learn from this? That the manifested or the grosser state is the effect, and the finer state, the cause.
- *The rise and fall of waves:* The TREE produces the seed, which again comes up as another TREE, and son and on; there is no end to it. Water drops roll down the mountains into the ocean, and rise gain as vapor, go back to the mountains and again come down to the ocean. So, rising and falling, the cycle goes on. So with all lives, so with all existence that we can see, feel, hear or imagine. Everything that is within the bounds of our knowledge is proceeding in the same way, like breathing in and breathing out in the human body. Everything in creation goes on in this form, one wave rising, another falling, rising again and falling gain. Each wave has its hollow; each hollow has its wave. The same law must apply to the universe taken as a whole, because of its uniformity.
- *The periodic nodes of turning or tropics:* There is one more fact about this rising and falling. The seed comes out of the TREE, but has a period of inactivity or rather a period of very fine unmanifest action. The seed has to work for some time beneath the soil. It breaks into pieces, degenerates (dies) as it were, and regeneration (resurrects) comes out of that degeneration.
- *Out of what has the TREE been produced?* Out of the seed; the whole of the TREE was there in the seed. It comes out and becomes manifest. So, the whole of this universe has been created out of this very universe existing in a minute form. It has been made manifest now. It will go back to that

minute form, and again will be made manifest. This coming out of the fine and becoming gross, simply changing the arrangements of its parts, as it were, is what in modern times called evolution.

- *Involution precedes evolution:* We have to go one step further, and what is that? That every evolution is preceded by an involution. The seed is the mother of the TREE, but another TREE was itself the mother of the seed. The seed is the fine form out of which the big TREE comes, and another big TREE was the form, which is involved in that seed. The whole of this universe was present in the cosmic fine universe.
- *A priori – Recognition of the involutionary principle in an evolutionary process:* This involution and evolution is going on throughout the whole of nature. The whole series of evolution beginning with the lowest manifestation of life and reaching up to the highest, the most perfect man (Anthropic Principle), must have been the involution of something else. The question is: The involution of what? What was involved?
- *Unfolding of involved a priori universal intelligence as evolving individual and social intelligence:* The TREE comes out of the seed, goes back to the seed; the beginning and the end are the same....applying the same reason to the whole of the universe, we see that intelligence must be the lord of creation, the cause. At the beginning that intelligence becomes involved, and in the end that intelligence gets evolved. The sum total of the intelligence displayed in the universe must, therefore, be the involved universal intelligence unfolding itself.
- *Complete or perfect anthropic principle:* This cosmic intelligence gets involved, and it manifests, evolves itself, until it becomes the perfect man.
- *Macrocosm and microcosm are built on the same plan:* Applying the law, we dwelt upon under macrocosm, that each involution presupposes an evolution, and each evolution an involution, we see that instinct – of the personal ego-animal level is involved or down turned reason. In this manner, each

lower level is an evolution of a preceding involvement of a higher level. The latest scientific man admits that each man and each animal is born with a fund of experience, and all these actions in the mind are the result of past experience.

1. Resurgence of waves
2. Inversions (collapse of the wave function)
3. Mirroring both and fractals (see Figure 6.24B)
4. One Force *(Shakti)* Field *(Adwaitam)*

The manifold waves of the sea are united on a backdrop – the sea itself, which is underneath and therefore beyond the waves. This backdrop is a calm and transcendental backdrop (position 10), with respect to the changing, resurging surface of waves (position 4). This is one side of the picture. At the same time, this backdrop is essentially related to the continuously changing surface – the various waves, big or small, appearing, collapsing and re-appearing and so on. Thus the backdrop is all pervading and immanent with regards to these waves. This is the other side of the picture. Four aspects are important here:

- All waves are parts of that one mass of water. That one mass of water is the Sea. As names and forms, the waves are separate (or diverse – the first stage).
- But seen as parts composed of water, they all in essence are the same (this is unity or the second stage).
- That water in essence is that great calm sea – the transcendental backdrop (the third stage or infinity).
- Finally, as a whole they co-exist together - the sea, the waves and the winds of change, which bring around the creative surges, the waves near the bank.

The water is the life and soul of all waves in space-time causation. All the waves are within that great sea, if the wave function is made to collapse. If they are made to re-surge, they emerge from that sea. Together, the four aspects represent a unique *Religion of the Sea*, which also provides the wonderful simile of Completeness. All waves are contained within the sea. The water of that sea, in essence, is contained in the waves. This iteration goes on eternally. The many, in essence, are in that one. The one, in expression, are contained by that many. This concept of iteration between the two brings forward an ancient wisdom found in the Isha Upanishad (sukta 8) and later in the unique sloka of Gita, which says:

'Who sees the whole universe within that self and the self everywhere in the universe – is the perfected personality – the great Yogi (Chapter 6.29).

So the consciousness of the great Yogi becomes all-pervading and embraces all aspects of creation – from the origin to everything that is manifested. That one calm sea is the origin – called *satchidswarupa* (the constant unchanging immutable basis of the ever-changing world) and it is linked with the *chidaananda-lahari* (the creative waves of this world) and this provides us the complete picture, the complete truth. Swami Vivekananda in this third deliberation on "Hinduism" in the Parliament of Religions at Chicago in 1893 had concluded by saying:

'Science is nothing but the finding of unity. As soon as science would reach perfect unity, it would stop from further progress, because it would reach the goal. Thus Chemistry could not progress farther when it would discover one element out of which all others could be made. Physics would stop when it would be able to fulfill its services in discovering one energy of which others are manifestations, and the science of religion become perfect when it would discover Him, who is the one life in a universe of death, Him, who is the constant basis of an ever-changing world. One, who is the only soul of which all souls are but delusive manifestations. Thus is it, through multiplicity and duality that the ultimate reality is reached. Religion can go no further. This is the goal of all science'.

'All science is bound to come to this conclusion in the long run. MANIFESTATION, and not creation, is the word of science today, and the Hindu is only glad that what he has been cherishing in his bosom for ages is going to be taught in more forcible languages, and with further light from the latest conclusions of science'.

Note that in the cyclic change from the preceding patterns of involution (return to multitude of waves) to evolution (collapse of the wave function), i.e. from (position 4: tree formation) to the sea without waves (position 10: back to seed) and returns to re-scaling (further evolutionary cycles), there are the relative grey scales that exceeds the supremacy of any absolute truth. The power in the cycle is the soul of the universe of which the absolute is only a stage in realization (see Figure 6.24C).

It is the unity (Adwaita) of the one Force-Field (Shakti).

6.11.4 Parallels in science: Truth of non-locality – its current evolution

To create an atmosphere of comparative analogy, here is a brief of the other side. These are the current changes in modern physics since the days of Sir Albert Einstein, which have led to the theory of our present discussion, the theory of non-locality. The brief outlines a sequence of events:

Figure 6.25 The architects of Cosmic Interconnectedness; Symmetry of polarization (non-locality) and its patterns (wave mechanics)

Note: Architects of the EPR Enigma; the Uncertainty Principle of Werner Heisenberg and the bi-polar experiment of Erwin Schrodinger (both – see left) inspired David Bohm (see middle) to forward his two-way explicate and implicate orders that finally inspired Alain Aspect and John Cramer (see right).

1. In May 1935, Sir Albert Einstein and two of his colleagues, Boris Podolsky and Nathan Rosen published the first description of a reality that is non-local (meaning traveling faster than the speed of light) as something unbelievable. Einstein called this 'spooky action' and this publication was eventually called the EPR paradox. It includes two major enigmas:
   - The collapse of the wave function as interpreted through the wave equation of Erwin Schrödinger
   - A probabilistic notion that every part of a quantum system responds instantaneously to a stimulus affecting any other part of a system. They suggest instantaneous connection with the universe as a whole.
2. The EPR experiment inspired other areas of research like polarization of light[20] seen from a quantum viewpoint. These emissions suggested information transfer in opposite directions to points far apart. Whether such transfer actually takes place at a speed exceeding that of light is another question.
3. Two later works emerged. One was of David Bohm (London, U.K.) in the 1950s and the other was by John Bell at CERN (European Center for Particle and Nuclear Physics, Switzerland) in the 1960s. Bohm proposed the 'Scattered-Matrix' theory and John Bell his 'Bell's Theorem' to take the notion of 'non-locality' further. But all these were theories.
4. In 1980s, Alain Aspect and his colleagues (in Paris) for the first time experimentally confirmed the EPR enigma and posed new avenues to review the Copenhagen interpretation of Schrödinger.
5. In the early 1990s John Cramer at the University of Washington, Seattle, pointed out a unique thing implied in Schrödinger's wave equation. Cramer reviewed the equation and explained a bi-polarity meaning a *conjugate of opposites*. His wave equation is based on the simple idea of complex numbers which is: $Y = A + Bi$

---

[20] It is a property of light giving it a kind of orientation vertically and horizontally across in the lines of motion.

And this stands for a complex number:

If $Y = A + B$ then $Y.Y = (A + B) \cdot (A + B)$

In case of complex numbers, we know that $Y.Y = (A + Bi) \cdot (A - Bi)$

In other words, this complex conjugate form implies backward and forward linkages of the B factor, which stands for Time in the wave equation.

So, implicitly or explicitly, the use and application of the wave equation involves backward and forward linkages in time (Gribbin, 1995)[21] in any quantum calculation or experiments.

Cramer's deliberations imply that a wave function has a bi-polarity of backward and forward linkages of time. Backward linkage of time takes creation backward to its roots, its origin. In other words, the linkage is one of anti-creation (deconstruction taking everything to its seed form). Forward linkages of time, on the contrary, take us to future. It takes us to the full bloom and the highest creative possibility. The two concepts are however juxtaposed in the above equation. The findings in ancient wisdom of the Vedas are akin to what is happening in Science. The religion of the rise and fall of waves holds the key.

6.12 Parallels in Iconography: Fractals and the Gandhaavyūha Sutra

In ancient sutra called the Avatamsaka Sūtra, which is one of the most influential Mahayana sutras of East Asian Buddhism, there is a great parable of the truth. In English it is known as Flower Garland Sutra, Flower Adornment Sutra, or Flower Ornament Scripture. The *Avatamsaka Sūtra* describes the cosmos as a reality of infinite realms upon realms, mutually containing one another. The vision expressed in this work is the basis of the philosophy of interpenetration. The last chapter of the Avatamsaka is the *Gandhaavyūha Sutra* meaning the 'flower-array' or 'bouquet', where there is a description of the "climax" based on the pilgrimage of the youth Sudhana to various lands at the behest of the bodhisattva Mañjuśrī.

---

[21] The idea comes from Schrödinger's parable of two kittens – Dead or alive (1995) – readers may refer John Gribbin in 'Down to Earth', August 15, pp. 29–36.

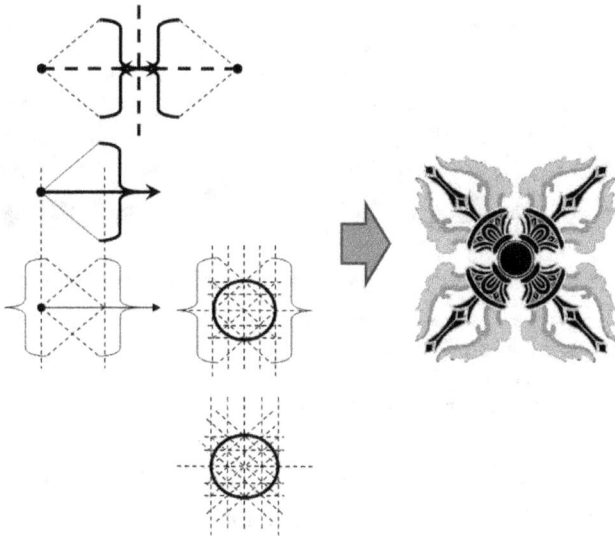

Figure 6.26 Double frame or double bow: Array of nodes (Marmas)

Note: See middle left and below; the Weft and spinning loom of two-way Vayu – see middle right; arrow and the bow and one-way frame – see top-left; Criss-Crossing or the two-way Vajra – see topmost left

Interpenetration is the doctrine of mutual containment and interpenetration of all phenomena, as expressed in Indra›s net. One thing contains all other existing things, and all existing things contain that one thing. In the words of Fritjof Capra in his seminal work 'The Tao of Physics':

The core of the Avatamsaka Sutra, one of the main scriptures of Mahayana Buddhism, is the description of the world as a perfect network of mutual relations where all things and events interact with each other in an infinitely complicated way. Mahayana Buddhists have developed many parables and similes to illustrate this universal interrelatedness, some of which will be discussed later on, in connection with the relativistic version of the 'web philosophy' in modern physics.

The cosmic web, finally, plays a central role in Tantric Buddhism, a branch of the Mahayana which originated in India around the third century A.D. and constitutes today the main school of Tibetan Buddhism. The scriptures of this school are called the Tantras, a word whose Sanskrit root means 'to weave' and which refers to the interwovenness and interdependence of all things and events.

Figure 6.27 The weaving (web) of the cosmic interwoven-ness

Note: Founded on a feeling of 'ALL in each and of each in All' (Imagery of the Flower Bouquet) As the Isha Upanishad says:
yastu sarvâni bhûtâni âtmanyevânupasHyati,
sarvabhûteSu câtmânam tato na vijugupsate (6)

But he, who sees everywhere the Self in all existences and all existences in the Self, shrinks not thereafter from aught (translations by Sri Aurobindo).

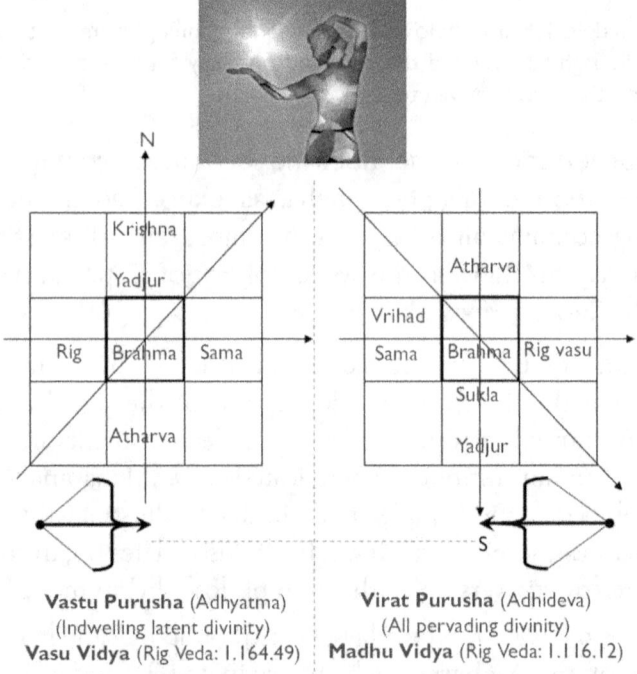

Vastu Purusha (Adhyatma)   Virat Purusha (Adhideva)
(Indwelling latent divinity)   (All pervading divinity)
Vasu Vidya (Rig Veda: 1.164.49)   Madhu Vidya (Rig Veda: 1.116.12)

Figure 6.28 The double intender – the Divinity within and the Divinity without

Note: Complementarities and interconnections as portrayed by the opposite but complementary positions of the four Vedas (note the position of Black (Krishna) and White (Sukla) of the Vedas of Vayu or Shakti – the two aspects or folds of the Yadjur Veda)

6.12.1 The two way diagonals: Regulating lines or the Karna Sutras

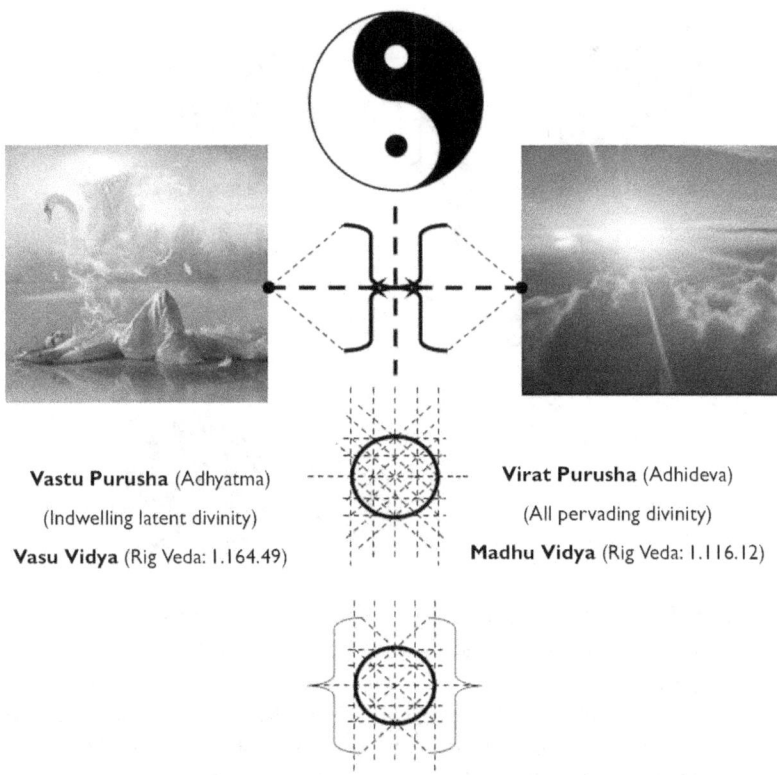

Figure 6.29A The fractals within and without – the Matrix containing all the parts and all the parts containing the Matrix

The idea is evident in the twin aspects of reality and architecture that needs to be bridged. It is the architecture of the Vast – the macrocosm and architecture of the Small – the microcosm, and the relationship between the two.

The idea of non-locality and interpenetration of the two stages of Schrodinger's experiment that the Creature is dead (transcendental and absorbed) and alive (immanent and resurrected) is an age-old idea of the schools of ancient realization (see Figure 6.25). In Figure 6.26, the same idea is portrayed by the Double frame or double Bow: Array of nodes *(Marmas)* that is based on the logic of Criss-Crossing and therefore is the basis of the two-way Vajra.

Fig 6.29B The fractals within and without a two-way ladder: Jacob's ladder and Escher's diagram — leading to fractalization

Genesis 28:10-17
Jacob's Dream at Bethel: From Beersheba to Harran, Jacob stopped at a point when sun was setting. He had a dream in which he saw a stairway resting on the earth, with its top reaching to heaven, and the angels of God were ascending and descending on it.

In Figure 6.27, the idea emerges as the weaving (web) of the cosmic interwoven-ness founded on a feeling of ALL in each and of each in All. It is evident in the parable of the Flower Bouquet, which is the basis of the *Gandhaavyūha sutra* or Brahmajala Sutra (called the Indra's net).

Figure 6.28 brings out the double intender in terms of the Divinity within and the Divinity without, i.e. the polarities in the microcosm and the macrocosm. The complementarities and interconnections as portrayed by the opposite but complementary positions of the four Vedas in view of the twin positions of Black *(Krishna)* and White *(Sukla)* of the Vedas of Vayu or Shakti – the two aspects or folds of the Yadjur Veda hold the key, the way or the Tao.

Finally, Figures 6.29A and 6.29B forward the fractals within and without a two-way ladder, based on an ancient parable – the Jacob's ladder and the Escher's diagram – leading to *fractalization*. Thus from the most ancient philosophy coded in the Vedas to modern images of nature and its inherent geometry, there lies the one and only interconnectedness and undifferentiated-ness that we may call divinity. In the simple words of Swami Vivekananda describing 'God in everything', we get the vivid description of the latest word of science:

We shall understand this better, when, later on, we come to the more philosophical portions of the Vedanta. But for the present I beg to state that in Vedanta alone we find a rational solution of the problem. Here I can only lay before you what the Vedanta seeks to teach, and that is the deification of the world. The Vedanta does not in reality denounce the world. The ideal of renunciation nowhere attains such a height as in the teachings of the Vedanta. But, at the same time, dry suicidal advice is not intended; it really means deification of the world – giving up the world as we think of it, as we know it, as it appears to us – and to know what it really is. Deify it; it is God alone. We read at the commencement of one of the oldest of the Upanishads:

– "Whatever exists in this universe is to be covered with the Lord."

The ideal of man is to see God in everything. But if you cannot see Him in everything, see Him in one thing, in that thing which you like best, and then see Him in another. So on you can go. There is infinite life before the soul. Take your time and you will achieve your end. "He, the One, who vibrates more quickly than mind, who attains to more speed than mind can ever do, whom even the gods reach not, nor thought grasps, He moving, everything moves. In Him all exists. He is moving. He is also immovable. He is near and He is far. He is inside everything. He is outside everything, interpenetrating everything. Whoever sees in every being that same Atman, and whoever sees everything in that Atman, he never goes far from that Atman. When all life and the whole universe are seen in this Atman, then alone man has attained the secret. There is no more delusion for him. Where is any more misery for him who sees this Oneness in the universe?"

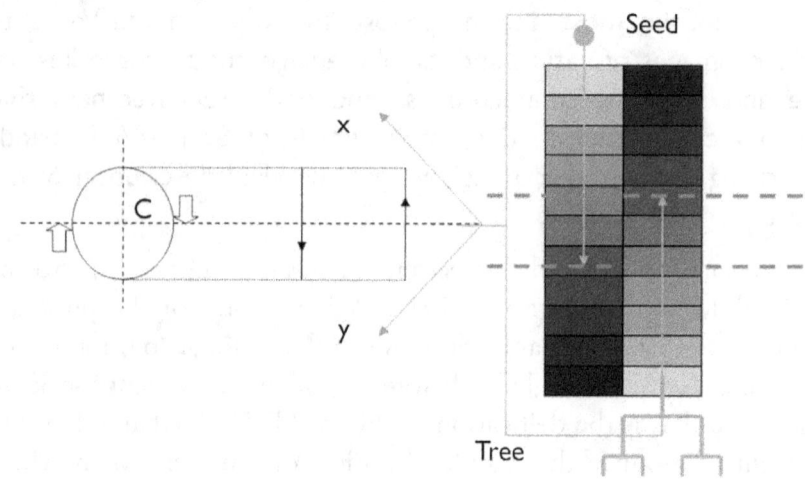

Figure 6.30

6.13 Conclusions: Cycles and lines – both and beyond

India of the ages is not dead nor has She spoken her last creative word; She lives and has still something to do for herself and the human peoples. And that which must seek now to awake is not an Anglicized oriental people, docile pupil of the West and doomed to repeat the cycle of the Occident's success and failure, but still the ancient immemorial Shakti recovering Her deepest self, lifting Her head higher toward the supreme source of light and strength and turning to discover the complete meaning and a vaster form of her Dharma.

– Sri Aurobindo

It is probably true quite generally that in the history of human thinking the most fruitful developments frequently take place at those points where two different lines of thought meet.

– Werner Heisenberg

'The modern physicist experiences the world through an extreme specialization of the rational mind; the mystic through an extreme specialization of the intuitive mind...to paraphrase an old Chinese saying, mystics understand the roots of the Tao but not its branches; scientists understand its branches but not its roots. Science does not need mysticism and mysticism does not need science; but men and women need both'.

– Fritjof Capra

'Epilogue: Tao of Physics'

In the progressive journey of civilization, we have finally reaching a climax.

The spiritual liberty is at all the three planes – the individual, the universal and the beyond. The reciprocating social and material liberties have to activate that spirit in matter so that all the three thresholds of material existence – the material, the mental and the vital correspond to the planes above.

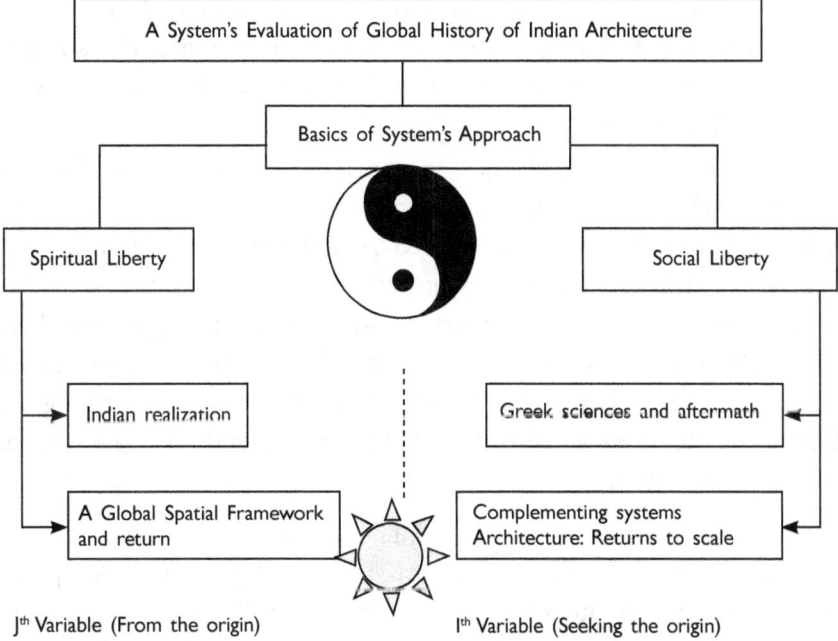

Fig 6.31 The complementarity of the two-way ladder – the system's framework of the two forces and their mutual interpenetration

In the words of Sri Aurobindo:

'The one principle of interconnectedness inhabiting every object in the universe and that every object is universe in universe, movement in the general movement, has been explained in the terms of complete oneness by the Brahman, transcendental and universal even in the individual, through – One in the Many, Many in the One, Stable and Motional, exceeding and reconciling all opposites.'

- There is an initial expectation from the current generation to transcend the unhealthy stage of mental idiosyncrasies and lopsided material excesses and move to levels of 'simple green living and higher to even higher thinking'.
- The education paradigm of the preceding century, which is still filled with urges of competitive and comparative exploitations and comparative flamboyances, needs to promote the greater cooperative platform to inspire the strands of high to higher thinking.
- Finally, our remaining obsessions with the plethora of a materialistic civilization have to be pushed beyond our physical and associated mental worlds to reach the sublime and the vast array of things interspersed in the beauty of the cosmos.

As a result, a simple-minded approach to enjoyment, life and livability, which have now taken a back seat, can be recovered. It is time that humanity needs to revert back to normalcy and touch the stage of simplicity in watching life and the universe as a poetry of rhythm, cooperation and an ever-growing love for each other. It is a match point of the two thought-forces, the Indian and the Greek and their interpenetration (see Figure 6.29). The need of the hour is finally forwarded in these words ['God in everything']:

'Who enjoys the picture, the seller or the seer? The seller is busy with his accounts, computing what his gain will be, how much profit he will realize on the picture. His brain is full of that...that man is enjoying the picture who has gone there without any intention of buying and selling and these foolish ideas of possession will be ended.

The money-lender gone, the buyer gone, the seller gone, this world remains the picture, a beautiful painting.

I never read of any more beautiful conception of God than the following:

"He is the great Poet, the Ancient Poet: the whole universe is His poem, coming in verses and rhymes and rhythms written in infinite bliss"

As the two master forces are beginning to meet and interpenetrate, there is a need to reach the climax of the present cycle of the 4-phase system of global civilization and the role of an ancient country to recreate the climax.

'The star arose in the East; it traveled steadily towards the West, sometimes dimmed and sometimes effulgent, till it made a circuit of the world; and now it is again rising on the very horizon of the East, the borders of San-po...

'And perhaps, in our own day, such a time for the conjunction of these two gigantic forces (Indian and Greek principles) have presented itself again.

This time their center is India'.

– Swami Vivekananda

References

1. Alexander, Hartley Burr, *The World's Rim: Great Mysteries of the North American Indians,* Lincoln (Nebraska), 1953.
2. Birge, John Kinsley, *the Bektashi Order of Dervisches,* London, 1937.
3. Basham, A. L., *The Wonder That was India,* London, 1971.
4. Boner, Alice, Sadsiva Rath Sarma and Bettina Baumer (Trans). Vastu Sutra Upanishad, *New Delhi,* 2000.
5. Bose, Ashish, 'Six Decades of Urbanization in India 1901–1961', Indian Economic & Social History Review January 1964 2: 23–41, 1961.
6. Breese, Gerald William, Urbanization in newly developing countries, Prentice-Hall (Englewood Cliffs, N.J), 1966.
7. Burckhardt, Titus, *Art and Thought,* London, 1947.
8. Burckhardt, Titus, *Le genese du temple hindou, in Etudes traditionnelles,* paris, juin, juillet, December 1953.
9. Banerjee, Arunendu, *Rabindranath Tagore and Patrick Geddes – the Ecological Cultural Visionaries,* Kolkata, 2005.
10. Behling, Sophia and Stephen Behling, Sol Power – The Evolution of Solar Architecture, Munich, 1996.
11. Brunn, S. and Williams, J. Cities of the World. World Regional Urban Development, New York, 1983.
12. Capra, Fritjof, *The Turning Point,* London, 1982.
13. Capra, Fritjof, *Uncommon Wisdom,* London, 1988.
14. Capra, Fritjof, *the hidden connections,* London, 2003.
15. Chambers, Robert, *Rural Development – putting the last thing fast,* Harlow, 1983.
16. *Complete Works of Swami Vivekananda,* 8 Vols, *Mayavati Memorial Edition,* 1989.
17. Caroutch, Yvonne, *La Licorne alchimique,* Paris, 1981. Champeaux, G. De and Dom Sterckx, S. (O.S.B.), *Introduction au monde*

des symboles, Paris, 1966. [Refer sections in page 31 and 429, mainly].

18. Champeaux, G. De and Dom Sterckx, S. (O.S.B.), *Introduction au monde des symboles,* Paris, 1966.

19. Champeaux, G. De and Dom Sterckx, S. (O.S.B.), *Introduction au monde des symboles,* Paris, 1966.

20. Chevalier, Jean and Alain Gheerbrant, the Penguin *Dictionary of Symbols,* Paris, 1982. [Translated from French into English by John Buchanan-Brown]

21. *Complete Works of Swami Vivekananda,* 8 Vols, *Mayavati Memorial Edition,* 1989.

22. Complete *Works of Sri Aurobindo,* Pondicherry, 2001.

23. Corbin, H., *L'imagination creatice dans le soufisme d'Ibn 'Arabi,* Paris, 1958.

24. Corbin, H., *L'homme de lumiere dans le soufisme iranien,* Paris, 1961.

25. Corbin, H., *Trilogie ismaelinne,* Paris and Tehran, 1961.

26. *Cultural Heritage of India,* 6 Vols., Ramakrishna Mission Institute of Culture, Kolkata, 2001.

27. Ching, Francis, D.K., and Mark M. Jarzombek and Vikramaditya Prakash, *A Global History of Architecture,* New Jersey, 2007.

28. David-Neel, A., *Initiations and Initiates in Tibet,* London, 1958.

29. Davy, M.-M., *Initiation a la symbolique romaine,* Paris, 1964.

30. Davy, M.-M., *Un traite de la vie solitaire: lettre aux Freres du Mont-Diu,* 2 Vols, Paris, 1940-6.

31. Diel, Paul, *Le symbolisme dans la mythologie grecque,* with preface by G. Bachelard, new edition, Paris, 1966.

32. Dorf, Richard, C., *Technology, Humans, and Society – towards a sustainable world,* San Diego, 2001.

33. Doxiadis, C. A., Ecumenopolis: World City of Tomorrow, Impact of Science on Society 19, 1969.

34. Durand, Gilbert, *Les structures anthropologiques de l'imaginarie,* Paris, 1963 [Refer page 137 where the two-way arrow has been the *Vajra*].

35. Durand, Gilbert, *Les structures anthropologiques de l'imaginarie*, Paris, 1963.
36. Durand, Gilbert, *L'imagination symbolique*, Paris, 1964.
37. Eliade, Micrea, *Patterns in Comparative Religion*, translated by Rosemary Sheed, London and New York, 1958.
38. Friedman, John, Urbanization, Planning, and National Development, MIT Press, 1972.
39. Granet, M., *Chinese Civilization*, London, 1930.
40. Granet, M., *Danses et legendes de la chine ancienne*, 2 vols, Paris, 1926.
41. Griaule, Marcel., *Symbolisme d'un temple totemique soudanais*, Rome, 1957.
42. Grimal, Pierre, *Dictionaire de la mythologie grecque et romaine*, with preface by Ch. Picard, Paris, 1963.
43. Guenon, R., *Le symbolisme de la Croix*, Paris, 1931.
44. Guenon, R., *Man and his becoming according to the Vedanta*, London, 1945.
45. Grodecki, Louis., *Symbolisme cosmique et monuments religieux*, Paris, 1953.
46. Hauser. P. *World and Asian Urbanization in Relation to Economic Development and Social Change*. Pp. 53–95 in Phillip Hauser (ed.), *Urbanization in Asia and The Far East. Calcutta: UNESCO.* 1957.
47. Jacobs, J., *Cities and the Wealth of Nations*, Random House, New York., 1984.
48. Johnson, E.A.J. *The Organization of Space in Developing Countries. Cambridge, MA:* Harvard University Press, 1970.
49. Lannoy, R., *The Speaking Tree: A Study of Indian Culture and Society*, London, 1968.
50. Evola, Julius, *Le Yoga tantrique*, Paris, Fayard, 1971.
51. Krugman, Paul R. and Anthony J. Venables. 1995a. 'Globalization and the inequality of nations.' Quarterly Journal of Economics, 110: 857–880. 1955.
52. Kuznets S. "Economic growth and income inequality", American Economic Review, 45, 1–28. 1955.

53. Hautecoeur, L., *Mystique et architecture*, Paris, 1954.
54. Hinnells, John R., The Penguin *Dictionary of Religions*, New York, 1984.
55. Hinnells, John R., *A Handbook of Living Religions*, London, 1984.
56. Macionis, J. J., and J. L. Spates, *The Sociology of Cities*, Belmont, California, 1987.
57. Moore, Gary, T., *Environment-Behavior Studies in Introduction to Architecture*, New York, 1979.
58. Mallmann, M.-T. de, *Les enseignements iconographiques del'Agni Purana*, Paris, 1963.
59. Massignon, L., *La Passion d'Al-Hallaj*, 2 Vols, Paris, 1922.
60. Massignon, L., *L'ame de l'Iran*, Paris, 1951.
61. Massignon, L., *Essai sur les origines du lexique technique de la mystique musulmane*, Paris, 1922.
62. Meyerovitch, Eva., *Les songes et leur interpretation chez les Persans*, Paris, 1959.
63. Monod-Herzen, G.-E., *L'alchimie mediterraneane, ses origines et son but, la Table d'Emeraude*, Paris, 1963.
64. Pseudo-Dionysus the Areopagite, The Divine Names, translated by the editors of the Shrine of wisdom, Godalming (Surrey), 1957.
65. Porter, Robert, Urbanisation and Planning in the Third World: Spatial Perceptions and Public Participation, Routledge, 1985.
66. Possehl, Gregory L., *The Indus Valley Civilization, a contemporary perspective*, New Delhi, 2002.
67. Ramanada, Swami, *Santa Prasanga*, 2004.
68. Rapoport, Amos, *Cultural Origins of Architecture in Introduction to Architecture*, New York, 1979.
69. Roux, Jean-Paul, *Fauna et Flore sacrees dans les societes altaiques*, Paris, 1966.
70. Rutten, M., 'Emblemes geometriques' in Revue d'historie des sciences 2, 1949.
71. Russell, Bertrand, *A History of Western Philosophy*, Sydney, 1979.

72. Scholem, G.G., *On the Kabbalah and its Symbolism*, translated by Ralph Manheim, London, 1965.
73. Sechan, Louis and Leveque, Pierre, *Les grandes divinites de la Grece*, Paris, 1966.
74. Seckel, Dietrich, *The Art of Buddhism*, London, 1964.
75. Sen, J., *Concept of Complete Religion*, Kolkata, 2006.
76. Stein, Rolf., 'Jardins (Garden) en miniature de l'Extreme-Orient, le Monde en petit', in *Bulletin de l'E.F.E.O.*, Hanoi, 1943.
77. Sri Aurobindo, *The Foundations of Indian Culture*, Pondicherry, 1995.
78. Tagore, Rabindranath, *Santiniketan*, Santiniketan, 1991.
79. Tyrwhitt, Jacqueline, *Patrick Geddes in India*, Bangalore, 2007.
80. *The Wordsworth Encyclopedia of World Religions*, Great Britain, 1999.
81. Virel, Andre., *Histoire de notr image*, Geneva, 1965.
82. Williamson JG. Regional inequality and the process of national development: A description of the patterns. Economic Development and Cultural Change 13(4): 1–84, 1965.
83. Zimmer, H. R., *Myths and Symbols in Indian Art and Civilization*, Princeton, 1971.

Index

A

Advanced HVAC systems
  capital-or-techno-intensive design ventures, 22
Ancient Indian architecture
  conception and application, 16
Anthropic principle
  Tagore–Einstein dialogue, 47–48
  Timothy Ferris' thoughts, 48–49
Anthropocentric realization, 62
Architectural parallels
  Ancient Buddhism and early Christianity, 204–211
    Buddhist Chaitya halls, 204
    Basilicas of the Greco-Roman world, 204–211
    Indo-Iranian deity 'Mithra', variety and spread, 207
    mansions of God and human, ecology of the architecture, 208–211
  'deep ecology', 58
  conventional value shift from the 'shallow' to the 'deeper', 58
  Cybernetic perspective, patterns of co-evolution, 6–8
  one-way' linear approach, 7
  cycles, turnings and regulating lines, 55–56
  design innovation and creativity, 56
  evolutionary system-driven system (ES-D-S), 57, 59
  factor-driven changes, 58
Architecture, 2
  and Indian civilization, 7
  seed idea and expression, 55–59
  seven sages, 61–62
Architecture history
  absolute impersonal Brahman, 81
  ancient Airyan Vaeja (Iran), Traces of Bahram, 84
  Ancient gardens of Adonis, ecological patterns, 92–93
  Archaeological evidences of 'Bahram' from Rajasthan, India, 85
  Armenian 'Vram', 83
  Ba or Vayu-yoga, 82–83
  Bahram amongst Mandeans (from ancient Sheba) of lower Iran and Yemen, 85–86

Bahram in head-crowns of Sassanids Kings, astral implications of, 84
Bahram traces in Southeast Asia, 84
Baul or Faqir, 86
cooperative language systems, 94–114
   Ancient ties: Phoenicians-Moors in Asia and Africa, 101–103
   anointment and resurrection of body for final transfiguration, 106
   early migrations to Egypt, 103–104
   India's spiritual double: Another version in Egypt (Elements of transmigration – KA and BA), 105–106
   Indo-European language systems, 94–95
   land migration: Indo-European Gypsy, 95–97
   marine linkages: phoenicians and the land of Punt, 98–101
   system of Al-Baka: Lost wisdom of Mother Goddess, 106–108
   system of immaculate conception: Virgin Mary, 109–111
   system of matrix: God as the mother, 108–109
   system of universal sacrifice, 111–114
   Unicorn, 112–114
Diwan-i-Khas, 79–80
Garden of Eden, intercontinental, trans-cultural and cross-religious perspective, 93
gardens as a cultural landscape, 91
impersonal Indo-Iranian solar symbolism, 83
holistic process-based systems-driven framework, 58
inspiration-driven innovation, 58–59
integral ecological economics, 58
inter-mixing of the two civilizations, India and Greece, 87–88
Iranian Zoroastrian 'Bahram' (Vedic – 'BRAHMN' and Orphic – 'BRIMO'), 83–86
Ka-Ba-Lah, 82
Kali and Al-Kali, connection between, 93–94
Lalon Shah and roots of 'Bahram' in undivided Bengal, 86–87
Land of SEBA', 146
Lord of Four Quarters, 79
Orphic idea of Erebus, 78
Parades, 90

paradise as a garden, immortal tradition, 93
pattern language systems' for the built environment, 91
reversal Al-Ba-Ka, 82
Rodasi, 74–75
'SABEANS', 146
Sassanid park, quadrangular pattern, 92
sequence cycle, 72–73
seven ears of the corn and the stream of life (shibboleth), 144–45
space of four divine quarters' /'Chahar-bagh', 91
system of converging realization and belief systems, 88–94
    afri' or 'apri'-sukta' of the Rig Veda, 89
    integral Vedic lore, 88
    Kabalistic tradition, 90
Lordship of four quarters, 90–93, 161–162
    Semitic stock from Persia, 89
system of death and resurrection: the parable of Corn spirit, 154–155
system of double intender: Cult of Tammuz, 149–151
system of immortal life principle, 143–144
system of immortal lordship, 81
system of inter-continental carriers and migrations, 114–121
    etymological over-laps, 116–120
    fire-traditions of 'Bahram' (Persia) and 'Varman' (South Asia), 119
    folk-anthropology and socio-normative belief systems of times antiquity, 116
    ichnographical evidence, 120
    migration of Mongoloid tribes to the Americas, 114–121
    resemblance between the Sanskrit word Ahi, 117
    resemblance between two important peaks of Mount Annapurna, 117
    resemblance between two words and places, 117
    resemblance of the word Maya, 117
    resemblance with the first of the twin rivers of Amu-Darya and Sur-Darya, 116–117
system of cooperative archaeology, 121–160
    'Atar-Ba-haram', 143
    Atharvans – An etymological extension in Azerbaijan, 124–125

Atharvans – Origin of Indo-Iranians (Airyan-Vaja), 121–122
Biblical 'Sabbath', 142
Chthonian basis of Orphic lore, 126–127
Chthonian Celtic-Caledonian festivals, 126
Chthonian Egyptian Sed festival, 126
chthonian immortality (Corporeal counterpart of Elixir of life: Soma), 133–135
Chthonian Indo-Iranian Mithraism, 127
Dithyrambic, 139
evolutionary symbolism of seven stages, 131–133
human evolution, folk-anthropology-based evolutionary purpose, 131
Iranian counterpart of the Atharvans, 122–124
Mithraic and Gallo-Roman pictures, symbolism of the Bull-killings, 130
Mithraic temples, 128, 127f, 128f
Sabazios, 142
sages *Kaushiki Viswamitras*, 135
Shivaji or *Sebazeo*, 130
'soma-sema' doctrine of Orphism, 136
Soma-Tawy doctrine of Egypt, 136–138

system of chthonian death and rejuvenation (Odin-Adonis-Eden), 125
system of festivals of Adonis in West Asia, 125
system of immortality in Orphism, 141
system of immortality or the symbolic Sabbath (roots in Sheva or Seba), 142–143
system of Soma – the doctrine of immortality in the Vedas, 135–136
system of triple foundations of Sabazius, 139
Zarathusthra doctrine of a 'future savior' (*Saoshyant*), 133
system of lordship of the third and fourth quarters: the Atharvans, 79–80
system of lower quarter: tala (tail), 78–79
system of myth and history, 71–75
system of reconciliation in the lower half, 78
system of seven from the land of Sheba (Saba or Shivah), 145–149
system of upper and lower world: Parable of Kora (Kore), 153–154
systems of historical–mythological recurrence – from India to Egypt, 75–88

concept of four quarters, 75–76
Persian-Semitic-Romaic tradition, 76
system of descent into lower quarter, 77
system of upper and lower Godheads (Sura and Ashura), 77
systems of historical–mythological recurrence – from India to Egypt, 75–88
three upper quarters or Tripadam – Aja-ekpadam (one lower quarter), 75–76
Tammuz in Orphism, System of original divinity, 151–153
tradition of garden in the Semitic tradition, 90–91
triple system of Sabazius-Bromius-Tammuz, 149
turning of the wheel or the Mandala, 82–83
Vahrām or Bahrām, 83
Vedic wisdom, 72
Verethragna, 84
Architecture of the cosmos system of completeness, 40
Architecture, systems' evaluation
spatial and historical dimensions, 23–24
Aranyakas' or the Vedic gurukuls, 24
green design, 24
macrocosmic changes, 24
microcosmic changes, 24
atma-vidya/direct truth-realization, 16
Avi-istaka'/ 'sacred bricks' in India, 62

B

Bacchic-Dionysiac element
origin, evolution and impact, 176–177
salient features, 177–178
Bio-social entropy, 46
Built-environmental design sciences, 28

C

Celto-Hellenic dissemination, 162
Chaitya, 16
Complementarities and co-evolution: India versus Greece, 35–37
one-way' linear approach to human progress, 36
Complete Anthropic Principle (CAP), 47
Complete system's approach (CSA), 37
Concept of space-time (Blowing in and the blowing out), 157–159
Convergent realization and belief (normative) systems, 162

Cybernetics, 2–5
  Aham (individual or isolated identity), 32
  architecture, built-environmental design, 5
  built-environmental design sciences, 4
  Carnot's Cycle in Physics, 32–33
  Cognitive memory sequence, 4
  Mahat (collective or cosmic identity), 32
  point of view of elements of design, 29–30
    aerodynamics, 29–30
    mathematics, 29
    philosophy, 30
  Tibetan Mandala in metaphysical reality, 32–33

D

Dorians and the Milesians: Traces of the second westbound movement, 178–182
  Milesian philosophy, 179–180
  system's framework, 181–182

F

First order cybernetics, 3, 27

G

Gaia myth, 69–70
Gaia's matrix, 69–71
  Patanjali's Kaivalya-pada, 70
  system of sacrifice and resurrection, 71
General system theory, 15
global history of architecture, Phase I, 60–172
  al-khemia or Alchemy, 62–63
  ancient system of, 62
  body of opinion, 67
  complementary conjugate, system of equal and opposite, 69
  cycle of seasons, 68
  death and resurrection, system of cycles, 68–69
  Gaia's hypothesis, 69
  Ka-Ba-Lah, 63–64
  life-and-death-cyclic system approach'(LCA), 65
  samavatsara, 68
  system of complementarities', 66
  system of cycles and renewability, 64–65
  system of iterations, 67
  system of opposites', 66
  system of unity of opposites, 66–75
  systems inquiry, cooperative approach, 65–66
  Yoga and kshema - conjugate system of the spiritual and the material, 63–64
  Yoga-sutra, 69

Global history of architecture, Phase II, 173–258
  Advaitic Vedantists', 231
  Indian architectural history: Evidences in the Eastern Mediterranean, 199–201
  missionaries of 'Dhamma' (or Domos), 234–235
  missionaries of 'Dhamma' to the Mediterranean, 196–204
  Phaistos Disc and other rock-cut architectural evidences, archaeology of, 203–204
  rock-cut caves, similarity between the construction styles, 201
  rock-cut monastic establishments in Anatolia, 204
  sect of *'Therapeutae'*, 235
  sending missionaries to the West, Indian history, 197–199
  Shape grammar and iconography based, 233–234
  timeline of architecture, 202–203
Global history of architecture, Phase III, 259–315
  Albigensian Crusade and the Cathars, 277–281
  Ancient Persian civilization, resurrection, 264–265
  Array of four quarters, cardinal realizations, 300–302
  black unicorn, Mari and her metamorphosis, 282–284
  Buddhist Iconography, Four quarters, 303–304
  Cardinal Principles of Architecture, revival, 288
  Char-bagh, evolution, 294–299
  Christianity during the Dark Ages, 260–261
  cult of ADONIS, 291
  Dark Ages, Barbaric invasion, 261–262
  El-KA-BA (El KAB) in pre-dynastic (3500 BC) Egypt (Mishrah or Magara), 294
  European civilization, making of, 284–286
  European Dark Ages: Asia and the Mediterranean, continuity of trade, 263
  European Renaissance', 260
  Fall of Granada and rise of France vide the Spanish Inquisition, 276–277
  Indian philosophy in the Judeo-Islamic order, 289–291
  Indian sources, 292–293
  Ka-Ba and El-Ilah, mysteries of, 293–294
  Korahites (Quraysh), legacy, 267–274
  Kore to the Carolingian, 274–276
  Kores, contribution of, 274–284

Liberalizing performing arts and architecture, 286–288

Lordship of four quarters: Origins in the Vedas, 299–300

Muqarnas, 287

Redepiction of the Garden of Eden: The Char-bagh, 291–304

Rise of Arts and Sciences, 266–267

Rise of Moors and the message of the Prophet of Arabia, 263–264

Spiritual phonetics, 288–289

Global history of architecture, Phase IV, 316–401

Akashic records: the universe as Mahat (Collective Mind), 350–355

   archaic evidences: The 1935 Yale–Cambridge expedition, 370–371

   architecture of co-evolution, 366–375

   Co-evolutionary Anthropology, Recognition of, 366–370

   Matariswan (Celtic *Matrice*), 374

   Narmada valley: Traces of advanced or an older cycle of civilization, 371–375

architecture of deep ecology, 362–364

architecture of evolution, 355–362

   cyclic evolutions of death and resurrection, 359

   evolutionary chemistry, 355–362

   Mahat, 360–361

architecture of interpenetration, 378–392

   all in one and one in the all, 379–385

   cycles and lines – both and beyond, 398–401

   fractals and holism: the double intender – the mirror (*vajra*), 378

   gandhaavyüha sutra, 392

   parallels in iconography, 392–394

   parallels in science: truth of non-locality, 390–392

   spiritual liberty, 399

   two-way ladder, 385–390

architecture of the cosmic matrix, 365–366

   co-evolution: cybernetics, 365–366

   universal gaia and recognition of an impersonal, 365

architecture of the mahat, 375–378

Bhrigu–Angirasa Samhita/ Atharva Veda, 329

challenges in transition between Phase III and Phase IV, 336–340
cosmic architecture, 350–355
cumulative causation of four phases, 318–336
   Angirasas, 329
   one-force theory, 321
   succession in systems framework, 318–332
   systems phase I question I, 321–322
   systems phase II questions, 322–323
   systems phase III questions, 323–324
   systems phase IV question I, 324–325
   Zoroastrianism and Vedanta, interconnection between, 328
delineating Phase IV: a system's approach, 332–333
evidences of the split, 340–345
   Charles Darwin's Theory of Evolution, 346
   deepening of the crisis, 343–345
   Judeo-Christian tradition, 344–345
     Logos, 341
     Rene Descartes, 346
     Sigmund Freud's realm of the sub-conscious, 346–347
   reductionism, crisis of, 345–347
   regulating lines or the Karna Sutras, 395–398
   restarting phase IV, 333–336
system's architecture: post-Cartesian departure, 347–348
system's architecture: post-Darwinian shift, 348–350
uncertainties or shades of distrust, 338

H

Hamsah, 87
Habit–habitation complementarities, 25, 25f
Habit–habitation' interdependence, 25
Holiest of Fires, 84
Human-mind-driven innovations, 24

I

Indian architecture, 6–7
   global history, interconnectedness, 20
Indian Cosmology, 40–41
   co-evolution, cultural aspects, 45–46
   co-evolutionary base, 46
   cognitive psychology and evolutionary biology, 43–44
   completeness of the cosmos (*the vrihad–aranyak*), 50

concept of completeness', 50
cosmic expanse, 49
decimal' system (dasam) of India, 54
Extended Anthropoligical Framework (EAF), 51, 52
fully blooming human personality, 44–45
Gaia hypothesis : pan-ecological/environmental studies, systems matrix, 46
Gaia hypothesis', 46
green consciousness, 52
Holistic 'spectrum', Ken Wilber, 44–45
modern sciences, recognition by, 43
Morphic resonance, 45
Orphic school of thought, 53–54
Post-Freudian years: Carl Gustav Jung, 44
principle of a priori, 53
psychic-transpersonal' and the 'spectrum-universal', 43
Swami Vivekananda's conceptual framework, 43–46
towards a psychology of being', 45
transpersonal objective, Abraham Maslow, 44
TREE as a primal archetype, 53–54
TREE structure, 52
Tree/Taru or bifurcation (troyi), 49–50

K

Karna-dhara', 25–26
Kore-Tammuz, Vedic origin, 157

M

'Machine-industrial order', 13
Meditation, 42
Megasthenes' Indica
    Bacchic-Dionysiac element: Origin, evolution and impact, 176–177
    godhead, 173
    Recasting the dates of a two-phase recovery, 174–175
Modern European civilization, 13

N

'Nadia-Murshidabad', 87
Naimesaranya, 335

O

One-way' linear approach to human progress, 36

P

Paradigm shift, 14
Participatory Anthropic Principle (PAP), 48

principle of Chi, 112
principle of Lin, 112
Puras' or 'Pharaohs, 107
Purusha, 16

R

RAMASES, 103
Renaissance, 13

S

Semitic 'Isaiah' or *Yeshua*, 108
System's approach (SA), 1, 14
    applied and social sciences, system of interconnections, 23
    basis, 21–22
    complementary events and impacts, 39–54
        emerging paradigms in evolutionary sciences, 40
        non-linear dynamism based on fundamentals of network, 40
    architecture of the cosmos, 40–43
    cybernetic perspective, 25–28
        knowledge systems, 27
        numerological sequence, 26
        philosophical sequence, 26
        principal factors, 26
        procedural sequence, 26
    evolution, 18–39
    foundations, 22–23
    holistic approach, 1
    holistic spirit, 21–22
    holistic viewpoint, 22
    interconnected truths, 22
    nature as a network, 18
    patterns of co-evolution, 8–11, 38–39
        global patterns and movements, 38
        gothic reformations, 9
        research and authorship, 9
        system's dynamism, 10
        system's framework, 10
        time-series, 8–9
    patterns of flow and measures, 54–59
    patterns of relationship between parts, 21
    premises, 1–2
    reductionist paradigm, 2
        sustainability, 1–2, 22–23
    system of human associations or organizations, 19
Scientist's Anthropic Principle, 47
Second order cybernetics, 3, 27
Shvetashvatara upanishad, 16
Strong version Anthropic Principle (SAP), 48
'Super-implicate order', David Bohm, 49

system of descent of Ishtar and the ascent of Tammuz, 156–157
system of Gnosis: the basis of deep ecology or spirituality, 159–160
system's evaluation, cybernetic perspective
   patterns of co-evolution, 34–35
system's viewpoint (SV), 18–19

T

The legend of Therapeutes Who were they?, 211–233
   archaeological implications of the dream, 220
   Clues from ancient Mediterranean, dream and events at Galilee, 218–219
   Epistles of St. Paul, 214–217
   Etymological evidences, 229–233
   historic reformulation, 219–220
   original sin: a global perspective, 212–214
   pointers of Swami Vivekananda, 223–227
   pointers to Cyclades, 220–223
   sect of Essenes, 227–228
   sect of Therapeutes, 228–229

St. Paul's letter to Timothy, 217–218
   universal resurrection through the Cross and the ideal of Bodhisattva, 211–212
Third order Cybernetics, 3, 28
   framework of, 4

U

Unity of opposites, 161
Universal Anthropic Principle, 46–49

V

Vastu Purusha Mandala, 15f, 16
Vedantic Cosmology, 43
Vrihad Aranyak, 49–54

W

Weak Anthropic Principle (WAP), 48
Widest social intelligence (WSI)
   TREE as a complete archetype, 54–55

Y

Year Sempiternal (Sana)' and AGNUS DEI, imagery of, 182–196
7 × 7 life principles or 'Marutas', 190–192

Agnus Dei, ancient Vedic image, 187–188
Esoteric Islam or Sufism, 195
in Egypt and in Tibetan Buddhism, 195–196
Movement in the Cosmic Wheel, imagery and the built form, 185–187
New Testament – Book of Revelations, 193–194
Old Testament, 188
physical and inner imageries, 182–183
root of the abstraction: 'Personified' and 'Impersonal', 183–184
Vedic foundations and the Alexandrian Theraputtas, 188–190
vedic imagery of the Lamb, 192–193

About the authors

Joy Sen is a Professor of Indian Institute of Technology, Kharagpur. He is currently Head of Ranbir and Chitra Gupta School of Infrastructure and Design (2014–17). His areas of research are Community and Regional Planning Analyses & Programming and Architecture and Planning related Heritage Studies and Documentation. He is  currently the Principal Investigator of two mega projects sponsored by MHRD Govt. of India: SandHI – Science and Heritage Initiative and the Future of Cities (2014–17).

Joy obtained his Bachelors in Architecture (1984) and PhD from IIT Kharagpur (2007). He obtained in Master's Degree in Community and Regional Planning from Iowa State University, Ames, Iowa, USA. Additionally, he received a Minor in Technology and Social Change (under UNDP-DAT program 1989) at ISU, USA. Joy received the Silver Medal for his Best Thesis Award and overall performance at the Bachelor's level and the Best Thesis Award from ISU, USA, at the master's level.

Joy received his spiritual initiation from Swami Ramananda, whose wisdom is epitomized by the two Forewords of the present book.

Joy has been associated with Asia Pacific Network of Housing Research (APNHR), Hong Kong as Associate Member; Reviewer (Editorial Board) Journal of Architecture and with CSVTU Research Journal as Associate Editor. He is member, Advisory Council Board, SPA Bhopal and the Aurora Design Academy, Hyderabad.

Joy has forwarded key talks at Sustainability Research Center (IR3S), the University of Tokyo; and Tokyo Metropolitan University in Japan (2008; 2010; 2012); International Society of City and Regional Planners (ISOCaRP) Congress (Athens 92002); Bilbao (2005); Istanbul (2007)]; Sains University, KL, Malaysia on various aspects of Indian Ecological traditions (2011; 2013); and SPURS

Program, Department of Urban and Regional Planning, MIT, New Cambridge, MA, USA (2015).

He has authored five books on Indian Heritage, Iconographic Documentation and a widely accepted text book on Sustainable Urban Planning by TERI (The Energy Research Institute), India Habitat Center, New Delhi.

Akshata Mohanty obtained her Bachelors in Architecture from IIT Kharagpur in 2015. Akshata has worked on her B. Arch Thesis on Varanasi with the author. *Akshata has contributed extensively in the making of various graphic features of the present book.*

Akshata has completed her schooling from Chandigarh. Her research interests are in the field of Architectural Software, Design Computation and Building Information Modelling. She has previously done projects in the same domain with Value and Budget Housing Corporation, Bangalore, Queensland University of Technology, Australia and across and Beyond Development Consultancy, Mumbai.

She is currently working as a Research Assistant at the School of Design and Environment in National University of Singapore, on an online visual programming environment for Architects. In her spare time, she likes to develop apps, read and paint.

www.ingramcontent.com/pod-product-compliance
Lightning Source LLC
Chambersburg PA
CBHW071234300426
44116CB00008B/1036